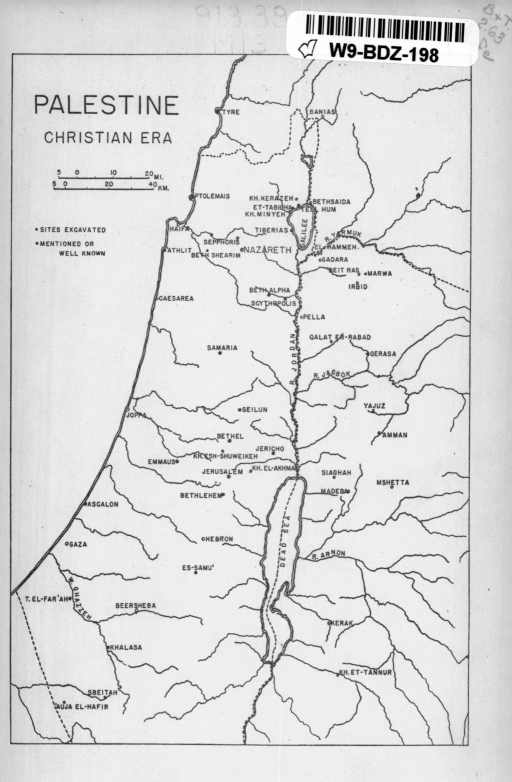

PALESTINE

CHRISTIAN ERA

5   0   10   20 MI.
5   0   20   40 KM.

- SITES EXCAVATED
- MENTIONED OR
  WELL KNOWN

TYRE

BANIAS

PTOLEMAIS

KH. KERAZEH · BETHSAIDA
ET-TABIGHA · TELL HUM
KH. MINYEH

HAIFA

TIBERIAS

GALILEE

ATHLIT

SEPPHORIS

NAZARETH

R. YARMUK

BETH SHEARIM

EL-HAMMEH

GADARA

BEIT RAS · MARWA

IRBID

BETH ALPHA

SCYTHOPOLIS

CAESAREA

PELLA

QALAT ER-RABAD

SAMARIA

GERASA

R. JORDAN

R. JABBOK

YAJUZ

SEILUN

JOPPA

BETHEL

AMMAN

JERICHO

EMMAUS

KH. ESH-SHUWEIKEH

JERUSALEM · KH. EL-AKHMA

BETHLEHEM

SIAGHAH

MADEBA

MSHETTA

ASCALON

HEBRON

DEAD SEA

GAZA

R. ARNON

ES-SAMU'

W. GHAZZEH

T. EL-FAR'AH

BEERSHEBA

KERAK

KHALASA

KH. ET-TANNUR

SBEITAH

AUJA EL-HAFIR

913.39
W9-BDZ-198
B + T.
2.63
Pel

B.+T.
2.63
Rife

The Ladder of Progress
in Palestine

Nympheum, or public fountain, at center of chief street (*cardo*) of Jerash; built 190 A.D.

DS1089
M3

THE LADDER OF PROGRESS

IN PALESTINE

A Story of Archaeological Adventure

by

Chester Charlton McCown

Sometime Director of the
American School of Oriental Research, Jerusalem
Director of the Palestine Institute
Pacific School of Religion

Publishers

HARPER & BROTHERS

NEW YORK *and* LONDON

Copyright, 1943, by Harper & Brothers
Printed in the United States of America

All rights in this book are reserved. It may not be used for dramatic, motion- or talking-picture purposes without written authorization from the holder of these rights. Nor may the book or part thereof be reproduced in any manner whatsoever without permission in writing except in the case of brief quotations embodied in critical articles and reviews. For information address: Harper & Brothers, 49 East 33rd Street, New York, N. Y.

SECOND EDITION

G-T

This book is complete and unabridged in contents, and is manufactured in strict conformity with Government regulations for saving paper.

To
WILLIAM FOXWELL ALBRIGHT
First Companion and Constant Mentor
in Matters Archaeological

34849

PREFACE

Unusually successful excavations have distinguished Palestine during the past two decades. Not all of them have as yet been fully described, but a spate of preliminary reports has poured from the press, while sumptuous—and expensive—volumes in a considerable number have appeared to give final and definitive accounts of what has been discovered. Even now others are anxiously awaited. But a time like this, when further work in the field is impossible, allows an opportune breathing space for surveying the large and rapidly growing mass of new information which has been dug out of the earth.

The purpose of this volume is to describe the methods and results of typical and important excavations so as to give an intelligent but nontechnical reader some appreciation of how the archaeologist works and what he discovers. The effort to understand what was going on amid the dust and dirt of excavation and to explain it to others, both in Palestine and at home, during these two decades has led to a desire to present the subject so that the reader or observer who is not an archaeologist will not see the archaeologist and his work through a glamorous haze, but will appreciate the difficulties and the limitations of archaeology as well as the values and the successes that have been won.

There is in archaeology the fascination of adventure, the seduction of a game of chance. But its real lure lies in the problems which are constantly appearing. Discovered materials which solve one problem usually raise several new ones. Archaeology, like all the social sciences, like all human effort, is constantly striving toward a moving goal. The archaeologist has the enduring satisfaction of making progress but never reaching the stagnation of finality. There are always new worlds to conquer. It is my hope that I have been able to suggest something as to the nature of the difficulties which must be met and the problems which have to be solved, both the practical dilemmas and tasks of the excavator's life and the historical questions which he is able to answer, as well as the character of the often recalcitrant materials he must use. While avoiding long and technical disputes on abstruse points, I have tried to exhibit the methods and achieved results of Palestinian archaeology so that the reader may be in a position to understand the reports which come to him from time to time and estimate their value.

This has been attempted through the rather full description of typical expeditions and the discussion of the outstanding problems rather than through a systematic and complete discussion. Exceptional opportunities due to connection with the American School of Oriental Research and, directly or indirectly, with a variety of expeditions running from prehistoric to Byzantine and Arab times have been exploited in the accounts here given. Almost every site discussed has been visited either before or during the period of excavation, or both. As full use as possible has been made of published reports and discussions, a burden of debt only partially acknowledged in the bibliographies. The chief difficulty has been the rapid growth of knowledge and the consequent change of opinions during the last twenty years and particularly during the dozen years while this volume has been in preparation.

To nearly every recent excavator mentioned in this book and to many others too numerous to mention I am in debt for repeated favors—hospitality, instruction, and hours spent in showing American School of Oriental Research students and myself over their excavations. I am especially indebted to Professor W. F. Albright for much advice in addition to the specific assistance mentioned in chapter VII, and to Professor John Garstang for assistance with chapter VI. Dr. T. D. McCown has read and criticized the chapters on prehistory and given other assistance. Dr. D. E. McCown read several of the earlier chapters and made many suggestions beside contributing many excellent photographs. Portions of the book have profited from criticisms by Dr. Beatrice McCown and my wife. Miss Margaret Harrison has made a large contribution to the final form of manuscript, plates, and plans.

January 31, 1943   C. C. McCown

CONTENTS

ILLUSTRATIONS

TEXT FIGURES AND MAPS

The Ladder of Progress
in Palestine

TABLE OF ARCHAEOLOGICAL PERIODS
WITH ABBREVIATIONS

	ALBRIGHT	WRIGHT		ALBRIGHT	WRIGHT
Neolithic	6th-5th millennia		Early Iron (Iron I)	1200-900	1225-900
Sub-Chalcolithic	late 5th millennium		EI i (Ia)	1200	1225
Chalcolithic	4th millennium		EI ii (Ib)	1150	1160
EC	± first quarter		EI iii (Ic)	1000	1000
MC	± second quarter		Middle Iron (Iron II)	900-530	900-500
LC	± 3500	± 3500	MI i (IIa)	900	900
Early Bronze	3000-2100	3300-2100	MI ii (IIb)	750	750
EB ia	+3000	3300	MI iii (IIc)	575	587
EB ib		3100	Persian, or Late Iron	530-330	500-330
EB ii	+2800	3000	LI	530	500
EB iii	2600	2700	Hellenistic		330-100
EB iv	2300	2300	Hellen.		330
Middle Bronze	2100-1500	2100-1500	Hellenistic-Roman	B.C. 100-100 A.D.	
MB i	2100	2100	Hellen.-Rom.		100 B.C.
MB iia	1900	1900	Roman		100-400
MB iib	1750	1750	Rom.		100 A.D.
MB iic	1600	1625	Byzantine		400-630
Late Bronze	1500-1200	1500-1225	Byz.		400
LB i	1500	1500			
LB ii	1350	1350			

It is to be understood that all of the above dates are approximate, referring to centuries and parts of centuries rather than to specific years. Early Iron I, II, and III was the terminology adopted by the Dept. of Antiquities and the archaeological schools in Jerusalem in 1921. The terms Early, Middle, and Late Iron were suggested in 1925 by Dr. C. S. Fisher and are here used because of their convenience and their uniformity in pattern with those for the previous periods. Iron I, II, and III are now preferred by both Albright and Wright. The terms Late Iron (LI) and Iron III are little used, despite their typographical convenience. Dr. Albright has recently revised his dates downward due to the discovery of the Khorsabad list of Assyrian kings; see Arno Poebel, *JNES*, I (1942), July and October; cf. Albright, *BAS*, 88 (1942), 28-36. The dates marked with a plus (+) are minimal dates. Wright's dates are given for convenience as used in his authoritative work on the earliest pottery, *The Pottery of Palestine from the Earliest Times to the End of the Early Bronze Age*. New Haven, 1937.

CHAPTER I

THE MAGIC OF METHOD

How Excavations Are Carried On

❖

BUCCANEERS AND TREASURE HUNTERS

PURPOSE usually determines method. The earliest excavators in the Near East were merely collectors of curiosities, often as aimless as pack rats. Kings, country gentlemen, and aspiring merchants adorned their palaces with objects which pleased their fancy, much as the small boy fills his pockets. Since, after the Renaissance, ancient art objects were regarded by collectors as peculiarly valuable, the earliest excavators dug with the sole purpose of uncovering golden treasures. Museums then were governed by the same desires and, too largely, the museums of today still are concerned with finding "museum pieces," objects which are beautiful or at least interesting to the common gaze. Inscriptions also were sought. But the budding historical interest of the period was concerned chiefly with inscriptions which carried names or dates that touched the great military or political or ecclesiastical figures of antiquity.

The prescientific excavators were, in fact, mere treasure hunters, and their methods were those of the looter. They sought mementos, not records, of the past. Where there was reason to suspect that jewelry or statuary or beautiful pottery was to be found, they ran trenches or dug pits. They threw away whatever was not unusual or had no aesthetic appeal and thus destroyed invaluable and irreplaceable historical data. They carted away to distant places or museums the objects they considered valuable in order to delight the eyes of their patrons, usually with no adequate record of the circumstances of discovery. The most beautiful objects out of their historical context have no scientific value. Only if one knows who made them, and where and when, do they contribute toward piecing out the story of man's upward climb from savagery to civilization.

Furthermore, material hidden away in private collections and unpublished has no historical value. Only a few years ago a French collector died who for over a generation had kept to himself a considerable number of inscriptions and other objects of artistic or historical value. He had never allowed any of them to be published because, so he said, he could not enjoy what had become public property by being made known to the world at large. Fortunately, even in earlier centuries, such unreasoning egoism was rare. Most collectors were glad to be advertised as owners of objects of historical or artistic worth. Fortunately, also, excavation was not undertaken on a large scale until its purposes had altered, its patrons had undergone some education, and its methods had been greatly refined.

It must be admitted that the buccaneering method of archaeology rendered services of value. If the looter from the West had not gone into the East and by bribes, diplomacy, or force carried off objects like the Elgin marbles, the chances are that the ignorance of the local inhabitants and the cupidity of antiquities dealers would have shattered many magnificent monuments and carried them away piece-meal as the Arabs broke up the "Moabite Stone." Any one who studies the descriptions former travellers have left of ancient sites or the pictures that were made fifty years ago and compares them with the meager remains of today can only thank the earlier excavator for removing and so preserving many objects which otherwise would have been destroyed. When one discovers indisputable evidence that beautiful marble statuary has been burned for lime, that magnificent reliefs have been taken down, smoothed off, and built into wretched modern hovels, that frescoes and paintings have been intentionally disfigured by iconoclastic fanaticism, one views the ancient looting collector with no small degree of tolerance. But one can be thankful that times and methods have changed.

SCIENTIFIC AIMS

The aims of the modern excavator are radically different. His purpose is scientific. He does not go into Bible lands to prove the Bible either true or false. He knows that his discoveries are sure to assist in the interpretation of the Bible, but he does not go to work with preconceived ideas which he wishes to establish. Like any scientist, he may have some hypothesis which he wishes to test, but the archaeologists I have known have not been more dogmatic or prejudiced than men in other fields. They have been seeking unwritten, material documents to put along beside the written documents of the past in order that the one may interpret the other.

Ostensibly at least the modern archaeologist has put away the childish collector mania. Even if he is representing a museum, he is no longer dominated by a desire merely to assemble statuary or bronzes or glass whose value is chiefly artistic or spectacular. His predominant purpose is historical, and that in the largest sense. His conception of history is radically different from that of a generation or two ago. He wishes to be able in the end to restore in model, picture, and writing the entire material civilization of the place and period with which he is concerned. He wishes to know the life of the people, to depict their buildings, public and private, to understand what tools they used and the technical processes of their artisans and artists. Their clothes, their household arrangements and furniture, their kitchen utensils and their diet, their industrial and commercial methods and organization, all of these are objects of investigation, and are of perhaps even greater interest than their political history or their military organization and accoutrements. The modern excavator wishes to restore in the mind's eye a complete civilization, an ancient society in all its details, and to follow its evolution from its meagre beginnings to its eventual dissolution. His dominant interest is in social evolution.

The modern excavator seeks historical data. Every scrap of evidence, therefore, must be noted and preserved. A broken pot dropped by a wayfarer as useless may be of much greater historical importance than beautiful statuary or imposing buildings. A copper coin may tell as interesting a story as a gold one. A broken potsherd may have a message of much greater value than a vessel that is whole. Finding a coin or a scarab or a characteristic bit of pottery above instead of below a floor level may change the history of a city. The style of the letters in an inscription may give the document its value. Happy as the excavator is to find an historical inscription, a graceful bit of statuary, an elegant and artistically decorated vase, or a rich collection of jewelry, the greater part of his work is given to "inconsidered trifles." His time is spent largely in registering bits of bone, metal, and baked clay that will never grace the show cases of a museum. He must note and record a hundred minor details which the uninitiated would not even see. Indeed, the excavators themselves have come to realize the importance of these less obvious matters only through long years of experience, and archaeological methods are being constantly improved and refined as the work continues.

BEFORE EXCAVATION BEGINS

The methods of the archaeologist will be illustrated in many ways in the subsequent accounts of various expeditions. There are, however, many items which are common to all and they may best be summarized in advance, in order to answer questions which would inevitably arise in a reader's mind.

How does the excavator know where to dig? There are four chief sources of information to guide to the kind of site that interests him: (1) ancient more or less contemporary references to places; (2) later but still ancient tradition handed down by Jewish, Christian, and Arabic writers; (3) modern Arabic tradition, which frequently preserves ancient place names, sometimes only slightly changed, and (4) the surface indications of walls and broken pottery, especially the latter, which afford the trained archaeologist a fairly accurate indication of the periods to which the site belongs. Sometimes a fifth means may be employed, a "trial trench," which is to determine whether the surface indications may be misleading. Where the identification of a site is disputed, the excavator hopes that his findings will eventually settle the problem. If he has two or three hypotheses upon which to work, the joy of solving a puzzle of historical importance may finally be his.

Having selected his site, the excavator's practical difficulties have only begun. How does he get permission to dig? In all countries of the Near East he must secure a permit from some official or department of the government. In Palestine the governmental department of Antiquities, with the assistance of an Archaeological Advisory Board consisting of representatives of various schools of archaeology, passes upon all applications. The prospective excavator must ask for his permit in the name of a reputable institution—a wholesome provision which prevents antiquities dealers and cranks from destroying historical data.

A true story will illustrate the need. An earnest individual came to Jerusalem with a divine revelation that the tomb of Christ was at Beth-shan in the necropolis where Mr. Alan Rowe had been excavating on behalf of the University of Pennsylvania Museum. To authenticate himself and his mission he could cite the fact that his name was mentioned in the Bible, for Isaiah (25.6) spoke favorably of "wines on the *Lees* well refined." (This is a fact!) The consul of his nation, finding him impervious to argument, sent him to the director of his national school of archaeology, who also could not dissuade him from his purpose. But a well-drawn Antiquities law and a quick-witted secretary proved a real safeguard to the ancient and much abused Land of Promise.

The law also requires assurance that the institution applying for a permit has sufficient funds to carry out a creditable piece of excavation, that the proposed staff is adequate, and that publication of results will be made in such fashion as to put the discoveries into the hands of all scholars. The removable "finds" are divided between the Palestine Museum, for the erection of which Mr. John D. Rockefeller, Jr., made a generous gift, and the institutions represented by the excavator, the Museum reserving the right to all unique pieces. By a wise and equitable administration of the law, a magnificent collection of great historical value is being gathered in Jerusalem, a collection which will eventually make the city more than ever a place of pilgrimage for scholars of all nations. At the same time, excavation is encouraged and objects are being scattered through Europe, Great Britain, and America to educate students and arouse the interest of patrons of archaeology.

One of the most trying hurdles the excavator faces, one which is sometimes extremely costly in time and money, is the negotiation for the land which is to be excavated. Beth-shan was government property, and so was part of the mound at Sepphoris (Saffûrieh). But few archaeologists are so fortunate. In a few cases the land is purchased outright, as at Megiddo. More often it is rented for a season or two and then restored to its former condition. Nearly every mound is agricultural land or contains fertile soil. Usually it belongs to peasants and to a large number, for family inheritances have been divided and subdivided until a field of two or three acres may have a dozen owners, each of whom the harassed excavator must satisfy. The Antiquities law provides that if the excavator and the owners cannot reach an agreement, Government shall appoint arbitrators to determine the proper sum. In recent years few serious disputes have arisen. At Jerash, part of the site had to be let alone during years of litigation caused by grasping claimants. The Palestine Exploration Fund expedition on Ophel was sadly "held up" by the arbiters appointed, to the advantage of a speculator in land values. At Malhah a small expedition of the American School of Oriental Research had to be abandoned because of the exorbitant demands of the owners. But such cases have luckily been rare.

The management of an expedition is a major business enterprise. The personnel is usually small in proportion to the variety

of tasks to be undertaken. The director should be a good execu-
tive and business manager in addition to being an historian and
linguist. Either he or one or more reliable assistants should be
competent archaeologists. Some one should know enough Arabic
to understand the feelings of the work people. An architect is
valuable, and he is necessary on a mound where there are buildings of more than the simplest construction. In any case there
must be a surveyor or draughtsman for planning and mapping
the structures uncovered. A competent photographer is demanded on every kind of dig, for a visual record of the various
stages of excavation is of infinite value when the archaeologist
needs to refresh his memory before writing his reports. As the
work progresses, levels change and buildings gradually appear.
A series of photographs will reveal a chain of developments
which escapes notice in the long spread of the excavator's labors.
Of real importance is the workman who puzzles over pottery
fragments till he restores whole vessels. If these tasks are left
until the objects are removed to the museum, the expedition
works more or less in the dark and may overlook important
evidence because the successive levels are not understood. Another laborious but essential task must be fulfilled by the re-
corder, for objects without their record are as good as destroyed.
One excavator nearly lost his permit because a lucky find so
overwhelmed him with pottery that he failed to keep accurate
records. Another has almost wrecked an important site because
the pottery fragments were neglected.

In addition to the staff of trained workers there must be a
large force of workmen who do the actual digging. Nearby
villages usually afford willing recruits. Even in the extreme south
on the edge of the "Wilderness of Sin" where there are no
settled villagers, Sir Flinders Petrie has found it possible to
recruit and train the seminomadic Bedouins of the region to
become reliable workmen. They come with their black "houses
of hair" and settle near the mound to work for four or five
months through the winter and spring. Everywhere the cash

which the excavator pays his workmen makes his intrusion most welcome to the larger part of the population.

The supervision of the workmen is carried on in different ways. Some excavators insist that a member of the staff must be in direct and constant charge of every significant section of the work. Others use native foremen, preferably Egyptians who have grown up with the great expeditions of Luxor or Memphis. Both methods have their good points. The staff member will understand the principles of archaeology far better. The Egyptian foreman has certain limitations. He will not understand so fully the ultimate aims of the excavator and the meaning of the objects discovered. But he usually knows the practical problems and understands the methods in use well enough for all ordinary purposes. He is more likely than a Westerner to be able to detect defections or deceptions on the part of the workmen. As an outsider, he is not likely to be in collusion with the indigenous workmen for the purpose of hiding and later profiting by finds of special value. He is less likely than a local foreman to racketeer at the expense of either his men or his employer. But some excellent Palestinian foremen have been developed. In any case members of the staff must be constantly "on the job."

To the distress of some lady visitors, the foreman usually carries a long and evil-looking whip. In the considerable number of excavations with which I have been very familiar, I have never seen the whip used with any direct effect. Its crack seems to stimulate activity—some stimulation is often necessary—and it serves as a symbol of authority. In the third millennium B.C. such a badge was in the hands of overseers by the Nile. The long lines of boys and women carrying their baskets of earth ply back and forth through the nine- or ten-hour day, usually to the accompaniment of a song which rings out over the hills with wearying monotony to Western ears but apparently with stimulating or narcotizing effect on the Easterner, and the occasional crack of the whip does not disturb it in the least.

Excavations are usually carried on in the country at a distance from any buildings which can be used for office or living quarters, and tent colonies are a frequent answer. Native-built houses of rough stone and mud roofs may be cheaply erected. The camp must be placed where it will be healthful, cool, and clean. It should not be directly east of the dig, because clouds of the dust will inevitably be carried to it by the prevailing westerly winds. Accessibility, water, and a dozen other factors are to be considered.

The commissary department is of basic importance. Water must be supplied for drinking and washing and for cleaning pottery. The health of the staff is a prime consideration. The excavator's day runs from five or six in the morning until ten or eleven at night. He may be in the field for only two or three months, but during that time he is working under extraordinary pressure. Nerves become frayed and quarrels within the staff, who are constantly treading on one another's heels both literally and figuratively, may seriously interfere with efficiency. Archaeologists are as human as any one—if not more so. Amoeba, dysentery, typhoid, and malaria lurk everywhere. Too great precautions as to sanitation, too careful attention to the removal of inconveniences and causes of irritation, and too abundant provision for comfortable living and nourishing food are impossible.

The office equipment and scientific instruments needed are no small financial burden. Tables and instruments for drafting and for recording, shelves and boxes for the storage of finds, a place for cleaning and assembling the thousands of potsherds, flints, coins, and other small objects, specially prepared paper and now a new rubber solution for making squeezes and tracings of inscriptions and carvings, paper for drawing and mapping, cards for recording, labels for baskets of pottery, caustic soda and zinc "tears" for cleaning coins or other bronze objects, these are some of the small worries. Cameras, photographic supplies, a dark room and its equipment, a surveyor's level, alidade, plane table, and other instruments, all must be at hand. The large, permanent expeditions have their own, often most elaborate equipment. In four or five Palestinian expeditions, a Decauville railway carries the earth and useless stone to the dump and saves hundreds of dollars in wages. The American School of Oriental Research has been co-operating with several smaller expeditions which do not work continuously by acting as a clearing house for the sharing of both staff and equipment of all kinds, thus obviating the necessity for sinking much capital in equipment which would through many months not be in use, while surveyors and other members of the staff as well as trained foremen also go from one expedition to another, thus securing steady employment and providing intelligent assistance to the excavator.

Work on the Mound

At last when the innumerable preliminaries are past and the camp is in order, the actual work can begin. Procedure will depend on the nature of the task. The large majority of Palestinian sites are tells, irregular oval mounds built up by long centuries of occupation. The first builders of cities usually occupied a limestone knoll or hill near a spring and built practically on the rock. Searching in the vicinity they found clay for sun-dried bricks or stones which, laid in mud mortar, would make the walls. On these they laid wooden beams covered with branches of trees or brush and then a layer of clay for the roof. The earth was their flooring. The predicament of the woman who lost a coin in the Gospel story is typical and suggestive. Streets piled up with debris and garbage. Floors also received a slow accumulation. The houses easily succumbed to earthquake or fire. If no such accident occurred, plague might drive the inhabitants away for a time, or a raid by enemies might bring destruction and temporary abandonment.

After lying for a few years only the upper parts of the walls would be visible and they would be too unstable to serve for new buildings. When the site was reoccupied, the new city was built above the old one with little attempt to clear away the debris except the visible building stone. Usually there was no digging of deep foundations. Such a procedure, repeated again and again in the course of the centuries, would form a mound of really imposing height. The debris of occupation at Beth-shan reaches a depth of at least 85 feet, at Megiddo 70. At Jerusalem the sacred rock at the top of the Temple hill has always been preserved uncovered by deposits, but in the Tyro-pean Valley there is an accumulation of at least 100 feet in some places.

In tombs and caves the deposits are partly due to materials carried in by man or washed in by rains, partly to constant deposits from the limestone ceilings. Though tombs were often cleared and reused, they usually have but one occupation which has left valuable materials. Occasionally the lower part will be partly filled with vessels from an earlier burial left when they were swept off the shelves where the bodies of new occupants were to be laid. One Tell en-Nasbeh tomb covers almost the entire history of Palestine. The floors of caves occupied by pre-historic man were littered with the ashes of his fires, the chips from his flint working, the tools he dropped or discarded, and the cracked and broken bones of the animals he had eaten. With deposits from the roof of the cave these gradually built up very respectable strata, and so here also clearly marked occupa-tional levels are found.

The more careful and ambitious the builders became, the more they erased the work of their predecessors, and thus the Greeks and the Romans have greatly increased the archaeologist's prob-lems by removing all of the superstructures of previous build-ings and digging deep foundations, with the result that Roman pottery may be found at the bottom of a fill with bronze-age pottery at the top. Cities which were continuously occupied, like Jerusalem, show numerous rebuildings on practically the same level, in the same style, and often with the reuse of old floors and foundations. In such cases it is often impossible for the archaeologist to disentangle the evidence.

When all the preliminary preparations are complete, the exca-vator faces a hilltop, a mound of earth, which holds all of his hopes. Where shall he begin? It is often a most perplexing problem. There may be outcropping walls to suggest where important buildings lay, but such indications may be misleading. A depression with a gentler slope on one side of the mound may point to the city gate, through which debris has washed away whereas elsewhere the city walls keep the top fairly level and prevent erosion. There may be nothing but broken pottery to mark the site. What can the excavator do?

Whatever the external appearance, in most cases the excavator digs one or more trial trenches from the bottom of the debris up to the top. This helps him to determine where he can discover valuable material, and it often inducts him at once into the chief problems of the site and points towards their solution. It gives him a bird's eye view of the long history of the mound, a preliminary cross section of the entire history of his tell, to which he can relate the various strata as they appear. While this preliminary work is going on, the surveyor will make a contour map of the tell showing its shape in all detail and indicating every outcropping wall. Sometimes an airplane picture assists. By these various means the point of attack is determined.

The archaeologist must also decide where he can safely dump the earth which covers the ruins he seeks. A spot must be found which can hold nothing of archaeological value and which is near enough to his seat of operations to avoid a long line of basket carriers to raise his aggregate expense for wages. It is not safe to dump even on neighboring fields or rock outcrop about the edge of the tell, for not infrequently investigation will show that tombs with extremely valuable deposits are concealed at just such points.

Another question is how to proceed on the mound itself. With the exception of the ideal expedition at Megiddo, excavators in Palestine have usually selected a certain section or sections of the mound for a season's work and have confined themselves to the part chosen. Here they dig to the underlying rock and then at the end of the season "fill in" again, restoring the plot to its owner ready for use. The next season an adjoining sector is similarly investigated.

The work begins with pick men going over the surface and loosening the soil to a depth of three or four inches. That is, the soil must be taken off layer by layer. Hoe men follow (the spade and shovel are almost unknown) and pull the earth into baskets which the women hoist to their heads or boys to their backs and toss upon the nearby dump or into the little railway cars. Under the steady work of a gang and a foreman a given section goes down and is recorded in stages of some ten inches. Every man is on the look-out for objects large and small. When beads or exceedingly small objects appear, the earth is carefully sifted. In tombs the earth near the floor is sifted. Once a "shalaby," a fine or fragile object appears, hoe and pick are banished for a small knife and a brush.

CONSERVING RESULTS

The area to be excavated is mapped out in arbitrary squares of say ten meters (33 feet), and also, if walls appear, by rooms which are systematically numbered. Tombs, cisterns, and grain bins are similarly numbered in series. As soon as any floor, door-sill, or other evidence of an occupational level is discovered, the work is directed toward clearing the whole area which belongs to this level, and all walls are carefully mapped, the very stones in the walls and on the floors being drawn to size on a large scale plan. Objects of importance are photographed *in situ* and drawn into the plans. Pottery and other small objects as found are collected in numbered baskets, minute objects such as coins and jewelry in cigaret boxes, all labeled so that the place and level of origin may be known. Only when buildings of one level are fully photographed and drawn and have been carefully described in the director's diary and notes are they removed so that work may proceed on the next lower level. In an ideal excavation the work is done with such care that a model of the original could be reconstructed from the plans, drawings, photographs, and descriptions. Thus no information of historical value is lost, though the whole may be destroyed.

While working on his mound the excavator will investigate

the neighborhood for other evidences of occupation which will throw light on his problems. He will inquire as to local traditions and names. Tombs are extremely valuable for two reasons, one scientific, the other practical. Because the ancients almost invariably deposited vessels containing food with the dead and also buried jewelry and other objects of value with them, tombs are likely to provide him with objects of value and with pottery which is intact. Coins, scarabs, and seals found in tombs will serve to date the pottery there found quite exactly, and a "tomb group" therefore becomes extremely useful in giving precision to the ceramic chronological scale. The stratified chronology of the tell and the tomb groups supplement one another in most desirable fashion. Moreover, the fine objects found in tombs will appeal to his patrons and make them feel that their money is well spent. Unfortunately nearly all tombs were plundered in antiquity, but ancient tomb robbers sought chiefly gold and silver, and that very hastily. Hence the excavator usually finds something of value to him.

When the labeled baskets of pottery and other objects are carried to headquarters, they are washed and cleaned. Careful washing will often reveal decoration that gives the expert pages of information. The fragments of pottery must be carefully spread out and studied by some one who has an eye for the solving of jig-saw puzzles. Often a practically complete vessel can be restored from a score of fragments which may be scattered through more than one basket. The shape, with peculiarities of base, neck, mouth, and handle, tells the pottery expert the date of the vessel. The texture, color, and baking of the clay are also important data. One or two excavators bite and taste their pottery—not an entirely sanitary procedure and not regarded by others as scientific. The gradual accumulation of innumerable details as to all of the factors above mentioned in stratified tells has made pottery one of the surest of chronological criteria. Beauty of decoration and form is of secondary importance to the archaeologist who is seeking scientific historical data.

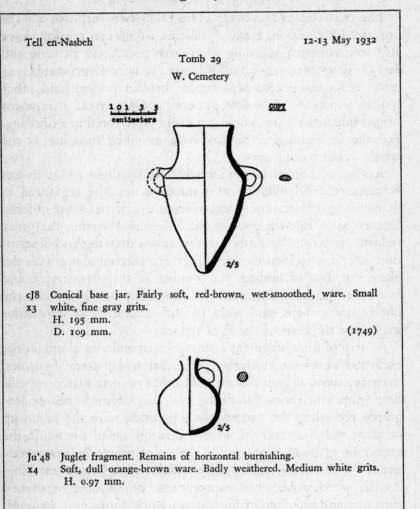

Tell en-Nasbeh   12-13 May 1932

Tomb 29

W. Cemetery

10 1 3 5
centimeters

COPY

2/5

cJ8   Conical base jar. Fairly soft, red-brown, wet-smoothed, ware. Small
x3   white, fine gray grits.
      H. 195 mm.
      D. 109 mm.   (1749)

2/5

Ju'48   Juglet fragment. Remains of horizontal burnishing.
x4   Soft, dull orange-brown ware. Badly weathered. Medium white grits.
       H. 0.97 mm.

A POTTERY RECORD CARD FROM TELL EN-NASBEH

Drawn to a $\frac{2}{5}$ scale for reduction to $\frac{1}{5}$ when published. When only one half
of a vessel is preserved, the other half can be restored, like the handle in the
upper drawing; but when both sides are wanting it must be left unfinished
as in the neck of the small globular juglet. Tomb 29 belongs to the period
of the Hebrew monarchy.

FIG. 1

The next step is recording. This takes two forms in a well-organized expedition. First, all objects which can possibly have any archaeological meaning are drawn accurately to scale and described on cards of a uniform size. A very large number of cards and photographs will record broken pottery and other objects which are not worth preserving. Often from a fragment of one side of a jar the whole can easily be restored in a drawing. For the archaeologist this has fully as much meaning as the whole vessel would have.

Second, all objects which are whole or by slight additions can be restored for exhibition in a museum must be registered in duplicate under serial numbers which are written on the objects. One copy of this list goes to the Palestine Museum, the other remains with the expedition. In this case a drawing and description sufficient to identify the object are entered along with the place and date of finding, the number of the photograph, and any other valuable information. These records, along with the photographs, maps, and plans of the excavation at its various stages, are the basis of the final report.

A "day of final judgment" hangs like an ominous cloud on the excavator's horizon. With the accumulation of pottery, figurines, statuary, tools, utensils, coins, and other objects in the expedition "museum," with the filling of boxes of cards and photographs recording the various kinds of finds, with the piling up of maps and plans and the written descriptions of the work, the excavator gradually approaches the point where he can reconstruct the life of the ancient city which he has been unearthing. As the weather becomes unpropitious, or his time or money runs low and the close of his season's work draws near, he sends for a representative of the Museum to divide the "spoil." He works feverishly from early morning till late at night to have everything ready. He seems usually to make some of his most important "finds" just at the last moment and it appears impossible to have all photographs and records in the hands of the Museum's representatives, as required by law, days in advance of the time for the division.

Photo by D. E. M.

Payday at Jericho. Money had to be brought from Jerusalem with a police escort.

A "Fantasia," a dance in celebration of payday.

Photo by D. E. M.

At center the white building is the Antiquities Museum at Jerusalem. Over its wing is the tower of St. George's Cathedral, and just to its left over the corner of the museum is the roof of the American School of Oriental Research.

The American School of Oriental Research at Jerusalem from the rear. Director's house to left of patio, main building at center and corner of the annual professor's wing at right.

Finally the day for the division comes and the whole staff and the workmen too wait "with bated breath" for the outcome. With regret that is barely tempered by a recognition of the justice of the law, the excavator sees his unique pieces, his prize discoveries, set aside for removal to Jerusalem. But he gives thanks for temporary loans of striking objects and for special concessions in the matter of duplicates which may to some extent balance the sequestration of the more beautiful or more unusual objects.

Then comes the long and uninteresting task of packing up his share of the finds, breaking camp, and journeying home. After that there looms the tedious and arduous labor of writing accounts of the season's work for various archaeological journals and a fuller "preliminary report" demanded by the Antiquities law. Only after some years and much more monotonous research can the final report appear with its story of the entire expedition, and most important of all, its reconstruction of a section of the life of the ancient world.

CHAPTER II

SEVENTY-FIVE THOUSAND YEARS BEFORE HISTORY BEGAN

❖

PALESTINE offers the most complete and continuous picture of prehistoric human evolution that is at present available in any part of the world. Even in single discoveries, China with *Sinanthropus peikinensis*, Java with *Pithecanthropus erectus*, Rhodesia and Kenya with their much debated skeletons from extremely early geological strata, have nothing more remarkable than recent finds in Palestine. Fifteen years ago almost nothing was known of the Stone Age in Palestine. The remarkable progress made in this brief period as well as the interest of the discoveries justifies an ample account.

In studying prehistoric cultures we are in the position of trying to piece together a book from fragmentary exemplars printed at different times and in different editions. One page is found in one place, a whole quire from a different version in another, a few pages from a still different account somewhere else. It is fortunate if there is enough overlapping to enable us to recognize the order of the pages. Before 1925 the prehistorian in Palestine was in position similar to that of an historian if his sources covering thousands of years were torn into fragments and piled here and there in heaps with no dates and no indication of authorship.

Until 1925 no human remains of the Old Stone Age and no superimposed and undisturbed strata exhibiting the industries of the Stone Age had come to light in Palestine. Innumerable flint tools of many types had been found, but only at surface stations where early and late types were often inextricably mixed together. Useful service had been rendered by many scholars in classifying such surface stations with their innumerable flint tools, but, without excavation, with no indications of date but the very precarious criteria of type and technique, no sure results were possible. Now, aside from human remains of ancient date in part not yet published, Palestine can boast a dozen more or less complete Neandertal or Neandertaloid skeletons. They were found where the bodies had been buried in the midst of the stone tools which the dead or their immediate ancestors had used. Moreover they were directly related to a most complete and satisfactory series of successive levels of Stone Age cultures, which have been handsomely and scientifically published by competent experts. Almost as important as the skeletons of people of the Old Stone Age were remains of over one hundred individuals of the Middle Stone Age, representing the arrival of modern man, *Homo sapiens*, in Palestine. Meantime the paleontological study of the animal remains discovered has painted in a part of the background against which early man must be pictured.

GALILEE MAN

The first epoch-making discovery was made in Galilee. In the year 1923 an Oxford student, Mr. F. Turville-Petre, abandoned the quiet of university life to seek adventure in the field of archaeology. Going to Palestine he prospected in Galilee and found attractive and promising sites near the Plain of Gennesaret. In 1925, on behalf of the British School of Archaeology in Jerusalem and under the general supervision of Professor John Garstang, director of the School and of the Department of Antiquities, he excavated two caves just at the edge of the plain at its northern side, Mughâret el-Emireh ("the cave of the Princess") and Mughâret ez-Zuttiyeh ("the cave of the Gipsy woman"). To reach Mughâret ez-Zuttiyeh one must climb some 130 feet above the present level of the oleander-bordered stream of Wad' el-'Amud to a bold limestone cliff.[1] In the cave and the large terrace in front of it, Mr. Turville-Petre dug down through

[1] See illustration facing p. 49.

various levels: the dung left by the sheep folded there in winter; hearth levels with Arab, Byzantine, and eventually Iron Age and Bronze Age pottery; then a layer of fallen rock, including one large boulder, which isolated a considerable portion from any possible disturbance. Below this stratum, in a bed of fine, reddish, argillaceous earth, were hard mineralized bones of many animals and flint tools definitely like those which are called Mousterian because they were found first at Le Moustier in France and which belong to the middle of the Old Stone Age. As one looked at the bank of earth and rock through which the excavator had penetrated into the past, seven levels of human occupation appeared. One moment the gaze might rest on objects in use within but a few centuries and the next the hand might touch a tool that some uncouth, shambling ancestor of man shaped eons ago.

Here, under the large boulder and deep down in the layer of man-made deposits, amid flints of the Mousterian type, Mr. Turville-Petre came upon four pieces of a skull now famous as the "Galilee man."[2] It was an epoch-making discovery, for, up to that time, no primate remains so old by tens of thousands of years had been found in Palestine. Indeed no careful skeletal studies had been made in Palestine except in connection with Macalister's excavations at Gezer (1908), where a "pre-Semitic" race of about 3000 B.C. was discovered and studied by the excavator's father, a surgeon who fortunately came that way at the right time. The Galilee skull dates back to at least 40,000, perhaps, even to 100,000 years ago and actually represents an entirely new species related to the genus *Homo*.

A popular preacher contrasted "Galilee man and the Man of Galilee." Yet it is not from a sentimental but from a scientific point of view that these four bits of human braincase are important. They were put into the hands of the famous English anatomist and (physical) anthropologist, Sir Arthur Keith, who identified them as coming from the skull of a young man of the

[2] For a time the skull was thought to be that of a woman, but further study has reversed the verdict.

Neandertal race. It was the first discovery of a member of that race outside of Europe. Over twenty skeletons, or more often parts of skeletons, of members of the race had been found in Europe, in Germany, Spain, Belgium, Moravia, France, Croatia, Italy, Gibraltar, and the islands of Jersey and Malta. The types of flint instruments made and used by the Neandertalers, the Mousterian, were well known in all of these countries. They had been found in North Africa, Syria, Iraq, and Palestine, and, it is now claimed, in China and Rhodesia. But, outside of Europe, who made and used them? When the boulder was tilted over and the brown fragments of skull lay revealed, a new chapter was begun in the prehistory, not only of Palestine, but of the world, for they proved for the first time that similar races were making and using similar flint tools in Asia as well as Europe. Sir Arthur Keith noted also that the skull was partly Neandertal, partly of a different type. Was Galilee man a true Neandertaler? The discoveries which Mr. Turville-Petre made opened up many new vistas, but left many questions undecided because they stood alone. Happily material looking toward a solution of these problems was not long in coming to light.

Shuqbah—A New Civilization

The second excavation in search of prehistoric materials was carried on by a joint expedition of the British School of Archaeology in Jerusalem and the American School of Prehistoric Research. In the spring of 1928 Miss Dorothy Garrod undertook the excavation of a cave at Shuqbah in Wad' en-Natuf on the edge of the Central Mountain Range some ten miles northwest of Jerusalem. The large and lofty cavern, which lay on the north side of the wadi over seventy feet above its floor, had been discovered in 1924 by an indefatigable explorer of Palestine, the late Father Alexis Mallon, S.J., director of the Pontifical Biblical Institute in Jerusalem, who kindly relinquished discoverer's rights to Miss Garrod. She came fresh from the discovery of the skull of a Neandertal child on Gibraltar.

Could such a discovery be duplicated in Palestine and answers found to some of the questions which Mr. Turville-Petre's excavation in Galilee had raised? Was it possible to add materially to the story of prehistoric man in Palestine? The fact that, as a result of six years of exploration and excavation in the Near East, chiefly in Palestine, Miss Garrod has been made the first woman professor at Cambridge University suggests the success she has had. Largely due to her efforts Palestine has become almost the classical land of prehistory, vying even with France. The single season at Shuqbah served as a most useful introduction to the search for Stone Age man in Palestine.

The physical task of recovering the evidences of prehistoric human occupation is simple. Their interpretation was then difficult, for in Palestine such excavation was almost entirely new. The ancient inhabitants of the cave had left their tools of flint and bone and the bones of the animals they had eaten mixed with earth, charcoal from their fires, and droppings from the limestone roof, all in confusion on the floor where they had lived. They had buried their dead underneath. The debris deposited had been unevenly distributed and often had been disturbed in various ways. In such deposits there are usually no marks by which to distinguish the remains of one period from those of the next except slight differences in the color and consistency of the earth, in the kinds of animal bones, and in the types of tools. Excavation has to be by layers of four or five inches. Everything found is carefully recorded and accurate statistics are kept. In some cases only a decided difference in the numbers of a particular tool in two neighboring strata serves to indicate a change in culture. Miss Garrod's intimate knowledge of European prehistory enabled her to recognize the variety of artifact types, for, though the European and Palestinian types differed, there were decided family resemblances. Eventually, in the hands of Miss Bate, the animal bones discovered in the strata of various excavations served to record the fluctuations of Palestinian climate in the Stone Ages.

At Shuqbah Professor Garrod discovered three layers of human deposits. The topmost stratum, as in all such sites, contained pottery and other objects of all ages. The second, which ranged from one and one half to twelve feet in depth, revealed a unique microlithic industry which Miss Garrod later named Natufian, because it was first found here, in Wad' en-Natuf. It is characterized by multitudes of tiny crescents, triangles, and trapezoids of flint and by various miniature knives, points, borers, and cores of flint. There were "carefully made bone points, . . . a few coarse needles, one with an eye near the point," and a "fragmentary bone plaque decorated with groups of parallel incisions engraved obliquely along the edges." The stratum contained numerous animal bones, black hearths, and eleven burials, of which at least seven were certainly contemporary with this industry. Some forty-five individuals were represented. They represent the oldest race of modern man yet found in Palestine.

Below this layer was another consisting of large quantities of animal bones in a tough, sometimes rock-like, breccia. The flint industry represented a vigorous phase of the Upper Levalloisian (Middle Paleolithic) period. Of human remains in this layer there were only a large molar tooth and a fragment of a skull of Neandertal type. Like one stratum at Mugharet ez-Zuttiyeh, the upper part of it had been washed and redeposited by a flow of water through the cave, indicating a period of heavy rains. Evidently a long interval elapsed between this Middle Paleolithic stratum and the Mesolithic Natufian.

These three unrelated strata raised more questions than they answered. Much as the Shuqbah excavation revealed regarding Stone Age man, the story would have been quite fragmentary and disconnected but for the further discoveries at Mugharet el-Wad which unexpectedly interrupted excavation at Shuqbah.

Mugharet el-Wad

By all odds the most important prehistoric site yet excavated in Palestine is to be found in the caves at the mouth of Wad' el-Mugharah (the "gorge of the cave") on the western edge of the Mount Carmel range, eighteen miles south of Haifa. Here were uncovered an astonishing series of superimposed and interrelated layers of prehistoric occupation, comprising seventy feet of deposits and, still more astonishing, the remains of a large number of skeletons. Ten of them constitute one of the most remarkable and valuable prehistoric discoveries ever made. Others supplemented and overshadowed the skeletal discoveries of Shuqbah. The story of this instructive site demands telling in some detail.

Wad' el-Mugharah cuts through the steep slope at the western foot of the Carmel range three and a half miles southeast of the beautiful Crusader castle of 'Athlit. The Coastal plain, which is only a narrow ribbon at the promontory of Carmel, slowly widens southward until at this point it is an expanse of nearly two miles of waving grain. Where the wadi cuts its way through the limestone cliffs that border the level plain, it leaves a jutting crag on either side. On the southern side are four caves, one of which had never been occupied and was therefore sterile. Three were remarkably rich in remains, Mugharet es-Sukhul (the "cave of the kids"), Mugharet et-Tabun (the "cave of the oven"), and largest of all, Mugharet el-Wad (the "cave of the gorge").[3] The last cave faces northwest at the angle between the wadi and the north-south line of the mountain side. Its entrance, which is half way up the cliff, looks out to the blue Mediterranean high above the trees at the mouth of the wadi, and can be seen from a considerable distance. These fine caves, in limestone strata full of nodules of flint ready for the making of smaller tools and of chert for hand axes, offered perfect homes for prehistoric man.

The region came to archaeological notice in the autumn of 1928 when the company which was building the Haifa breakwater thought of using the cliffs as a source of supply for stone. When blasting was begun in order to sample the stone, numerous flint tools were uncovered. This was reported to the Department of Antiquities, and the director, Mr. E. T. Richmond, sent a member of the department to investigate the archaeological value of Mugharet el-Wad. His soundings proved it to be un-

---

[3] Arab ingenuity in inventing names nodded here. The "cave of the gorge" is in the "gorge of the cave."

expectedly productive. Not only did he find numerous artifacts running back into the Stone Age, but also what appears to be a young calf, or deer, carved in the round on the end of a bone and evidently coming from a very primitive period of art. Burials were discovered in connection with a stone industry characterized by pigmy flints like those at Shuqbah. Better stone for the breakwater was found on the coast near the railroad, and, therefore, no clash arose between commercial and archaeological interests.

As a result of the successful soundings, Mr. Richmond asked Miss Garrod to transfer her expedition to Mugharet el-Wad. This she did in the spring of 1929 and the task was completed in seven periods of about three months each, spread over the years 1929-1934. The three caves were excavated at Wad' el-Mugharah and, in 1931, another, called Mugharet el-Kebarah ("the big cave"), was partially cleared near the railway station of the Jewish colony, Zichron Yaqob, formerly Zammerin.

In such an out-of-the-way place, provision for the household needs of the staff was a problem which was not immediately solved. The first season the staff lived somewhat uncomfortably in the caves. Later, camp was made in tents, eventually with the addition of a stone building, erected native fashion, to serve as cook and store house. The workers, most of whom were women, came chiefly from the nearest village, Jeba', which lies a mile or more to the south. They welcomed the opportunity to earn ready cash, and the relations of staff and workers were most cordial.

Minor difficulties enlivened the excavators' often monotonous labors. One morning one of the excavators was suddenly struck and stung just over the eyebrow by a small but very fast-flying bee. He thought nothing of it at the moment but soon began to feel faint and numb in his extremities. He was helped to his bed in his tent and was laid on the shelf for the day. The next day the one eye was swollen shut, the following day the other. In two or three days the effects were entirely gone and he suffered no subsequent ill effects. The cook had recently been stung on the ear by a similar bee and had suffered no evil consequences. He concluded that Europeans were inferior to Arabs.

Another morning one of the Arab women workers yawned so tremendously that she threw her jaw out of place. Immediately all the workers were in tremendous excitement. As Dr. Martha Hackett, who was looking after the health of the camp, was in Haifa, the excavators feared to attempt to replace the offending mandible lest they break off the ascending ramus. However the people themselves had less dangerous remedies to propose. Since a *jinni* must have caused such an unusual accident, it was necessary to resort to magic. As they crowded about the frightened girl, someone suggested putting a copper coin in her mouth, someone else that they call a sorcerer. All was excitement and distress, until suddenly the offending member slipped into place of itself. The only troublesome consequence was that for a time the other women refused to work with the unfortunate one lest the same *jinni* get them also. Unless the reader of archaeological reports pictures the excavator's life as continually punctuated by half-amusing, half-troublesome incidents, he will have no complete idea of what actual excavation involves.

The plan of work followed at such a site and in such remains is naturally very different from that adopted in a city ruin. The total amount of earth to be moved is small. The artifacts are very small. A man was employed to dig out basketfuls of deposit, and carry them to groups of three or four women who sat together and sifted material from the baskets. They were taught to save every bit of stone, bone, shell, or other material which could possibly be of archaeological interest. The staff supervised the work of the women closely and, from what they had saved, selected all worked flints and other objects of human handiwork as well as fragments of bone which might serve to determine the fauna of the periods from which the remains come.

Professor Garrod found that Mugharet el-Wad consisted of three parts, two lofty chambers near the front and a long corridor running over 200 feet back into the mountain. In front of the cave was a terrace built up of the deposits from millennia of human occupation. Soundings in the corridor found it to be unstratified, relatively sterile, and also very wet. It was, therefore, ignored. The floor deposits in the large outer chamber had been extensively disturbed, but in the smaller inner chamber seven distinct layers, six of them prehistoric, were eventually distinguished. Within two of these layers there were sufficient differences between the upper and lower parts to justify subdividing them, making actually nine strata of civilization in all. They were not separated by sterile strata; in other words the cave had been continuously occupied and there were here almost no distinct breaks in the story of social evolution during 75,000 or 100,000 years. Thus rung after rung in an almost complete ladder of civilization was discovered.

The Natufian at Mugharet el-Wad

After an uppermost mixed stratum, Professor Garrod found herself plunged into the familiar microlithic culture of Shuqbah, and, during the first two seasons, it occupied the center of the stage. It appeared in both chambers of the great cavern and in the terrace in front of it. In this stratum (B) at least six items may be picked out as specially significant: peculiar microlithic flints, sickles for cutting grain, numerous carvings in bone and the bone implements, various ornaments in bone, the burial of at least sixty-four individuals in the cave and terrace of Mugharet el-Wad, and finally certain cup holes cut into the rock in connection with these burials.

During 1929 and 1930, the Natufian at Mugharet el-Wad was regarded as homogeneous. Only when, in 1931 and the following years, a wider area was dug in the terrace, was it discovered that there were two phases of Natufian culture here, the earlier distinguished from the later by greater care in the making of the implements and by a different kind of retouching. In general the classes of implements were the same in all. In bulk the most impressive group of artifacts was the microliths. Of greater significance were the long bones, such as rib bones of deer, with grooves along one side into which little flint blades a half or three quarters of an inch long were set. The outer edge was often polished, evidently by the stalks of grass which the blades had cut. They are evidence of agriculture of a kind, at least the reaping, if not the sowing, of grain, long before pottery was known. Many fragments of basalt mortars and pestles suggested the making of flour.

Some of the primitive sickles had carved handles and their shape indicated that possibly they were for ceremonial, not actual, use. Some of these carvings in the round seemed to be intended to represent goats or deer. The number of bone tools, such as barbed harpoon or spear points, awls, and pins was large. Bone ornaments, chiefly pendants, and dentalium shells made into caps and circlets were numerous. There were a few small phallic objects. One crude carving of a human head in calcite was found near an infant burial.

Within the cavern the skeletons, which included all ages and both sexes, were laid on their backs in the extended position. The larger number, in the terrace, lay on their sides with limbs loosely flexed. They were variously oriented. Some, both old and young, had dentalium caps or circlets about their heads. The oldest interments were distinguished by three group burials, one of four, one of five, the other of eleven individuals, by a tightly flexed position, the knees being drawn up to the chin.

As the clearance of the terrace in front of Mugharet el-Wad continued in 1930, the rock underneath its upper part was exposed. It sloped gradually down for some thirty-two feet and then dropped away rapidly. In the lower part a small area (5 x 7 ft.) had been partially leveled and here were found a sort of pavement and in the rock itself a series of cups, or basins, which were evidently artificial. One in particular was like a perfect inverted cone about 16 inches in diameter and 16 inches deep, set off by a rim carefully carved in relief. As it went down to a perfect point and showed no signs of wear, it could never have been intended for any practical use. The inescapable conclusion is that this installation was for ritual purposes and, in view of the numerous burials, served some cult of the dead.

STRATA AT WAD' EL-MUGHARAH

PERIODS	STRATA	DIAGRAMMATIC SECTION	CLIMATE & FAUNA
I Recent Bronze Age	All Caves A		
II Upper Natufian	M. Wad B1		
II Lower Natufian	M. Wad B2		very dry, warm gazelles abundant
III Atlitian	M. Wad C		increasingly dry conditions, warm
IV Middle Aurignacian	M. Wad D		slightly moister, warm
V Middle Aurignacian M. Wad-	M. Wad E		change to dry climate
VI Lower Aurignacian	M. Wad F		warm
VII Upper Levalloiso-Mousterian	M. Wad G		heavy rainfall
	Tabun Chimney		perhaps slight fall in temperature
	Tabun B		great faunal change
VIII Lower Levalloiso-Mousterian	Tabun C		warm & dry, approach of wet conditions
	Sukhul B		at close permanent rivers
IX Lower Levalloiso-Mousterian M. Sukhul-	Tabun D		becoming drier Gazella & Dama equal
	? Sukhul C		
X Upper Acheulean (Micoquian) Tabun-	Tabun E- A		warm & damp, growing somewhat drier
	B		mixed fauna
	C		
	D		survivals from Level F Rhinoceros & Hippopotamus present Dama plentiful
XI Upper Acheulean	Tabun F		damp and tropical microfauna of primitive species
XII Tayacian	Tabun G		
Bedrock			

FIG. 2.

The excavation of the Natufian in Palestine wrote an entirely new chapter in the history of the Stone Age, but it was an isolated chapter. The industry has certain resemblances to the Capsian of Gafsah in North Africa, but it is so different in its general character as to be independent of any direct connection with that part of the world. It is likewise without any close analogies in Europe, and, when Professor Garrod finished her second season at Mugharet el-Wad in the summer of 1930, it was without connections either below or above in Palestine. Like Melchizedek, it lacked both forebears and offspring, and, unlike him, it seemed to have no contemporaries. It required excavation at other sites, as well as further labors at this one, to fill in the connections both below and above, both before and after the Mesolithic of Mugharet el-Wad. At Mugharet el-Kebarah and notably at Jericho, where some of the missing cues were discovered, the story is continued.

CHAPTER III

THE SEARCH FOR THE EARLIEST INHABITANTS

❖

PALEOLITHIC CULTURES

As MISS GARROD dug under the Lower Natufian of stratum B, she found an unrelated civilization out of which the Natufian could not have developed. There was no sterile layer, but stratum C was peculiar. It belonged to the Paleolithic, not the Mesolithic period. It was marked by the intrusion of a type of curved flint points which were more primitive than any in the preceding stone industry, differing in this from the Upper Aurignacian of Europe. It was so peculiar that Miss Garrod gave it a distinctive name, Atlitian, from 'Athlit, the site of the Crusader castle not far away.

The three strata next below partially explained what had happened at the end of the Old Stone Age, and how stratum C had received its peculiar character. Up to that time Palestine and Europe had belonged to one cultural area. Strata D, E, and F represent the long accumulations of the Middle and Lower Aurignacian periods in Europe, when man's technical skill increased and his fashions changed very slowly. The last of the three (D) at Mugharet el-Wad differs from its contemporary European industry in that it contains a large amount of charcoal but no bone tools, which are common in Europe. Apparently Palestine was then more heavily forested than Europe. Its forests increased still more in the period represented by stratum C.

Whether as a result of its heavy forests or not, stratum D deteriorated toward its close and was unable to resist the intrusion of the more primitive culture which appears in stratum C. This shows that the cultural unity of the western and Near Eastern worlds was broken, with the result that Palestine began to develop along a path of its own.

The lowest Aurignacian stratum (F) contained only a mass of flint instruments and chips, the majority of them "rolled," that is abraided, or worn, by the action of flowing water. They were so numerous that, when the three or four little gangs of workers began to shift the materials from this stratum, flints came out by the hundred every day. Miss Garrod had to add a fourth to her European staff of three to keep abreast of the output. How explain this "all-flint" stratum, as the Arab workers named it? Miss Garrod believes that the heavy rains of a pluvial period produced a large spring in the "corridor" in the back of the cave and that the stream from it leached out all the lighter materials. That similar evidence of periods of heavy rainfall has appeared at Mugharet ez-Zuttiyeh, Shuqbah, and Mugharet el-Wad does not prove that the period was the same or that it was contemporary with any European ice age. But it is possible that eventually the data will be found so correlated as to establish such an identity.

The next stratum at Mugharet el-Wad, which was Levalloiso-Mousterian in its cultural character, rested directly on the rock. But the excavation of this cave was far from having exhausted the riches of Wad' el-Mugharah or from having reached the beginning of human occupation, for the two other caves, Mugharet es-Sukhul and Mugharet et-Tabun, carried the story on down for thousands of years. Fortunately there were no questions as to chronological relations. Mugharet et-Tabun had as its uppermost unmixed layer (B) an Upper Levalloiso-Mousterian industry like the lowest (G) in Mugharet el-Wad. Mugharet es-Sukhul paralleled the Lower Levalloiso-Mousterian of strata C and D in Mugharet et-Tabun, and this last cave carries the story of man's slow progress toward civilization back through three more successive strata with various phases to a primitive Tayacian culture which rests on bedrock.

MUGHARET ET-TABUN

The "Cave of the Oven," excavated in 1929 and 1931-34, serves thus to fill out the long history of man's progress. Some seventy-five yards southwest of Mugharet el-Wad, facing almost due north lies the cave which owes its name to a chimney-like hole that opens the inner part of it to the sky. Both the inner and the outer chambers had surprisingly deep deposits left by human habitation and in front was a steeply sloping talus (rather than a terrace) which also had preserved a large amount of material.

Its peculiar value lay first in the fact that it evidently had not been abandoned until after men began to live in Mugharet el-Wad. It is the combination of overlapping levels which renders the discoveries at Wad' el-Mugharah so interesting and important. The sections of the ladder of civilization fit together admirably. Mugharet et-Tabun was valuable for a second reason. No skeletal fragments of man of the Old Stone Age, aside from a tooth or two, appeared in Mugharet el-Wad. But in the inner chamber, the "Chimney" of Mugharet et-Tabun, a considerable number of bones were found, chiefly skull fragments and both adult and milk teeth in layer B, and several bones in layer C, while one complete and well preserved skeleton of a woman came from layer C.

The skeleton lay just outside the cave entrance on the west side of the talus with the head pointing due west. It rested on its back, slightly turned to the left side, with the legs loosely flexed and the left arm bent at right angles to the body. The skull was crushed and the right arm was fragmentary. The bones, which showed a number of breaks probably due to the roots of a carob tree which grew near, were hard and colored mahogany brown. The skeleton lay only a little over a foot below the surface of level C and it is not possible to say whether it belonged originally to layer C or had been buried from layer B, but it certainly was an intentional burial.

MUGHARET ES-SUKHUL AND CARMEL MAN

The chief skeletal remains, however, came from a much smaller and less promising site. At about the level of Mugharet el-Wad, a few yards to the east up the wadi, lies the cave, or

rock shelter, called Mugharet es-Sukhul, the "cave of the kids."
Excavation discovered three layers. First were 50 to 70 centimeters of mixed recent, Upper Paleolithic (Aurignacian), and
Mousterian material. There followed a Mousterian industry of
the same type as that in the other caves, with abundant animal
bones, subdivided into two layers differentiated by slight peculiarities in the artifacts and in the type of earth in which they
were buried. The basal layer consisted of abraided flints with
no bones. The distinction of Mugharet es-Sukhul lies in that
its middle layer (B) harbored a larger number of better preserved Old Stone Age skeletons than had ever been found in
one place.

A sounding made in the floor of Mugharet es-Sukhul in 1929
confirmed the surface indications of the presence of a Mousterian industry. In the spring of 1931 the presence of a larger
staff made it possible for Miss Garrod to assign the clearing
to the cave to Dr. Theodore D. McCown, of the University of
California and the American School of Oriental Research in
Jerusalem, who, in 1930, had joined the expedition as representative of the American School of Prehistoric Research.

The cave faces almost due north and runs back into the rock
only some twenty feet. In front of it is a terrace sixteen by forty
feet in area. The limestone strata overhang the deposits in the
characteristic fashion of the European "rock shelter." Unfortunately the terrace was partly covered with great blocks of
rock deposited by the blasting operations at the time when the
Haifa breakwater company were prospecting for materials.
In many places the earth which had covered the deposits had
solidified into a breccia almost as hard as concrete. The work
was, therefore, alternately slow and rapid. The clearance was
made by horizontal stripping in arbitrary levels of ten centimeters (four inches). In the breccia chunks had to be broken
off by pick or with hammer and chisel. The women then broke
up the chunks with a blow of a hammer and the flints came
out quite clean.

This monotonous labor, with an ever increasing harvest of

Mousterian flints, had been going on for six weeks, and, by the middle of May, 1931, the stripping had reached a level about six and a half feet below the surface and just above the lower Mousterian layer, when the workmen early one morning came upon part of a lower jaw with teeth which Dr. McCown immediately recognized as clearly human. Shortly another part of the jaw appeared. A little later the pick man, who was breaking off the chunks of breccia, disclosed the skull. Dr. McCown then chiseled out a twelve-inch cube of breccia. This he carried to camp and began to chisel down to lessen its weight. On one side he came upon a humerus and, on another, upon a part of the pelvis and ribs.

As tools were not at hand for clearing the hard incrustations of lime from the fragile bones, the whole block was shipped to Sir Arthur Keith in London, where in the laboratories of the Royal College of Surgeons, the skeleton was freed from the covering which has preserved it these tens of thousands of years. It has been found to be almost completely preserved and to belong to a girl of some four or five years. It lay in one corner of the block with limbs tightly flexed. Apparently it had been wrapped or tied up and then deposited in a kneeling or squatting position in a hole in the floor. It was, therefore, clearly an intentional burial. Thus "Sukhul I" came to be. One cannot forget the excitement at the American School of Oriental Research in Jerusalem one May afternoon when a telegram came saying, "Neandertaler found!"

The skeleton showed many definitely Neandertal characteristics, but certain anomalies, especially the fact that the back of the skull was more human in shape, raised questions, first, whether the Neandertal race of Palestine was identical with that of Europe and, second, whether *Homo neanderthalensis* might not after all have developed, via such a race as this, into the modern human race, *Homo sapiens*. These questions could not be answered from the skeleton of an undeveloped child, and, therefore, it was hoped that eventually adult skeletons more complete than that of the "Galilee man" would be found. This hope was abundantly fulfilled in Dr. McCown's discovery of the remains of seven adults and two children of Neandertaloid type in Mugharet es-Sukhul during the month of May, 1932.

Professor Garrod was unable to go to Palestine that spring but very generously allowed Dr. McCown to continue his excavation of Mugharet es-Sukhul. Before any considerable progress could be made a large boulder had to be blasted away. This was successfully accomplished with the help of one of the managers of the breakwater company. Then on April 30, after less than three weeks' work, some bones and bits of skull came to light. When the skull was pieced together, the heavy supraorbital ridges characteristic of the Neandertal race were plainly to be seen. On the same day the workmen uncovered leg bones in the breccia at one side of the terrace. On this one day three individuals, Sukhul II, III, and IV, were discovered. On May 2, the top of an adult male skeleton (V) appeared in the middle of the terrace, the next day the incomplete remains of another (VI). During the next ten days no new individuals were found while the area where the bones had been discovered was being very carefully cleared away to expose the complete skeletons. On May 13 two more (VII and VIII) came to light, and on May 19 still another (IX). In addition to teeth and bits of bone which may have belonged to these individuals, fragments of a tenth skeleton (a four-year-old boy, judged by the teeth) were eventually found embedded with No. VII, the burial of which had probably destroyed the child's other bones. An ox head was also found, it would seem intentionally buried.

The problem of excavating and preserving the skeletons was a puzzling one. It was clearly impossible to dig out the fragile bones one by one, for they were imbedded in the hard breccia, from which they could be freed only with the greatest care. Both tools and time for such a task were lacking. The incomplete skeletons and single bones could be removed in chunks of breccia. It was decided to uncover each more or less complete skeleton (IV, V, VII, and IX) and lift it with the encasing breccia in one piece.

As soon as the workmen discovered human remains, the staff

went to work with fine chisels and light hammers to discover their position and extent. The skeletons to be lifted were greased, covered with silver-foil paper, and completely encased in plaster of paris. Since they lay practically on the limestone rock under the terrace, it was necessary to undercut them and take them out on a slab of limestone. The blocks thus made, one weighing as much as two tons, were transferred to a sledge which was slid down the sloping talus of debris of excavation and then dragged 150 yards to camp. Each was then boxed, the spaces left about the edges filled with cement to prevent slipping, and the whole transported on stone trucks to the port at Haifa. Thence they were shipped to England where in the laboratories of the Royal College of Surgeons in London and of the Buckston Browne Research Farm near Downe, the bones were carefully cleaned and removed under the supervision of Dr. McCown and Sir Arthur Keith. The task occupied Dr. McCown and one or more assistants from the autumn of 1933 until the end of 1937.

Some of the skeletons were quite fragmentary, but Nos. IV and V were remarkably complete even down to the tiny bones of the fingers. In the case of these two and also some of the less complete individuals, it was perfectly clear that the burials had been intentional and careful. Since they were all near the surface when buried, it is strange that there had not been more disturbance of the remains. This remarkable cemetery is all the more important because it is associated with a phase of Lower Levalloiso-Mousterian industry which can be exactly paralleled in strata C and D of Mugharet et-Tabun and thus "their chronological position is made certain with regard to the prehistory of western Asia and Europe," while the enormous number of animal bones found allows a full correlation with paleontology.

MUGHARET EL-KEBARAH

That the discoveries at Shuqbah and the fine succession of industries at Mugharet el-Wad do not give a complete picture of the evolution of civilization is clear. The three caves at Mughâret el-Wâd have made the chief contribution to the story of primitive man, but the Stone Age on Mount Carmel would not be entirely intelligible if other less productive sites had not contributed here and there a page or a chapter to the account. One of the least publicized, that at Mughâret el-Kebarah, has not been one of the least valuable.

While excavation was going on at Wâd' el-Mugharah, the neighborhood was searched for other promising sites. Evidence of a more complicated historical process was found only a few miles away at Mughâret el-Kebarah, situated like Wâd' el-Mugharah just on the edge of the coastal plain. Soundings made in 1930 revealed its wealth of material. Its partial excavation by Mr. Turville-Petre and Mrs. Charlotte Baynes in 1931 uncovered four ancient levels, running from Lower Natufian to Lower Middle Aurignacian.

The Natufian was especially rich in bone carvings. Its chief contribution was "a well-defined and peculiar microlithic industry," tentatively named "Kebaran," which lay below a layer like the Natufian of Mughâret el-Wâd B2 and prepared for it. Its distinction lies in its remarkable carved sickle hafts. It lay above a Middle Aurignacian industry similar to that of Layer D in Mughâret el-Wâd. Its chronological position and relationships are thus clear and serve to confirm the conclusions reached at the other two Natufian caves, at Shuqbah and Mughâret el-Wâd. It fitted into and practically closed the gap between strata B and C of Mughâret el-Wâd.

Other Expeditions

If the expeditions of the British School of Archaeology at Jerusalem and the American School of Prehistoric Research have been the most fortunate in startling discoveries and unexpected additions to the scientific aspects of Palestinian prehistory, nevertheless scholars of other nations have made indispensable contributions. In 1936 and 1937 an expedition consisting of Professor M. Stekelis and other members of the Hebrew University investigated gravels in the bed and on the shores of the Jordan River below Lake Huleh. Bones of an elephant which Miss Bate identifies as a Pleistocene species were found with implements of basalt and flint of Lower and Upper Acheulean types, some of them exhibiting a technique which resembles stratum E of Mugh[aret et-Tabun. Along the Jordan, then, man seems to have been living in the open as early as the second interglacial period.

As might be expected, French scholars have shown great interest in the field of prehistory, in particular M. René Neuville, French vice-counsel at Jerusalem. In part with the assistance of Dr. Stekelis he has carried on, in the name of the Institut de Paléontologie Humaine of Paris, important prehistoric excavations at various caves in Judea.

One of the most fruitful of these was at the cave called Mugharet Umm el-Qatafah. It lies southeast of Bethlehem near Jebel Fureidis, or Frank Mountain, on the left side of the Wadi Khreitun and opens toward the west-southwest about 130 feet above the valley floor. It is now elliptical, about 40 by 50 feet in area, but was some 30 feet longer until Chalcolithic times, when part of the roof fell, crushing three of the inhabitants.

Excavations carried on in the summer and autumn of 1928 discovered within the cave five geological levels which were divided into nine archaeological strata. Below a mixed layer which contained materials ranging from modern times back to the Early Bronze Age were two sterile layers differentiated by the color of the earth, which contained only masses of rodent bones. The two lowest geological strata, each about 7 feet thick, contained five archaeological levels, distinguished by the gradual evolution of the types of flint artifacts which they had preserved. All were Acheulean in general character, but only one, the third, closely resembled the European Acheulean.

The fauna was clearly Pleistocene, according to M. R. Vaufrey, who identified the remains. The number of different animals was small, amounting only to eighteen and varying little as to type. M. Vaufrey regarded the fauna as "completely arctic." "African forms," he says, "are exceedingly rare." He suggested that arctic fauna had been displaced to the south by the advent of the glacial epoch. Since the very much larger variety of species and number of specimens from the Galilee and Carmel caves tell a different story, one must conclude that chance played too large a part in the preservation of the Umm el-Qatafah remains.

The other most productive excavation of M. Neuville was undertaken at Jebel Qafseh, the "Mount of the Precipitation" of late monkish legend, a mile and a half southeast of Nazareth. In land belonging to the Franciscan Custody of the Holy Land opposite the "Sanctuary of the Precipice," the Fathers of Beth-arram discovered an almost completely covered cave which seemed to promise valuable prehistoric materials. They reported it to M. Neuville and he carried on excavations in 1933, 1934, and 1935 for brief periods.

Below remains of medieval date and of the Bronze Age were ten strata of the Paleolithic period. In the highest of these, which was Upper Paleolithic, were parts of a female skull cap and lower jaw and of a masculine forehead. In the lowest of all, below five other Levalloisian strata, were the remains, some quite fragmentary, of seven individuals. Whether they are decidedly different from Neandertal and Carmel man, as some have claimed, and belong to an earlier level than the latter is a matter which can only be settled when they are fully published. Some would date the deposits in the second interglaciation, which, on the longer chronology, would make them 500,000 years old. But possibly they were contemporary with Carmel man and, therefore, belonging only 100,000 years ago.

Sir Flinders Petrie believes that his expedition at Tell el-Far‘ah discovered evidence of occupation along the Wadi Ghazzeh in Paleolithic times. On the basis of purely typological studies and, as he expressly notes, without having seen the sites, Mr. Reid Moir, the eminent English specialist in Lower Paleolithic industries, identified a series of Chellean, or, better, Abbevillean, and Acheulean coups-de-poing, or fist-hatchets, of rostro-carinate type. He argued that the presence of this type in England, Rhodesia, India, and Palestine argues for a much longer time and a much higher organization during the Lower Paleolithic period than has formerly been assumed. He would push the Abbevillean back to the First Interglacial, and the Acheulean into the Second Interglacial period.

The question, then, as to the earliest inhabitant of Palestine is still in dispute and may not be settled for many years. Indeed discoveries in Syria recently announced but still unpublished further complicate the problem. For the Paleolithic and Mesolithic periods and their correlations Miss Garrod had hoped for stratified deposits of archaeological materials in geological contexts in the Jordan Valley and on the seacoast. No doubt such will eventually come to light, for a beginning has already been made. Thus it will be possible to introduce better chronological correlations. There can be no doubt that other sites will add new details to our knowledge of the tools man used in the Stone Ages and that new horizons will appear.

However, another period of peace, as fruitful of discoveries as the last twenty years have been, can hardly bring results more astonishing. The prehistorian is 100,000 years nearer the Palestinian Adam than he was when the last war ended. From 6000 B.C. to 75,000 or 100,000, not to mention 500,000 years ago, is a tremendous leap. Careful stratigraphical excavation, the wearisome study of thousands of flint instruments shaped by human hands eons ago, the examination of countless fragments of human and animal bones, all of them deposited in chronological sequence in the strata of human occupation, have determined the outlines of human history for this immense period.

Even far back of human occupation the story of the ancient Near East can now be carried. To understand the history of any country, one must begin with geology and paleontology. Geologists have long been giving attention to Palestine, depending chiefly on surface observation. Owing to the extreme disturbance of the geological strata, Palestine and Syria are a geologist's paradise. But since there have been no mines and no deep well borings, the geologist has labored under a certain handicap. During recent years excavation in Palestine has made its contribution, especially to paleontology. The paleolithic caves have been remarkably rich in animal bones. And the last published prehistoric excavations made before war again began reached still earlier materials.

A chance find in a garden at Bethlehem led the late Mr. John L. Starkey, director of the Wellcome Research Archaeological Expedition, to arrange with Miss E. M. Gardner, geologist, and Miss Dorothea M. A. Bate, paleontologist, of the South Kensington Museum, to undertake excavation there, for two seasons in the winters of 1936 and 1937. Laid down in water-borne gravels, the deposits, the oldest yet investigated in Palestine, include bones of various feline and bovine types, species of elephant, hippopotamus, and rhinoceros, a gigantic and a diminutive tortoise, and, most interesting of all, the *Hipparion*, diminutive horse already known from Tertiary deposits in Asia and America, India and Africa. The fauna belongs to the earliest Pleistocene and, while of Asiatic origin, forms a link between Asia and East Africa. Broken flints were found which some anthropologists regard as eoliths of pre-Chellean times, similar to those found in England and elsewhere. Others believe that their flaking was due merely to the pressure of the accumulations above them.

The deposits, now on the top of the hill at Bethlehem 2500 feet above sea level, on the watershed between the Mediterranean and the Dead Sea, were laid down in floods of water. Chalk-like *nari* limestone above them proves that the period must have been early. Evidently land which had been above sea level was again submerged before the final movements which caused the Jordan rift and put this stream bed on a mountain top. Such discoveries will eventually give a secure dating for the various steps in the long process which made Palestine geographically unique.

CHAPTER IV

MAN'S SLOW ASCENT

❖

WHAT now has been the outcome of all of these labors on remains of ancient man? The methods of the prehistorian archaeologist and the process by which he reaches his conclusions may
be made clearer by a more systematic presentation of some of
the outstanding results of his labors. Professor Garrod, M. Neuville, and others have devoted much thought to the relations
of the various industries discovered one to another and to their
correlation with geological and climatic changes. None would
claim finality but progress has been made.[1]

PALEONTOLOGY AND CLIMATE

One of the great contributions of the Wad' el-Mugharah expedition has been the recovery of innumerable bones of animals
in the various layers of occupation. As they were found they
were all carefully labeled according to their place in the long
series. Thus although Miss Bate, to whom they were entrusted
for study and interpretation, had not had a part in the excavation, she was able to trace the fluctuations of Palestine's prehistoric climate with very considerable certainty and to reach
interesting conclusions on the life and habitat of early man.

Other investigations have added data which aid in solving
these problems. No single site can solve the problems of an excavator. Miss Bate's study of the paleontology of Mugharet
el-Emireh and Mugharet ez-Zuttiyeh had already made an important contribution. The studies in the Jordan Valley by Dr.
Stekelis and others have added their part. The extremely early

[1] See the chart, fig. 2, p. 29 for a combination of Miss Garrod's and Miss
Bate's conclusions, *RB*, XLIII (1934), pl. XV, for M. Neuville's.

material of the Bethlehem deposits provided an introduction to this chapter of human history. The detailed study of the animal remains found in the caves and terraces at Wad' el-Mugharah and the other sites mentioned reveals some remarkable correlations between changes in the climate, the fauna, and the cultural levels. Along with the bones of other animals, the relative frequency of bones of *Dama mesopotamica*, a deer which loved forests and moisture, and of the gazelle, which prefers a dry climate, proves that there had been remarkable fluctuations of prehistoric climate. Palestine never had an arctic climate. In the Upper Acheulean period, the earliest but one discovered, tropical conditions prevailed.[2] During the period to which the remarkable skeletons of Mugharet es-Sukhul belong, gradual desiccation brought a warm, dry climate but with abundant rivers, for the crocodile, the hippopotamus, and rhinoceros are found. Then follows an abrupt break in the nature of the fauna, though not in the flint industries, for the great pachyderms disappear permanently. Wet conditions with a slight fall in temperature reach a high point in the Upper Levalloiso-Mousterian period. From that time on there was a gradual recession toward a dry, warm climate, which, with one minor oscillation, continued down to the Natufian (Mesolithic) period, when the deer practically disappear.[3] The caves offer no certain indications as to the climate after the Mesolithic period. The remains show that Palestine was the scene of very considerable evolutionary activity at times, and that it was in the path of migration from Asia to Africa, and therefore subject to great immigrations. It has always had a highly varied fauna.

The animal bones which have been found beside the hearths of ancient man, hacked and broken by his flint axes and knives, indicate the creatures with which he had to contend, from which he sought shelter beside the fires in his caves, and from which he secured his food. Thirty-five species, including several birds, a few reptiles, and some amphibians, were identified

[2] See the right-hand column of the chart on p. 29.
[3] See above, chapter III.

in the deposits of the Galilee caves. Fifty-two mammals were identified in the Carmel caves in addition to a few reptiles, birds, and amphibians. Of the large and dangerous animals, such as the elephant, rhinoceros, and hippopotamus, not many bones were found in the middens of the caves. Man's food was made more largely of less formidable creatures. Evidently the deer and gazelle were popular, but many small mammals, such as moles and shrews, were present. Strangely enough, there is little evidence of the use of sea food. One of the most striking discoveries was the lower jaw of a wild boar which had been placed in the arms of Sukhul skeleton V when it was thrust into its rather small grave. Its significance, whether as a trophy, an amulet, or a food offering, can only be guessed.

Character and Relationships of Carmel Man

The character and relationships of Carmel man, whose bones were found in the Levalloiso-Mousterian strata of Mugharet es-Sukhul, Mugharet et-Tabun, and Mugharet es-Zuttiyeh, will doubtless be long debated. The conclusions which Dr. T. D. McCown and Sir Arthur Keith have reached may be briefly stated. The Mugharet et-Tabun skeleton, which is typically Neandertal, proves the existence of that race in Palestine as a contemporary of the other species of primitive man found at Mugharet es-Zuttiyeh and Mugharet es-Sukhul.

The skeletons showed a range of structural variation such as could be found in no local group in the world today. They ranged from the Neandertal woman of et-Tabun to a man (Sukhul IV) who could be a primitive European, from one with a Roman nose to another that was almost negroid. The early reports misrepresented them. At first sight the heads appeared to be distinctly Neandertal because of the heavy supra-orbital ridges and the prognathous face and jaws. But closer inspection disclosed the fact that the ridges were different, that there were real chins and moderately full foreheads, which the Neandertaler lacks, that the dome of the skulls was higher, and that the occiput projected beyond the line of attachment of the neck muscles. Just as Sir Arthur Keith had guessed from the fragmentary skull of the Galilee man and the child, Sukhul I, the Carmel heads showed a decided development toward *Homo sapiens.* In a large number of characteristics Carmel man resembles the earliest modern type known, the Cromagnon, in others the Neandertal race, in still other certain simian types. Nature was experimenting at the foot of Mount Carmel in the effort to discover what types could best survive her selective processes.

There were no giants in those days. But the men were larger than the Neandertal type, ranging from 5 ft. 8 in. to 5 ft. 11 in. The women varied from 5 ft. to 5 ft. 4 in. They walked as we do, not with a shambling simian gait. Their chests were ample and they were probably long-winded runners. Yet certain details of their feet, legs, arms, and vertebrae were simian. The finding of a perforation made in the hip joint of one of the men by a four-sided wooden spear head points to a hitherto undreamed-of warlike strength and ability on the part of Paleolithic man. Their brains were as large as ours and there is every indication that they had the capacity for speech. The care with which the dead were buried is significant of their mental and cultural development. Does not the jaw buried with Sukhul V suggest a boar's tongue for a dinner in the future world, as Sir Arthur Keith intimates?

The new information regarding human evolution which Carmel man has given is so revolutionary that Sir Arthur Keith and Dr. McCown propose an entirely new nomenclature and classification of fossil races. Instead of *Homo neanderthalensis* and similar specific divisions of the genus *Homo*, they separate palaeoanthropic from neoanthropic man and list, in the order of their evolutionary development, (1) *Palaeoanthropus heidelbergensis,* (2) *P. ehringsdorfiensis,* (3) *P. neanderthalensis,* (4) *P. krapinensis,* and (5) *P. palestinensis,* the last including the Mount Carmel and Mughâret ez-Zuttiyeh remains.[4]

4 See McCown and Keith, *The Stone Age of Mount Carmel,* II (Oxford, 1939), 18.

In Palestine, then, 100,000 years ago, before the last glacial epoch began, that is in the third interglacial period, when Europe was inhabited only by the Neandertal race, there was already living a race which was far superior to it and in some of its members closely approached the earliest European representatives of *Homo sapiens*, Cromagnon man, who first appeared in Europe fifty or seventy-five thousand years later. But, as Sir Arthur Keith says, that does not prove that the Garden of Eden is located in Palestine. Various characteristics prove that Carmel man is not to be thought of as a direct ancestor of modern man, *Homo sapiens*, but he was closely related to the ancestors of the Caucasian race and illustrates the process of evolution by which it was produced. Rather, as discoveries in other regions suggest, the original home of modern man is to be sought perhaps in western or central Asia, possibly in eastern Africa.

The Arrival of Modern Man

It is a far cry from Carmel man with his lingering primitive, even simian, characteristics, to a race of men such as live to-day. The thick layers deposited in the caves of Wad' el-Mugharah during the long stretches of the Aurignacian period, when Cromagnon man appeared in Europe, tell what tools men were making and what animals they were eating, but they have preserved neither his bones nor any other record of the evolution or invasion which eventually made a new race master of the great cave. When the new race appears, it is a different kind of man who lives in a different world.

Although the study of the Natufian skeletons of Shuqbah and Mugharet el-Wad is not yet complete and little has been published, it can be said that it has been possible for Sir Arthur Keith and Dr. T. D. McCown, who is to publish the final study on the subject, to determine that they undoubtedly belong to the Mediterranean race which forms one of the chief constituents of the peoples living today about that inland sea. In other words, by 10,000 or 8,000 years ago, Palestine was inhabited by a fully developed *Homo sapiens* of the Caucasian, or white, race. As yet they had no metals and not even pottery, but they were making a beginning in agriculture, and they already had domesticated the dog. Human bones broken while they were fresh testify that the Natufians were cannibalistic. It is quite impossible to determine the nature of their religious worship, but they must have believed in a life after death and practiced burial rites much more elaborate than those of Paleolithic man.

Natufian man was something of an artist. The extent of his proficiency is still a matter of uncertainty. At one excavation, in uncertain cave light, an inexperienced assistant of the excavator thought that he descried on the walls a remarkable series of animal pictures. A slight retouching produced figures that photographed well and even were reproduced in a famous weekly.[5] Later examination by experts proved that they were the product of a vivid imagination and overenthusiasm.

In 1932 Professor Nelson Glueck, then Director of the American School of Oriental Research in Jerusalem, discovered some excellent animal drawings on rock surfaces in Transjordan.[6] As they are in the open and nothing in connection with them offers an unquestioned date, their age cannot be positively determined. They are thought to belong to the Mesolithic or Neolithic period, probably the latter.

The earliest evidences of art that can be surely dated come from the Mesolithic period. The fine conical cup hole at Mugharet el-Wad reveals an excellent sense of geometric form. The carvings in bone and stone found at Shuqbah, Mugharet el-Wad, and Mugharet el-Kebarah in stratified deposits clearly show the beginnings of artistic interest, if not of any considerable skill during this period. The prize piece is a small deer in limestone found by M. Neuville at Umm Zweitina. The well shaped body partially reclines on its side with its legs drawn up under it in a most natural position, evincing careful observation, a sense of form, and technical skill.

---

[5] *The Illustrated London News*, Nov. 5, 1932; *AJA*, XXXVII (1933), 161 f.
[6] See below, chapter XIX.

Photo by T. D. M.

Excavating Mugharet el-Wad. Cave openings at right, dump at left with women and sieves. Terrace of deposits from mesolithic (Tahunian) occupation in foreground, Wad' el-Mugharah in background.

Mesolithic (Natufian) cup marks, platform, and skeleton of modern Mediterranean type, in terrace (seen above) before Mugharet el-Wad.

Photo by D. E. M.

Mugharet ez-Zuttiyeh, where "Galilee Man" lived in a cave running back into the face of the rock back of the terrace.

Skeleton of Paleoanthropus palestinensis; as uncovered in terrace before Mugharet es-Sukhul.

Photo by T. D. M.

THE CULTURAL SIGNIFICANCE OF THE NATUFIAN

The cultural significance of the Natufian discoveries is immense in other matters than that of art. The Natufian Mesolithic lies immediately above the latest Upper Paleolithic level (C at Mugharet el-Wad), which is a peculiar industry (Atlitian) without close analogies in Europe, Africa, or Asia. The Natufian, likewise, stands by itself, without close European analogies, not only because of the character of its flint instruments, but still more because it represents the hitherto unknown stage of agriculture without pottery. Doubtless it developed out of the Upper Paleolithic as the Tardenoisian is believed to have done. The Mesolithic represents a further movement in the same direction of independence, or rather provincialism, as does the end of the Paleolithic.

Here begins also agriculture (in a sense) and probably the domestication of animals. Moreover, man moves out of the caves into the open. It is significant that while there were four inches of Mesolithic deposit within Mugharet el-Wad, there were ten feet in the terrace outside. The characteristic microlithic crescent has been found also in many other open-air stations. The climate was evidently so dry during this period that cave life no longer had attractions. Whether huts or tents began to be used cannot as yet be determined, but, even if men still used caves during part of the year, their life was chiefly outside in the sun and fresh air. This period Miss Garrod would date as late possibly as 6000-5000 B.C. Comparison with Babylonia and Egypt would suggest an earlier date. But in any case the Mesolithic period, with its agriculture and its eventual introduction of pottery, marks the longest stride taken by prehistoric man toward the city civilization which was already in existence when history dawns.

The fact that the greater part of the deposit at Mugharet el-Wad was found outside the cave proves conclusively that it belongs to a period when the floods and cold of the ice age were forever past, and man needed no longer the year round to seek refuge in caves from rain but did welcome the warmth of the sun. The use of agriculture, however, proves something more—the development of a dry climate and an increase in population which together drove man, or possibly woman, to work for his bread in the sweat of her brow. That is, the climate was essentially what it is today, and, though still a hunter and fisher, as arrow and lance heads, harpoons and fishhooks show, man was no longer content or able to secure sufficient food by such limited means only. The presence of the characteristic microliths, or pigmy flints, of the Natufian, not only in the caves mentioned, but also on the surface at many other places in Palestine, shows that people using that type of industry were scattered all over the land just as the Tardenoisian, its nearest European relative, is widely spread over Western Europe and North Africa.

The finds at the 'Athlit and Zichron Yaqob caves which show that by this time man was progressing in his tastes for personal adornment and in his desire for artistic creation, crude though his efforts in these directions were, prove that his mind had developed far beyond its simian beginnings. Pins of bone and similar articles show the development of efforts toward clothing, doubtless still only with skins as the material. The complex of burials, pavement, and cups cut in the rock at Mugharet el-Wad testifies to the development of ceremonies of some kind, doubtless connected with the burial of the dead, indicating another long step in intellectual development.

The Natufians and others who lived in the Middle Stone Age had made long strides on the upward climb toward civilization. Their manual skill and patient endurance are shown by the stone implements they made, their intelligence by their increasing mastery of their environment. Perhaps too much credit should not be given them. Changing climatic conditions may have made their advance possible and the pressure of an increasing population may have forced them to seek foods in new directions and by other methods than hunting and fishing. Still further changes were forced upon them and the next period reveals an entirely new form of social organization.

Relations of Late Stone Age Cultures

Certain excavations disclosed the extent of the still-unsolved problems and of the present ignorance of data for their solution. The order and relationships of various Stone Age cultures one to another were far from clear. A very careful examination with excavation of numerous sites along the Wadi Ghazzeh published by Mr. Eann MacDonald, one of Sir Flinders Petrie's assistants, in 1932 disclosed remains of old huts, caves, and camp sites with a remarkable series of prehistoric cultures belonging to the Chalcolithic and Early Bronze periods. Sequence datings based upon the artifacts and pottery coincided roughly with the Egyptian series which Sir Flinders established. The evolution of the stone hoe could be traced. Traces of the microlithic industry characteristic of the Mesolithic period were frequent and at one site (A) highly developed. This was probably a chance survival from earlier times. In the mound of Tell el-Far'ah itself, above a pavement belonging to the Ramesside period, was a flint factory which Sir Flinders ascribed to the Israelites, on the quite probable supposition that they came in from the desert still living in the Stone Age and continued to use flint tools long after their entry in the land of Canaan. As other excavations also show, flints did not go out of common use until after the beginning of the Early Iron Age. Here were long vistas, but few fixed points upon which the student could base a sketch plan of more recent prehistory.

The length of time and the nature of the process which transformed the Stone Age into that of metals in Palestine have been, until recently, matters of great uncertainty. Little was known of the Chalcolithic period, when stone and copper were both in use, and it was denied that there ever had been a Neolithic period such as is known in Europe, when men had no metals but manufactured pottery and polished stone tools, had many domesticated animals, and engaged in agriculture. The problem is one to which Miss Garrod, M. Neuville, and others have devoted fruitful labors. Through various excavations and the study of surface stations, valuable data have been accumulated.

An important surface station was found in 1928 in Wadi Tahuneh, some three kilometers south of Bethlehem, a region especially rich in Stone Age remains. Père Denys Buzy, the discoverer, classified the industry as Mesolithic. He found hatchets, or chisels, scrapers, knives, and arrow heads, none of them polished and all of Mesolithic character. There were also microlithic flints and even mortars, pestles, pottery, and other implements which suggested to him an agricultural civilization still partially in the hunting stage.

M. Neuville found a very similar stone industry at el-Khiam, in Wadi Khreitun, not far from Wadi Tahuneh. It lay above an Upper Paleolithic industry and a Mesolithic of late Natufian type. Misled by fragments of pottery and copper such as are found at surface stations, M. Neuville called it Chalcolithic (*énéolithique*) but remarked that its earliest phase did not differ from the highest Natufian stratum except in the presence of these two characteristics of later civilization. He had found in its earlier phase no polished stone implements and, therefore, denied to it the name "Neolithic." Some polished stone tools appeared in a higher stratum at el-Khiam, but since they seemed to be associated with metal, they were not a Neolithic industry. As late as 1934 it could still be maintained that precocious Palestine had stepped directly from the Mesolithic period into an age when metal was already beginning to be used.

It was believed by the majority of prehistorians that Palestine, Egypt, and all of the Near East in fact had never had a true Neolithic period. Polished stone tools are found in Palestine in relatively small numbers and almost always in connection with copper or bronze. It appeared that somewhere in the Near East, or not far from it, the use of copper and then of bronze was discovered before the use of polished stone tools became widespread or perhaps known at all. The much superior metal tools made the long labor to produce polished stone tools superfluous, while the use of the much more quickly and cheaply made chipped stone tools continued among the poorer classes and for less important purposes.

However, excavations at Teleilat el-Ghassul had introduced a very puzzling culture, which had Neolithic characteristics, but which was elsewhere entirely unknown. Also M. Neuville had himself distinguished at surface stations, in the lowest levels then known at Jericho, and elsewhere another unrelated industry belonging to the Early Bronze Age, which, for want of a better name, he called Cananean. The various Stone Age cultures, Natufian, Tahunian, Ghassulian, and Cananean, did not fit together, and the absence of a Neolithic was perplexing. In 1935, excavations at Jericho in still lower strata brought a solution for these problems. It is necessary, therefore, to turn to Teleilat el-Ghassul and Jericho in order to follow the steps by which Mesolithic man reached civilization.

CHAPTER V

MAN BUILDS CITIES

❖

CIVILIZATION is an ambiguous term. For many people it means a mode of life essentially like their own. In scientific language it is often used to mean the way in which men live. In that sense one may speak of various stages of civilization, even from the Old Stone Age to that of steel and electricity. But the word is commonly used in the sense of the establishment of social order, interdependence, and co-operation with a consequent advance in the arts and improvement in living conditions. The "beginnings of civilization," then, may be regarded as marked by the domestication of animals and efforts at agriculture, which are surely man's first great strides upon the tremendous journey from the cave to the "city," *civis*, which the Greeks and the Romans regarded as the only "civilization."

Long as the Stone Ages were (surely much more than a hundred thousand years), they came to an end with man just emerging from his caves and only beginning to cultivate the soil, while still depending for food and clothing chiefly upon the fruits and nuts he could gather and the fish or game he could catch. The next few thousand years, up to the beginnings of written history, saw progress in the achievement of civilization which, compared to its heritage, was far more astonishing than that of the age of the radio and cinema. The building of cities, the organization of states, the growth of great religious systems, the discovery of the calendar, the invention of writing and of numerous crafts, such as weaving and metallurgy, the development of architecture and of art, the organization of commerce and the beginnings of legal codes, these were a few of man's early achievements. The part which Palestine played and the experiences of its peoples in this long process can now be described in vivid, if incomplete, detail and constitute a new and fascinating chapter in the story of man's conquest of civilization.

These developments, in greater part, are still far back in the prehistoric period, for no written documents older than about 1600 B.C. have as yet been found in Palestine and the allusions to that little land in Egyptian and Babylonian documents do not begin before the third millennium B.C. Until recently the oldest cities unearthed in Palestine had not gone back beyond 2500 B.C. But now the picture has been entirely changed by the discoveries at Jericho and Teleilat el-Ghassul, lying some 20 miles apart in the Jordan Valley. These two recently excavated sites have illuminated the period when real civilization was being achieved, beginning in the latter part of the age that knew only stone tools, when men left their caves, built huts side by side, and gradually developed a city civilization.

The recent discoveries re-establish a Neolithic period, not long, nor exactly as commonly known and described, but at least as a cultural stage analogous to European Neolithic. After it comes a Chalcolithic period, that is a period when objects of copper or bronze and tools of stone were used side by side, with a preponderance of stone. Then finally, a little before 3000 B.C., copper began to take precedence over stone, although in Palestine flint tools were in use in agriculture until after iron was introduced.

Père Mallon has the credit of being the first to unearth an entirely new and most remarkable Neolithic and Chalcolithic stage of Palestinian civilization. Thus, although he did not know it, he began to fill in part of the gap between the Mesolithic period and the Bronze Age. Père Mallon, M. Neuville, Father Robert Köppel, and, after Père Mallon's death in 1934, his successor, Père Marc. Lobignac, have carried the enterprise through eight seasons during the winters of 1929-38.

On a wide expanse of desolate "sagebrush desert" a couple of tents and later some wooden shacks served to protect the staff and their rapidly accumulating finds from the burning sun and

occasional storms. Very modest equipment has served to secure
very valuable results. Geological and stratigraphic studies by
Father Köppel, who is by training a geologist and geographer,
have made important contributions. He has shown that every
expedition needs a binocular microscope.

The very discovery of the site was a triumph of keen observation, for the little mounds which have been excavated
hardly show above the surface of the ground. It was a mere
chance which brought them to Père Mallon's attention. In
January, 1929, on a school field trip, the Pontifical Biblical Institute party stopped for lunch on a little hillock in what seemed
uninhabitable desert. While they rested, Father Mallon noticed
that countless flint artifacts and potsherds strewed the ground.
Few archaeologists would have undertaken the apparently
thankless task of exploring in the forbidding region just back
from the "bad lands," those barren and deeply eroded hillocks
of chalky marl which border the Jordan. The soil appears to be
only a combination of rocks and sand with a sparse and inter-
mittent covering of small desert shrubs. No region could be less
promising. The site of Teleilat el-Ghassul ("little mounds of
the washing plant") lies three miles east of the Jordan and four
and a half miles north of the Dead Sea, at the edge of a plain
which runs back of them northeastward to the brown mountains
of Moab. To the southwest, strata of gray marl drop away
rapidly toward the shores of the blue sea and the muddy Jordan
and are cut into fantastic shapes by the rains of unnumbered
millennia.

On the surface, stones marking an occasional Bedouin burial
are to be discovered and innumerable heaps of ashes, doubtless
remains of Bedouin campfires and of the crude soapmaking
which gives the tells their name. In a few places vestiges of
walls appear. The mounds cover a very considerable area, half
a mile long by a quarter of a mile wide. Each little mound contains the remains of a few houses, sometimes only of one or
two. Between some of the houses there were apparently narrow
streets, but nothing seems to connect the different groups, and

no encircling wall is reported. The place probably represents
a large unorganized village or a small city.

These little tells would be quite unimportant but for two reasons, one scientific, the other biblical, or exegetical. Jesuit
scholars at first maintained that they represent the site of the
pentapolis of Genesis 14, to which Sodom and Gomorrah belonged. This would place their destruction at 2100 B.C. or
later. From the first Dr. Albright saw in them a Chalcolithic or
Neolithic civilization, which would demand a very much earlier
date. Whether Sodom and Gomorrah lay at the north end of
the Dead Sea or at its southeast corner and is now under its
heavy, salt-laden waters, as Père Mallon formerly held, and
as Dr. Albright still believes, is a matter of relative unimportance,
though the matter caused much discussion and "went over big"
in the newspapers. But since, as now all scholars agree, the
mounds do represent a very early phase of civilization, which,
as also at Jericho, preceded the other great Palestinian cities,
their scientific importance is incontestable. Excavation there has
brought to light few beautiful specimens of human artistry.
But as examples of very early and very primitive efforts of man
to build himself houses and cities and to create for himself the
comforts that are supposed to make life worth living, the crude
walls, paintings, and utensils which Father Mallon's workmen
have uncovered are pathetic and instructive illustrations of
man's slow and laborious climb toward the empyrean.

GHASSULIAN CIVILIZATION

It must be admitted that, when the best is said for their progress in handicrafts and arts, the Ghassulians do not represent
a very high development of civilization. Yet they did some
things remarkably well. There is no evidence that the place
possessed any system of defense, which of course may mean
that they were still savages who knew nothing of the cultural
blessings and ennobling glories of war. The few buildings
excavated show fairly regular, rectangular plans with orientation east and west or north and south in a majority of instances.

But the walls are extremely crude. They begin with a course or two of rather small, entirely unshaped stones, above which there are piled rude sun-dried "bricks" shaped by hand into rounded or flattened lumps, sometimes unduly dignified with the term, plano-convex. In some cases, all, including the lowest, courses were of brick. As in practically every Palestinian city the houses were destroyed by fire. The timbers which formed the upper part of the walls and supported the earthen roof fell and deposited the earth on the contents of the rooms.

The greater part of the pottery was handmade, but it is far from representing the earliest stages of ceramic art. The clay was good, fairly clean, and usually well burnt to a clear red throughout. The best paste appears to belong to the earliest period. Naturally many pieces were rough and poorly shaped, but others again show real skill and a sense for artistic form. Some showed a regularity of shape, a thinness of wall, and an evenness of horizontal decoration which indicate the use of the potter's wheel or some method of turning which approximated it. One of the most characteristic shapes was an ugly conical vase or cup, sometimes called a "cornet." It could only stand when thrust into the sand. Specimens of well-shaped chalices, or goblets, set on stems with broad, flat bases were found. Another characteristic of the pottery was the frequent use of very small lug, or ear, handles, while the customary loop handle is rare and the ledge handle, which belongs to the Early Bronze Age, is wanting. In the process of their manufacture, various vessels had been set on woven material. Many were painted in bands, wavy lines, and criss-cross, or net, patterns. Others were decorated with applied serpents in clay.

Only a very few pieces of copper were found. There were large numbers of stone implements, bowls, mortars, pestles, saddle querns, rubbing stones, spindle whorls, and loom weights. The flint implements were of various kinds, chisels, scrapers, knives, drills. In contrast to Jericho in the same period, practically no arrowheads were found. Microlithic drills abound. Many polishers and some partially, some wholly, polished stone instruments were found. There were bone drills and needles as well as pendants and other ornaments. Beads of stone and mother-of-pearl, pendants, pectorals, and other ornaments were found. There were many animal bones, especially of the pig.

One peculiarity of Teleilat el-Ghassul was the number of burials or at least of skeletons found within the houses. The bones of many infants were uncovered, usually within pottery jars or among potsherds indicating that they had been buried within jars. Apparently the jar was placed under the floor of the house. A few adult skeletons were found, but none of ancient date so placed as to indicate regular burial. In one case an adult lay with his head under the wall of a house. In some cases the bones were calcined, doubtless by fire, and scattered. The decapitated head of a child of six or seven years was found very carefully enclosed in a jar which had been cut in two, then put together with the head inside, and covered with a stopper of clay. Examination of the head showed that it had been struck off by a blow which had crushed the left side of the face and head. As the jar was laid against the base of a wall, it might appear to have been a foundation sacrifice. This inference may be wrong, but there can be no doubt that some religious or superstitious value was attached to the burial of this head. The infants in jars, however, were probably not foundation sacrifices but merely burials of stillborn, or very young, children in the hope, possibly, that the spirit would return soon to animate another. These burials cannot be supposed to represent all of the dead of the settlements. The excavators believed that they found the necropolis nearer the hills in a group of cist and tumulus burials.

The depth of the deposits was first revealed in December, 1930, by Father Köppel's studies of the topography of the region and by his use of a geological auger. It was found that the original natural ground level was fifteen feet under the present surface. From the clear stratification in three of the little mounds, from the floors, foundations, and other structures found at various levels, the excavators have distinguished two chief periods, one representing a Neolithic, or Chalcolithic, culture and beginning before 4000 B.C., the other, more truly Chalcolithic, falling between 4000 B.C. and 3500 B.C. Each was divided by a bed of ashes into two sub-periods, and the last city (IV) had two phases. The changes which appeared prove the existence of the settlements for several hundred, perhaps a thousand, years.

The same general type of civilization runs through the whole of the deposits, and there are no sharp breaks, but there is a definite development and improvement marked by enlargement, especially in the highest level, in spite of apparent deterioration in the pottery. The two cities, or settlements, of the earlier age were quite small and occupied only the central part of the area. The third and fourth cities, of the second age, grew to at least double the size of their predecessors, and pottery of this period was found at a distance of two miles, representing, possibly, suburbs of the city. Throughout the deposits both flints and pottery show a steady change and development.

THE CHRONOLOGICAL PROBLEM

A few specimens of pottery belonging to the Middle Bronze Age and some bronze objects (with 7% tin) which at the beginning were found in the upper stratum seriously confused the chronological problem. But the great mass of the pottery was eventually seen to belong to a much earlier time and most of the few metal fragments to be pure copper. The fact that the pottery entirely lacked the ledge handles which are typical of the Early Bronze Age, as Father Köppel saw, reduced the problem to a simple dilemma: before 3000 B.C. or after 2000 B.C. Once the dilemma was faced, there could be but one conclusion: before 3000 B.C. Observation of the action of the wind has convinced him that the earliest and latest strata cannot be regarded as separated by a thousand years or more but at best by only a few hundred.

In the beginning a serious aspect of the chronological problem was the absence of comparable material elsewhere. Here, in the center of a desert, were four strata full of pottery, flints, and bone instruments, with nothing but sand above and below them and with no similar artifacts elsewhere in stratified deposits by which to date them. In 1935 and 1936 Professor Garstang completely demolished that obstacle to the interpretation of Teleilat el-Ghassul by discovering at Jericho material which very closely paralleled the Ghassulian and by finding other cultures above and below which gave an excellent series of sequences even if no absolute dates. In several other places also, parallel material in both pottery and flints has now been recognized and the order of development made clear. Teleilat el-Ghassul is robbed of neither priority nor uniqueness, but it no longer suffers from complete isolation.

Various competent persons now agree that the upper stratum, city IV, is to be equated with cultures found in Wadi Ghazzeh, at Umm el-Qatafah, at Khudeirah in the Plain of Sharon, at 'Affuleh on Esdraelon, in the lowest levels at Gezer, in the lowest pottery-bearing strata at Mugharet el-Wad, and in Salhah in northern Galilee. Much more important is the fact that it has affinities with strata VIII and IX at Jericho, with stratum XVIII at Beth-shan, and with stratum XIX, the next to lowest, at Megiddo. Since these all lie far under Early Bronze Age strata, there can be no doubt as to the period of the Ghassulian culture. It is Middle or Lower Chalcolithic, even at first Neolithic, and belongs before 3500 B.C. Its flint industry is contemporary with the later Tahunian and falls before Cananean. Far from being isolated, the Ghassulian culture was paralleled by various cultures all over Palestine and in some particulars related to them.

The date thus agreed upon precludes all possibility of identifying these little mounds with the ruins of the pentapolis to which Sodom and Gomorrah belonged. No one can name the ancient city, but nevertheless it has added 500 or 1000 years to the history of the Jordan Valley. More than that, it has revealed a civilization with hitherto undreamed of capacities.

GHASSULIAN FRESCOES

One of its glories blossomed but to die. Certain peculiarly inscribed pebbles and potsherds created a real sensation when they were "discovered" during the second campaign. Apparently they came from all levels and they resembled Sumerian and other early types of writing. Eventually, however, M. Neuville discovered an ink mark on one. He is said to have remarked to a workman who handed one to him that it was strange that they were all so small. A few days later a large one appeared. Father Köppel examined them with his microscope and discovered from traces of steel in the incisions that practically all were forgeries. It is supposed that they were made in Jericho, and planted by bakhshish-hungry workmen. It need hardly be said that Father Mallon dealt sternly with the workmen who had made the "discoveries." There remain some marked potsherds which were found under circumstances that put them beyond suspicion, but which cannot be interpreted. This is the first significant attempt at forgery for a generation and its speedy detection speaks well for the perspicacity of the three excavators.

If one of the expedition's sensations has proved to be a fiasco, another of equal proportions and incontestable authenticity has taken its place. On the crude mud-brick walls of the next to last city (III), well preserved fragments of frescoes were discovered. Father Köppel cleaned them himself millimeter by millimeter with the greatest possible care. Many walls were so completely destroyed that it could only be seen that they had been decorated. On the standing portions and on fragments of clay found on the floors was plain evidence that the walls have received four or five coats of paint, and apparently that the scenes had been changed when the new coat was applied.

On one wall a painting, in white, black, yellow, and light and dark red, ran a length of over thirteen feet. Unfortunately the upper part of the wall had been destroyed and only the lower third or quarter of the panel was preserved. It appeared to begin at the left with the rays of a large sun, in front of which was a small upright figure facing right. Then follow, as it were hanging in the air, seven pairs of feet facing left and growing gradually smaller toward the right. It appears to represent some cultus act. A wall in another house shows a rather well-drawn, if impressionistic, bird in black. It certainly is not stiff or conventionalized, but quite naturalistic. Almost equally remarkable was a highly complicated, many-colored, eight-pointed star found in still another room. It is quite indescribable, both in the ingenuity of the arrangement of its various parts and in the impression its full-sized reproduction makes. On the wall are various cubist drawings also in color, with some very excellent cubist faces.

Since a series of decorated rooms has now been found rising slightly above the first discovered with the painting of the series of feet, it seems clear that this complex represents a shrine. Possibly the rooms are connected with the cult of the dead as in Egypt, but burials have not been found to prove it. In none of the rooms recently discovered was enough preserved to throw any light on their purpose. Future excavations here or elsewhere may eventually solve the riddle.

Origin and Relationships

These remarkable paintings raise the question of the priority and relationships of Ghassulian civilization in an acute form. Nothing of the kind had ever been found in Palestine and no suggestion of such art appears until far down in the Late Bronze Age. In Babylonia there are no early parallels. At Cnossus the earliest frescoes belong to Middle Minoan II, 1900-1750 B.C., and are of an entirely different technique. In Egypt similar scenes can be found in the third millennium B.C., but Teleilat el-Ghassul belongs to the fourth or fifth millennium. In Persia painted frescoes on house walls found at Persepolis in its prehistoric settlement in one of the earliest painted-pottery phases (ca. 4000 B.C.) save the Ghassulian frescoes from complete isolation, but no geographically intermediate stages bridge the thousands of intervening miles.

The flint industry has fair parallels at a predynastic settlement discovered at Ma'adi in Egypt south of Cairo, but not close enough to prove direct relationships. It can hardly be derived from the contemporary Tahunian, nor is it an ancestress of the Cananean. Ghassulian agriculture, again, did not develop out of any now known previous phase in Palestine. Mesolithic agriculture, as found at Shuqbah and Wad' el-Mugharah, depended upon rainfall. That the Ghassulians were farmers is clear. One characteristic of all strata is the number of round silos, or grain bins, which were found. Mortars and flint sickles likewise indicate an agricultural community. But there could not have been enough rainfall to grow anything. Yet water is abundant in the wadis that come down from the eastern mountains, and is still used extensively for irrigation. The Jordan had then not dug itself so deeply into the alluvial lake bed. The Ghassulians, like dwellers on the Nile and the Euphrates, were undoubtedly dependent on irrigation.

Their house roofs must have used wood extensively, if one may judge from the amount of ashes which separate the strata. Wood was available in any quantity along the Jordan and on the hills of Moab. But the roughly contemporary structures at present known from Palestine (Khudeirah and Jericho) suggest no such lavish use of wood, while the "brick" walls have their only possible parallels in crude mudbricks of a similar age in Babylonia. Thus both wooded mountains like the Taurus and river bottoms are suggested as the place of origin of the race.

The conclusion is inevitable that some elements in Ghassulian culture were intrusive. Pottery and tools, houses and frescoes show a high development when the site was first occupied. If intrusive, the Ghassulian culture must have come from Egypt, Babylonia, or Syria. The frescoes and the painting on the pottery suggest connections with some phase of the early painted-pottery cultures of the Fertile Crescent. Since relationships are to be seen between Teleilat el-Ghassul and stratum V at Ras esh-Shamrah, Syria at present seems the most promising source for the peculiar features of Ghassulian culture. Other evidence for or against this hypothesis will doubtless come to light.

Possibly, then, some of the people who founded these "cities of the plain" came from a land where irrigation was practiced and found this warm river valley exactly suited to their needs. With them they brought their strange methods of construction, their peculiarities of technique in flint and pottery, and their knowledge of painting. They influenced their neighbors and borrowed from them. Their forwardness in some matters, their backwardness in others suggest emigrants from an advanced civilization who found themselves isolated from stimulating cultural contacts. If, as now appears, their earliest pottery was their best, possibly the effects of isolation and certainly those of an increase in numbers and of an enervating climate upon population in a relatively high civilization, caused gradual deterioration in some elements of their culture.

The earlier phases of the settlement were ended by conflagrations. Wind erosion, which is especially effective here in the Ghor because of the downward sweeping air currents from the heights, might conceivably have removed traces of fire on the surface of the last occupation if it had suffered the same fate. Probably the place was gradually abandoned and quietly fell into ruins leaving it to the Jesuit fathers 6000 years later to resurrect this lost civilization.

PRIMITIVE HOUSE MODELS

A remarkable confirmation of the antiquity of Ghassulian civilization comes from Khudeirah on the Plain of Sharon. A necropolis plainly marked as Ghassulian by the nature of the few vessels preserved was found in a layer of sand under about a meter and a half of *kurkar*, a type of rock which is, geologically speaking, most recent, but, humanly speaking, very ancient. The geological problem must be left to geologists. Professor Sukenik, Père Vincent, and others who are competent to judge, place the pottery in the fourth millennium, and probably near the beginning of it. In general the settlement seemed more primitive than that at Teleilat el-Ghassul.

The most astonishing feature of this discovery was that it included a group of burials in small models of houses in poorly baked clay used as ossuaries. A model round house appeared at Jericho.[1] Those at Khudeirah were rectangular, about 18 or 20

[1] See below, chap. VI.

inches long, and almost as high. Some had gabled roofs; some had four long solid feet which raised them above the ground level. Some were decorated with horizontal bands and with friezes of triangles separated by perpendicular lines that suggest triglyphs. In two or three, on each side of a door in one end, was a loop through which a bar could be thrust. In the opposite gable in one there were three small rectangular holes which may represent windows or the substitute for a chimney.

Ossuaries in house form suggest many things. First of all those with feet point to houses set upon corner pillars in a region such as Khudeirah probably was. By their shape they imply a house made of reeds or branches set erect and then tied together at the top. The gabled roof may mean a more rainy climate than at Teleilat el-Ghassul, where a flat roof supported on beams, sometimes held up by pillars, was assumed as normal. The models, like the house plans at Teleilat el-Ghassul, were rectangular, it is to be noted. These were far from primitive builders in the earliest stages of house construction.

The care taken in the permanent disposal of the bones of the dead, the deposit of pottery with them, and perhaps especially the fact that these are secondary burials point at once to belief in a future life. The house form of the ossuary is religiously even more significant. It means that a house was prepared in which the dead relative might live. Doubtless also it is a survival which points to a time when the dead, as at Mugharet es-Sukhul, were buried in the dwelling. Whether that was impossible here because the houses were elevated, as in lake dwellings, or other reasons caused a change of custom it is impossible to say. In any case the paintings of Teleilat el-Ghassul and the house ossuaries of Khudeirah point to a very considerable progress in the manual and the mental activities of ancient man.

During the greater part of the years in which excavation was in progress at Teleilat el-Ghassul, the place seemed entirely isolated. The distant resemblances between its pottery and its flint industry and those of other similarly isolated sites could have meant little in intepreting the progress of civilization and the connections between periods but for the discoveries at Jericho in the last two seasons of excavation there. Jericho gave the prehistorian and the historian also solutions for some of Palestine's most perplexing historical problems. Jericho, therefore, is the next site to be considered.

CHAPTER VI

JERICHO, PALESTINE'S OLDEST CITY

❖

TYPICAL EXCAVATIONS

Two Palestinian excavations provide a systematic and continuous story of man's cultural development from the meager beginnings of civilization down to recent times. Few sites have been occupied from the dawn of city civilization, none continuously. The excavations of Jericho and Tell Beit Mirsim together provide typical illustrations both of continuous historical evolution and of orderly, scientific archaeological method. These two mounds are selected because of special circumstances, in part the writer's familiarity with the sites and his acquaintance with the excavators, in part the character of the mounds, but most of all the competence of the excavators and the completeness of their reports.

Jericho covers the long ages from the Mesolithic period down to the invasion of Palestine by the Israelites. Tell Beit Mirsim takes up the tale about 2200 B.C., meagerly parallels Jericho for 800 years, and carries it down to the end of the Hebrew kingdoms. Other sites have their peculiar problems and their striking contributions to make. No two are alike. These two provide an excellent introduction to both matter and method. Neither produced a vast number of "museum pieces," but each has made remarkable contributions to modern knowledge of antiquity.

The results of excavation at Jericho have proved of the highest value, not only to the student of the Bible, but also to the scientific historian. The questions as to both the why and the when of the fall of Jericho have been answered. But, more important than that, excavation of the site has revealed a succession of cultures running back through the earliest city civilization

68

in Palestine to the primitive settlements preceding walled cities and even to a much earlier microlithic Middle Stone Age occupation which, in some measure, approximates the Natufian of the Mount Carmel caves. Wad' el-Mugharah and Jericho together assemble the sections of the long ladder of civilization from 100,000 to 1400 B.C. almost without a break. The revelation of primitive man's efforts to struggle upward has been instructive and amusing, not to say pathetic.

THE PROBLEM OF JERICHO

Few sites more brilliantly illustrate the progress which archaeology has made in the last century and even in the last decade than the great mound which represents ancient Jericho. The story of its excavation has been as full of dramatic surprises as the familiar biblical account of its capture by Joshua. The first investigators thought it not worth digging. The last has found the oldest and longest series of civilizations and the clearest and most complete stratification yet known. In 1831 Edward Robinson, looking for Jericho, decided that the mound above the bountiful spring, 'Ain es-Sultan, was only rubbish. In 1869 Charles Warren saw that it was "formed by the gradual crumbling of great towers or castles of unburnt brick," but doubted whether it could be Jericho. Frederick J. Bliss, in 1894 recognized its importance, but Professor Ernst Sellin was the first to undertake its excavation, with Dr. Carl Watzinger, in 1907-09. Their excavations were scientifically conducted and were reported in a stately volume (1913) with careful descriptions and excellent plans and plates. But they themselves were soon dissatisfied with the dates they had given to the walls and strata discovered. As new evidence came to light from other sites after 1920, Albright and Watzinger independently reached the conclusion that the city wall which had been called "Israelite" and assigned to Hiel actually was a thousand years older and had been destroyed about 1600 B.C. by the incoming Israelites.

The new hypothesis was much more satisfactory, but had certain evident disadvantages. It introduced too long a gap into the city's history, and discredited the biblical account of Joshua's conquest. It did not seem possible that a site so strategically located, with a marvelous spring flowing beside it, should lie unoccupied, or at least unfortified, for 600 years, especially during the Late Bronze Age, a period when, according to Egyptian records, the land was populous and prosperous.

During his seven years (1920-26) as director of the Department of Antiquities of the Palestine Government and director of the British School of Archaeology at Jerusalem, Professor John Garstang of the University of Liverpool had been constantly occupied with the problems of the Bronze Age, largely because of previous excavations and studies in Egypt and the Hittite country. He once remarked to me that everything after the Bronze Age was "post-history," as all before it was prehistory. In 1926 he returned to his post in Liverpool, but in the winter of 1928 he was again in Palestine with a commission to excavate Jericho. His sounding convinced him and Albright that there was clear evidence of occupation during the Late Bronze Age, that is, well after 1600 B.C. In January, 1929, Professor Garstang began the systematic excavation of the site as the only means of untangling the snarl of problems which the German expedition had dumped into the lap of archaeology. The work was continued during six more campaigns, every winter or spring until 1936, with the exception of 1934.[1]

The mound presented some unusual advantages and equally unusual difficulties. The presence of the village, a hotel, and empty houses easily solved the problem of living quarters for the staff. Workers were found in part in the local population.

[1] I owe Professor Garstang very hearty thanks for the privilege of spending many hours with him at Jericho during his campaigns of 1930 and 1931. In 1936 I repeatedly went over the new excavations at the northeast end of the mound with him and he was kind enough to give his arguments for the date shortly after 1400 B.C. at some length to one American School party. In 1941 he repeated these to me in Chicago. He has been so kind as to read this chapter and make correctional suggestions, although the content and conclusions are my own. See now his article in *AJSL*, LVIII (October, 1941), 368-72. Regarding this account I have consulted at length with Dr. D. E. McCown, who took part in the work of the first two seasons at Jericho.

But a very large number, men and women, boys and girls, came from Deir Diwan, just southeast of et-Tell (Ai). The pottery was washed, 40,000 pieces of it yearly, under Mrs. Garstang's supervision, by setting the baskets in the flowing water of the concrete irrigation channels that run from the spring. Abundance of water is most unusual in a Palestinian dig. But the constant stream of visitors, while it brought a few whose advice the excavator valued, operated to interrupt the work continually. Professor Garstang, wearing dark goggles and two wide-brimmed hats for protection against the sun, had frequently to interrupt his careful observation of what was happening in order to show individuals and groups over the mound. Fortunately the weather at Jericho during the winter and early spring is almost ideal. During no campaign, each of about two months, was the work halted by rain or wind for more than two or three days, and the heat was never prostrating.

The previous excavation constituted the initial problem. Carefully as its work had been done, it had necessarily destroyed much evidence and its great tip heaps sometimes covered the hitherto unexcavated sections of the city. The new excavations had to clear the old trenches, to verify former observations, and to open new areas in order to estimate all of the evidence *de novo*. It was not easy to discover virgin material, since, after lying for twenty years, the old dumps had consolidated until it was difficult to distinguish them from the debris of the ancient city. I can remember Professor Garstang telling, early in the campaign, how he had set men at work on what he judged to be an untouched section. As they had gone down and down, his hopes had risen till he was certain he could now get at the evidence sought, when, far down in the debris, they unearthed, not a relic of the wars of Israel, but a modern tin helmet. It is no reflection on the previous excavation to say that no little patience and no little keenness of observation were necessary to take up again the half-finished task and carry it through to successful completion.

One of the most significant pieces of work was done at the

north end of the mound where a great dump from the former expedition had buried an unexcavated portion of the city walls. First a long trench was dug extending both outside and inside the city. The earth was removed in half-meter layers and all objects, chiefly potsherds, carefully registered according to their levels. Out of some 20,000 fragments, representative selections were made and examined independently by Garstang, Fisher and Vincent, who agreed substantially as to the periods to which the sherds belonged. The find spots of the sherds were then charted on millimeter paper and gave a consistent stratification. Later the entire northeast corner, which lay under the towering dump, was excavated down to the water table at the level of the spring and here some of the most startling discoveries, to be described below, were made.

In other places pits were sunk to the Stone Age stratum at the bottom of the debris. The walls also were followed and sections were cut through them and through the debris around them in order to discover the character of the walls and what had happened when they were destroyed. On the top of the mound, below the Israelite houses, which could be recognized from their pottery, were two earlier cities, rightly called Canaanite, one with a double wall and another beneath it with a single wall, represented on the German map by dark and light blue. At the north, under these and projecting beyond them, the Germans had found a still earlier wall which was colored purple on their map.

The "dark blue" double wall Professor Garstang found to rest upon debris of the Middle Bronze Age into which its foundations hardly penetrated. But a great wall of polygonal stone (shown in red), which the German expedition had assigned to the Israelites, was found at one point to have destroyed a house of Middle Bronze i or possibly of Early Bronze iv and was thus proved to have been older than the double wall, which rested on much later debris. Thus the historical relations of the walls had to be reversed, as Watzinger and Albright had already concluded. As the digging proceeded from year to year, the picture became more and more clear. But as some uncertainties disappeared, new problems arose and new, unexplained materials were discovered.

In the dig of 1930 a shaft had been sunk far down into the debris in order to guide the excavator in making his further plans. At a level many feet below the surface Neolithic flints were found and dull-red floors of puddled clay and lime. There were crumbling fragments of colored clay, but no pottery in the lowest levels, though there was unbaked pottery above. Similar discoveries were made elsewhere in deep cuttings. Whether the floors belonged to houses or grain bins could not then be determined.

This mystery was not solved until 1935, when a considerable area in the northeast corner of the mound reached a succession of seven such floors, one above another, in areas large enough to discover house walls and the plans of houses and shrines. Various implements of stone and bone, along with clay figurines, were discovered, enough to make out the character of the various levels of civilization which developed beside the abundant spring during successive cultures.

The Archaeological History of Jericho

It would be fruitless to record in detail the process by which Professor Garstang slowly disentangled the confused data. Not all of the difficult problems which arose are even now settled. But the main outlines of the history of Jericho are fairly clear.[2]

Even to seasoned archaeologists, the most unexpected and astonishing discoveries were those just mentioned, made in the lower strata of the mound. Above sterile earth some eighty feet below the top of the acropolis, there were about three meters of deposit marked by microliths as belonging to a Mesolithic (Middle Stone Age) civilization somewhat like the Natufian of Mugharet el-Wad. There followed in the next four meters the seven painted and polished floors just described. In all these lower strata (from IX down to XVIII), which totaled some

---

[2] See the chart on p. 83 for a chronological outline.

twenty feet in thickness, there were flints of the Tahunian type already mentioned.

From stratum X upward pottery appears, and in stratum VIII it shows distinct resemblances to Ghassulian types. In stratum VII there appears the flint industry called "Cananean" by Neuville, which runs all through the Chalcolithic and Early Bronze Ages. Thus, as already noted, the lower strata which Professor Garstang uncovered at Jericho reach down almost to the top of the Mesolithic strata at Mugharet el-Wad and settle the relative position of the strange civilization at Teleilat el-Ghassul. As the strata are followed upward, one occupation succeeds another until the coming of the Israelites. Together the two sites, Jericho and Wad' el-Mugharah, provide a fairly complete skeleton of the history of Palestinian civilization from 1400 B.C. back for 100,000 years.

Besides filling in a gap of some thousands of years, the lower strata at Jericho are extremely interesting in themselves. Only a few features can be mentioned here. The seven painted and polished floors, with their worn polishing stones, should serve as a bond of sympathy between the modern housewife and the women of primitive Jericho. However, the men may have had a hand in the polishing also, for in one place the highest of these floors seems to have held a temple, in plan like a Homeric *megaron*, but having, instead of a hearth, a central pillar supporting the roof. It was simple, merely a rectangular room, with a wide porch supported by six posts in front.

In its neighborhood were numerous small clay figurines of animals; the cow, goat, sheep, pig, and possibly the dog. Other models resembled a cobra's head, the male organs, and small cones. All these suggest that the building may have been the shrine of a pastoral fertility cult.

A lime-faced bin in stratum X, 23 feet above sterile earth, may be regarded as the first step toward pottery. In the lowest phase of the next stratum above (IX), a basin scooped out of the earth and lined with a coat of marl three or four inches thick marks what Garstang calls the first timid appearance of pottery. A little later the coat of marl was carried up above the floor level. Still later, in the second phase of stratum IX, un-baked, sun-dried pottery vessels, in which the clay was mixed with chopped straw, appeared. In the third phase, fine grit and sand were mixed with the clay, the vessels are sometimes decorated with paint, and they are partially baked.

Technologically less interesting but culturally more so was a strange bee-hive-like structure of clay which appeared partly in this stratum and partly in stratum X below. It stood 40 inches high and was 30 inches wide. On a base nearly six inches thick was a floor of stone slabs. A dummy doorway was blocked inside by a round, flat stone which rolled in a frame. Higher on the wall was a recess with solid floors and walls. A central pillar supported a floor running entirely across the structure at about two thirds of its height, and another pillar supported the roof. Professor Garstang notes a resemblance to the Argive Heraeum. It may be a miniature shrine.

This peculiar structure, which possibly preserves the chief features of the houses of that far-off age, was carefully photo-graphed, drawn, and recorded. Fearing he might destroy an object so unique, Dr. Garstang called upon the Department of Antiquities to send a Museum expert to preserve and remove it. The official took all proper precautions to consolidate it with paraffin ("wax" as the English call it) and prepare it for moving. One can imagine the general dismay when, in the heat of the sun, the paraffin melted and the unique structure suddenly crumbled into dust.

Stratum IX provided a still more bizarre discovery, the earliest known attempts to model the human form. The plastic figures of mud and clay found with the *megaron* in stratum XI prepared for this much more ambitious undertaking, which is repre-sented by fragments of clay statues modeled on "skeletons" of reeds. Fortunately they held together better than the "house model" and could be almost completely restored in the Museum workrooms at Jerusalem. Two groups were found, each appar-ently representing a man, woman, and child. Viewed full face the representation is remarkably life-like. Viewed from the side, the heads are flattened almost to disks. The bodies and limbs, however, are rounded and show realistic observation, even if not perfect proportions.

There can be little doubt that, even in this early period perhaps 7,000 years ago, the figures are to be taken as representations of a divine triad. It is significant that there was no emphasis on the sexual features of the figures and therefore no such development of the fertility cult as later marked much Near East religion. Set in connection with the wall paintings of Teleilat el-Ghassul, the figures suggest a long previous period of religious development.

In stratum VIII the flints begin to deteriorate slightly, though fine pieces appear. But pottery improved. Potters learned to turn their vessels on mats and thus produced much better shapes. In the next two strata (VII-VI), a new age (City I) begins, which falls in Early Bronze Age i, 3250-2850 B.C. It is marked by linear painted decoration on pottery, by rounded houses in groups, but, most significant of all, by a city wall which enclosed an area of perhaps four acres.

Babylonian influence appears in various matters, most strikingly in a shrine. It was an almost rectangular building with a platform covering one end and solid benches running around the other three sides. In this stratum, probably connected with the shrine, were a small libation altar and a long, smooth rounded stone which may be a primitive massebah, or sacred pillar.

The flints continued to deteriorate. With the exception of one arrow head, they were all for domestic use, for scraping skins or cutting grain. Sickle blades were especially numerous. Though, for convenience sake, this is called the Early Bronze Age, there was no bronze and, though copper was known, no tools of that material were found.

The city walls and house walls were built of irregular sundried brick, laid in thick mud mortar. The rooms and courtyards were large with ample provision in round clay bins for the storage of grain. Remnants were actually found of millet, barley, lentils, and grapes. Even a few fragments of cloth were recovered. Clearly, 5,000 years ago Jericho was, for many generations, the home of a peaceful agricultural and pastoral population which had made no small progress in the arts of civilization, in communication with distant lands, and even in art. In addition to the decoration on their pottery, one piece of evidence for artistic progress is a bull's head carved in blackened ivory, perhaps used as the head of a staff. The technique of the workmanship was Babylonian and the head copied a Babylonian species of bull. A second and third phase of this civilization (strata V-IV) began about 3000 B.C. or somewhat later. They are marked by still more highly developed pottery forms and by more numerous silos, or grain bins.

These 500 or 600 years of peaceful progress seem to have come to an end before 2500 B.C. in a catastrophe, for the remnants of walls discovered showed traces of fire and the city was completely rebuilt. This next city (II) is much better preserved. The walls were heavier, as much as ten feet thick, and built of firmer, better-shaped bricks. Possibly an outer screen wall was added in places. The chief monument of the ancient builders was a great tower overlooking the spring, built doubtless to defend the spring and the gate, which must have stood here. The tower was thirty feet wide, sixty feet long, and over thirteen feet high. Once built it was used during many succeeding ages. The population must have greatly increased during this period, for rooms were smaller, houses were more crowded together, and one wall, which stood sixteen feet high and points to a three-story building, suggests enlargement vertically as well as horizontally.

A great sepulcher (tomb A) in a cave which lay less than 300 yards west of the mound had received generations of burials from some family or clan of this period. When it was cleared in 1931 and 1932, there came out of it some 800 pottery vessels representing possibly 500 burials. There was the greatest variety in the pottery. Crude and fine vessels appeared side by side. There were interesting specimens of bone flutes such as have also been found at Ras esh-Shamrah. The dead had been adorned with an abundance of amulets and crude jewelry of semiprecious stones, faience, and bone, but no precious metals. Archaeologically such a "tomb group" is extremely valuable since the pottery types are strictly determined by their interconnections. Similar pottery was found in certain rooms of this period as well as elsewhere on the mound and thus the tomb and stratum III mutually assist in arriving at a proper date for both, which falls in EB iii, a little later probably than the first Khirbet Kerak ware, which appears in tomb A and on the mound early in this period.

The rapid progress which archaeology made in the early thirties is shown by the fact that this tomb, which was, at the time of its discovery in 1931, dated about 1800 B.C., was the next year thrust back a century or two by the evidence and placed in City II. Further evidence, collected in part by Dr. Albright at Tell Beit Mirsim, showed that the tomb must belong to the EB Age. At the same time it was discovered that the City II wall also was much earlier than at first supposed, since it likewise belonged to the EB Age, and thus the tomb and City II are now put at the still earlier date.

After 400 or 500 years, about the end of the Early Bronze Age, the second city perished in some social convulsion and, for a century or two, the site probably lay uninhabited, as is indicated by a washed and eroded surface, over which another city (III) was built on an entirely new plan. This began the most glorious period in the history of the site. A great stone glacis, surmounted by a mud-brick parapet and enclosing a large area, and an imposing "palace" with great store rooms testify to the city's wealth. It was succeeded by another city (IV) following the narrower lines of the older cities and with a lofty mud-brick *migdal*, or tower, at its northwest corner, a characteristic Canaanite structure which might well seem, to the invading Bedouins who became known as Israelites, to reach to heaven. The double wall which surrounded this city was, however, far from equal in strength to that which preceded it.

City III belongs to the Hyksos period, as scarabs clearly show. City IV was evidently under control of the Egyptians who expelled the Hyksos. A scarab of Kames, the Pharaoh who first raised the standard of revolt against the Hyksos, was found in one of the tombs. It is clear that early in the fifteenth century, probably at the time of the campaigns of Thothmes III (ca. 1482-50), the city came completely under Egyptian domination and the cultural changes due to contacts with Egypt brought in the Late Bronze Age. Imperial signet rings in tomb 5 indicate that the local dynast was a vassal of the Pharaohs, and eventually a "cremation pit" points to the presence of Egyptian mercenaries of the "sea peoples," Sherdens or Philistines. An Astarte figurine points to the later development of fertility cults in Palestine, and an unfortunately illegible and undatable cuneiform tablet recalls the fact that imperial correspondence as in the period of the Amarna letters had begun.

The Fall of Jericho and the Israelite Conquest

There can be no doubt that it was the fourth city which the invading Israelites captured and devoted to destruction. When and under what circumstances did this take place? That is the question which Professor Garstang set himself to answer and about which dispute still rages. But the new evidence has shifted the center of discussion. The date is no longer set between 1600 and 1200 B.C., but is narrowed down to little more than a century between 1385 and 1250 B.C.

Professor Garstang's statement of the case for a date about 1400 B.C. or shortly thereafter is this: (1) Scarabs of Amenhotep III (1412-1375) and pottery attributable to his reign are abundant. (2) No later scarabs, either ordinary or royal (with one exception to be mentioned below), were found. (3) Typical Late Bronze Age ii pottery is extremely rare on the site and is apparently confined to a single building described below. Except for a fragment found on the site of this building, Late

Mycenean pottery, which began to be imported about 1400 B.C. and was in full tide under Ikhnaton (1375-60) is wanting. (4) Only two tombs (4 and 13) had any deposits which can be dated later. A very careful search in all the region for a mile around the necropolis during one whole season succeeded in discovering only one more tomb and it belonged to the Middle Bronze Age. (5) There is no mention of Jericho in the Amarna tablets. (6) The mention of Israel in the Merenptah stela (1231 B.C.), far from indicating the date of the Exodus, proves that the Hebrews had long been settled in Palestine.

On the mound itself over the palace area there was a building which continually puzzled the excavator because it was higher than the latest stratum elsewhere and its plan did not conform to that of the city. Its pottery, like that in tombs 4 and 13, seemed later than that of the upper stratum of the city, yet typical pieces resembled Beth-shan pottery which was then dated in the fifteenth century. When, however, the Beth-shan strata were redated and stratum IX was seen to belong to Harmhab or Seti I, not to Thutmose III,[3] the difficulty was resolved. It is now clear that this "Middle Building" did not belong to the pre-Israelite period at all, but was an isolated structure standing on the ruins of the city destroyed by the Israelites.[4] Above it was another building with very heavy walls. The German excavators had cleared it and called it a *hillani*, from its resemblance to a type of building found in Syria. When Professor Garstang investigated its walls, he found them to contain both Late Bronze and Early Iron Age potsherds. It must, therefore, belong to the beginning of Early Iron Times. Professor Garstang believes that the "middle building" may represent the rule of Eglon, king of Moab, over the "City of Palms" (Jdg 3.13 f.). He attributes the late scarab found in the "cremation pit" and some of the LB ii and EI i potsherds with the *hillani* building to the presence of Sherden mercenaries of a Ramesside Pharaoh for whom the building served as a

---

[3] See below, chap. XI.
[4] See Garstang's article, in *AJSL*, LVIII (1941), and *Joshua-Judges*, 270 f.

The "Plains of Moab" where Père Mallon discovered Teleilat el-Ghassul; mounds showing on the horizon. The expedition tents at the right (1930).

Teleilat el-Ghassul: Room in which four infant burials in jars were found.

Jericho: Northern half of mound in 1921, looking north.

Across northern end in 1930, looking east. Workers at breakfast. Neolithic Jericho
many feet below.

military post. Thus both the "middle building" and the *hillani*, with their associated pottery on and off the mound, point to a partial reoccupation of the site by intruders after its destruction by the Israelites, not to a continuation and a destruction long after 1400 B.C. Joshua's conquest should fall not after 1385 B.C.

Albright differs only slightly from Garstang, putting Jericho's fall less than a century later. He has thought that the pottery suggests a somewhat later Canaanite occupation of the whole city. The purely negative evidence of the lack of any royal scarab later than Amenhotep III does not seem to him conclusive. The discovery of another tomb might easily fix another date. But he agrees that Jericho was uninhabited beginning in the latter part of the fourteenth century for, aside from the few exceptions already mentioned, the characteristic types of pottery in use during that century are wanting.

Jericho, therefore, was destroyed by the incoming Israelites, but not 440 years before Solomon began to build the Temple, as one might calculate from the Massoretic text of 1 Kings 6:1, nor 400 years before, as the Septuagint text would set it. The problem is complicated by our ignorance of Solomon's exact dates. Thus, while the literal accuracy of the biblical text is by no means established, the general dependability of the non-miraculous features in the record is rendered probable, and, though problems remain unsolved, it also becomes somewhat easier to frame a historical account of the Israelite conquest of Canaan, for the principal incidents need not now be spread over four centuries. The following chapters will show that they can by no means be telescoped into a single man's lifetime as the Book of Joshua does, but the decisive phases of the conquest at least can be compressed within a century or two.

What now was the manner of Jericho's fall? It need hardly be said that no ram's horns were found nor other evidence to substantiate the miraculous items of the story in Joshua 6.

Professor Garstang, however, did find evidence which intimates how the miraculous elements in the story arose.

As might be expected of a city lying in the deepest rift valley in the world, the excavations disclosed repeated evidence of the action of earthquakes. From Neolithic times on, fissured floors and cracked and fallen walls were frequent. The workmen from Eriha (modern Jericho), who live in mud-walled houses, remarked, when they were clearing the walls of City IV, "These walls look like the walls of our houses after an earthquake."

During the earthquake of 1927 the Jordan was dammed up by the fall of a cliff twenty miles up stream near ed-Damieh. A similar incident is recorded by an Arab historian as happening in 1267 A.D. It is easy to imagine the nomadic Israelites camped in the 'Araboth Moab, the plain north of the Dead Sea, by the bountiful streams that flow down from Gilead, and longing to cross over and plunder the rich city amid its green verdure at the foot of the western mountains. Suddenly the waters of the river cease to run and they hastily break camp and pass over, to find the city walls in ruins and the houses on fire. They would march around it in wonder and, believing that the calamity which had come upon it was due to divine wrath, would devote it to Yahweh as accursed and assist in spreading the fires that were destroying it.

The completeness of that destruction became evident as the excavations went on. The city walls which appeared so lofty and so formidable had been carelessly constructed on old walls and foundations. Houses had been built against the walls and even between the main wall and the screen wall. Their pressure aided the earthquake and pushed the walls out so that they were found often sprawling many feet down the slope of the mound. The fires burned so fiercely that some of the sun-dried brick seemed almost like baked brick.

As in nearly every Palestinian "dig," charred or carbonized grain and food were found. In one house at Jericho, when the earthquake came, bread had been laid out for baking along

PERIODS	MEGIDDO		JERICHO	BETH-SHAN	AI
Wright	*Albright*	*Shipton*	*Garstang*	*Albright FitzGerald*	*Albright Wright*
3750 MC	3500 XX		Str VIII	XVIII	
3500 LC	3250 XIX	3300	City I	XVII–XVI	
[Esdraelon ware]	Stages		Str VII–VI	XV	
3300 EBia	VII–VI				
3100 EBib		Stg V–IV	Str V	XIV	III 3000
	3000 XVIII	3000			Necropolis
3000 EBii		Stg IV–III	Str IV		II 2900-2700
	2800 XVII	2500	City II	XIII	
	Stg II?		(2500)		
2700 EBiii	XVI		Str III		I 2600–2200
	Stg I?			XII	Later shrine
[Kh.Kerak ware 26–2400 Wanting]				Kh.K. ware	and palace
[Tomb A pottery	"	]	Tomb A	T.A. ware	———
				XIB	*T.BEIT MIRSIM*
2300 EBiv			Tomb 351		*Albright*
					2500 J
2100 MBi	2050 XV	1950	[Deserted]		2300 I–H
				XIA	
1900 MBiia			City IIIa		1900 G
	1850 XIV	1850	Stone glacis		
	XIII	1800			F
	Hyksos			XB	
1750 MBiib	XII	1750	City IIIb		1700 E1
	Hyksos				E2
	XI	1700			
	Hyksos				
1625 MBiic	X	1650		XA	1600 D
			City IV		
1500 LBi	1525 IX	1550			1550 Gap
	1469 VIII	1479			1450 C
1350 LBii			Destroyed	IX 1350	1350 C
LB–EI	1300 VII	1350	Middle Bldg	VIII 1325	1230 B1
			(1320)	VII 1275	
1225 EIi			Block house	VI 1230	
1160 EIii	1140 VI	1170		V 1150	1150 B2
	1090 Gap	1100	Gap		
	1050 V	1060			
1000 EIiii					
	950 IV	1000	Rebuilt	Gap 975	1000 B3
900 MIi			City V		920 A1
	Gap	800	(900–700)		800 A2
750 MIii	733 III	780			
	IV	650			
587 MIiii	600 I	600			
530 Persian					
	450 End	350	(All dates are approximate)		

TENTATIVE TABLE FOR COMPARISON OF SITES AND DATES

with vegetables and dates. The falling beams and branches that supported the mud roof ignited along with the oil and grain in their vessels and charred the food. But the mud of the roof, falling, put out the fire, and the charring prevented rotting. Still today one can see the burned dinner of some Jericho family that was driven out by the earthquake and probably slaughtered by the ruthless Hebrews.

In such a summary as this there is no possibility of describing the small finds and the pottery in detail. But entirely without that, surely something of the wider historical implications of an excavation such as that at Jericho must be clear. Having traced the development of human architecture, art, and artisanship at a single site from 5000 B.C., or earlier, down to 1400 or 1300 B.C., from their first blossoming in a river-valley, irrigation-sustained culture complex down to the time when the nomadic Hebrews were settling in Palestine, one is better able to appreciate how far man had climbed up the ladder of civilization, even in such an isolated enclave as the Jordan Valley must have been.

CHAPTER VII

TELL BEIT MIRSIM

An Introduction to Excavation[1]

❖

Although far from finished, the excavation of Tell Beit Mirsim has been carried on and reported systematically and with unusual attention to the synthesis of its historical results. At the same time it represents a clearer stratification than any other excavation. Though absolutely conclusive topographical and archaeological evidence is wanting, its excavators believe it to be the ancient Debir, or Kiriath Sepher, the "city of the book, or scribe," the most important of eleven towns in the sixth district of Judah. Having been a Canaanite royal city, it was captured by the Israelites and became the seat of Othniel, first "judge" of Israel. It was occupied until well toward the time of the Exile, as its mention in the list of towns in Joshua 15 shows. Such a city offers an excellent introduction to Palestinian archaeology in the Old Testament period.

Tell Beit Mirsim, "the mound of the house of the fast camel driver," lies in rather barren foothills some 13 miles southwest of Hebron at the edge of the southern Shephelah, on one of the main routes from Egypt up into the mountains of Judah. It is a large tell with masses of Middle Iron Age pottery on the surface and with an ancient city wall and revetment that could be followed almost the whole distance around, even before excavation began. Dr. W. F. Albright, then Director of the American School of Oriental Research, visited the mound in April, 1924, with the annual spring exploring party of the school. His description of the mound so impressed the late Dr. M. G. Kyle, then president of Xenia Theological Seminary,

[1] This chapter has profited by corrections from Dr. W. F. Albright.

that Dr. Kyle decided to undertake its excavation. Accordingly in the spring of 1926 a co-operative expedition was organized by President Kyle for Xenia Seminary and Dr. Albright for the American School. Excavation was carried on for two or three months in the spring or summer of four years, 1926, 1928, 1930 and 1932.

According to the excavators, the summer season has certain real advantages. The heat was not found unsupportable, for the winds from the sea blow up daily and at 1600 feet above sea level the air is fresh and bracing. At that time of the year the country is so dry that malaria is unthinkable. Since the harvests are practically over when operations begin, there is no difficulty in finding workers and nothing is growing on the mound except *durrah* (millet), or other summer crops, which are not costly. During the summer vacation, scholars from Europe and America are glad to join the staff as honorary workers. The value of such a vacation to the student, one who plans to enter the ministry, for example, is questionable. But a man with the proper historical and philological preparation and interest can find no better opportunity to learn the methods and value of archaeology than to spend a summer thus in the bright sunshine and invigorating air of Palestine under the direction and instruction of an expert archaeologist.

DISAPPOINTMENTS

Like every other expedition, this one provided the excavators with numerous disappointments. Long ago Professor Sayce suggested that Kiriath Sepher, the "book city," should have stored valuable archives. If Tell Beit Mirsim represents Kiriath Sepher, it has as yet failed to deliver up any archives and has proved bare of cuneiform tablets, ostraca, or any considerable inscriptions. At the very beginning of the excavations what had been supposed to be a sanctuary turned out to be a private house of a common type. In digging down to the underlying rock to study the structure of the west gate, the excavators came upon a narrow rock-cut tunnel filled with debris con-

taining only Middle Bronze Age pottery, which they followed
with high hopes. One can imagine their disappointment when
they emerged, not into a necropolis of the time of the Patri-
archs, but into an empty Israelite cistern. The Hebrews had
cleared out the Bronze Age tombs and made them into a fine
series of cisterns.

North of the east gate a similar cleft in the rock was discovered. The workmen were ordered to widen it to admit a
man, and then excavators and workmen crept in. The Arabs
were convinced that they would find buried treasure—they can
imagine no other motive for digging—and Dr. Albright heard
one of them suggest that as soon as they found the gold they
should cut the throats of the *khawajat* (the "gentlemen") and
make the treasure their own. Eventually they came into a
cavern which had been used for the storing merely of prosaic
grain, straw, and oil. The Arabs, bitterly disappointed, crept
out, saying, "Poor people, they were peasants like us," a very
true remark. The sanguinary individual disappeared for some
weeks, but his friends never allowed him to forget the episode.

This group of caverns proved also to be Bronze Age tombs
reused. They had been entered from the interior of the city by
a typical Bronze Age doorway of megalithic construction. Apparently all of the Bronze Age tombs were within the city walls,
but all were cleared and used by later inhabitants. Up to date
no search has been made outside, because of despoliation that
the inhabitants might carry out if the necropolis should be discovered. Consequently no untouched tombs have been opened
and few "museum pieces" have been discovered.

Yet, because of Dr. Albright's unusual experience and competence, the expedition has been remarkably fruitful. During the
four successive campaigns, the long panorama of Palestinian
history from the third millennium B.C. down to the Exile has
gradually unrolled before the eyes of the excavators. The mound
is particularly favored in one regard. Through a large proportion of its history, for much over a thousand years, indeed, it
appears that a great deal of wood was used in the construction

of Tell Beit Mirsim and that the city was repeatedly burned to the ground. Sometimes after such a destruction the place lay uninhabited until wind and rain had smoothed over the surface. Sometimes new walls were laid at once in the ashes of the preceding city. In either case a light or heavy layer of ashes usually separates one layer of occupation from the next and gives the excavator unmistakable stratification. For this reason the mound has been remarkably instructive.

The History of the City

The Tell represented at least ten clearly marked periods, and several of these layers have to be divided into subordinate phases because of evident differences of pottery or reconstruction of buildings.[2] The lowest strata, J, I, and H, covering Early Bronze Age iv (2300-2100 B.C.) and the transition to Middle Bronze (2100-1900 B.C.), were represented chiefly by their pottery. Beginning with level G, which falls in the 19th and 18th centuries, the remains are better preserved and the historical picture clearer. Among small finds, a limestone mold for casting bronze ax-heads and lance-heads was notable. The city wall, which was built of small stones and was only about eleven feet thick, seems to have enclosed the greater part of the hill. In level G a type of courtyard house, or "palace," appeared which was characteristic also of the three strata above it. The best example stood at the side of a large rectangular walled court with a street entrance too narrow for horses and chariots. Two doors from the court gave access to the ground floor. Though stratum G was totally destroyed, there was no change in civilization in the succeeding stratum, F.

Dr. Albright tried an interesting experiment with the pottery of the G level. He himself first determined its date roughly by comparison with that from a somewhat later Gezer tomb excavated by Macalister (28 II), which, according to its scarabs, belongs to the thirteenth Egyptian dynasty and, therefore, allowing an ample margin, can be placed between 1850 and

[2] See the chronological chart, p. 83.

1750 B.C. He then asked Père Vincent and Dr. C. S. Fisher to give independent judgments as to the date of the G stratum pottery, without knowledge of the stratification of the tell. Dr. Fisher said it was earlier, but not much earlier than 1800 B.C. Père Vincent placed it in the 19th century. Surely a brilliant verification of the reliability of the ceramic index to chronology, when used by experts!

The next two strata, E and D, have an entirely new type of culture. They clearly belong to the Hyksos period, that is, the time of the barbarian invasion which entered Palestine in the 18th century and occupied Egypt throughout the 17th. During this period and until the Hebrew invasion, the city was surrounded by massive defenses consisting of a sloping revetment and an upper wall of adobe brick. It closely resembles the great wall of Jericho, already mentioned, which was built also in the 18th century.

A large house, or "palace," of this period had a great court with a gate wide enough to admit a chariot, a trough for feeding animals, and quarters on the ground floor for a chariot and horses. This suits the Hyksos age when the horse was first introduced into Palestine. In the house there were five rooms on the ground floor, two for storage, two for horses, and an anteroom, besides a small back court with a gate. The walls, built of adobe on stone foundations and covered with white lime plaster, were four feet thick. From models of houses found at Beth-shan and elsewhere, Dr. Albright infers that there were two upper stories, in which the family lived.

In this house various unique objects were found. One was the lower part of a limestone stela, badly calcined in the fire which destroyed the building. Presumably it had stood in a niche in a private shrine in an upper story of the house. The stela portrayed a relief of a goddess, a draped figure wearing a robe which reaches to her ankles. A large snake, probably a python, comes out of the earth and coils about her limbs with its head between her thighs. When found, during the second campaign, it was the first representation of a serpent goddess to have been found in Palestine. Since then another has been found at 'Ain Shems, which, along with other evidence, shows how widespread the serpent cult was in Palestine. The goddess appears to be a fertility deity and the serpent a symbol of the fecundating power.

At the opposite end of the house, during the third campaign, a very different kind of discovery was made, a little ivory die and a set of ten blue faience playing pieces, with which charioteers may have whiled away their time while awaiting their masters' pleasure. The set was then absolutely unique, though parallels of a kind were known from Egypt and Assyria and have since been found in Palestine. Fragments of the ivory inlay of the game board and of other ivories, some of them again inlaid with ebony, were found. Bronze weapons, jewelry, and vessels of faience and alabaster, indeed a great quantity of objects, indicate a high level of culture at this period.

The Hyksos city of level D fell, doubtless before the arms of Ahmose I, between 1560 and 1550 B.C. according to provisional calculations, and the people perished in a bitter struggle accompanied by a fierce conflagration. The skeletons found, which were examined by Dr. Paul Culley, a member of the staff during the second campaign, were those of elderly persons and children and of men of fighting age who lay where they had fallen in the struggle. No clear traces of looting were found. Numerous remains of inlaid furniture and boxes indicated that the place was subjected to destruction, but apparently the women were enslaved.

Level C belongs to the late Bronze Age. The former inhabitants were thoroughly scattered, for the site apparently lay unoccupied for some time. When it was rebuilt, a new wall a little over eight feet in thickness was erected just behind the old revetment. The deposits of stratum C were three feet and a half thick in places and were divided into two phases by ashes found in various parts of the ruins, indicating a partial destruction and then a rebuilding of the city. A scarab of Amenhotep III (1412-1375 B.C.) found in the upper layer proves the destruction of the earlier city after 1400. A scarab of the time of Rameses II (1299-1232) proves that the city was still occupied down to the 13th century. The pottery found had already indicated the same periods before the discovery of the scarabs.

Two of the most striking discoveries made at Tell Beit Mirsim belong to this period and come from the third campaign. Early in the season the workmen came upon a stone platter, or table, for offerings, a slab that had been hollowed out like a shallow basin and decorated with crude feline heads which, by courtesy, could be ascribed to lions. Just before the end of the campaign at a spot in the debris not far from that where the platter was found, a crude animal figure some two feet long came to light. At first the Moslem workmen called it a pig, but eventually one of them, after examining its tail, which curved around over its back, announced that it was not a pig, but a lion. With this wise judgment the excavators agreed. The lion is not an artistic or anatomical triumph, though one side of the upper lip shows a most successful snarl. But, as the earliest example of such a sacred object, as indeed the only pre-Roman lion in the round to be found in western Palestine, it is extremely interesting. Doubtless both objects belonged to the shrine that was destroyed when the Israelites took the city.

On the whole the C city was less prosperous than the preceding one. The houses so far excavated have been relatively good but less numerous, and no unusually fine ones have yet been found. There were many grain silos within the city during this period. Apparently the nobility were not so important as in the previous period and consequently, perhaps, the country was less settled and less ably defended. Egyptian rule also was weak and the Khabiru were ravaging the country.

THE ISRAELITE CITY

About 1250 B.C. the Israelites destroyed the city. The break in the continuity of culture was complete, but the city was immediately reoccupied, possibly under Othniel (Jdg 1.1 ff; 3.9 ff.). The pottery at first was very poor. The city walls, which

varied from eight to fifteen feet in thickness in the Late Bronze
Age, were only five feet thick in the Iron Age and were hastily
and poorly constructed. To strengthen the defense there was
introduced a series of casemates consisting of closed or open
chambers formed by thin transverse walls between the outer
wall and a thin inner wall, two and a half feet thick. Most of
the casemate rooms served as store chambers for the adjacent
houses. These thin city walls are typical of early Israelite cities.
Since the Hebrews were free tribesmen, and the corvee was
unknown except in Solomon's time, there was no social organization which could develop the strength and cohesion necessary to erect such massive structures as characterize the Middle
Bronze Age.

Stratum B was marked by a large number of silos, or grain
pits, within the walls, some as much as ten feet in diameter.
There were a few in level C. In level A, after its earliest phase,
they disappear entirely. In other words, during the period of
level B, the city was sparsely inhabited. There was room within
the city, and agriculture must have flourished. Under the
Hebrew monarchy the city became more densely populated,
industry developed and silos became less numerous. In stratum
B for the first time iron sickles and plough points appear, while
flint tools which had been common even in the Late Bronze
level (C), disappear completely. The presence of Philistine
pottery marks the middle phase of stratum B (1150-1000 B.C.).

The invasion of Shishak (shortly after 922 B.C.) probably
was the occasion for the destruction of this city along with
many others. Apparently the citizens escaped to the hills, for
no skeletons from this destruction were found in the debris.
The city was thoroughly destroyed, the city gates being almost
completely demolished. However, the people returned immediately and rebuilt their houses in the ashes of the conflagration,
sometimes on the old foundations. The immediate rebuilding
resulted in the destruction of all but the floors of the previous
city. By way of contrast the new city which then arose, though
houses were rebuilt from time to time, is well preserved because,

after its destruction in 588-586 B.C., the site was never used again.

This second Hebrew city was characterized by a new type of house, which can hardly be derived either from the "hearth house" (*megaron*) of the north or from the "courtyard house" of the south. This new kind of construction is marked by a row of pillars, three or more often four, set along the axis of a large rectangular room as supports for the ceiling. The pillars were cut in a roughly rectangular, sometimes oval shape, and were five or six feet in height. Sometimes they were set on rude bases. In other cases, doubtless, their length was increased by stone or timber. In some cases several stones were used much like column drums. From two to four rooms, doubtless for storage, were to be found alongside the large room. Living quarters were in the second story, which was reached by an outside staircase. In some cases the solidity of the lower floor suggests that there may have been a third story. The walls of the lowest floor were of stone, the upper stories of adobe. Since this type of construction goes back to Solomon's time, as witnessed by the stables at Megiddo, it may have been introduced from Phoenicia. The use of rude monoliths which weighed from 1800 to 3000 pounds each gives one new respect for the energy of Hebrew peasants in the time of the monarchy. To hew them in the quarry and drag them to the mound and up its slopes required no little strength, industry, and perseverance, as well as co-operation.

During the period of the Divided Kingdoms (900-700 B.C.) the city was densely populated. The streets were narrow, usually seven feet wide or less, and were only occasionally paved with small stones. There were no large courtyards, only narrow passages and tiny open spaces at the entrances. The area of the town within the walls was about eight acres and contained from 250 to 350 houses. Dr. Albright estimates the population at from 2500 to 5000. The houses spilled out over the walls, as at Tell en-Nasbeh and 'Ain Shems. There were no grain pits inside. Both facts illustrate the relative prosperity and security of this period. Since animals were not kept within the walls, the sanitary conditions were better than in the typical modern Arab town. No refuse heaps were found. The numerous cisterns were provided with settling basins. If, like modern inhabitants of the mountains of Judea, a large part of the population spent two thirds of the year in the open, living in tents, following their flocks, and camping by their fields, probably the health of the people was good.

During its whole history apparently the city gates remained in the same places, one on the east, the other on the west. Both of the Iron Age entrances were so constructed that one approached with his left side to the city wall, passed in through one gate, and then turned at right angles to enter the city itself by a second gate, an indirect mode of ingress which is still to be seen in the Damascus and Jaffa gates in Jerusalem and, in a sense, in the great gate at Megiddo. That on the east, which is barely wide enough for a chariot, opened upon the ancient road running southeast into the hill country. The west gate, which opened upon an ancient road that ran north and south along Wad' el-Bayyarah, was only three feet wide, and therefore could have admitted only pedestrians and asses. Yet a large and well-built tower by this gate was probably the meeting place of the city magistrates. Several standard weights found here were doubtless used by them to settle disputes.

Another evidence of the prosperity of the city during the later Israelite period was discovered in a number of dye-plants, most of them constructed on a standard plan. At the end of a rectangular room ten by twenty feet in area, were two massive stone dye-vats with shallow basins of cement beside them, and in the two corners nearest the vats were large-mouthed jars for lime to use in fixing the color. The dye-vats were hollowed out of single blocks of stone about three feet across and three feet high, flat at top and bottom. The interior was a roughly spherical basin about a foot and a half in diameter, and the mouth was about six inches across. Around the flat rim ran a deep circular channel with a hole opening into the interior, for collecting and returning the precious dye that might be spilled when the cloth was lifted out. In the room there was generally also a series of large stones pierced with a hole in the center. Their purpose could not be guessed, unless they served in some way to press the surplus dye from the cloth. A study of modern dyeing methods showed some improvements but essentially the same process for simple dyeing. Modern installations are much more flimsy.

The presence of dye-vats suggested that weaving must have been an important industry. The discovery of numerous loom weights in almost every house proved that the ancient city would have been a place after Gandhi's own heart. Nearly all of the population must have been both agriculturalists and weavers. The Negeb was always a grazing country. In David's time it was the country of Nabal, who "had three thousand sheep and a thousand goats" (1 Sam 25.2). The ancient city gathered the wool from its multitudinous flocks and sold its cloth to the caravans that passed by its western gate.

Objects illustrating the life of the people were numerous. A group of figurines representing a female deity, and called by newspaper reporters the "bobbed-haired Venus," is regarded by Dr. Albright as portraying the coiffure of the period, which was not bobbed hair, but an elaborately plaited and curled mass which hung down below the ears. There were numerous little cosmetic palettes, or rather miniature stone bowls, or mortars, with a small hemispherical cavity in the top and a small flat bottom. Around the cavity in the upper surface the wide flat rim is decorated with incised geometrical figures, in some cases colored dark blue, in some cases inlaid with a dark blue gem. They were used for the grinding and mixing of the various mineral substances which went to form the face paints. One haematite spatula for this purpose was found. There were quantities of iron tools and numerous toys, animal and human figurines, some of them hollow, rattles, and whistles that still are as effective as when the ancient Israelites blew on them.

Few inscriptions of any kind were found—as yet not a single

ostracon, that is a potsherd inscribed with ink. Five fragmentary inscriptions incised on pots before they were broken came to light, four evidently names of persons, and one containing the Hebrew word *bath*, the ten-gallon liquid measure. The characters were of the type of the Siloam inscription and therefore of the eighth or seventh century B.C. Dr. Albright notes the apparently common use of writing in this period. Amphora handles were found of the now well-known type bearing the stamp, "belonging to the king—Hebron." These were from wine or oil jars of standard size originally intended for the receipt of taxes in kind and later used as standard measures. Since these stamps belong to the period before Hezekiah, they prove that the city was destroyed by the Chaldeans at the time of the Exile, not by the Assyrians at an earlier time.

Even more conclusive evidence on this point was discovered in two stamped jar handles bearing the legend "Belonging to Eliakim, boy (steward) of Yokin." An identical stamp was found by Professor Grant at 'Ain Shems in 1930. As Père Vincent, who was visting Tell Beit Mirsim on the day the first was discovered, pointed out, Yokin or Yaukin, is an abbreviated form of Joiachin, the name of the king who was carried to Babylon by Nebuchadnezzer in 597 B.C. and is mentioned in Babylonian tablets as Yaukinu. Eliakim was probably the steward who administered his property, perhaps during the reign of his uncle, Zedekiah (598-587 B.C.).

On religious matters light was thrown by various discoveries, though no Israelite sanctuary has been found. It is to be hoped that some future campaign may uncover the pre-Israelite sanctuary from which came the lion and lion platter already described. One interesting discovery in stratum B was the top of a miniature limestone altar of incense measuring two and three-quarters by three and one-half inches in horizontal section, and having at its corners four projections which the Hebrews called "horns." Similar but larger altars have been found at Shechem and Megiddo which are at least 250 years younger than this specimen. Some years back Dr. Ingholt discovered an inscription on an altar at Palmyra which proves that such an altar was called *hamman*, a word hitherto rendered "sun-pillar." These discoveries prove that incense was used in popular worship during the whole Hebrew period.

Tell Beit Mirsim has been particularly prolific in figurines of female deities. They began to appear in stratum E, of the Middle Bronze Age, but are more numerous in stratum C. There were some six of a type common in Late Bronze Age sites, showing a naked goddess without headdress, with spiral locks, and with a long-stemmed lotus flower in each hand. A second type differs from the first only in having a lofty feather crown. Other types in the C stratum are fragmentary except one which represents a nude goddess with her arms hanging at her side, her hair in two heavy masses which hang down her shoulders, and with ten round marks in a circle around her navel. The figurines of the C level have a distinctness of form which seems to indicate that they were modeled directly or indirectly from specific idol figures. Doubtless they were used for magical purposes. Such figurines represent fertility goddesses who would magically induce fertility in crops, beasts, and human beings.

The "Astarte figurines" of the B level, the Early Israelite period, were not so numerous as in levels C and A. They were quite distinct in type from those of the Canaanite level (C). Some were amulets to assist women in childbirth. In a silo of the Philistine period, and therefore probably of the eleventh century, was found a hollow figurine of local clay, which portrayed a naked woman with prominent breasts pressing a dove with outstretched wings to her breast. As the dove was sacred to Astarte in Palestine, Syria, and Cyprus, there can be no doubt as to the interpretation of the figurine. The dove, like the serpent on the relief already described, represents the fecundating power.

Astarte figurines seem more numerous in the A level than in any other, nearly forty in all having been found. They are all of one type, a "pillar goddess," consisting of a woman's head, bust, and arms set upon a simple column which spreads at the base so that it may stand erect. The woman, who holds her hands under her prominent breasts as if presenting them to a nursing infant, undoubtedly represents the goddess, Astarte, as a nursing mother. Some specimens are very carefully and artistically executed. The type seems to originate in Phoenicia and Cyprus in the tenth century and then to spread southward. Whether Israelite woman regarded these figurines as images of Astarte or simply as potent amulets is a difficult question. Allusions to Ishtar worship in Jeremiah 44.17 ff. seems to point to its conscious practice by Hebrew women in the last days of the monarchy.

If the numerical proportion of Astarte figurines is an index, it would appear that the simple Hebrew worship in the earlier period was less impregnated with this element of Canaanite religion than in the period when the great prophets were fulminating against it. But this does not by any means prove that the earlier nomadic period, or "Mosaism," was therefore essentially higher or purer than the religion of the eighth century. Many other factors have to be considered. The tremendous increase of prosperity which is discovered in Tell Beit Mirsim in the ninth, eighth, and seventh centuries certainly meant new temptations due to increased wealth and wider international contacts. In particular Assyrian influence is to be considered. The increase of luxury and of population would result in new fashions and in more numerous objects in the deposits. Bedouin religion is now much simpler than that of the towns and villages, but it can hardly be said to be more truly monotheistic or more ethical.

Tell Beit Mirsim displays the history of southern Palestine before the eyes like a panorama in a motion picture. It begins dimly, and the first centuries pass quickly and indistinctly. First in the Middle Bronze period the character of its buildings becomes clear, when a large house, or "palace," appears. Three major breaks in the continuity of civilization are to be noted. The beginning of the Hyksos period marks one, its end another, with a subsequent drop in prosperity. The third appears at the

Hebrew conquest, which on the ceramic evidence, according to Dr. Albright, comes toward the end of the thirteenth century, that is after 1250 B.C., and results in the sharp lowering of culture and prosperity. A minor variation is indicated by the prevalence of Philistine pottery probably during part of the twelfth and the eleventh century. Thereafter the city climbs gradually to a truly high degree of prosperity, to decline at the end of the seventh and beginning of the sixth century, and to fall immediately thereafter at the Exile, never again to be reoccupied. When the prosperous Byzantine period came, a new city was founded at what is now called Khirbet Beit Mirsim on another hill a short distance away.

CHAPTER VIII

THE QUEST FOR AN ALPHABET

❖

THE alphabet is one of the most valuable of the inheritances which the western world received from the Near East. Its origin has long been under debate. The two decades between the two world wars can unfold a fascinating story of progress in solving that riddle and of chance discoveries and unexpected coincidences which contributed toward the solution. Nothing could better illustrate the devious paths of progress.

THE GEZER POTSHERD

On a day in December, 1929, a party of students from the American School of Oriental Research in Jerusalem visited the mound of ancient Gezer, which Professor R. A. S. Macalister excavated in Turkish days, between 1902 and 1909. Professor W. R. Taylor of the University of Toronto, who was in charge, was already famous among the students for his affection for inscriptions. As the party walked over the mound Mr. Douglas James picked up a broken bit of pottery and remarked, "Here is an inscription for Professor Taylor." The potsherd measured two by two and one-half inches. On what had been the outside surface of the vessel were three characters which had been scratched into the clay before firing.

The discovery was unusual. No other person had ever picked up an inscribed potsherd on the surface of a tell, yet no one then had any suspicion of the significance of that bit of pottery. But in March, the late Father Romain F. Butin of the Catholic University at Washington came to the American School fresh from an expedition (to be described later) to the puzzling alphabetic inscriptions at Serabit el-Khadem in the Sinaitic

Peninsula. He saw the Gezer potsherd and remarked the likeness of the characters to the Proto-Sinaitic script which he had just been studying. Inquiries were at once made from various pottery experts as to the character of the potsherd, and independently but unanimously they agreed, Père Hugues Vincent, Professor John Garstang, Dr. C. S. Fisher, and Professor W. F. Albright, that it belongs to Middle Bronze Age ii (1900-1500 B.C.). According to Professor Kirsopp Lake, leader of the Serabit el-Khadem party, it was "a most interesting, and perhaps the most important, discovery" of that expedition.[1] Its larger meaning and importance can best be understood after the other early materials bearing on the alphabet are described.

THE 'AIN SHEMS OSTRACON AND OTHER DISCOVERIES

Another potsherd of perhaps equal interest was discovered less than six months later. On May 6, 1930, Mr. and Mrs. Alan Rowe rode with me down to 'Ain Shems to see Professor Elihu Grant's excavations. When we had walked over the tell and climbed down to the chief seat of operations, the foreman handed Dr. Grant a potsherd and pointed out the spot where it had been found. Professor Grant remarked, "That is our 1400 level." We immediately noted that both sides of the piece were marked with characters in ink. Mr. Rowe, being an Egyptologist, naturally attempted to find hieratic characters in them, but soon abandoned the effort as fruitless. Their meaning has not been made out fully, but several of them quite plainly resemble later Phoenician-Hebrew letters and there can be little doubt that they belong to some Semitic alphabet.

After these fortuitous beginnings in 1929 and 1930, discoveries bearing upon the alphabet multiplied with bewildering rapidity. Some of the inscribed objects were found along with other materials which securely date them: a bronze dagger at Lachish (Tell ed-Duweir) and a limestone plaque at Shechem (Tell Balatah) in the seventeenth or sixteenth century, a limestone plaque at Byblos (Jebeil) in the fourteenth, two inscribed pot-

[1] HTR, XXV (1932), 99. See fig. 3, p. 109 for a copy of the characters.

tery vessels at Lachish in the fourteenth or thirteenth century, a skinning knife at Byblos in the twelfth century. A potsherd inscribed with three characters, found in 1892 by F. J. Bliss at Tell el-Hesi, then supposed to be Lachish, belongs in the same series. It is to be dated in the thirteenth or twelfth century, as is a bronze dagger found at Rueisseh in Syria. These all have short inscriptions, most of them with from three to a dozen characters. All are so short or fragmentary as to be uncertain of interpretation. But they show definite relations to the later Semitic alphabet. It is to be noted that they cover all of Palestine and Syria and the period from 1700 to 1100 B.C., when the stabilized alphabet appears.

Discoveries of inscriptions in hitherto unknown characters have also been made in Transjordan at Balu'ah and in Syria, especially at Byblos, the modern Jebeil, and at Ras esh-Shamrah. Some are related to the hieroglyphs of Egypt, some to the cuneiform of the Tigris-Euphrates valley. Some of the former seem to date in the third millennium. At the Nineteenth Congress of Orientalists, held in Rome in the autumn of 1935, M. Maurice Dunand, excavator of Byblos, showed examples of unknown scripts, hieroglyphic and cuneiform, possibly syllabic, possibly alphabetic, which he had found. And no one in all that highly competent company could decipher them. Had modern scholarship lost all cunning? By no means! Undecipherable alphabets only prove the fecundity of alphabetic invention in those far-off days.

The Stabilized Alphabet

As the two thirteenth-century inscriptions from Tell ed-Duweir show, some time about 1300 B.C. an alphabet began to take shape in Syria and Palestine in a form sufficiently like the later alphabet to make it possible to read almost any document that contains more than two or three letters. It was not stabilized in the sense that it made no further changes or development, but it was used in much the same form all over Syria and Palestine. There is a considerable body of Phoenician material which has been fully deciphered. It begins with the recovery in 1923 by M. Dunand of the sarcophagus of King Ahiram of Byblos, originally assigned to the thirteenth century, but possibly as late as the eleventh. Various discoveries made in Palestine and Syria cover the tenth century, the time of Samuel and Saul, David and Solomon, and the ninth down to the period of the Moabite Stone, in the time of Omri and Ahab. Hebrew-Phoenician paleography is complicated and not too well known, but enough materials to make its development clear are available down to the time when at the latest in the eighth century, perhaps two hundred years earlier, the Greek alphabet was borrowed from the Phoenician variant.

In Babylonia the cuneiform characters which the Sumerians had developed were still in use. Egypt had its hieroglyphs. In the Hittite country, in Crete, and in other Aegean lands pictographs of different kinds had long been the means of writing. In Palestine and Syria the cuneiform of the Mesopotamian lands was still in use, the Amarna letters and many tablets found in Syria and Palestine being witnesses. Thus not one but many kinds of script were on trial: hieroglyphic, cuneiform, linear pictographs, and alphabetic characters. It was about the eastern end of the Mediterranean, according to the multitudinous evidence of which I have given samples, that there was no static system. Here invention was at work. Where was the alphabet invented?

Before 1914 the alphabet could not be traced back of the Moabite Stone—about 830 B.C. In that inscription it apparently sprang into life full-fledged. Some inscriptions, the Gezer Calendar for example, were dated in the ninth century because no other earlier than the Moabite inscription was known. There were various speculations regarding the "prehistory of the alphabet," but there was no means of checking the contradictory hypotheses. Suddenly the revisiting of Serabit in 1927, the Byblos and Ras esh-Shamrah excavations, and the Palestinian and other discoveries, beginning in 1929, brought to light the unsuspected existence of these numerous attempts during the second and perhaps the third millennium to construct alphabets and suggested two possible origins.

The two most widely used kinds of ancient writing, the Mesopotamian cuneiform and the Egyptian hieroglyphic, yielded to the persistent labors of numerous scholars during the nineteenth century, and both of them opened up hitherto unimagined vistas into the distant past. Both of them were ideographic and syllabic, with tentative and abortive steps toward alphabetic writing. A character stood for an idea or a syllable and often was a recognizable picture of an object. That is, both were based on an aboriginal pictographic writing. Neither people saw the convenience of making a character represent a single vowel or consonantal sound or of combining such characters to represent a word. Instead of the highly abstract method of representing ideas by combining twenty-odd letters, hundreds or thousands of individual characters were necessary. The explanation of the origin of the alphabet, in the face of the flock of new linguistic enigmas, would have appeared hopeless, but for light from two directions: one from far to the north, in Syria, the other from far to the south, in the Sinaitic Peninsula; one from Babylonian cuneiform, the other from Egyptian hieroglyphic. It is possible that other centers, Crete for example, made contributions. But once more the Nile and the Euphrates are the chief rivals.

A Cuneiform Alphabet

In a cuneiform alphabet was found one mass of documents in sufficient quantities to make decipherment possible. The story of that triumph of practical ingenuity and linguistic scholarship is a romance. The discovery is one of the most astonishing and, from a literary and folklorist, as well as religio-historical, point of view, one of the most valuable of recent years. The success of the effort at decipherment proves that given sufficient material, no such problems are forever insoluble.

Sometime before 1400 B.C. Semites in north Syria had caught the idea of an alphabet and, because clay tablets were the only easily available writing material, they constructed a series of alphabetic characters out of various combinations of little wedges such as were impressed on wet clay tablets with the square stylus of the cuneiform script.

At Ras esh-Shamrah, the ancient Ugarit, on the coast of Syria, an expedition headed by MM. F. A. Schaeffer and George Chenet of the Strasbourg Museum, excavating in the necropolis near the harbor, Minet el-Beida, found tools and weapons and in the mound clay tablets inscribed in an unknown cuneiform character. The first were published by M. Ch. Virolleaud in the periodical *Syria* in the spring of 1930. The late Professor Hans Bauer of Halle and Professor Paul Dhorme, then at the École Biblique in Jerusalem, began to work on their decipherment. Both of them had had much experience with ciphers during the World War. The French Government had decorated Professor Dhorme for his successful solution of an enemy cipher on the Salonika front.

Both men were highly trained Semitists. They applied their two techniques, of the linguist and the cipher expert, to their peace-time task. They soon saw that there were twenty-seven or twenty-eight characters. This fact as well as the number of characters in the words, which were separated by vertical strokes, suggested a Semitic language and proved that the script was alphabetic. Professor W. F. Albright was excavating at Tell Beit Mirsim in 1930 when Bauer's solution was printed in the now lamented *Vossische Zeitung*. Albright's international acquaintance bore fruit, for, discovering the newspaper in the hands of Professor Kurt Galling of Halle, at that time head of the German Evangelical Archaeological Institute in Jerusalem, he took it to Dhorme. Dhorme had arrived independently at the same identification for all but two or three characters. He immediately recognized the value of some of Bauer's suggestions and was able to advance beyond him toward a final solution of the puzzle. Bauer accepted some of Dhorme's proposals and both published practically identical sign lists.

Meantime Virolleaud, himself an Assyriologist of distinction, was working on the problem and with the aid of still more tablets discovered in the excavations of 1930 and of the contributions of Bauer and Dhorme, he was able to improve upon the work of both, and in *Syria* for 1931 he published a brilliant study of a remarkable "Epic of Aleyan and Mot," an astonishing piece of Semitic mythology which is not by any means complete but quite evidently is an early variant of the myth of Adonis.

Albright and many others have contributed further refinements to the work of Bauer, Dhorme, and Virolleaud. The excitement of the scholars concerned and the vigor, not to say acerbity, of their discussions can be easily imagined. Nothing could better illustrate the advance which Semitic philology has made nor the advantage of international co-operation in matters of scholarship than the successful publication of such a text within two years of the time when the first tablets were discovered. But it is worth noting that this alphabet was recognized and the texts deciphered easily and quickly because the materials were full and the texts continuous.

Other texts too numerous to mention were discovered. Some were in the newly discovered Hurrian language. Some were of religious, some of secular interest; one on animal husbandry, for example. Such discoveries bid fair to revolutionize knowledge of Hebrew lexicography, grammar, and poetic usage. They make contributions to the understanding of the origins of Hebrew literature and the development of Hebrew life and thought comparable to the contributions of Assyriology. These documents exhibit far closer parallels to biblical ideas than appear in the cuneiform documents from Babylonia, for here the language is really only an earlier dialect of Hebrew and the social and intellectual background is that of the Hebrews themselves.

How far the use of this alphabet extended is not yet known. Another example was uncovered as far south as 'Ain Shems in Palestine. A peculiar feature of the long, narrow, oval plaque found there is that it must be read in a mirror, as Albright was the first to discover. This tablet suggests that the cuneiform alphabet was far from an isolated or local affair and, with the

'Ain Shems potsherd mentioned, shows the two alphabets, that which eventually became the Hebrew-Phoenician and this cuneiform invention, actively in conflict.

The relation of the cuneiform alphabet to the Phoenician is difficult to determine. Some of the cuneiform letters bear a remarkable resemblance in general outline to some "Phoenician" letters and appear to imitate them. But some scholars would reverse the relationship. In any case it is most fortunate that the inventor perfected his invention, because it has saved for modern study a mass of materials which only the clay tablet could preserve. May good fortune present the world with many more tablets of the Ras esh-Shamrah type!

THE ALPHABETIC INSCRIPTIONS OF SERABIT EL-KHADEM

In the very years when the Ugaritic alphabet was being deciphered, a much more likely line of alphabetic descent was being investigated. It ran back into the region of the legendary source of Hebrew law, the Sinaitic Peninsula, to the place already mentioned, Serabit el-Khadem, a spot within fifty miles of the traditional Mount Sinai.

The belief in the possibility of an alphabet at so early a date as 1700 or even 1400 B.C. rests upon a discovery made by Sir Flinders Petrie as long ago as 1904-05, when he went to Serabit el-Khadem to study the remains found at the famous turquoise mines which once furnished jewels dear to Egyptian hearts. He copied 344 Egyptian inscriptions and eleven more which he recognized as being "in unknown characters." These were extremely difficult and were not published until 1917, when the English Egyptologists, Alan H. Gardiner and T. Eric Peet, essayed a tentative decipherment. Since then many scholars have been working on their interpretation. Dr. A. Cowley, Bodley's librarian at Oxford, and Professor Sethe of Berlin, deserve especial mention. In 1923 Professor Hubert Grimme of Münster achieved notoriety for himself and newspaper publicity for the inscriptions by discovering in them a supposed allusion to Moses and an Egyptian princess who rescued him from the Nile. Unfortunately for drama, romance, and biblicistic literalism, no other competent Semitists or Egyptologists agreed with his readings. Gardiner's methods and in general his results hold the field.

In the spring of 1927 Professors Kirsopp Lake and Robert Blake of Harvard University with Mrs. Blake were on their way to the Monastery of St. Catherine on Mount Sinai to study some of the manuscripts for which the monastery is famous. In Cairo they met Alan Gardiner, who begged them to visit Serabit and, if possible, bring Petrie's inscriptions to the National Museum in Cairo. On their return trip and on a second expedition organized for the purpose by Professor Lake, several new Egyptian texts and twenty-three additional alphabetic inscriptions were discovered, nearly all of the latter, unfortunately, fragmentary. All were brought to Cairo but three. Two found in the mines could not be cut out without danger of bringing down the roof, and one small graffito was discovered when it was too late to remove it. A fragment had previously been recovered also by a Finnish expedition in 1928. One similar inscription, apparently a dedication to Ba'alat, which was found by Palmer in 1868 at Meghara, ten or fifteen miles southwest of Serabit, where there are other famous turquoise mines, is now known only from Palmer's copy and squeeze. Thus sixty years and scores of individuals of a dozen races have been needed to prepare for the solution of the problem of the origin of the alphabet.

Practically all of the alphabetic inscriptions were found in one place, the hieroglyphic in another. In considerable part the recovered inscriptions are on loose stones or small stelae and were found in what are supposed to have been the sleeping quarters of the miners. Apparently the majority of the alphabetic inscriptions contain the names of the persons who occupied the shelters and their petitions for protection to "Ba'alat," the goddess Hathor, "the lady of the turquoise," as the Egyptian inscriptions name her, whose temple is on an eminence near the mines. Five inscribed sphinxes, busts, and statuettes dedicated to Ba'alat were

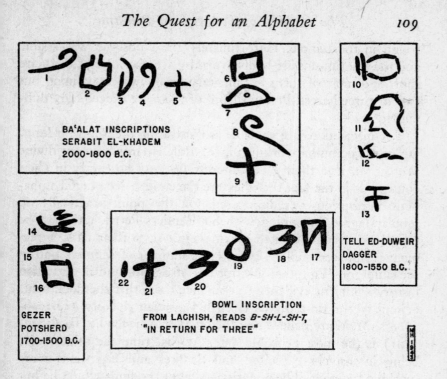

EARLY ALPHABETIC FORMS

KEY TO CHARACTERS

1, 4, 8, 19. An oxgoad, *lamedh* (*l*)
2, 6, 16, 17. A house, *beth* (*b*)
3, 7. An eye, *'ayin* ('), *a guttural*
 sound without English equivalent
5, 9, 21. A mark, *tau* (*t*)
10. Uncertain
11. A head, *resh* (*r*)

12, 15. A snake, *nahash* (*n*)
13. Uncertain
14. A hand, *yadh, yodh* (*y, i*); or teeth,
 shin (sh); or (best) a palm, *kaf*
 (*k*)
18, 20. Teeth, *shin* (*sh*)
22. A word divider

FIG. 3

found in the temple. Unfortunately the sandstone was friable and the inscriptions are badly worn by weather. All of them are short and most of them fragmentary, some now containing but two or three letters. Practically all of them are exceedingly difficult to read.

The inscriptions are valuable as illustrating the poignant longing of the common workman in a hostile environment for divine protection. But their chief interest lies, not so much in their content, as in the fact that they are the earliest deciphered alphabetic inscriptions yet discovered. On this point practically all scholars agree, beginning with Sir Flinders Petrie, although he refuses to become excited about them. As to their date, agreement is not so complete, but a large number of scholars find in the numerous Egyptian inscriptions of Serabit and in Egyptian history sufficient evidence to convince them that the documents belong to the time of the twelfth Egyptian dynasty (*ca.*2000-1800 B.C.). Many believe that the reign of Amenemhet III (1849-1801) is the most probable date. At that time the mines were being intensively exploited and Semites and Egyptians were working together. The scientific value of the finds would be but slightly modified were it shown that they belonged three hundred years later under the eighteenth Dynasty, as Petrie still insists. But the history of Egyptian mining operations points rather to the end of the nineteenth century, and, moreover, the Gezer, Tell ed-Duweir, and 'Ain Shems potsherds, and still more the stabilized alphabet of the Rueisseh dagger and the Ahiram sarcophagus can hardly be explained if the very primitive Sinaitic alphabet of Serabit el-Khadem is made later than or contemporary with them.

THE EARLIEST KNOWN ALPHABET

What now do these documents teach about the alphabet? It has long been a generally but not universally accepted principle that the "Phoenician" alphabet was invented on the principle of acrophony with a conventionalized picture as the letter. That is, each character, originally a picture, represents the sound of the first letter of a common word, and this word gave its name to that character. Thus *aleph*, the name of the first letter, is the Hebrew word for "ox," and the letter was an ox's head. *Bayith* or *beth*, the second letter, was the floor plan of a "house." *Daleth* (d) was a "door." *Yodh* or *yadh* (*y* or *i*) was once a "hand." It is as if the nursery rhymes by which children were taught the alphabet had been standardized so that *a* were called "apple," *b*, "bat," and *c*, "cat," and a picture of each formed the respective letter.

It has also been widely held that the alphabet arose by modification of Egyptian hieroglyphs; that is, the pictures which in Egypt had very early come to represent syllables and sounds as well as ideas and by the principle of acrophony had come to stand for the first sound of the word they represented, were gradually simplified and adopted as alphabetic characters, while the number was reduced to cover only the consonantal sounds. The South Semitic and North Semitic languages and their various branches did not adopt the same name and character for each sound. The hieroglyphic signs were sometimes misunderstood or reinterpreted. Experiments were many, and the results were various. No one could apply for a copyright, and there was no Academy to standardize procedure.

The Sinaitic characters are recognized as representing a very primitive form of this acrophonic development and as assisting very materially in unravelling the tangle of possible explanations. In several instances they are almost pictures; the oxhead, which occurs seventeen times, for example, is almost as clear as the hieroglyphic character. The fish, or *samekh*, is quite plain, as is also the eye, or *'ayin*. Unfortunately the fragmentary and weatherworn stones offer too few distinctly legible, connected words for the decipherment to be easy or absolutely certain.

The long story of the valiant, but sometimes ludicrous attempts which scholars of many nations have made to solve the puzzle cannot here be told. A happy inspiration of Gardiner's seems clearly to have marked the longest step toward the final solution of the riddle of the inscriptions. In working over the materials he had noticed a recurring set of four symbols. The first, second, and fourth were relatively easy, a house, an eye, and a cross, that is *b*, '(*'ayin*), and *t*; the third he discovered was like a North Semitic *l*, turned upside down. The peculiarity did not disturb him, because "the comparison of Greek *lamda* and Latin *L* showed that the character *L* did in fact possess this acrobatic peculiarity." The four letters, therefore, made *ba'alat*, and "with amazement" he recollected that the goddess Hathor was called Baaltis in Greek. "Hundreds of hieroglyphic inscriptions at Serabit el-Khadem mentioned "Hathor, lady of the turquoise."[2] The method suggested in this "discovery," for such it was, is that which must be followed, Gardiner rightly insists. The characters must be explained individually so as to bring them into the line of evolution from Egyptian hieroglyphs or hieratic characters to the Semitic alphabetic characters. At the same time the individual letters thus discovered must fit into words and phrases which give a sense that suits a group of Semites mining turquoise in the desolate Sinaitic Peninsula. A solution must be found which "satisfies both philology and common sense." [3] The most involved cross-word puzzle is baby's work compared to the complications of this problem.

As to the origin of this alphabet, Professor Martin Sprengling of the University of Chicago has suggested that some Semitic mine foreman who had to keep account of the men he was bossing discovered something of the methods of Egyptian scribes and applied them to his own language. Gardiner remarks that the invention of the alphabet "was the deliberate achievement of some man of genius," not an ignorant mine boss. Not Sinai but a region farther to the south and east appears to him the "real home of the original Semitic alphabet of which the Sabaean and Minaean inscriptions retain a greater degree of the original character."

Two French scholars who are especially competent in this

---

[2] *PEQ*, 1929, p. 49 f.; cf. Jensen *Die Schrift*, Glückstadt u. Hamburg: Augustin, 1935, p. 178. See fig. 3, p. 109 for examples of the characters.
[3] It was common sense that Grimme's sensational interpretation lacked.

Photo by D. E. M.

Tell Beit Mirsim; house walls (late Hebrew), standing columns used as roof supports showing in various places.

Dye vats of Hebrew period at Tell Beit Mirsim.

Photo by D. E. M.

Photo by D. E. M.
Gezer potsherd with three Proto-Sinaitic characters,
about two-thirds actual size.

Tablet with characters of Ras esh-Shamrah alphabet, found at 'Ain Shems.

Courtesy of Professor John W. Flight

field, MM. René Dussaud and Maurice Dunand, believe that a script of the late third millennium found on stone and copper at Byblos and resembling a simplified hieroglyphic writing may be ancestress of the linear alphabet which later appears in Syria and Palestine. It is a cogent argument that the Syrian coast, with its relatively high culture and its long and close contacts with Egypt, would be much more likely than the barren Sinaitic Peninsula to produce the alphabet. The numerous alphabets discovered in Syria suggest that here were the "variations" upon which "natural selection" worked. The Byblos script is not yet deciphered and the connection not yet proved. However, not all of the characters in the Phoenician alphabet continue the Sinaitic tradition. The *samekh* of Sinai, for example, is a real fish. In the later alphabet it has a very different form. The probabilities of Syrian contributions are great.[4] If Egyptian hieroglyphics are the original ancestors of the alphabet, it must have arisen at some point where Egyptians and Semites were long in close contact, and where a Semitic language was in common use. At present the Proto-Sinaitic inscriptions seem nearest to the original source of the South and North Semitic alphabets, both of which can be in part derived from it. As a friend of mine remarked, "An ignorant mine boss might be a genius."

One *caveat* must be entered. Too much honor should not be laid on the brow of the man of genius. Professor Frank R. Black of Johns Hopkins University has remarked that "progress in the early development of any human activity is largely the result of . . . accident and imitation" rather than "outright invention," which he thinks extremely rare.[5] On the other hand, modern examples of such "inventions" are known which constitute instructive parallels.

STIMULUS DIFFUSION

A well-known case is that of the Cherokee Indian, Sequoya, or John Gist, who, though he never learned English, used the

[4] Here and elsewhere my account owes much to discussions with Dr. Ray Bowman of the Oriental Institute at the University of Chicago.

[5] *JAOS*, 60 (1940), 391, note 1.

English alphabet in part in a set of signs for the syllables of his own language. His syllabary, developed about 1821, is perhaps the best parallel to the origin of the Phoenician alphabet as I have explained it, for he adopted only part of the letters and entirely misused those employed, giving them quite new and different values. In fact he was much more original than Sprengling's putative mine foreman, who took his characters directly from Egyptian hieroglyphs and certainly understood some of them.

A somewhat similar enterprise was undertaken about 1900 by Njoya, sultan of Bamun in the Cameroons. He invented a purely ideographic system which, however, he changed four times in a dozen or fifteen years, ending with an alphabet of seventy characters. His country was Mohammedan, and Arabic as well as European languages was more or less understood in it. It is perhaps pure coincidence that both Sequoya and Njoya claimed to have received the first suggestions for their systems in a dream or trance. Still another example of the indigenous invention of an alphabet or syllabary by illiterates is that of the Vey, or Vaï, a people of Liberia, whose undertaking was discovered by Commodore Forbes in 1848 and was later published by the missionary Koelle.

All of these differed from the original Semitic invention by taking the retrograde step from an alphabet to ideographic or syllabic writing. But all of them belong in the category, not of direct borrowing or imitation, but, to use a phrase of Professor A. Kroeber, of "stimulus diffusion."[6] In each of these cases a language which was never learned by the originator of the new system stimulated him to an invention in which borrowing was at a minimum. No application of a copyright or trademark law could have found him guilty of infringement, unless the intangi-

---

[6] See his article, "Stimulus Diffusion," in the *American Anthropologist*, 42 (1940), 2-6. Professor Kroeber discusses Sequoya, the Vey language, and the Phoenician alphabet as examples of "stimulus diffusion." This reference I owe to Dr. T. D. McCown. I owe further material to Miss Frieda Fliegelmann of Berkeley.

ble idea of putting words and ideas upon paper by means of signs could be copyrighted.

TENTATIVE CONCLUSIONS

Other older examples of alphabetic inscriptions and other "connecting links" may yet be found. The great variety of Semitic alphabets proves that scores of inventive minds tried to profit by the principle of acrophony which the Egyptians discovered but never carried through in their writing. Whoever the discoverer, it certainly is true that these fragmentary and half-illegible lines from the poor miners of turquoise in desolate Sinai have contributed magnificently toward solving the problem of the origin of the alphabet and have established for it a hitherto-undreamed antiquity, while the fragmentary inscriptions on pottery, stone, and bronze from various places in Syria and Palestine are the connecting links which exhibit the slow and tentative, sometimes retrograde, steps in its development.

Whether the Greek alphabet was derived directly from the Phoenician or not is a question which is under debate. This much at least is clear: there is no need for pushing the origin of the Greek alphabet down to so late a period as the eighth century, if it is derived from the Phoenician, since the latter is now shown to begin long before the Mesha stone of 830 B.C. That the Phoenician alphabet greatly influenced the Greek is certainly to be granted.

The Neandertaloid skeletons found at the western edge of Mount Carmel at Mugharet es-Sukhul exhibited the most remarkable variations. As Sir Arthur Keith pointed out, they showed evolution in progress 75,000 years ago, trying numerous experiments on the way toward *Homo sapiens*. In the various alphabetic scripts discovered in Palestine, we again see evolution at work. *Homo sapiens*, having emerged slightly from the reign of seemingly blind variation and natural selection, was experimenting, more or less blindly yet with no little ingenuity, on the best way in which to record his ideas and his words on something more durable than the impalpable air. Whether he was at first trying to bind gods and spirits and magical forces to do his will or was merely moved by the purely utilitarian desire to record prosaic business transactions, he was unintentionally creating the means by which to store up for the future his intangible cultural achievements. He was making possible literature, philosophy, mathematics, and science. Above all he was making progress possible in all that has moral and spiritual value. The Gezer potter and his three-letter inscription, the crabbed characters cut into rough and friable sandstone by the crude workmen in the Sinai mines open up to our eyes 3500 or 4000 years later entrancing vistas down the long aisles of time.

All the choicest elements of the cultural inheritance of the western world receive their full meaning and value because inventive geniuses of the third or second millennium B.C. struggled to develop an alphabet which would easily record and transmit human ideas. One long double line of western cultural tradition came down through the Greek and the Latin modification of the Phoenician alphabet. Another came through the Hebrews' adaptation of the same original alphabet.

HEBREW PALEOGRAPHY

It is remarkable that the land which cradled the alphabet and the people whose literature has become one of civilization's chief treasures should have left so few contemporary documents. The only Hebrew inscriptions of any considerable length which have been preserved are that of Mesha, king of Moab, not a Hebrew at all, and that scratched by some unknown engineer in the darkness of the Siloam tunnel. The first, discovered in 1868 and now, sadly disfigured, in the Louvre, dates from about 830 B.C. The second, discovered in 1880 and now in Constantinople, is usually ascribed to the time of Hezekiah, about 700 B.C. A much shorter document was an agricultural calendar on a limestone tablet found at Gezer and probably dating in the tenth century.

While in the Phoenician cities, at Samal and elsewhere in Syria, at Teima in Arabia, and at many Nabatean sites, numerous somewhat lengthy inscriptions have come to light, nothing more of the kind has been found in Palestine. The Hebrews may have written on parchment and papyrus; they did not on stone. However, ostraca—potsherds containing receipts, letters, and lists written in ink with a reed pen—were discovered at Samaria, on Ophel, and recently a few letters of extraordinary interest at Tell ed-Duweir. Numerous seals, and seal impressions on pottery,[7] some graffiti on pottery, and a few other brief inscriptions, have served gradually to build up a sufficient knowledge of the evolution of Hebrew writing to give paleography in the hands of an expert no small dating value.

It is clear that, during the period of the monarchy, the Hebrews developed the Canaanite-Phoenician alphabet into a handwriting of their own (though not a new alphabet) with two varieties, one used at Samaria, the other at Jerusalem. During or after the Exile they changed to the Aramaic alphabet, which had developed along different lines from the Hebrew, though they grew from the same stem. For certain purposes the Jews continued to use the old Hebrew forms. The coins of the Maccabees and Hasmoneans and of the two revolts are decidedly archaistic.

The original traditions of the Hebrews were doubtless written down in the Canaanite-Phoenician alphabet, which had reached a fairly stable form before the Israelite tribes entered Palestine. Various books were written in a variety of dialects and characters as the evolution of the language and of the alphabet went on. Eventually, in the post-Exilic period, the sacred books were put into the antique Aramaic alphabet and then, when that alphabet assumed the "square" form, the biblical text was eventually "frozen" by the Masoretes essentially in the Hebrew alphabet known today. Thus the Hebrew Bible came to the Christian world by a process of previous development lasting over two thousand years.

[7] Fifteen years ago Hans Bauer counted only 40; now much over 100 are known.

CHAPTER IX

ON THE EGYPTIAN FRONTIER

❖

AFTER forty-five years in Egypt Sir Flinders Petrie decided to turn from it to investigate the influence of that land upon Palestine, a question which had often been thrust upon him by discoveries of traces of Semites in Egypt. Already a famous archaeologist, he had made a short exploratory trip through southern Palestine in 1890 and at Tell el-Hesi had excavated a small portion of one of the great mounds which dominate so many vistas in the Negeb. Forty years later he celebrated his archaeological Jubilee at another mound. Going to Gaza the last of November, 1926, he soon discovered that he could do nothing at the site of the city itself and decided to begin work at Tell Jemmeh, a large mound on Wadi Ghuzzeh, eight miles from Gaza. For eight successive winters his expeditions worked with fruitful results at this and two other large mounds standing beside the same wadi, Tell el-Far'ah and Tell el-'Ajjul, and then at Sheikh Abu Zuweid, just beyond the border in Egypt.

During all of this period up to 1932-33, Mr. J. L. Starkey and Mr. Lankester Harding bore the "burden and heat of the day," while other workers came and went. The local workmen and women were recruited from the mobile Bedouins, who followed the expedition from one place to the other. The expedition was housed in huts with corrugated iron roofs and expended a minimum upon equipment and conveniences, for Sir Flinders has always made it a point of honor to achieve the largest possible results with the smallest possible expenditure and the simplest equipment. Doubtless his long experience gives him some excuse for dispensing with equipment which most modern excavators require. He insists, for example, that a surveyor's level is unnecessary. A staff and a clear view of the horizon will sufficiently determine the levels of a tell.

Sir Flinders must have appreciated and understood the fact that other archaeologists find it difficult to use his materials and to trust his results, for he rarely used theirs. All the rest of the world is out of step with him. His entirely different system of chronology before 1500 B.C. often works havoc in comparative studies, such as Duncan's *Corpus of Palestinian Pottery*. He has had different methods of working and of reporting results—a shorthand method, on the one hand, evolved through years of tedious labor, and a popular method on the other, due to the necessity of raising funds by private subscription. His reports often, not always, enable the critic to reach his own conclusions.

All four expeditions have worked beside what may be regarded as the southern boundary of Palestine, for Wadi Ghuzzeh rises near the Dead Sea, and, making a wide bend southward, passes by Beersheba and then runs northwestward to fall into the sea near Gaza. The three mounds along Wadi Ghuzzeh are immense piles of earth rising on what were low limestone or sandstone hillocks. The earth accumulated on them from houses and walls of mud brick, from great ramps of earth raised to defend them, from vegetation, and from wind-blown sand and dust until they became very respectable strongholds. The region is one of wide-sweeping desert vistas. There are now no settlements from Gaza to Beersheba, a distance of about thirty-five miles. The population lives in "houses of hair," as they call their black tents, and they have found it easy to follow the excavator from one mound to another when they had once learned the joy of earning ready money.

At none of the mounds did Sir Flinders do more than make a series of glorified soundings. He followed a system which, he believes, enables him to find the most productive part of the mound. He excavated the northern section where the coolest summer winds blow and where the governor's palace and the best buildings would therefore lie. He followed the walls around and discovered the gates. He usually excavated as many tombs as possible. Thus, he admitted, he could quickly disembowel a mound of its treasures and its historical secrets.

TELL JEMMEH—GERAR

It is generally agreed that Tell Jemmeh is ancient Gerar, a southern site which appears in folk tales about Abraham and Isaac, but otherwise has no known history.[1] Soundings begun by Phythian-Adams in October, 1922, were interrupted after three days by a clash between police and salt smugglers near the mound. As a Bedouin was killed, the neighboring Bedouins were highly incensed at foreigners in general, and the little expedition forthwith returned for safety to Gaza. The incident serves as an apposite illustration of the purpose which these mounds on the edge of the desert have always served. They were fortresses guarding the frontier and collecting toll from passing caravans. Only a hundred yards east of the tell runs the caravan route from Egypt to Beersheba and the Negeb. As Phythian-Adams says, "How many caravans must have paid their toll at the Wady under the watchful eyes of the sentinels on the walls! How many feet must have passed over it into Palestine, wearing down its backs with the traffic of innumerable beasts and men, till today you must descend to the dry bed through a steep gulley with high precipitous sides!"[2]

The history of Gerar, so far as revealed by the two excavations, begins in the Late Bronze period, with uncertain debris still lower down. There was little evidence of the presence of the Hyksos. Occupation continued down into the Persian period and was renewed at intervals, especially in Byzantine times. Three disputes have arisen over important matters which illustrate problems of the archaeologist.

One of the startling discoveries at Tell Jemmeh was the presence of great grain pits under fortresses of the Persian period. Sir Flinders attempts to date the last fortress at the time of the

[1] See Gen 20.1; 26.6, 20. According to Albright it is to be put in place of Gezer in 1 Kg 9.16, an attractive hypothesis. But see Alt, *JPOS*, 15, pp. 294-324; 17, 218-35.

[2] *Quarterly Statement*, 1923, p. 145 (now the *Palestine Exploration Quarterly*).

Persian invasion of Egypt in 457 B.C. and supposes the granaries to have been intended to hold supplies for the Persian army. As Professor Kurt Galling pointed out, he based his dating upon a red-figured Attic vase found in one of the pits which, according to classical archaeologists, belongs to the third century, not the fifth. With similar perversity he dated a lower stratum by a scarab of Thutmose III to the reign of that king. But it is notorious that this powerful monarch's cartouche was used as an amulet for centuries after his death. In any case a single object cannot be decisive as to a date.

The misdating of the Thutmose scarab and its stratum was partially responsible for giving Sir Flinders an early date for the introduction of iron and for the Philistine invasion. He discovered iron knives in strata which, after his Thutmose stratum, he placed as early as 1300 B.C. Even if his early datings were acceptable, the presence of small quantities of iron does not make an Iron Age. Since his dates are largely based upon a too-mechanical and, as he seems to admit, a conjectural reckoning of chronology in terms of depths of debris, they cannot be regarded as weighty enough to overbalance conclusions based upon a mass of evidence from other quarters. Even he dates very interesting iron-smelting furnaces which he found at about 1175 B.C. The beginning of the Iron Age and the occupation of Palestine by the Philistines must, therefore, still be placed at about 1200 B.C.

The third dispute has to do with the cultural relations of Gerar and Palestine with the East and the West. For example, Sir Flinders found a problematical set of objects which he regards as small clay models of chariots. They are rude clay boxes, two of them containing sitting figures. Near them were found wheels, two of them with teeth set all around the "tire." The teeth are explained as intended to penetrate the loose dry sand to the harder substratum, which seems of doubtful value. Perhaps they were intended to prevent "skidding." But are they chariots at all? Galling again doubts it. When Petrie points to similar clay models found by Pumpelly in Turkestan, Galling points to parallels in the Cyclades and at Sakje Göze and Boghaz Köi.

The point at issue is whether Gerar shows most the influence of the East or the West. Petrie draws practically all of his materials for comparison from the East, Galling discovers even closer parallels in the West. It is evident from the literary records that the seacoast and the maritime plain had been occupied by immigrants from the West before the Hebrews settled in the hills. Who they were and whence they came is one of those questions about which much has been written because the literary data allow no certain conclusion. It is not for a moment to be denied that traders and armies from the East came to Gerar and passed through it on their way to Egypt. But its closest connections were with Egypt and the Mediterranean lands. One of the most striking evidences of this is to be found in the multitude of fibulae which appear. Almost all are of the form common in Palestine, Syria, and even in Asia Minor in the Middle Iron Age, in which the back is bent instead of curved.

Only a careful study of the seventy-two fine plates of photographs and drawings in Petrie's *Gerar* can give one an adequate impression of the multitude of objects to be found in a great mound such as Tell Jemmeh. Only such a study can give one some conception of the richness and fullness of life in these ancient civilizations. Scarabs, seals; jewelry of rings, earrings, bracelets, pectorals, beads, and pins; weapons of flint, copper, bronze, and iron; including spearheads, arrowheads, knives, and swords; ivory and bone work; kitchen and other household utensils and tools; agricultural implements; figurines, divine, human, and animal; and a tremendous mass of pottery of all sorts and all ages—such a list poorly suggests something of what was found on a site which Sir Flinders regarded as worth only a single season of excavation.

One cannot avoid begrudging Sir Flinders the disemboweling of so important and instructive a mound and then leaving it. One can only sympathize with him in his disappointment at finding that the Persian grain pits had destroyed so much of the earlier strata and that the lowest levels offered little material bearing on the Egyptian civilization in which he and his constituency were most interested. It is unfortunate that this and other mounds which might contribute richly toward a solution of the Philistine problem have not yet been adequately studied.

TELL EL-FAR‘AH

The second great mound which Petrie attacked was Tell el-Far‘ah (or Fari‘ah), which lies half way between Gaza and Beer-sheba, about ten miles southeast of Tell Jemmeh. What its ancient name may have been is unknown. The modern name means "mound of the mountain top," or the "lofty tell." Hearing the name as *farah* (not *far‘ah* with the ‘ayin which is so difficult for Western tongues to speak and ears to hear), Petrie took it to mean "flight," or "escape," from Arabic *farra*. This he equates with Hebrew *palat*, "escape," apparently on the assumption that the Arabs understood the Hebrew word and translated it. He also operates with the well-known fact that *f* and *p* are identical and assumes that *r* and *l* have interchanged. What has become of the *t* in Pelet is not indicated. By a philological miracle, Tell el-Far‘ah thus becomes Beth-Pelet (Jos 15.27, Neh 11.26), on the identity of a single consonant in the names. By another miracle, Pelet, then, changes its inserted *teth* into a *tau* and is connected with the Pelethites, the foreign bodyguard of David (2 Sa 8.18; 20.7, 23; 1 Kg 1.38, 44), and Tell el-Far‘ah thus becomes the headquarters of the Pelethites. It need hardly be said that such etymological juggling exhibits more of ingenuity than philological method. However helpful such an identification might be in collecting funds, it has no scientific value, and it is unfortunate to have it blazoned abroad in all Sir Flinders' publications as if it were settled fact.

Fortunately this does not alter the interest of the results of the actual excavations. Albright would suggest that Tell el-Far‘ah, not Tell esh-Sheri‘ah, is the Sharuhen which figures frequently in ancient records. Sharuhen was an important Hyksos center and was occupied in the time of Shishak, both facts true also of

Tell el-Far'ah but not sufficient to establish the identity beyond all doubt.

Whatever the name of the place in antiquity, it was an important center for 2000 years, from the period of the Hyksos invasion, or before, down to the time of Vespasian. Its tremendous bulk towers above the bank of the wadi, piling fifty feet of debris upon the top of a hill 100 feet high, and, as the expedition uncovered its levels, it was as if the great dusty pages of history were turned back before one's eyes. The walled enclosure at the top of the mound is a half moon measuring some 750 by 400 feet at its greatest dimensions, and excavation disclosed an interesting series of structures. Yet it would have proved dull digging but for the hundreds of tombs which were found at its base and in the plain on all three sides of it. The area actually excavated to the lower levels equaled only about one quarter of that cleared at Tell Jemmeh, hence less was to be expected, but even so the hill was relatively barren. It was a military post, not a trading city. The excavating was done chiefly at the northeast corner.

The history of human settlement along Wadi Ghuzzeh begins far back in the prehistoric period. The Stone Age settlements along the wadi have already been mentioned.[3] A scarab of the Twelfth Dynasty appeared and two strata below the Hyksos remains were found, but apparently were not excavated over any considerable area.

So far as present information goes, the history of the mound begins with the Hyksos. The hill towered above the wadi with a small gully on either side of it. These the Hyksos deepened and connected at the rear by a great fosse, eighty feet wide. They piled the earth in a characteristic ramp behind and put the gate at a point where it was easily defended. Upon this ramp the Egyptians placed mud-brick walls which made the place almost impregnable. Against the wall on the northeast corner the Egyptian governor built a luxurious residency with a bathroom and a wine closet by the bedroom. An ivory panel from a box delicately

[3] See above chap. III, pp. 40 f.

carved with an Egyptian scene testified to His Excellency's elegant taste. During the Egyptian period the fosse was partially filled with blowing sand, and the steep, high slope of the ramp served as an excellent location for the digging of tombs. Other tombs in greater numbers were dug vertically into the plain back of the mound. The tombs produced the most interesting museum pieces as well as many items of historical information.

These tombs in the plain were in small groups which had been dug at different times or by different classes of people, beginning with the Hyksos. The Philistines had a group of their own, distinguished by five which were larger than the rest and must have belonged to "lords of the Philistines." Two of them contained "anthropoid sarcophagi," cigar-shaped clay coffins with removable lids at the large end shaped to resemble a human face. With the lid removed they look like a pointed slipper. Such slipper-shaped, or anthropoid, coffins have been found at several places in Palestine and also in Egypt. Their crude representation of the face and head with arms that start behind the ears and clasp hands under the chin gives them a most un-Egyptian appearance. They probably belong to foreign mercenaries.

Between the Hyksos and Philistine tombs, chronologically speaking, comes the great group found in the sides of the Hyksos fosse—six large and fifty small ones. Although plundered in antiquity, they still contained a very respectable collection of Late Bronze Age pottery, bead necklaces, and scarabs, and personal effects of Egyptian type.

Another group of tombs, discovered during the first campaign at the southern side of the mound, belonged to a variety of periods. One tomb lying just a little apart from the rest distinguished itself by fittings of unusual magnificence. It seems to have been a chamber cut into the ground and walled with adobe brick. It was entered from a shaft at one end by a door which was found walled up with bricks. It had been plundered, but there remained the bronze posts of a bed frame and two fine pieces of silver ware which Sir Flinders misdated, but which have been proved to be of a Phoenician type widely spread in the Persian period. One was a silver bowl nearly two inches deep and seven inches in diameter and formed into what would now be called a sun-flower pattern. The other was a silver ladle eight and one-half inches long with a handle made in the shape of a long slender swimming girl with an Armenoid nose. Bowl and ladle are beautifully executed.

An interesting series of interments consisted of cremation burials in urns. They are probably to be dated in the eighth or seventh century and ascribed to Phoenician immigrants. Two other groups of tombs, found northwest of the mound, are also to be dated in the Middle Iron period. In one, evidently a family burial place, 116 adults and six children had been crowded into a space measuring about 13 by 4 by 6 feet. A large proportion of the graves in the plain were shafts six or seven feet long and four or five feet deep with a shelf for the body dug into the west wall at the bottom.

A very large portion of the mound remains unexcavated and a large number of questions remain unanswered. A later excavator may find that the juice of history has been sucked out of the mound. Yet Sir Flinders frequently followed other excavators in Egypt and discovered remarkable objects and valuable facts which they had missed. Others, again, have followed him and repeated his fortunate experience. In any case a future excavator at Tell el-Far'ah will still find much to do.

Tell el-'Ajjul

The third mound undertaken by Sir Flinders Petrie is Tell el-'Ajjul, the "mound of the little calf," which lies on the north side of Wadi Ghuzzeh where it runs into the sea about five miles south of modern Gaza. In outward appearance it is not now an attractive site. Its height is not imposing. Sand dunes are drifting up against its seaward side and partly cover the fig groves which are planted on its edge. It is washed into irregular gullies by the rains of centuries. But it covers 28 or 30 acres, a large city in ancient times, six times the size of Troy, and more than three times the size of David's Jerusalem, twice the size of

Megiddo. The mass of material discovered is such that according to Sir Flinders, it would take fifty years to excavate the mound properly.

The strategic importance of its location can hardly be over-emphasized. Yet, strangely enough, what the ancient name of the city was cannot now be determined. Petrie believes it to be the original site of Gaza, abandoned because of malaria. The conclusion was suggested to him by the sad sufferings of his expedition during its first year, when one hundred of his work-men were in hospital with that most unpleasant scourge. His argument is that the ancient city lay in the most accessible place, at the mouth of the great wadi, which then formed a natural harbor. In the course of time the wadi silted up, marshes formed, and malaria was the result. The population then gradually shifted to the site of modern Gaza at about the begin-ning of the Late Bronze period, leaving this great "mound of the little calf" providentially ready for him to dig into it, undis-turbed by the debris of later settlements. Whether this theory is correct or not, the site has proved to be remarkably rich in remains, particularly of the Hyksos.

Excavation began in the autumn of 1930 but because of the malaria was adjourned to Tell el-Far'ah. When cold laid the mosquitoes, it was possible to return to Tell el-'Ajjul once more. During that winter the wadi bed was canalized so as to drain the marshes, and the excavations were continued unhindered each winter for four years. At the end of two years Mr. Starkey and Mr. Harding began excavation on their own account at Tell ed-Duweir. A fifth campaign, which was to have been undertaken in January, 1938, under the direction of Dr. Ernest Mackay and Miss Margaret Murray, was prevented by the destruction of the expedition houses and equipment at the hands of marauders. Since Sir Flinders' chronological results are so completely at variance with those of other excavators, Dr. Albright, who had recently visited the site and studied its pottery on the mound and in the Palestine Museum, undertook a revision of dates. The beginning of occupation, Sir Flinders' "Copper Age," he places in the twenty-second and twenty-first centuries, "Palace IV" in the fourteenth and thirteenth centuries, and "Palace V" with several tombs in the 1000 series in the tenth-ninth centuries.

Apparently the original hill which led to the selection of the site was very low indeed, perhaps only fifteen feet above the plain. On the south side it was a sandstone bluff rising fifty feet above the wadi, which perhaps was an estuary in ancient times. The defenders, in true Hyksos style, cut a fosse three-fourths of a mile long around the other three sides, leaving only a gangway at the city gate, and threw the earth upon the hill. When it was finished, an approaching enemy found an almost vertical drop of twenty feet into the fosse and then a slope of a hundred and fifty feet at an angle of thirty-five degrees up to the crest of the bank. If there was a west gate, it has been washed away. The chief entrance found was on the northeast side, where the ground is such as to render the approach easiest. Here a peculiar system of pits, trenches, and tunnels was uncovered which, so Mr. Starkey concluded, were sappers' tunnels and siege works of an enemy.

Within the city during the first campaign there was found an area of remarkably well-preserved houses belonging to the last occupation of the city. Walls stood to a height of eight feet with doorways intact, all buried in the debris of the two or three upper stories. Streets seem to have been laid out with regularity, walls and floors were stuccoed, and there was every evidence of greater neatness than in a modern oriental city. At the entrance to a shrine was a shell-covered brick platform with a drain in the center apparently intended for the washing of the worshiper's feet before entering. In a large building was a hall twenty-four feet long with a raised hearth in the center about which the notables of the city may often have gathered to warm themselves.

In the second and third campaigns, following his theory as to the site of the best buildings, Sir Flinders worked at the northwest corner of Tell el-'Ajjul with complete success, for he found stratum after stratum of large and finely constructed buildings, five in all. Under the fourth palace was a unique foundation sacrifice. According to Sir Flinders' interpretation of the discovered remains, a horse was killed and, after the removal of the shoulders and left thigh, probably for a feast, it was buried in a pit five feet deep. Two other horses were killed and eaten along with the parts of the first, and their bones were scattered beside the pit. Such hippophagy, or horse eating, is otherwise unknown in Palestine. Since the Hyksos were famous for first bringing horses into Palestine, it is possible that they were responsible for this foundation sacrifice and feast.

Various strange burial customs seem to be attested by discoveries made at Tell el-'Ajjul. Horses or donkeys and men were found buried in the same tombs. Bones of men and animals in some cases were found crushed together in complete confusion, in one case along with gold earrings and scarabs. Objects of gold, silver, copper, ivory, and basalt were deposited together, the metals fused by fire. Do these destroyed objects and crushed bones point to superstitious rites like the cursing of Achan and the treasures of Jericho? Are they sacrifices to avert a plague or to placate a deity's supposed anger?

The period covered by the strata in the mound runs from the end of the Early Bronze Age down to Late Bronze ii with a later extension into Early Iron ii and iii, but appears to be chiefly Middle and Late Bronze. Among the portable objects discovered, pottery, bronze weapons, and jewelry, there are many which point to importation from Cyprus, Crete, and the Aegean. As all excavations in Palestine show, the Middle and Late Bronze Ages were times of the liveliest intercourse between Palestine and the countries to the west and northwest. This is especially true of seacoast towns but is not confined to them. If the Hyksos came from the northeast, they brought very little of culture with them, and all of the time active commerce with the Aegean world continued.

What Sir Flinders Petrie has discovered at these three sites whets the appetite for more. The puzzling problems set by that strange folk, the Hyksos, are multiplying. The strange horse burials, the evidence of the sacrifice of the horse and of hippophagy, and the other peculiar customs begin to fill in the picture of southern Palestine with entirely unexpected lights and shadows. The variety of tombs and burial customs raises problems as to the identity of the various races who inhabited this part of the world. Few more interesting puzzles can be found than the ancient history of Palestine.

Tell Abu Selimeh

The volume which Sir Flinders Petrie called *Anthedon* (1937) marked his "century" of publications. One hundred books on archaeological and historical subjects are no mean achievement. Sixty years of labor lay between the first and the hundredth volume. And the hundredth volume bids fair to be his last to describe a new enterprise of excavation.

At periods in the spring, winter, and late autumn of 1935-1936, with a corps of self-sacrificing assistants, Sir Flinders and Lady Petrie excavated "about 100 feet across" the mound of Tell Abu Selimeh near the police post of Sheikh Zuweid. It was not a glorious climax to a long career, for the civil strife of 1936 rendered the final brief campaign in December difficult and the situation of the place itself was not auspicious. It lies between the sea and the desert in an unfrequented region. The weather was extremely unpropitious. Out of 188 days spent at the mound, a third was lost because of heavy gales, rain, and influenza. The party suffered from still other handicaps.

The site lies just across the present border between Egypt and Palestine but north of el-'Arish and the River of Egypt, the traditional border. The mound did not at first present the Egyptian materials sought. With an eye that twinkled in appreciation of my interest in later periods, Sir Flinders told me that they had to dig through a mass of "Hellenistic rubbish" before they reached Egyptian remains. The area excavated was not large but gave an excellent idea of the successive occupations, and the objects found emphasize the varied cultural contacts of the Palestinian seacoast.

Sir Flinders distinguished twelve or thirteen superimposed

cities running from the Roman occupation about the beginning of the Christian era back to the Nineteenth Dynasty—at least to Ramses II, possibly to Harmhab. The cities were built almost entirely of brick, as is to be expected in a region far distant from the mountains. A difference in the sizes of the bricks used often gave the clue to difference of date. This, of course, was supplemented by changes in styles of pottery, ornament, and the numerous Egyptian scarabs and amulets. Layers of wind-blown sand and the debris of conflagrations frequently assisted materially in distinguishing strata.

The most prosperous city of all seems to have owed its expansion to Hellenistic influence, one may suppose to that of the Ptolemies, since Aramaic ostraca of Ptolemaic times were found. Another important period was marked by a chamber approached by wide steps, all paved with baked tiles 14.4 inches square and 4 inches thick. Sir Flinders thinks the structure a shrine and ascribes it to the time of Nebuchadrezzar, but it might well be Persian. Another prosperous stratum Sir Flinders equates with the reigns of Jehoshaphat and Joash, but the date may be wrong for that was not a time of such prosperity as the age of Uzziah, a century later. The very small collection of Cretan, Cypriote, and Philistine wares proves that the site was little occupied from 1400 to 1000 B.C., or that the excavators did not find the part occupied during those centuries. Beside the Aramaic scribblings on pottery already mentioned, numerous Greek and Latin stamped impressions on pottery, which came from the tell and its neighborhood, rehearse the often-told story of the close cultural and economic connections between Palestine, even this bare and sandy coastal region, and the more attractive lands to the northwest.

In spite of numerous disagreements between Sir Flinders and other archaeologists on matters of chronology and interpretation and the many lacunae in methods both of excavation and reporting, the ten years of excavation, carried on by the British School of Archaeology in Egypt "in Egypt over the border," have been fruitful of valuable results. Very important additions have been made to knowledge of both the Hyksos and the Egyptian occupation of Palestine. Sir Flinders was himself persuaded by his discoveries to cut out one thousand years—not yet enough—from his long chronology.

Another fascinating vista into the past has been opened. It bristles with unsolved problems, but it is clear that the material lies at hand for the solution of many of these problems and that the tells on the edge of the Sinaitic desert have many secrets to reveal.[5]

[5] The above was written while Sir Flinders Petrie was still alive. He passed away in Jerusalem on July 28, 1942, at the age of eighty-nine.

CHAPTER X

BORDER CITIES OF THE SHEPHELAH

❈

JERICHO had certain decided advantages. Because it lay off the chief highways of ancient Palestine, it had an opportunity to develop through hundreds of years without disturbance except from its earthquakes. It came late and perhaps less directly under Egyptian rule. The cities along the coastal plain, in the level Negeb, or "South Country," and in the Shephelah, the foothills paralleling the mountains of Judea, have a different story. Unfortunately no important coastal city has had more than a surface scratching. Much more attention has been given the Shephelah.

The first systematic excavation in Palestine under Sir Flinders Petrie's direction took place at Tell el-Hesi, which is not Lachish, as was then supposed, but perhaps Saruhen or possibly Eglon. Tell ej-Judeideh, Tell es-Safi, Tell Sandahanneh, and Tell Zakariyeh followed, then Gezer, and later 'Ain Shems, all before 1914. Since 1919 there have come various soundings, some brief campaigns at Askalon, the resumption of work at 'Ain Shems, the series of forays by Sir Flinders Petrie on three imposing mounds along the Wadi Ghuzzeh, and finally a magnificent attack upon one of the most impressive and richest sites in all Palestine, Tell ed-Duweir.

TELL ED-DUWEIR—LACHISH

When J. L. Starkey, Lankester Harding, and H. Dunscomb Colt decided to leave the expedition of the British School of Archaeology in Egypt and embark on a joint British-American enterprise, they had two chief sites in mind, Tell esh-Sheikh Ahmed el-Areini, which might be Gath, and Tell ed-Duweir, which Albright had identified with Lachish. Their three chief British donors, Sir Henry Wellcome, Sir Charles Marston, and Sir Robert Mond, were farsighted enough to decide for the larger and more expensive of the two sites, Tell ed-Duweir. The outcome has more than demonstrated the wisdom of their choice. Tell ed-Duweir has proved to be one of the most fruitful and still is one of the most promising sites in Palestine.

The expedition has been very unfortunate in the loss of its leader, Mr. Starkey, at the hands of a group of marauders near Hebron on January 10, 1938. The task of completing the publication of results falls largely on his successor, Mr. C. H. Inge, and on Miss Olga Tufnell, who for many years was a member of the expedition staff.

Thus far only two final volumes have appeared, one recording the great find of the expedition, ostraca written a little before or during the final siege of Jerusalem under Nebuchadrezzar, and the other describing three very important Canaanite sanctuaries. Mr. Starkey made fairly full reports each year in the *Quarterly Statement* of the Palestine Exploration Fund and was always most generous in giving information to fellow archaeologists, with the result that other outstanding results of his work are already known.

At the beginning he explained that his larger purpose was "to trace, if possible, the sources of the various foreign contacts which influenced the development of Palestinian culture in the early pre-Hellenistic periods," especially the "foreign elements . . . introduced from the north and east," as exemplified particularly in the potters' craft.[1] This general aim was to be carried out by a series of excavations, for which Tell ed-Duweir was chosen as the beginning because of its size and its commanding position in the lower Shephelah on the chief route from Egypt to Hebron and central Palestine. Here he hoped to establish a full series of clearly stratified levels as a basis for further study. The breadth of Mr. Starkey's interests was illustrated by his inclusion of a "Geological Section" in his organiza-

[1] *Quarterly Statement*, 1933, p. 190.

tion with the very successful undertaking at Bethlehem as its first fruits.[2]

Excavation at Tell ed-Duweir was carried on through six seasons, each of about six months during the winters from 1932 to 1938. Mr. Starkey's untimely death was a serious loss to Palestinian archaeology, for he had demonstrated unusual organizing abilities with which to serve his high aims and ideals as an excavator. The work was continued through the spring of 1938 under the direction of Mr. Inge and Mr. Lankester Harding, who was granted leave, as necessary, from his recently assumed post as Chief Inspector of Antiquities in Transjordan. Both had been with Mr. Starkey from the beginning of the expedition, Mr. Harding for some years before.

The history of occupation at Tell ed-Duweir begins with the Chalcolithic and Early Bronze Ages, when there was a considerable community, of which the chief remains thus far discovered were on the hill west of the mound. Here were cave burials in what had first been cave dwellings with stone door frames and (probably wooden) doors that swung on pivots in stone sockets. Since the metal objects analyzed were almost pure copper, Mr. Starkey preferred to use the term "Copper," instead of "Early Bronze," Age, for the third-millennium culture. The Middle Bronze Age, including the period of Hyksos occupation, is marked by characteristic walls, pottery, and scarabs. The Late Bronze Age, under Egyptian rule, was the most prosperous of all.

So far as excavation has gone, the sections of the city's history which have been most fully illuminated are those which fall just before the Exile and during the Persian period. As yet the periods of the Hebrew conquest and monarchy to 600 B.C. have hardly been touched except in tombs. Much more may be expected. After the Persian period the mound seems not to have been occupied except by squatters who did no serious building. Some Byzantine graves were found, perhaps burials from elsewhere. A fine Roman road, doubtless the one over which

[2] See above, chap. III, p. 42.

Eusebius traveled, was uncovered under five feet of earth on the neighboring hillside. It is an index of the ravages of erosion in Palestine.

It is difficult to give an idea of the richness of Tell ed-Duweir and its adjacent tombs. In a single large tomb of the late Hyksos period 200 scarabs were found. In another were ivory rods whose use, according to the excavators' best guess, must have been as "curling irons." Assyrian reliefs show the city officials who surrendered to the invaders as wearing closely curled hair. In other areas baked clay rods of similar shape suggested that the poor as well as the rich curled their hair. One prized discovery, occurring under a Hyksos burial and a lime-plastered floor, was a complete skeleton of a dog. It is regarded as a "seluki," the type brought from Palestine to England by the Crusaders from which the greyhound was bred. The strata above and the pottery with it date it to the third millennium.

Besides numerous items of minor interest, the outstanding discoveries made at Tell ed-Duweir are various: a series of three Late Bronze Age temples; inscriptional material in hieratic and hieroglyphic, in the Proto-Sinaitic script, and in Hebrew; the "Lachish letters," the ostraca already mentioned; fortifications including a "Hyksos fosse and ramp" with a sappers' tunnel and Hebrew walls and gates with various rebuildings; two later historical periods, seen in a Persian palace, house, and sanctuary, and in part of the Hebrew city under the Persians; a "great depression," a tremendous rectangular "hole" cut into the hillside on the east side of the mound; tombs of various ages, some untouched; and two large collections of skeletal material. In an account devoted to methods more than to results it is impossible to describe these discoveries with any fullness or adequacy.

The three sanctuaries found in the Hyksos fosse were one of the chief centers of interest for five seasons. Progress in excavation was slow because the fosse was too wet for excavation during most of each winter. Eventually the plans of the three temples and much of their furniture were uncovered. The fact that they lay in the Hyksos fosse proved them to be Egyptian or later. Pottery under and on their floors proved them to belong to the Late Bronze period, between the fifteenth and thirteenth centuries. The first two had apparently not been destroyed but rebuilt to form the second and third. The third was violently destroyed by fire, probably by the invading Israelites. Unlike the Beth-shan temples, these contained no important Egyptian stelae or inscriptions and they were much smaller, but more of the furniture and offerings were in place.

Though, strangely enough, at this southern site no long official Egyptian inscriptions have come to light, early alphabetic texts have been numerous. The most important have been mentioned in the chapter on the alphabet. They prove that the Canaanites were literate before the Hebrew invasion. The first five letters of the Hebrew alphabet, scribbled in their still-conventional order on a step of the seventh-century Hebrew palace are equally significant as to Hebrew literacy. They do not prove that the ancient Hebrews had schools but they were the preface to the still more remarkable "Lachish letters."

THE LACHISH LETTERS

The most sensational discovery of many a decade in Palestine was the inscribed potsherds already mentioned, eighteen of which came to light at the end of January, 1935, three more a little later. Sixteen were found in a small room outside the city gate. Nos. I and XIX are lists of names, in no. XIX with numbers following them. No. XIII seems to be a military order, no. XX, a label written on an unbroken jar. The remainder are probably letters, of which several are almost illegible.

Of the five letters which are most completely legible, two (II, VI) are addressed to "my lord Ya'osh," and one (III) begins, "Thy servant Hosha'yahu (Hoshaiah) sendeth to report to my lord Ya'osh." Ya'osh is clearly a governor, or military commander, at Lachish, and the small room outside the gate where they were found should be his field headquarters, while Hoshaiah is probably a subordinate commander in some small city or important outpost. Recent events give poignancy to Hoshaiah's complaint (Letter VI) that "the words of the princes are not good, but to weaken your hands and to slacken the hands of the men who are informed about them."[3] It is uncertain whether they all came from the same hand. A slave or secretary may have done the writing. It cannot be proved that all came from Hoshaiah. However, in his "signed" letter and some of the others, the writer evidently is clearing himself of charges of disloyalty or neglect of duty. The contents suggest a single author. That several came from the same person or "office," is proved by the fact that five (II, VI, VII, VIII, XVIII) are fragments from the same vessel and can in part be fitted together to restore a wide-mouthed jar. They are an apt illustration of the practice, familiar from Greek ostraca in Egypt, of using for letters and receipts any broken pottery that lay to hand.

The difficulty of identifying a city which has been lost is well illustrated here. Letter IV comes as near to completing the demonstration that Tell ed-Duweir is Lachish as any one can reasonably ask. One sentence reads: "We are watching for the signals of Lachish according to all the indications which my lord has given, for we cannot see Azekah." Given the various reasons for believing the site to be Lachish, there is hardly a chance in a hundred that such a sentence could have been written to any other city.

In two letters a prophet was mentioned, in one of them by name, but, by one of those fatalities which seem to afflict archaeology and epigraphy too often, only the too-common ending -*yahu* (-iah) has been preserved. Some would identify him with Jeremiah, others with Uriah (Jer 26.21 ff.).

The sixteen letters outside the gate were found in a stratum of destruction dating from the final Babylonian invasion. They doubtless belong, therefore, to the decade between the first and the second invasions. Whether Jeremiah was mentioned or not, the letters give a stimulating, even if tantalizing, glimpse

[3] Albright's version, *BAS*, 82 (1941), 22.

into the conditions that surrounded his labors during the final years of the monarchy, possibly during the final siege of Jerusalem. They show how Hebrew characters were written at their exactly dated period. They give a first-hand view of non-literary prose as it was spoken and written just before the Exile. It was good classical Hebrew, differing from the earlier biblical books, such as Joshua, Judges, and Samuel, and equally from postexilic products such as Nehemiah, with their neologisms and Aramaisms.

The four inscribed potsherds found on the mound give basis for the hope that still more are preserved in the great mass of debris. The ostraca are far from representing all of the epigraphic material found, for there were numerous Hebrew seals and seal impressions. An impression reading, "Belonging to Gedaliah who is over the house," is ascribed to the Gedaliah who later, as governor, died at Mizpah (2 Kg 25.25). On the back of the clay lump which carries the stamp is the clear impress of the papyrus on which the document sealed had been written—a most valuable indication of the fact that leather, or parchment, and potsherds were not the only writing material in use.

FORTIFICATIONS

One of the earliest discoveries of the expedition was a deep fosse with perpendicular sides before a great ramp of clay and lime thrown up around the tell after the Hyksos fashion. Since under the ramp certain burials with pottery were sealed, it may eventually be possible to date it with some exactitude. A tunnel run through it was so clearly the work of sappers, probably during an Egyptian siege, that its discovery served to clear up the puzzle of similar tunnels at Tell el-'Ajjul.[4] It was in this fosse below the ramp that the three Canaanite-Egyptian temples were found. They give a date *ad quem* for the fosse.

The great wall which surrounded the mound in Hebrew times has been followed in its full extent. The rebuildings at the city gate were especially interesting as they have served

[4] See above, chap. IX.

materially to assist in dating the "Lachish letters." A detailed study, with the careful removal of one feature after another, made it clear that the large and imposing gate had been destroyed and the adjoining houses burned about the time of the Exile in Babylon, and that a smaller gate had been immediately rebuilt above debris eight feet thick and then again destroyed within a short time. The letters were found in the debris of this last destruction. Mr. Starkey, therefore, believed that the earlier destruction took place in 597 B.C. (2 Kg 24.1-17), on the first Babylonian invasion, the second at the beginning of the final siege of Jerusalem in 588 B.C. Later, in the Persian period, the gate had again been rebuilt on a still smaller scale. The city preceding the destruction of 597 B.C. had been much better built and more fully occupied than either of the succeeding cities.

PERSIAN AND HEBREW CITIES

On the top of the mound was a courtyard "palace" based upon, but not entirely covering, a large platform. It could be definitely dated to the Persian period by a fragment of red Attic ware which belongs between 470 and 425 B.C. Besides other buildings of the Persian period, what appeared from its plan to be a temple was uncovered at the northeast corner of the mound. It was oriented to the east so that the rising sun might be worshiped as it shone into the cella, which lay on a higher level back of a court. Unfortunately squatters of Hellenistic times had cleared it of any cult paraphernalia, as well as of means of arriving at a definite date. The Persian "residency" had been a fine structure, with round tile drains and other appurtenances of comfort, but, like the Persian city gate, it was not the equal of the Hebrew palace which preceded it.

When the Persian "residency" was removed, there was found under it a layer of debris which showed a destruction by fire. A large structure, seventy yards long, evidently a "palace fort," a real acropolis, had been built upon an artificial platform ten or twelve feet above ground level. The excavations of 1937-38 discovered that a row of poor houses had been built upon debris of this "palace fort" and that, according to the chronology adopted, this palace, which had been built in the seventh century, had not been rebuilt after the destruction of 597 B.C. This earlier destruction had everywhere been more ruthless and accompanied by much fiercer heat than the last destruction, that of 588 B.C.

In the neighborhood of the "palace fort" were various buildings which housed commercial or industrial establishments. A loom and a dyeing establishment were found in one, querns for grinding grain in another. One region had many handles with *lemelekh* ("belonging to the king") stamps from Hebron, Ziph, Sokhoh, and Memshat, the four places which are named on such handles all over Judea. They are proof, if proof were needed, that Lachish belonged to pre-exilic Judah. Do they mark the receiving depot for taxes in kind "for the king"? Another vessel, found near the gate, had on its shoulder, written in the clay before firing, *bath lemelekh*, the "bath of the king," or "royal bath," which means, not what it seems to say, but that the vessel was the standard *bath*, the measure of about 40 liters.

The wide stairway leading to the "palace fort" was laid over an earlier stairway, of which two steps were uncovered. On the upper one were drawings of a lion and of small concentric circles made with a compass, and the first five letters of the Hebrew-Phoenician alphabet already mentioned.

The "Great Depression"

In front of the "palace fort" was an open area more than 90 feet across, which may have been a parade ground or market place. It was paved with pounded limestone chips, as was also the main street of the seventh century which led up from the gate. The source of the paving material was discovered in a "great depression" which lay to the southeast of the open area and, like a similar "hole" at Megiddo, went through several excavation seasons as an unsolved riddle. Unlike the Megiddo puzzle, this one was never solved.

After removing tons of earth and rocks Mr. Starkey and Mr. Inge resorted to tunneling and at long last found merely a huge rectangular pit cut in the rock just inside the southeast corner of the city, and measuring eighty by seventy feet by eighty feet in depth. It suggests a new appraisal of the organizing ability of the ancient Hebrews. When finally the archaeologists' tunnels had followed all of its walls at the bottom and gone out to its center, the conclusion was reached that, in view of its extremely uneven floor, it was unfinished and that, therefore, its purpose will never be known. Perhaps it was to have been a great cistern into which the paved area was to drain. Possibly the Babylonian invasion interrupted this colossal undertaking.

Near the bottom at the northwest corner an amusing discovery was made. A projecting boulder, too hard to be cut away easily, had presented the appearance of a human profile. Some ancient Borglum had added a few touches which converted it into a very passable life-sized face with the stylized beard of seventh-century Assyrian sculpture. Three weeks after the digging was finished, the tunnel caved in and this unique piece of Jewish sculpture is no longer on exhibition, for it now lies under 80 feet of rock and earth.

Tombs and Skeletal Material

The scarabs, pottery, and jewelry found in Lachish tombs have great value for cultural history. They are too numerous for description here. But two discoveries merit special mention. One is the finding of three "slipper," or anthropoid, coffins of clay, the kind with lids molded to represent a face. Such have been found at Beisan, Tell el-Far'ah, in Transjordan, and in Egypt. One of them was unique in bearing a badly written and only partially preserved inscription in hieroglyphs. These coffins are believed to represent mercenaries of Aegean origin.[5]

[5] See chapters IX and XI.

Among the many tombs excavated, two provided extremely gruesome discoveries. Two neighboring caves, originally Bronze Age tombs, and later used as dwellings, had been cleared out and reused for the deposit of the remains of hundreds of persons. One contained the bones of some 500 individuals. The other had on top, under its broken roof, a deposit of animal bones, largely pig. Below was a conglomerate mass of some 1500 human skeletons which had obviously been dumped through the roof after the flesh had decayed, so that the skulls rolled down the sides of the heap as it grew. Many of the bones in both huge ossuaries had been partially calcined, a fact which suggested that they may have been cleared out of the burned city when it was reoccupied after a terrible massacre and fire. Strewn among them were much broken pottery and some small vessels that were whole. The latter may have been offerings from surviving relatives. The pottery sets the date in the eighth or seventh century. Some wholesale destruction of the city and its inhabitants, perhaps in an Assyrian, perhaps in a Babylonian, invasion must have been responsible.

A very careful study has been made of the cranial remains which Mr. Starkey was able to bring to England. Nearly 700 individuals were represented. Unfortunately, according to Sir Arthur Keith, the method used does not get at some of the significant facts and obscures others. The conclusion was that the Lachish population was Egyptian, and Upper Egyptian at that. This unexpected judgment Sir Arthur doubts, believing that, then as now, the Caucasian Mediterranean, not the Hamitic type, must have been dominant in southern Palestine. Clear evidence of trephining on three excellently preserved skulls has aroused much interest. In one case at least, the patient had lived long enough for the bone to make some growth.

Some of the problems which Tell ed-Duweir presented will be solved when the results of the present excavations are worked out and published. Others await further excavation, or further study, as in the case of the skeletal material. There are still great masses of material for the future archaeologist and it is to

be hoped the expedition can eventually be resumed. With truly
scientific foresight Mr. Starkey had spent a considerable part
of his six seasons clearing ground outside the mound where the
debris from the city itself might be dumped and preparing the
necessary plant and paraphernalia for this main task. The inter-
ruption caused by his death and the war came just as the main
task was to be undertaken.

'Ain Shems—Beth-Shemesh

Beside Tell ed-Duweir, the modest mound of 'Ain Shems,
or Tell er-Rumeileh, is almost infinitesimal. Yet, after many
vicissitudes, it has proved most interesting and instructive. It
was one of those which were attacked before the first world
war. Three short campaigns (1911-12) reached conclusions
which have not proved sound in all particulars. But the Palestine Exploration Fund was fortunate in choosing as a director
Duncan Mackenzie, an experienced excavator already familiar
with Aegean archaeology, for 'Ain Shems proved to be especially rich in imports and imitations of Aegean wares. Great
advances have since been made in the archaeology of Cyprus,
Crete, and the Mycenean region. Yet Mackenzie's chronology
for the major strata of 'Ain Shems has proved remarkably satisfactory. Only the dating of certain tombs has had to be altered
by a century or two. The fine "Philistine ware" which Mackenzie found has whetted the appetites of other archaeologists,
and the discoveries of the recent American expedition have
more than justified its efforts and expenditures.

In 1928 the Palestine Exploration Fund generously ceded its
rights of priority to an expedition from Haverford College, organized by Professor Elihu Grant, who had had long familiarity
with Palestine. He has had the skilled assistance of Dr. C. S.
Fisher, Mr. Alan Rowe, Mr. A. J. Tobler, Mr. J. C. Wampler,
and others in the digging through five campaigns (1928, 1929,
1930, 1931, 1933), and of Dr. G. Ernest Wright in the two final
volumes of the sumptuous six-volume publication. The student,
if he wishes it, has rich materials for a restudy of the problem
of the site.

Tell Jemmeh, probably ancient Gerar. Wadi Ghazzeh in the foreground.

Tell el-Far'ah, Wadi Ghazzeh at right. Expedition houses in foreground; excavations showing on top of mound at left and right.

Tell ed-Duweir (Lachish) from the east. A path runs up from the left just below the line of the Israelite wall.

Temple (?) of the Persian period; court and steps leading to the sanctuary.

Ancient Beth-shemesh lay in one of the happiest landscapes in Palestine. Being on the border between Philistine and Israelite territory, it was the natural place for the ark to halt on its return from Philistine captivity (1 Sa 6). Its excavation has disclosed an interesting story of the conflict of races and cultures. In 1929 the excavators lived through a new episode of this eternal conflict, when their workers, during the unfortunate riots of August and September, took leave for two or three days to plunder the hastily abandoned colony of Spanish-Hungarian Jews at 'Artuf, just across the railroad to the northwest. Here in the Shephelah, the Hebrew "lowlands," Canaanite and Egyptian, Canaanite and the "sea peoples," Israelite and Philistine, the East and the West, were ever at war.

The five major strata discovered on the tell, which run from about 2200 B.C. to the time of the Exile do not exactly correspond to those of other excavated sites or to the conventional archaeological periods.[6] The ancient enemies of the city were thoughtless enough to destroy it at odd times between periods. In general, however, the city's history corresponds to that of Tell Beit Mirsim, which lies some twenty miles to the south. The stratification was not clearly marked and was not properly clarified until the final season of excavation in 1933. The earlier part of the city's history was not well represented. But the Late Bronze Age (stratum IV) was more prosperous than at Tell Beit Mirsim and was distinguished by important and beautiful importations from the Aegean region. The Philistine ware of the Early Iron Age was especially abundant. 'Ain Shems quite overshadows Tell Beit Mirsim in the beauty of the pottery found, but that is probably due to the fact that no tombs have yet been opened at Tell Beit Mirsim.

SPECIAL DISCOVERIES

The most interesting objects came from the tombs of Beth-shemesh, all of which were found along the edges of the mound. Mackenzie made some of his finest discoveries in tombs and Grant was even more fortunate than he. Indeed his Tomb 11

[6] The Byzantine remains, called stratum I, are here omitted.

(called Tomb 1 in his *Beth-Shemesh*) completely overwhelmed him with an embarrassment of riches. The tombs were valuable supplements to the cultural history of the city as read on the mound, and the tomb groups assisted greatly in determining the chronology.

No building which was clearly a shrine or temple was found, but a cigar-shaped stone 5 feet long and a base in which it could be set were found reused in walls of stratum II. They may have come from a shrine in stratum III, the Philistine period. There was no lack of "Astarte" figurines. A beautiful, molded terra cotta plaque was found in 1928 in the Late Bronze Age city. It shows a nude figure of a goddess, or a sacred courtesan, standing with a long-stemmed flower in each hand. Her hair, carefully combed and parted, is pushed back over her ears, and a serpent crawls down over her left shoulder with its head at her left hip.

An interesting type of tomb closure was repeatedly illustrated. As in many places, the tombs of the Middle Iron Age were entered by square passages set at ground level and just large enough for a person to crawl through. This hole was plugged with a large rabbeted stone block which fitted into it. Against this block was rolled a stone cylinder, about the size of the stone rollers used on mud roofs. It represents a less familiar type of rolling stone for tombs.

The household pottery, the mortars and querns for grinding grain, the jewelry, the farm utensils, and all the various objects commonly found appear. A jar of jewelry showed so many diverse forms which might be supposed to belong to different periods that it was tentatively assigned to an ancient tomb robber.

A previous chapter has mentioned the two invaluable inscribed objects which were found: the potsherd with Proto-Sinaitic characters from the fourteenth-century stratum and the clay tablet with cuneiform alphabetic characters of the Ras esh-Shamra type found between strata V and IVa, that is, in a late sixteenth- or early fifteenth-century context. Their chief value is the evidence which they afford of widespread experiments in alphabetic writing.

A considerable number of jar handles with *lemelkh* stamps proved that Beth-shemesh belonged to Judah up to the Babylonian exile. Evidence even better, if possible, was discovered in an impression from the same seal as two stamps found at Tell Beit Mirsim and reading, "Belonging to Eliakim, boy (steward) of Yokin," or Joiachin.[7] Evidently property of the exiled king was to be found at Beth-shemesh as well as at Kiriath Sepher. Since the stamp was found in the uppermost level at Tell Beit Mirsim, it is clear from this also that Beth-shemesh was occupied down to the Babylonian exile.

Ancient Beth-shemesh, the "house of the Sun," should have revealed evidence of sun worship. It might have been expected to exhibit more numerous traces of Egyptian and Philistine occupation. But it was not a place that could be strongly defended and, despite its favorable location, it never became strategically important, nor large and prosperous. It is an excellent example of a rural city in the Shephelah and makes a valuable contribution to the history of the development of Hebrew culture.

EARLIER EXCAVATIONS

Between Lachish and Beth-shemesh lay various cities of the Shephelah, four of which, at Tell Sandahanneh, Tell ej-Judeideh, Tell Zakariyeh, and, on the edge of the martime plain, Tell es-Safi, were investigated, rather than excavated, by Bliss and Macalister in 1898-1900. At Tell ej-Judeideh only one twenty-fourth of the mound was touched, and the work resulted merely in gathering specimens of Jewish pottery—undated—and stamped jar handles. At Tell es-Safi a doubtful pre-Israelite sanctuary was found, but little else. At Tell Zakariyeh a large fortress was traced, though only half excavated, and the rest of the city hardly touched. Only at Tell Sandahanneh was the entire Hellenistic city (Marisa) uncovered.

[7] See above, chap. VII.

Many pottery types were recovered and are well published in the volume describing the excavations. Many other objects are likewise recorded. But no careful records of provenience are given and no such stratification as at Tell el-Hesi was discovered. It is perhaps fortunate that so much is left for future excavators.

A chance discovery made later just under the shadow of Tell Sandahanneh has revealed something of the wealth that belonged to ancient Marisa. Two profusely decorated tomb complexes, first publicly reported in June, 1902, were found to have belonged to Sidonian immigrants who settled here, probably in the third century B.C. The paintings which adorned the walls are not remarkable artistic productions. A frieze of animal figures which decorates one of the largest chambers is more indicative of imagination than zoological learning, but the inscriptions, some dated, were long unique, and they throw light on the architecture, the religious conceptions, and the cultural relations of the developing Hellenistic population of Palestine.

Other more beautiful tomb paintings and evidence that the practice was common through four or five centuries have since been discovered, but for twenty-five or thirty years the Marisa painted tombs were among the chief archaeological marvels of Palestine. A "columbarium" near by is another interesting evidence of Hellenistic occupation. One of the unique discoveries in the city was a series of limestone tablets bearing Greek magical formulae of execration such as are elsewhere usually found on sheets of lead. On the doorpost of one of the tombs are scribblings in Greek that appear to belong to a clandestine correspondence. The Greeks of Marisa were far from illiterate.

GEZER

The one great prewar undertaking in this region was at Tell Jezer, or Tell el-Jezereh, seventeen miles southeast of Jaffa, near the village of Abu Shusheh. For once there can be no problem of identification, for five different inscriptions have been found, the first two by Clermont-Ganneau in 1873, which appear to mark some boundary about the city. They bear the Hebrew words *t-h-m g-z-r*, "boundary of Gezer," and the name Alkios in Greek. The latter must be the city official under whom the boundaries were so marked.

Dr. R. A. S. Macalister carried on the whole enterprise, which covered the years 1902-08, without assistance except from a loyal and trustworthy Arab foreman. The results, published in three stately volumes, are a remarkable evidence of Macalister's industry and skill. Considering the little knowledge which anyone then had of Palestinian archaeology, it is no surprise that his conclusions have often had to be amended.

In one particular he was badly deceived, by a hiatus in the occupation of the site between the 9th and 6th centuries. Since no other excavated site had exhibited such material, he could not know that three centuries were wanting. Naturally his chronology went astray and lowered many of his dates disastrously. He also confused other painted pottery, some of it Middle Bronze, some of it Persian, with Philistine pottery. As a consequence, a large number of his tombs, as well as his strata, have to be redated between 1200 and 300 B.C. Fortunately, in spite of his lack of helpers, his records were so well kept and his reports so well published, though without adequate descriptions of the pottery in some cases, that it is possible to arrive at satisfactory results on the basis of the new information now available. Full statistical information, indeed, is not reported, and pottery wares are neglected. But that is equally true of the majority even of recent expeditions.

Some of Macalister's finds were sensational. The contents of over 200 tombs made a stately show. The Troglodytes, cave dwellers on the mound before 2500 B.C., were entirely new to Palestinian archaeology. The tunnel of the Middle Bronze Age, leading from within the city to a water supply underneath, was then paralleled only at Jerusalem. The great reservoir of a much later period, with a capacity of 2,000,000 gallons, has since been paralleled only at Tell ed-Duweir. The "sanctuary" with its row of standing monoliths was much more impressive and has a stronger claim to genuineness than that found at Tell es-Safi. Gezer was an extremely rich and instructive site.

A recent attempt was made by Mr. Alan Rowe on behalf of the Palestine Exploration Fund in 1934 to excavate part of the one third of the mound which Macalister did not attempt. For various reasons the results were not so exciting as to attract funds for the continuation of the task. Only a sustained effort with no expectation of sensational results and covering several seasons could adequately supplement what Macalister did.

The new discoveries that have now done so much more for Palestinian archaeology should not entirely efface the memory of these earlier efforts. Any adequate history of Israel must take full account of the results of the infant efforts of Palestinian archaeology, even though necessarily at the expense of redating the results and reinterpreting the conclusions then reached.

CHAPTER XI

BETH-SHAN

❖

Two great fortress cities in Central Palestine, Beth-shan and Megiddo, have been scientifically studied, but both are still far from fully excavated. Both are in positions of unusual strategic importance. Both played leading roles in the history of the Bronze and Iron Ages as fortresses guarding great trunk lines of commerce and military communication. In each case the present results of the excavations, both historical and archaeological, fully repay the efforts spent, for both were in expert hands. Much more may be expected from further digging. The expedition of the University of Pennsylvania Museum at Beth-shan did not assemble elaborate and permanent equipment as did that at Megiddo, but the reported results were at first much more spectacular and the first permanent publications came more rapidly. Therefore, for some time Beth-shan spoke more loudly than Megiddo.

Tell el-Husn, in ancient times Beth-shean, or Beth-shan, is one of the most imposing mounds in all the land. Beisan, the name now given to the modern Arab village which lies on the hill south of it, can be followed back through Aramaic to the Hebrew name, which means "house of (the god) Shan." Who "Shan" was no one knows—possibly a serpent god, but whoever he was, his city was one of the most strategically situated in all Palestine. From the standpoint of either economic or military strategy the position of Beth-shan is difficult to surpass. Especially in the Bronze Age, when the Jordan Valley was rich in cities, Beth-shan played a most influential role, as the discoveries of the last ten years have abundantly shown. The modern Arab name of the mound, Tell el-Husn (Hisn) "mound of the fortress," describes its character exactly. Quite in keeping with the strategic situation and commanding appearance of the mound have been the discoveries of the expedition, which has reveled in tombs, pottery, reliefs, inscriptions, and temples of striking interest and historical value. The tell has gathered and preserved a remarkable epitome of Palestine's crowded history and valuable souvenirs of its varied races.

The mound stands like an island on a low limestone hill in a narrow valley which the River Jalud, on its way to the Jordan, has worn in the plain that lies east of Mount Gilboa. The top of the tell before excavation began was 346 feet below sea level. As the land around it slopes rapidly from the south down to the River Jalud, which runs just north of the tell, the mound is 133 feet high on the south side and 212 feet on the north side, while the river itself is fifty feet lower still. The base of the oval mound is 900 feet long. Excavation has gone down through over 70 feet of debris.

The great necropolis on the hillside north of the river has proved to be of equal importance with the mound. Here tombs of all ages have been found and the booty has been unusually rich and historically instructive. As will be seen later, the finds in the necropolis have supplemented those on the mound in a remarkable fashion, from prehistoric times down to remarkably interesting Byzantine Christian remains. The city of the Hellenistic, Roman, and Christian eras, called Scythopolis, spreads far over the valley and plain to the south and west of the hill and much awaits the excavator there, a theater, a hippodrome, churches, and other buildings of the Roman and Byzantine periods. There must be somewhere an undiscovered Hebrew settlement. The expedition has worked only on the mound and on the ridge to the north where the necropolis lies.

A five-line notice in the University of Pennsylvania *Museum Journal* for March, 1921, announced the first large archaeological undertaking in Palestine after the first world war. It merely stated that Mr. C. S. Fisher would leave in May for

Palestine *via* Egypt to undertake excavation at Beisan. Thus unostentatiously one of the most productive excavations of recent years was inaugurated. Dr. Fisher, who finished his long course of service to archaeology in Jerusalem in the summer of 1941, had already had experience with the one great American expedition of prewar times in Palestine, the Harvard excavations at Samaria. He had also labored long in Egypt and Mesopotamia and had developed a comprehensive system for excavation and for the recording of results. This was, therefore, an auspicious beginning for American enterprise in Palestine.

For three years, from June, 1921, to the autumn of 1923, Dr. Fisher carried an almost impossible schedule, excavating in Egypt during the winter, and, when it was too hot to continue in Egypt, migrating to Beisan, where it was only less unpleasant. Dr. Fisher was succeeded by Mr. Alan Rowe and he by Mr. G. M. FitzGerald, both seasoned excavators. Altogether between 1921 and 1933 there have been ten campaigns of from two to five months each, about forty months all told.

Excavating in the necropolis was always dangerous because the stone of the hill, really only a marl, is very rotten, and casualties from caving roofs occurred. To the staff the greatest threat was malaria due to the spreading marshes about Beisan. Another difficult problem which the excavators faced at Beisan was that of securing small change for the payment of the workers. As the nearest bank is at Haifa, a trip of thirty or forty miles each way had to be made by slow train with an inconvenient schedule which spoiled two days, or else by automobile over most indifferent roads. In many an expedition the task of having a large sum in cash on hand each week-end is a really serious burden. A day or more on the road, sometimes with a police escort, is often required. At Beisan as many as 400 persons were on the payroll and much of the money had to be paid out in small silver coin. Every excavator has a multitude of small worries which waste time and strength in addition to others which are more strictly archaeological.

THE COURSE OF THE EXCAVATIONS

In the course of its ten campaigns the expedition has ranged through over 4000 years of history. At the beginning of the first campaign a trench was run down the north side of the mound in order to get some understanding of the chronology. The top level was then attacked and removed but, as digging went on, it became increasingly difficult to date some of the upper levels because of objects found which had been taken from lower strata and reused. A doorsill in a Byzantine building proved to be made from an Egyptian stela, probably of Seti I. Moreover, foundations and cisterns of the Byzantine, Roman, and Hellenistic periods went far down into Egyptian levels.

To remedy the confusion a smaller section on the south side of the tell was attacked and excavation carried down to a level dating at about 1500 B.C. This magnified sounding, measuring about 200 by 250 feet, and going down 43 feet, gave a chronological system which can now be used with some confidence, although it has not proved complete or final, and disclosed ten major periods, or strata, running from Arab times, after 636 A.D., back to the Hyksos, to about 1800 B.C. In 1933 a smaller sounding went down to virgin soil through 28 feet more of debris over an area measuring 52 by 80 feet, and added eight more strata, carrying the history of the mound's occupation back to the Middle Chalcolithic Age, before 3500 B.C.

THE ARAB, BYZANTINE, ROMAN AND HELLENISTIC CITY

The story of the "dig" is one of frequent surprises and continually expanding knowledge. First came the house walls of a town built by the Arabs after their conquest in 636 A.D. The houses, which showed at least two phases, were small and poorly built. One room used two small columns and white stucco to construct a *mihrab*, or prayer niche, which pointed in the direction of Mecca, and it may, therefore, be regarded as a mosque.

Under the rooms surrounding the "mosque" the excavators

came upon one of their great surprises. Curved walls and mosaic floors began to appear and eventually the plan of a magnificent circular cathedral emerged. This was quite unexpected because there had been no literary allusion to such a church at Beth-shan. Moreover the plan proved to be much more elaborate and better proportioned than those of the Anastasis (Constantine's Church of the Holy Sepulcher) or the famous cathedral at Bosra.

Beside the church was a monastery and a bishop's house and below it the remains of a rectangular basilica of early Christian times. On the hill to the north above the necropolis a more pretentious monastery, built of basalt blocks and given by (or for) "our Lady Mary," was found. It had numerous mosaic floors elaborately designed and bearing inscriptions which date it probably in 568-9 A.D. The nave of the monastery chapel was paved with mosaic medallions containing 82 birds of many kinds. The central court had a large circular panel, at the center of which was a medallion showing busts of figures representing the sun with a rayed crown, and the moon with a crescent, each holding a flaming torch. Radiating from this center were twelve panels each showing a human figure engaged in an occupation characteristic of one of the twelve months. The name of each month and the number of its days is given. A noteworthy discovery was a hoard of gold coins of Tiberius, Phocas, and Heraclius and a gold chain, or girdle, "with a filigree medallion and flat leaf-shaped links bearing a faintly incised design." There was also a gold bracelet and a bronze censer. It is supposed they were hidden at the time of the Arab conquest.

With the second and third campaigns, in 1922 and 1923, it began to appear that the great Christian basilica on the mound had usurped the place of a pagan temple, which had been razed and broken up to provide a site and building material for the church. The temple may have been built originally at the beginning of the third century B.C., for two columns bore finely executed inscriptions containing the name of Demetrius while a hoard of silver coins of Ptolemy Soter I suggest that this Demetrius was Polyorcetes, King of Macedonia from 294-289 B.C. There was much evidence of rebuilding in Roman times. A fine head, two gigantic toes, and a finger joint show that a statue 25 feet high, possibly of Dionysus, possibly of Zeus, probably adorned the temple. In a tomb in the necropolis a sarcophagus was found bearing the name "Antiochus son of Phallion son of Baboas," who may have been an uncle of Herod the Great. The little that was found agrees with the various literary allusions to Scythopolis in indicating that the city in Graeco-Roman times must have been one of the most important in Palestine. In the Byzantine period its walls, which are mentioned in two Greek inscriptions of the time of Anastasius, dated between 508 and 510 A.D., went far out around the monasteries on the northern hill and the city on the southern plateau, giving it a truly magnificent area.

The Hebrew, Philistine, and Egyptian Periods

The difficulty of arriving at satisfactory chronological results by the trench method, even when the trench is as large as that here excavated, is emphasized by the fact that the dates of several strata in the Late Bronze Age had to be revised in the light of evidence discovered only a few months after Rowe published the first volume of the final report.[1] But Albright and FitzGerald have agreed on a fairly satisfactory chronology. When the Philistine stratum (V) begins is uncertain. Its temples were standing in the time of Saul, according to Rowe, and may have continued in use in Hebrew times. Therefore, it appears that the period comes to an end at the latest when the Israelites took the city, probably in David's reign. FitzGerald found walls which seem to belong to the Israelite period and it is to be hoped much more may appear to fill in the great void which makes up stratum IV, a shallow layer in the section first excavated. Surely so important a site cannot have lain unoccupied during all the period of the Hebrew monarchies.

[1] Reference to the chart on p. 83 will assist in following this discussion.

Something ought to appear also to mark the presence of the
Scythians, if it was they who gave the city the name Scythopolis, by which it was known during the Hellenistic, Roman, and
Byzantine periods. The uncovering of the remainder of the
mound and excavation on the plain to the south may provide
sensations equal to those of the campaigns which have already
been undertaken.

The finds in strata V to IX are so rich as to defy summary
description. Their invaluable contribution to Palestinian history can be best presented by briefly describing various features: temples, defenses, stelae and inscriptions, tombs, and
pottery; and then recapitulating the history of the city.

TEMPLES

The great mound has preserved a remarkable series of religious edifices. A Moslem mosque, below that a Christian
church, and below that again a Roman and Hellenistic temple;
then after a long hiatus the most complete series of Canaanite
temples yet discovered, five different levels and periods and at
least six sanctuaries. What may appear elsewhere in the mound
and at still lower levels remains to be seen. Surely an Israelite
sanctuary will come to light in some other place. It was remarkably good judgment which led Rowe to choose, not the
northwestern edge of the mound as Sir Flinders Petrie does,
but the southern end for his plunge into its depths, for he hit
upon the citadel of the successive periods of Egyptian rule
and therefore uncovered its most important buildings, sacred
and military.

The temples throw a flood of light upon the religion of the
Canaanites whom the Israelites supplanted and absorbed, for
they were built during a period when Egypt was strongly under
Syrian influence and, though erected by Egyptian officials,
they exhibit Canaanite worship under a thin veneer. As the
Egyptians loved to describe and picture themselves, their life,
and their gods on their monuments, the stelae which they
erected at Beth-shan furnish invaluable information regarding

the Semitic deities who were venerated there. There are remarkable similarities between the arrangement and furniture of these sanctuaries and those of the temples of Solomon and Ezekiel. Rowe was fortunate in having excavated in Egypt, for he recognized at once striking parallels with that land. Evidently the worship of the Hebrews was not unlike that of their neighbors, except in details.

The temples, all of which were of adobe brick, were quite irregular in plan and unmethodical in structure. Two belong to stratum IX (late fourteenth and early thirteenth century), one each to strata VII and VI (thirteenth and twelfth centuries), and two to stratum V (twelfth and eleventh centuries). To describe each of these would require a disproportionate amount of space. Usually there were stone foundations, but in spots these might be wanting. In the earliest temples (stratum IX) not enough was preserved to determine the roofing. But, in the others, walls, steps, and stone bases for pillars of stone or wood were sufficiently preserved to enable Mr. Rowe and Père Vincent, guided by the better-preserved ruins of Egyptian temples, to reconstruct their walls and roofs as well as floor plans with a high degree of probability. The uses of the various rooms, and many details such as the altars, offering slabs, places of sacrifice, and fire places for cooking the meat for sacrificial feasts could be determined.

Numerous cult objects came to light. In a small room or courtyard of stratum IX at one side of the southern temple there was a perfectly preserved massebah, a plain truncated cone of basalt, about a foot and eight inches high resting on a base of unhewn stones. It shows a type of the baetyl, or *bethel* ("house of God"), such as Jacob worshipped and anointed with oil (Gen 28.18-22) and the prophets so vehemently denounced.

This simple phallic emblem was enough for a Canaanite, but the Egyptian demanded something more realistic. A stela found in 1925 not far way in stratum IX not only names the deity but pictures him. He was Mekal, "lord of Beth-shan," a name entirely new to the Palestinian pantheon and heretofore known only from Cypriote inscriptions of a thousand years later, which identify Reshep-Mekal with Apollo Amyclaeus. Seated on a throne, he holds the *was* scepter of "happiness" in his left hand, and the *ankh* sign of "life," the crux ansata, in his right. His face is Armenoid, or Semitic, with a long pointed beard. He wears an ornamented collar and a high conical hat with two small horns in front and two long streamers behind. One streamer falls from the lofty point of the cone, the other from the lower edge behind. His attire relates him to Babylon and also to Sutekh, or Seth, as pictured on a Nineteenth or Twentieth Dynasty stela found by Petrie in Sinai. In front of the god stand Amenemopet (or Amanappa), the "builder," and his son, Paraëmheb, who set up the stela for his father. Below the figures is a prayer in hieroglyphics asking for prosperity, health, honor, and love. The stela thus set up by the baetyl, or massebah, shows that the temple is a Canaanite high place adapted to Egyptian uses. The deity and his attire illustrate the striking syncretism of the period of Akhnaton and the Ramessides, to which the stratum belongs.

Near by another discovery was made which is artistically much more imposing. A great wall which enclosed the southern end of the tell just beyond the corridor of the temple ended in three towers. In debris between the outer two was found a basalt slab three feet high with a remarkably fine relief. In the upper panel are a dog and a lion apparently in fierce combat. In the lower panel the dog is biting the lion above his withers and the lion is apparently roaring and trying to make off with his tail between his legs. According to Rowe, the lion is the animal of Nergal, god of plague and pestilence. The dog was widely regarded in various parts of the Near East but especially in Assyria as a defense against evil. Here he is the guardian of the temple against the attacks of Nergal. This interpretation has been attacked on the grounds that, since the stela was found in debris, its connection with the temple is uncertain and that there is nothing in the scene itself to give it religious significance. Kurt Galling regards it as a purely decorative scene and would apparently give it a later date. The relief should have religious significance or a mythological reference. But Rowe's explanation seems forced. The art of the panel is, in any case, closely connected with that of the Mitannian country, or with Assyria and Babylonia. Garstang says, "This carving is a veritable link between Babylonia and Egypt, indeed between East and West; and the nearest prototypes are to be found in northern Mesopotamia."[2]

In stratum VIII many cult objects were found but no sacred edifice. The next temple belongs to the period of Ramses II, stratum VII. Apparently the city had shrunk in importance and in size, for the temple, the residence of the commandant, and a little fort all together cover hardly more ground than the great irregular temple that belongs to stratum IX. So small a fort and temple suit the decadent Nineteenth Dynasty. They reflect the weakness of Egyptian rule in Palestine and the revival of Palestinian influence. The temple, set up above the ruins of the preceding one and probably sacred to Mekal, was little more than a small shrine and must have closely resembled tomb chapels and shrines which have been found in Syria at Marath and in Egypt at Amarna, and dating from the time of the heretic king, Akhnaton. Since many of Akhnaton's peculiar religious ideas may have come from Syria or Palestine, it is an attractive surmise that these temples are indigenous to Syria and borrowed by Egypt.

Though in this level no separate second temple was found, undoubtedly the goddess who is called 'Anat, or Astarte, was worshiped, for there was a stela, dedicated by a woman worshiper, showing "Astarte of the two horns," who wears a lyre-shaped headdress with two horns at the base and a long flowing robe, while in her right hand is the *ankh* and in her left a scepter. Of the pottery serpent-cult remains found, nearly all represented an upright uraeus-like serpent on a small stand. On one of the serpents the breasts of a woman were represented

---

[2] *Hittite Empire* (London: 1929), 331.

with a cup below, unambiguous symbol of an earth-born goddess of fertility.

The temple erected in stratum VI stood exactly over that of stratum VIII, of which it was almost a copy, with minor modifications of the outlying court and storerooms. Under its walls was a foundation deposit containing scarabs with cartouches of the ephemeral pharaoh, Ramses I (1315-1314 B.C.), Seti's father and predecessor. The date of building must, therefore, be placed after the time when father and son reigned conjointly for a year in 1314 B.C., whether immediately or many years thereafter depends upon the pottery and other objects found, and they point to a century later, as Albright and FitzGerald agree.

It is difficult to determine when this temple was destroyed and the next built. Stelae of Seti I and Ramses II, set up beside the temple in the next level, with a statue of Ramses III and inscriptions mentioning him, at first suggested that a city which Ramses II built over the ruins of that of his father persisted without radical change for nearly 300 years (1292-1000 B.C.). This conclusion, a startling one in view of the short life of the previous cities, has been altered by consideration of various facts, including the pottery. A lintel bearing the name of Ramses III, at first explained as representing a rebuilding, is now regarded as the original lintel of the temple in stratum V. It must therefore have been built after the accession of Ramses III in 1198 B.C. It could not have remained under Egyptian control long after his death in 1167 B.C. and apparently fell into the hands of the Philistines without a struggle. They held it perhaps for three-quarters of a century, until David overthrew their rule sometime after 1000 B.C.[3]

For several reasons the temples of stratum V are among the most interesting discoveries made at Beisan. The larger part of the many cult objects which shed a flood of light on the history of Palestinian religion came from above the floors of these

[3] The dates given in the table on p. 83 are those of Albright and FitzGerald, which lower Rowe's original calculations by a century or more.

buildings. They give, therefore, an unparalleled exposition of the type of worship in which the Israelites of the times often joined and from which the prophets could not fully rescue them.

The temples were built on the same spot which had long been sacred, but instead of being oriented roughly north and south, as the previous temples had been, they now faced the east—a significant change. They were much more spacious than those of strata VII and VI and better built than that of stratum IX. The southern temple may have still been dedicated to Mekal as in the Amarna period, but there is no evidence except a serpentine cylinder seal which pictures Ramses II shooting at two bound captives—brave king!—and opposite him a deity who in some particulars resembles Mekal, but was thought to be Reshep. However, Rowe now regards him as Seth.

The northern temple was clearly that of a goddess, for in it an Egyptian gentleman named Hesi-Nekht had dedicated a stela showing a tall slender figure with a high plumed crown, the *was* scepter of "happiness" in her left hand, the *ankh*, the crux ansata, or sign of "life," in her right. Before her crown are two lines of hieroglyphic text reading, "'Antit ('Anat), the queen of heaven, the mistress of the gods." She is essentially the Astarte whom Jeremiah's compatriots were worshiping hundreds of years later (Jer 44.19), the Astarte also of stratum VII, though her name and some of her attributes may have varied.

The objects found on the temple floors reveal the peculiar character of the Beth-shan goddess. She was of a type that had not before been discovered in Palestine, a serpent goddess of fertility. Her reptilian character was indicated by several incense or flower stands of pottery, models of buildings, and boxes over which spotted snakes molded in clay were crawling. Not less significant were numerous clay models of serpents of the uraeus type, some with female breasts represented on the lower part of the expanded hood. A considerable number of these were found in Level VIII, where no temple was discovered.

The serpent stone at 'En-Rogel, the Nehushtan in Solomon's temple, the serpent stela found at Tell Beit Mirsim,[4] and various objects with crawling serpents from 'Ain Shems and Jericho show how widespread was the serpent cult of which Beth-shan may have been the center. Future discoveries and the complete study and publication of results may make it possible to follow the development of the various cults. Probably one feature predominated at one time, at another some other peculiarity of ritual or iconic representation. Throughout the history of the site, however, the Ba'al and Ba'alat were worshiped under various forms.

Pottery stands for flowers or for incense, some ornamented with figures of doves, or other birds, and a ring-shaped *kernos*, a circular tube with six small vases at even distances opening into it, also doubtless for flowers, suggest something of the more beautiful side of Canaanite worship. The dedication of wealth to Ba'al is illustrated by the discovery of a pot full of gold and silver ingots weighing six pounds avoirdupois against the stone base of the central column of the temple of stratum V, and against the opposite base on the south side a pot with five pounds of silver ingots and jewelry.

Peculiar interest is lent to the temples of stratum V by the fact that they were standing when Saul's headless body was affixed to the walls of Beth-shan after his tragic death at Mount Gilboa only five miles away. Rowe supposes that the temple of 'Anat which he uncovered is the very "house of the Ashtaroth" in which Saul's armor was presented as an offering, while his head was carried about, as a visible evidence of victory, through the Philistine cities which then spread widely throughout all the plains of Palestine. That the "southern temple" at Beth-shan is to be called the "house of Dagon," as suggested by 1 Chronicles 10.10, has no evidence to support it. To the writer of Chronicles, Dagon was the Philistine male deity while Ashtaroth stood for female deities in general, and, since Ashtaroth

4 See above, pp. 89 f.

is a Canaanite, not a Philistine, word, he puts "gods" in its place.[5]

Strangely enough, on this "mound of the fortress" no enclosing walls earlier than Byzantine times have been found. But a *migdal*, or "tower," was found in stratum VII. It had extremely heavy walls and buttresses. Egyptian pictures of Canaanite cities make a restoration possible. It was probably the redoubt in which foreign mercenaries could defend themselves against revolts from within or incursions from without.

STELAE AND INSCRIPTIONS

Beth-shan has been remarkable for Egyptian stelae and inscriptions. Several have already been mentioned because of their religious interest. Royal historical inscriptions have been equally valuable. As yet none of Thutmose III have come to light, although a fragment probably belonging to the great conqueror has been found at Tell el-'Oreimeh by the Plain of Gennesaret only twenty-five miles away to the north and another at Byblos.

With the reign of Seti I there begins at Beth-shan a series of remarkable stelae which have been among the most highly prized discoveries of the expedition. Two belong to Seti I. They prove that the records which Seti's scribes wrote of his conquests were no idle boasts, and they also throw interesting light on various topographical and historical problems.

Most intriguing of all are possible references to the Hebrew tribes. The second stela mentioned above, which is dated in the first year of Seti's reign, is the account of the repulse of a coalition of local dynasts who were threatening Egyptian rule. The cities mentioned are in the Jordan Valley and include Pella, just across the river to the southeast of Beth-shan. The other, very fragmentary stela, in a passage which is badly

---

[5] The succession of phrases beginning with *beth* would explain such an omission. Cf. Eissfeldt in Baudissin, *Kyrios*, IV (1929), 212; G. P. Hedley, "'The Temple of Dagon' at Beth-shan," *AJA*, XXX (1929), 34 ff. Dr. Hedley argues plausibly that the two temples of the verse are not at Beth-shan, but in the "land of the Philistines."

broken, seems to refer to the " 'Apiru of the mountain of the Jordan." And the 'Apiru, who are mentioned elsewhere in Egyptian texts are, in all probability, the Habiru, or Hebrews. Probably, therefore, the passage refers to Hebrew tribes from the mountains who are seeking more room either west of the Jordan in the plains of Jezreel or eastward in the Hauran. Is it possible to identify these 'Apiru with the tribe of Manasseh, who "did not drive out the inhabitants of Beth-shan and her towns"?

A nine-foot stela of Ramses II, dated in his ninth year, is so worn as to be illegible in places. Much of what can be read is the ordinary commonplace of Egyptian royal inscriptions, vainglorious boastings of the power of the king, the fear he inspires, the enemies he overcomes, his care for the widow, the weak, and the poor, and his might as a warrior. A reference to the city Per-Ramses was reported to confirm the biblical story that it was built by the Hebrews, and was immediately seized upon by the press as a most significant matter. Unfortunately, though the city is mentioned, and also "the Asiatics," there is no allusion to the building of the city, nor are Asiatics, or Shashu (the "Bedouin"), mentioned in the same connection with the city. The strange distrust of the Bible, which leads many good people to seek "confirmation" of its history with such indiscreet avidity, constantly betrays them into the false position of accepting any apparent corroboration, whether based on fact or not. The desire to appeal to support from this direction not infrequently leads excavators to discover such "confirmations" in their imaginations.

The city of stratum V was decorated with a remarkable array of Egyptian monuments. Besides two complete stelae of Seti I and Ramses II, there had been at least two other royal stelae, for their bases were found. Various other fragments came to light. In 1925 a funeral stela bearing the name of another Amenemopet, a royal official, was found near the west end of the southern temple. Strangely enough Amenemopet is the name of a trained Egyptian scribe, called a *maher*, a Canaanite word meaning "swift," who, in an Egyptian piece of light literature, is taunted with his ignorance of Palestine, where he is to lead an Egyptian army. "Let him instruct us regarding the appearance of Kanah," runs one sentence, "acquaint us with Rehob, explain Beth-shan and Tirkel. How does one cross the Jordan? How does one pass Megiddo?" Could it be that the Amenemopet buried in Beth-shan lost his life because of the ignorance and incompetence which made him eventually the butt of the Egyptian satire? Unfortunately for the identification, the name is a common one.

TOMBS

The necropolis of Beth-shan, on the north bank of the River Jalud, had preserved most interesting finds. The hill consists of a soft marl, rendering the excavation of tomb chambers easy, but their destruction equally so. Later tomb builders dug into earlier broken chambers, and often left the floors or ceilings too thin. Therefore, the slope reveals a mad medley of early and late, with Byzantine stone sarcophagi lying in Bronze Age burial chambers.

The earliest tombs, of the Early Bronze Age, were rude, more or less circular chambers. They were followed by Late Bronze or Early Iron chambers which were roughly rectangular, sometimes with several connecting rooms.

In 1922 Fisher found the first of the anthropoid, slipper-shaped coffins to be discovered in Palestine. Others were found by Rowe in 1926 and by FitzGerald in 1930. Those at Beisan were of the same general type as those found at Tell el-Far'ah and already described, but they have been much more numerous. Some of the faces have the eyes opened, others closed. Some wear a sort of crown or frontlet. A beaded band encircles the forehead. The nose is long and Armenoid. One in which a woman's skeleton was found was much more feminine in appearance, with a broad flat nose. Practically no jewelry was found in any of the sarcophagi, but there were stirrup vases, pilgrim flasks, and other Mediterranean pottery, along with

Canaanite lamps, and Egyptian amulets and scarabs. In one there was found a lozenge-shaped gold-foil mouthpiece with a hole at each end by which it was to be tied over the mouth of the deceased. Similar mouthpieces have been found in Cyprus and other places which had been under the influence of Egyptian civilization. In some of the burials were Egyptian *ushebti* figures. This remarkable mixture of Aegean, Palestinian, and Egyptian articles is exactly what could be expected of mercenaries from the Aegean isles serving Egypt under Egyptian officers in the land of Palestine. It is a parallel to the use of the Mekal and 'Anat sanctuaries by Egyptians and later by the Philistines. As these mercenaries must have been in Beth-shan long before the coming of the "sea-peoples" at the beginning of the twelfth century, so-called Philistine pottery and weapons may antedate the Early Iron Age, but there is no stratigraphic evidence for this assumption.

From the point of view of the scientific excavator, Beth-shan has been remarkably fruitful because its stelae and its multitude of scarabs, seals, and other datable objects have allowed a fresh study of the chronology of Palestinian pottery, and that in a part of the country where no considerable excavation had hitherto been undertaken. All is far from simple even at Beth-shan, as the difficulty with the dating of stratum V and the meager returns from stratum IV indicate. The mixture of pottery in the tombs due to the intrusion of later tombs into the areas of earlier burials has been confusing. Flat-bottomed, ledge-handle jars of the Early Bronze Age have been found along with the slipper-coffins of Aegean mercenaries. But the pottery from the four temple levels can usually be dated with remarkable accuracy and its early publication has been a great boon to other excavators.

THE EARLIEST REMAINS

In several places in the neighborhood Stone Age remains had been found, and all three excavators came upon evidence here and there of prehistoric occupation. Nothing definite was known, however, until, in his last brief campaign in 1933, Fitz-Gerald went down to virgin soil on the south side of the mound.

He found the strata in the lower part of the sounding practically horizontal, as if the original surface had been artificially leveled. First there were pits of unknown origin. Then follow six strata (XVIII-XIII) which may cover over a thousand years. The next stratum (XII) is marked and dated—relatively if not absolutely—by the lustrous burnished red and black pottery called Khirbet Kerak ware because it was first noticed by Albright in the mound of that name just at the southern end of the Sea of Galilee by the Jordan outlet. This period and the next (XI), therefore, can be equated practically with stratum III, City II, of Jericho. Juglets with stump bases show them to be contemporary with Tomb A at Jericho, while the folded-over, or envelope type of ledge handle suggests stratum I at Tell Beit Mirsim. All this places the two strata between 2600 or 2500 and 1900 B.C.

Stratum X was first discovered in 1931 during the inception of the sounding completed in 1933. As the workmen dug down below stratum IX, the fragments of Cypriote painted ware and milk-bowl fragments characteristic of the Late Bronze Age gave way to an entirely different type of pottery, carinated bowls and bowls with three loop feet, lamps without pronounced spout, characteristic Hyksos scarabs, and at a low level "Syro-Hittite" cylinder seals. There was much rebuilding, yet apparently no destruction, but only continuous occupation running back possibly into the nineteenth century. A stamped jar handle and many scarabs of Hyksos origin were found also in the necropolis in 1931.

In all of these strata, from X to XVIII, the areas excavated were not sufficient to establish any city plan, and the objects of intrinsic interest discovered were comparatively few. But, compared typologically with strata in other mounds, they were sufficient to show the general character of the occupation of the mound and to assist materially in defining ceramic chronology.

Like the discoveries in the necropolis and elsewhere on the mound, they promise much to the future excavator.

THE HISTORY OF BETH-SHAN

The excavations have revealed the checkered fortunes of the city through over 4000 years. The earliest settlement falls between 4000 and 3500 B.C., and parallels the earliest stratum at Megiddo. As it is contemporary only with stratum VIII at Jericho, it falls far short of the antiquity of that city, which is only sixty miles south of it. Apparently the city's fortunes followed much the same pattern as those of Jericho and Megiddo until the beginning of the Eighteenth Dynasty in Egypt. It was occupied by the Hyksos as were other Palestinian cities. But when the Egyptians conquered it, it passed into a new phase of history which is not as yet paralleled elsewhere, though Megiddo should reveal the same conditions when its strata VI to X are more fully excavated.

During three or four hundred years in the most critical period of its history (1350-950 B.C.) the series of temples and migdals uncovered on the southern end of the mound show how important Egyptian relations and Egyptian rule were. But the discoveries on the mound and in the necropolis prove that the Hittites and Babylonia also were competing with Egypt. Babylonian influence is typified in the lion-dog relief from the Mekal temple in stratum IX. An ax and dagger of typical Hittite pattern, between forty and fifty Syro-Hittite cylinder seals, and a small bronze figure that seems to represent Teshub, the Hittite storm deity, testify to the penetration of Hittite culture especially in the age of Ramses II, stratum VII. The anthropoid sarcophagi show that Aegean civilization, probably through mercenaries fighting for Egypt, was also making its impression on Palestine. That the Philistines controlled this part of Palestine for a long period, after the death of Ramses III and the withdrawal of Egyptian control, is not proved by the discoveries. So-called Philistine pottery is wanting. Neither has any considerable evidence yet been discovered for Israelite settlements on the mound. Its history is a blank until Hellenistic influence appears perhaps in the third century B.C.

Then the main occupation, as probably in the Hebrew period, lay elsewhere and so continued until this day, although the mound itself testifies to intensive occupation by its important buildings and eventually its walls all through the Hellenistic, Roman, Byzantine, and early Arab periods.

The deep foundations laid for Hellenistic, Roman, and Byzantine structures above have destroyed much of the evidence for all of these later periods and may be responsible for the thinness of the Israelite period of Level IV which succeeds. At the moment, archaeology is compelled to leave the history of Bethshan practically a blank for 700 years, from 1000 to 300 B.C., when the Hellenistic buildings appear, just as the Bible and other written records do. It had its brief period of glorious life during Egyptian rule, and waited long for a resurrection, which again came, not from an indigenous population, but from a foreign occupation.

CHAPTER XII

ARMAGEDDON AND SOLOMON
THE HORSE TRADER

❖

THE well-trained eyes of an Egyptian *reis* made the first important discovery during the excavations of the Oriental Institute of the University of Chicago at Megiddo. While the local workmen were moving a dump heap left by Schumacher's expedition of 1903-05, the Egyptian foreman discovered fragments of a stela in the rubbish. In this case, the hieroglyphics named Sheshonk as the monarch in whose honor it was erected and for the first time provided contemporary evidence that the attack in the reign of Rehoboam by Shishak, as the Bible calls him, was not a mere raid for booty, but resulted at least in the temporary establishment of Egyptian garrisons on Palestinian soil. Possibly this very campaign was due to the horse trading of which the new expedition was to uncover the evidence. The discovery of this fragmentary stela was a happy augury of the eventual success of the expedition undertaken at the instance of the late Dr. James H. Breasted, premier American Egyptologist.

Megiddo, although merely one of several imposing mounds which dominate the southern edge of the plain of Esdraelon, is by far the most famous of all. The first battle ever so described as to render its strategy intelligible to modern study was fought at Megiddo on April 18, 1479, and according to the Book of Revelation, the last great battle is to be fought at Armageddon, the "mountain of Megiddo." Apparently the role which it played in Palestinian history for over a thousand years was so important and the battles fought around it were so momentous that its reputation remained when its site was forgotten. Eusebius, for example, had no suggestion as to where it lay. Yet the mound which the Arabs know as Tell el-Mutesellim so exactly fits all the data of the literary sources that no dispute as to its identification has arisen.

Like Beth-shan, Megiddo lay at a crossing of the ways. North of it stretches the plain of Esdraelon, which is alike one of the ancient world's great battlefields and one of Palestine's richest grain fields. South of it the great prolongation of the Central Mountain Range which ends in the imposing promontory of Carmel runs like a mighty wall of defense across the roads which connect Africa and Asia. Just behind it is the mouth of the Wadi 'Arah, which is the most direct of the three or four passes across the ridge. Megiddo closes the gate through the wall. Through the pass came Thutmose III on that first historical battle of Megiddo. At Megiddo Josiah lost his life. Through the pass came Allenby in 1918 to turn the enemy flank and drive the Turkish army, with its commander in his pyjamas, in disorder from the field. If General von Sanders had known his history as well as Allenby did, he would not have left this narrow wadi unguarded, just as the Canaanite allies opposing Thutmose III did 3500 years earlier.

When the present expedition began, the mound was not a virgin site as was Tell el-Husn at Beisan. From 1903-1905 Gottlieb Schumacher with some assistance from Immanuel Benzinger, conducted excavations at Megiddo for the Deutsche Orientgesellschaft. The labors of Schumacher and his editors Professors Carl Steuernagel and Carl Watzinger, have not been entirely fruitless. But he really introduced confusion and darkness instead of order and light into Palestinian archaeology and history, just as the excavations at Jericho had done. The excavators who have now undertaken the task find that the trenches dug across the tell have destroyed evidence which in many places they urgently need in order to explain the facts they discover. It gives one pause. Will archaeologists a generation hence pronounce the same blessing on the excavators who have recently been so ruthlessly ravishing the mounds of Palestine and blithely reconstructing its history out of their imaginations? It has been suggested that the Antiquities ordinance should require a small but essential part of each tell to be left to future generations.

THE ORIENTAL INSTITUTE EXPEDITION

The Oriental Institute expedition is using every precaution to secure a favorable verdict from posterity. Schumacher worked for but two years. The Chicago expedition was organized on a twenty-five year plan. It was equipped with every scientific device and conducted according to every rule that should insure correct historical results and a favorable verdict from posterity. No similar expedition could show a better equipment or more systematic method, and the work was conducted with necessary thoroughness. It was no hasty holiday for a bored professor. Indeed Mr. Guy once confessed, in a moment of pessimism, that it seemed as if it would require, not twenty-five, but fifty years. Archaeologists complained of the paucity of published reports. But why should an expedition which did not depend upon public subscriptions rush into print with ill-digested theories and sensational blurbs which, if the excavator is honest, are only to be retracted in the final scientific report? The recent publication of elaborate and magnificent reports and of several smaller studies now places Megiddo in advance of all other Palestinian expeditions.

Simple but comfortable stone buildings were erected in which the staff could live with comforts such as they enjoy at home. When it is remembered that year after year they spent nine or ten months at this spot in the country miles away from the nearest city, Haifa, which to an American is not a cultural center, and that they were cut off from contacts with other people except for visitors who rushed in for an hour or two to be led over the tell and told a story which, however thrilling to the listener, must become old to the director, it is possible to appreciate the need for some of the amenities of civilization. There is now a macadamized highway to Haifa, but there was one winter when the roads were impassable, except on horseback, for two months. Archaeologists also have nerves. The ladies who followed their husbands to Megiddo deserve unlimited sympathy. In the beginning malaria was a deadly menace. During the 1926 campaign the High Commissioner of Palestine, the late Lord Plumer, called on the expedition only to find every member of the staff in bed with fever. This enemy to human life in Esdraelon was finally restrained, if not defeated, by the combined attacks of the Government, the expedition, and the Jewish colonies.

A manual on archaeological method would describe the scientific equipment of this ideal expedition in detail: long ranges of shelves to store the pottery and other small objects; the excellent library; well-lighted rooms with tables and all other equipment for drawing and recording; the fine studio for photographing and reconstruction on the north side of the building; the large, airy, and fully equipped darkroom. It is impossible even to enumerate the various devices for insuring accuracy in the records. There was even a captive balloon which carried up a camera to do the aerial photography which so greatly assists the excavator in getting a true and comprehensive conception of the scattered and confusing structures on his large area. After starting with half the mound and excavating to some two or three meters of depth, through three layers of occupation, the expedition purchased the mound from Mrs. Laurence Oliphant —to become eventually the property of the Palestine government—and a complete stratum over the entire tell was removed before the next was attacked.

The task of excavating Tell el-Mutesellim is really a formidable one. To be sure, it cannot compare with Tell el-ʿAjjul or Tell el-Qedah (Hazor). Yet the summit covers about fifteen acres, and the slopes add perhaps thirty-five acres more. The depth of deposit runs as high as seventy-two feet. The mound was under excavation from 1925 to 1939, fourteen of the contemplated twenty-five years, when the war brought the work to an end. Dr. Fisher in 1926 and 1927, then Mr. P. L. O. Guy until 1934, and Mr. Gordon Loud from 1935 to 1939 as directors conducted campaigns each autumn and spring, for some five or six months a year. All had had sufficient previous experience to be entirely competent and they had groups of capable assistants, many of them Americans trained at the Oriental Institute. But the task is actually only well begun.

If one is to move a mountain, he must consider where it is to be put. When Dr. Fisher undertook the excavation of the tell at Dr. Breasted's request in 1925, his first care was to find a place for the tremendous mass of earth of which the hill consisted. He decided upon the slopes to the east, where there is considerable rock outcrop and not much depth of earth. But as there were tomb entrances already visible, this space had first to be investigated lest valuable materials be hidden beyond hope of recovery. Through all of the subsequent campaigns the gradual clearance of these tombs provided a constant stream of skeletons, pottery, and other objects which tell their stories of the people who have lived on the hill above. They provided also the first great volume of reports. A light railway was used to carry the earth and discarded stones across the mound itself. To carry the debris down the steep slope of the mound a wooden chute and later two large round chutes of steel were constructed. At the bottom the earth dropped through a sort of damper into cars on another light railway by which it was carried out to the edge of a constantly growing mound. After the stones came to rest, they had to be piled by hand in places where they would not interfere with new arrivals.

THE HISTORY OF THE TELL

The soundings of the prewar expedition and the finds in the tombs and on the slopes of the tell, along with the literary sources, gave a sufficient outline of what the excavator might expect to find. Open-air stations in the plain are thought to tell of Acheulean occupation. Polished stone implements in the lowest stratum and on the slopes of the mound come from Late Stone Age or Chalcolithic peoples. The tombs on the eastern side of the tell and a large sounding in the mound itself have recorded the presence of men in all periods from Early Bronze down to Hellenistic times. Indeed, an early Byzantine tomb with fine glass vessels was found, but its occupants must have come from the neighboring Roman city, now called Lejjun, from the Roman "legion" which had its camp near by. Occupation on the top of the mound ceased in the fourth or fifth century B.C.

Publication has now exhibited many illustrations of the wealth of the material which was found in the tombs and on the mound. Early Bronze Age jars with their wavy ledge handles, a scarab of Sesostris I (1980-1935 B.C.), pottery of peculiar shapes showing Mesopotamian or Persian influence, fine tomb groups with numerous Hyksos scarabs, Cypriote pottery with its characteristic shapes, decorations, and wish-bone handles, seals of the Israelite period, all of these and much more have been found.

There were numerous infant burials in jars which had been broken so that the tiny body might be inserted along with small jars or jugs to provide the soul with food and drink on its long journey. As Guy rightly insists, these are not sacrifices. Indeed, the burials often suggest the love and care which followed the dead long after their departure. Basalt libation bowls were sometimes left above the tombs so that the living might return with frequent offerings. A mother was found buried with an infant in her arms and a child at her feet.

Excavation over the entire tell went down to the fourth stratum. The agricultural soil at the top was so thin that plowing and the taking of stones for building in nearby villages had seriously disturbed stratum I.[1] English pennies, Hellenistic lamps, and Iron Age pottery all were found within a few inches of the surface. Obviously, however, though the pottery showed evidence of Greek influence, the city had not been occupied during the Hellenistic period and had been an unwalled town of small importance after the Babylonian conquest, for the foundations discovered did not point to buildings of consequence.

According to the most recent publications, stratum II, which

[1] See the chart on p. 83.

Beth-shan: Mound before excavation began. Excavation began toward the left (north) end of picture, went over top, and deepest at right (south) end.

Megiddo: Moving a mountain. Margin of mound full of tombs cleared for the dump which grows beside the mound at right. Automobile road in right foreground.

The hill of Samaria from the south.

A portion of the Roman basilica; figures in the apse.

belongs to the last half or two thirds of the seventh century, and stratum III below it actually represent one long period, perhaps 125 or 175 years, of continuous occupation. The stratum II city followed its predecessor in being regularly laid out in blocks of houses, and both were prosperous, crowded places. Both strata, and especially the later one, show much, often planless, building and rebuilding of individual houses. There was no general destruction at any time. Apparently the country was either fairly safe, or the energies of the people fell to a low level, or, more probably, the Assyrians prohibited repairs to the great city wall, for it was allowed to fall into ruins and city II had no protection except a fortress which in part overlaid the wall on the east side of the mound. It is the city in which Josiah met his fate at the hands of Pharaoh Necho, ally of the Assyrian monarch whom Josiah had been antagonizing by his religious reforms. Possibly city II was destroyed in 609 B.C., when Josiah was killed.

Stratum III was built upon the ruins of city IV after no great lapse of time, for the debris between the two was nowhere deep. It may owe its rebuilding to the prosperity of Jeroboam II. But it was not distinguished by any remarkable buildings, though the walls of city IV seemed to have survived. It seems more likely, therefore, that city IV was destroyed in one of the earlier Assyrian inroads (733 B.C.?) and rebuilt when Israel's glory had departed.

Stratum IV represents the city of Solomonic times. As the excavators slowly dug down into it, discoveries multiplied. A large building on the south side of the mound may have been a fortress begun by David. But other buildings corresponding to it were not found, and it seems to have been taken over, perhaps torn down, and incorporated into the great city which arose in the prosperous days of Solomon.

Stratum V has not been so completely excavated as those above it, and below it only small areas, in the nature of glorified soundings, have been undertaken. The original plan of Dr. Breasted, for the complete excavation of every stratum one by one, had to be abandoned because of prohibitive costs, especially after his death in November, 1935. However, the results of the soundings, though provisional, have made a fairly complete history of the tell possible. Enough has been found on the mound to relate the tombs on the slopes to the stratification and to carry the occupation of the site back through sixteen more strata, twenty in all, to the Middle Chalcolithic period, before 3500 B.C., to the same period as the earliest found at Beth-shan.

The interesting features of these twenty ancient cities, ranging through more than 3000 years of history, are innumerable. A few of the more significant discoveries were the city wall and gate, the "stables of Solomon," and the temple or house beyond them, all belonging to strata IV or III; the elaborate "water system"; the temples and palaces of the still lower strata; and the great collection of ivories from stratum VII.

Many questions regarding the structures uncovered are not as yet settled. Mr. Crowfoot, the recent excavator of Samaria, argues for Dr. Fisher's original dating of the Solomonic buildings to the time of Omri and Ahab because of the close resemblances between the masonry of the buildings at the two sites. According to his view, gate, walls, buildings, and pottery all point to the ninth century as the date of stratum IV, while stratum V was built by Solomon and runs, in round numbers, from 960 to 870 B.C. Mr. Crowfoot has put his finger on certain inconsistencies —paradoxes he calls them—in the dating of the materials from these strata, but masonry is one of the most deceptive of chronological criteria and cannot serve as a dependable basis for dating.

Dr. Albright differs from the recent excavators in his dating of some of the levels. The difficulties here are due in part to the variety of heads and hands which have had to do with the excavation and the study of the pottery—four different directors, including Schumacher, and at least six assistants and editors. However, Albright's ultimate conclusions lower the dates of strata IV and III only by fifty or seventy-five years. In so doing, although he had not seen Crowfoot's review, he seems to me to meet Crowfoot's objections while leaving the inception of stratum IV and the erection of its chief buildings still in Solomon's reign. He is thus able also to return to Mr. Guy's date for the great gate as Solomonic, instead of ascribing it to stratum III as Mr. Loud has done. Mr. Crowfoot's theory would ruin the title of this chapter—a minor casualty—and would alter, although it would not lessen, the contribution which Megiddo makes to the cultural history of the Hebrews. Even if what is here said of Solomon's chariots and horse trading proves incorrect, these differences of opinion do not affect the imposing impression which the ruined city makes.

Stratum IV, as it began to appear when stratum III was disentangled from it, showed itself to be a large, well-planned, and well-constructed city, with excellent buildings and a mighty defense system. Around the edge of the tell ran a stone wall twelve feet thick, which was so strong that it had apparently served also the next succeeding city.

The great city gate, whether belonging to stratum IV or III, is characteristic of the whole. The chariot road ran up from the west along the north side of the terrace and made a curve to the right which brought it along beside the city wall before a double gate set at right angles to the wall. An enemy who forced this gate found himself, not inside the city, but in a small paved and walled enclosure with the great walls and the bastions of the real city gate towering above him. This gate also was double and much more massive, with guard rooms on either side before one passed through the second passage into the city. The stone sockets on which the two wings of the gate turned were still in place, and also a second set placed much closer together, which testify to a later rebuilding, perhaps for stratum III.

THE STABLES OF SOLOMON

A wide paved street led upward from the gate by a gentle slope southward and then southeastward toward what are the most interesting structures uncovered—the "stables of Solomon" and the massive building behind them. Every tourist is shown the "stables of Solomon" at Jerusalem, subterranean structures under the Temple area which Solomon probably never saw and which were stables only for the Crusaders. Megiddo has real stables of Solomon, as the archaeological evidence abundantly proves. They were built on a standardized plan and stretch out in regular rows and sections on both sides of the great central street. On each side of a hard lime passageway are rows of stalls set face to face and paved with cobblestones. At the head of each stall was a stone manger and on each side of it a stone pillar which served both as a tie post and as a support for the roof. In a corner of the pillar toward the passage is a hole for the tie rope. Usually the stalls are in groups of twenty-four each, thus making twelve chariots the size of a squadron. In the north stables there were ten such and two stables with room for thirty horses each. On the south side of the mound were five more stables, each for thirty horses. Here there was also a great court or parade ground. Altogether 450 or more stalls have been found.

Beside the stables, on the highest part of the mound and close to the eastern wall of the city there is a large building which Schumacher called a *Tempelburg* and near which Fisher located a temple of Astarte in stratum III (7th century). Mr. Guy thought it the residence of the commander of the chariot detachment in the neighboring stables. Professor May argued that a large room in it (338) was a temple. Mr. Shipton and Dr. Engberg have returned to Mr. Guy's opinion. At one corner of it was a tower which would have given a view out over the city and, what is more important, over all the country to south, east, and northeast. Beside it and built against the city wall was a row of small rooms which could have served as barracks for troops while their flat roofs would have allowed them to deploy to meet attacks. Stables, barracks, and general headquarters are conveniently arranged for the chariot battalion.

The discovery of the stables explains structures found at various places in Palestine which excavators have been at a loss to understand. Schumacher had regarded the few hitching posts of the stables which he uncovered as *masseboth*, sacred pillars, and therefore thought the building a *Tempelburg*, a combined castle and temple. Watzinger had recognized the doubtfulness of the description of the pillars. It is clear that other *masseboth* which Schumacher found are merely tie stones or roof supports.

As Guy has pointed out, the same conclusion applies to *masseboth* which Sellin found at Ta'annak and dated between 1000 and 800 B.C. I myself examined the stones there after Mr. Guy called them to my attention, and I found a similar sandstone post with tie hole at Tell el-Far'ah. Nearly forty years ago at Tell el-Hesi Bliss found similar rows of pillars and later Macalister found them at Gezer, in both cases in buildings which had the same ground plan as the stables at Megiddo and are dated by both archaeologists to about 1000 B.C., although neither recognized their true character. Garstang uncovered a similar row of pillars at Tell el-Qedah.

Thus the evidence accumulates for Solomon's chariots and 12,000 chariot horses (if the stables were Solomon's and not Omri's or Ahab's) and for chariot cities from Beersheba almost to Dan. It is not likely that 12,000 stalls could be found, and surely not all of those discovered were built by Solomon, but enough have been found to substantiate abundantly the claim of the writer of the Book of Kings (1 Kg 10.26-29) that Solomon was a great horse trader, accumulating a force of no mean proportion for the defense of his kingdom and at the same time using the increase from his stables to add to his wealth. The discovery of the same telltale rows of pillars at Gezer, Megiddo, and Hazor exactly agrees with the statement of the writer of Kings that Solomon built, or rather rebuilt, these three cities.

All of the finest structures at Megiddo, those of stratum IV, have been assigned to the time of Solomon. By clearing the mound as a whole, the street and floor levels could be tied together with certainty. The previous excavators had dated the *Tempelburg* in the next later period after the "palace" which they found just a little to the southwest of it, because the "palace" was several feet lower down than the *Tempelburg*. But the upward slope of the main street, now that it has been traced in its full length, shows that the argument based upon the absolute level was erroneous.

The character of the masonry does not serve to distinguish the Solomonic stratum from buildings of the next period. The buildings of Omri and Ahab at Samaria were finer than most of the buildings at Megiddo, but the methods of the masons were practically identical, so much so that one is compelled to recognize the Tyrian tradition in both cases. In the commandant's residence a peculiar combination of ashlar and rubble was used. The corners are built of carefully squared stones and at regular intervals along the wall groups of them appear. Between is a rubble wall. There is a regular alternation of headers and stretchers in the ashlar sections. Moreover, on the lowest course of the dressed stones there is a red line running at the same level around the building as a datum line for the masons. And on one of the dressed stones of the southeast corner, faint but indubitable, has been cut in double lines that famous combination of interlaced triangles called the "shield of David," or "Solomon's seal," which is now known from other parts of the ancient world. Proto-Ionic or Proto-Aeolic columns adorned one room of the "residency." As Guy remarks, these buildings were "the work, not of peasants, but of skilled craftsmen."

One remarkable fact about nearly all of the building in this stratum, both in the houses and in the city gate, is that above the foundations there are "three rows of hewn stone." Upon the upper surface of the three courses, wherever they remain *in situ*, was indubitable evidence that they had been finished in mudbrick, and there were also traces of blackening by fire. In one place a chunk of charred wood was found which microscopic analysis discovered to be cedar. Just how the walls and roofs were finished cannot be determined, but Guy is certainly justified in calling attention to a sentence from 1 Kings 7.12 which describes Solomon's building: "And the great court round about had three rows of hewn stone and a row of cedar beams."

THE MEGIDDO WATER SYSTEM

Any number of problems arose to lure the excavators on. At the west side of the mound a very narrow passage lined with fine ashlar masonry and barely wide enough to admit a horse, runs straight through the great stone courses which formed the base of the city wall. At the point where the Solomonic city wall crosses it and again at the inner end, it had been filled in with rubble. No gate of any kind appeared. Was it a postern entrance? Unexpectedly, excavation into lower levels eventually answered this question along with another apparently unrelated problem.

A long-standing puzzle in a spot where he found no bottom lured Mr. Guy below his carefully observed self-limitation to stratum IV. As stratum III was being cleared away an area of several yards was found in which there were no walls, floors, or other evidences of occupation although there were buildings all around it. Again and again on my more or less periodical visits in 1930 he led me to his "bottomless pit" and discussed possible explanations. Once some stones appeared, and he thought they might mean a pavement, but they proved to have no connection one with another. Before the rains began, he had to fill the hole in lest it gather a pool and breed mosquitoes. Next season he went at it in earnest, determined to solve the mystery even if it led to lower levels. And this it eventually did—with a vegeance—down 125 feet into the rock on which the city was built.

What he found he guessed correctly long before he had the proof, that it was one of those internal water systems for which the Middle and Late Bronze Ages in the Near East are famous. Under some engineer who had no little skill in planning and execution, a vertical shaft was run down through some 45 feet of city debris and then through 35 feet of soft limestone rock. It then ran at an angle of 45 degrees another 35 feet down a long flight of steps and finally through 165 feet of tunnel to reach an underground cave with a perennial supply of water.

All of this labor was done by hand, it must be remembered. The final tunnel was cut from both ends, with a vertical error of only about three feet and an even smaller horizontal error. It was no small achievement when one considers that the underground cave and its pool of cold water were far in (65 feet) under the mound and some 50 feet below the surface of the ground at the foot of the irregular slope. Stairs ran around the deep vertical well and down the slope that succeeded it to reach the long tunnel. At its end the women could dip their pitchers in the pool of the cave.

It would appear that Megiddo must have had some other provision for water at an earlier period. Since the city stood upon a great heap of debris, cisterns were impossible even if they had been known in the Bronze Age. Some other such tunnel may have existed on another part of the mound. But one of the chief supplies of water had probably always been a spring at the foot of the mound on its southwest side. Because of a gradually lowered water table this spring was repeatedly cleared and its pool deepened, driving it back into the hill. Eventually the women of the city had to clamber down the side of the hill outside the wall and then down a long flight of steps in the rock.

The external entrance exposed the spring and the women to enemy attacks, and it became necessary to make some better provision. This was at first done by building what had so puzzled the excavators, the narrow covered passageway through the city wall, and then continuing it down to the spring. But this proved a fruitless endeavor. It also was exposed to attack by any resolute or cunning enemy.

Inside this outer entrance in a little alcove was found the skeleton of a man who probably had been on guard when some enemy came, surprised him, and took possession of the city's water supply. After this misfortune, the much more ambitious enterprise of the shaft and tunnel was undertaken. In the alcove under the guard's body, pottery of the twelfth century was found. A wall and a filling which blocked the outer entrance showed pottery of the same period, stratum VII. A bronze statue base bearing the cartouche of Ramses III (1198-1167 B.C.) confirms this dating. This then must be the period when the elaborate system was constructed. It does real credit to the engineering ability of some one, Hittite or Egyptian or Canaanite, in this pre-Israelite period.

Later it was decided to bring the water to the foot of the deepened vertical shaft by extending the horizontal tunnel. In this case the engineer was less skilled. He miscalculated and overshot his mark by several feet.

Another change occurred in the Solomonic period. Apparently during the period of stratum V, when the city had no strong defenses, the whole water system was forgotten and allowed to fill up with silt and debris. In Solomon's time the shaft and tunnel were cleared, and the silt was used to level up the great parade ground by the southwestern stables. But at the bottom of the vertical shaft enough was left to form the base of a masonry stairway leading up again to the stairs that went up about the vertical tunnel. In Josiah's reign it is possible that the system was still in use and some rebuilding done. But after that time, the grandiose effort of the twelfth century fell into permanent disuse.

THE MEGIDDO IVORIES

Artistically speaking, the most spectacular discovery at Megiddo was made in the spring of 1937. Just inside and west of the city gate on the north side of the mound lies a palace that exhibits five building periods running through four centuries, from the sixteenth down to the twelfth. The last palace was destroyed about or a little before 1150 B.C., and apparently at its destruction its treasures were rifled, but so hastily that much, including remarkable carved ivories, was left behind. They had been stored in a half-subterranean treasury of three rooms.

The ivories, found chiefly in one of these storerooms, rank high among the show pieces of the Megiddo expedition. The nearly 400 objects registered make the collection one of the largest ever found, and the variety of objects, of design, and of style render it culturally one of the most significant, for it indicates a large number of cultural relationships. There were boxes, bars, medallions, disks, plaques, and panels carved in relief; game boards, bowls, lids, cups, and combs carved or incised; figurines, game pieces, beads, spoons, rings, carved in the round or decorated in relief, a vast variety. Both animal and human figurines often had eyes of glass inlay. Incised lines were filled in with black or blue paint, but there was none of the rich inlay of the Samaria ivories to be described later. One plaque with incised designs has been interpreted as possibly picturing a triumph of some prince of Megiddo.

The pieces were found nearly all close together within about 9 square meters, but scattered about in complete confusion. While many pieces were marked by dowel holes and tenons as clearly intended for use as inlay, the condition in which they were found proves that they had not come immediately from furniture. Mr. Loud suggests that they were a connoisseur's collection and may have been produced during a longer time than that represented by the period of the palace.

The stratum in which they were found is dated by the discovery of the name of Ramses III (1198-1167 b.c.) on a probably imported model pen case. The decades 1170 to 1150, therefore, become the lower limit for the date. A small plaque, with a Hittite eagle and other clear indications of Hittite derivation, points to the beginning of the collection as about 1350 or 1300. It is a remarkable fact that a stylistically related group of ivories has been found at Enkomi (Salamis) in Cyprus and another, now in the Metropolitan Museum of Art, at a North Syrian site. Both of these are independently dated at about the same period. Another quite different fragment, from a round cylinder beautifully carved in relief in zones, came from stratum VI.

A discovery almost as attractive as the ivories was made under the floor of the previous stratum (VIII). A magnificent hoard of objects in gold and electrum had been buried either by the princes of the stratum VIII palace or by those of the first stratum VII palace. A beautiful, heavy gold bowl in the shape of a sea shell, cosmetic jars of serpentine and hematite having gold leaf applied over mouth and neck, a ceremonial whetstone made of sandstone capped with gold, and twin crowned heads of gold over a paste base are emphatic testimony to the wealth of the princes of Megiddo in the period of Egyptian suzerainty, between 1475 and 1200 B.C.

RELIGION AT MEGIDDO

The fact that numerous *masseboth* turned into hitching posts and temples into stables does not mean that there were no evidences of religious worship at Megiddo. On the contrary, the large number of cult objects found indicates a high development of religious ritual. Wherever stratum V has been touched, objects implying worship have been so numerous that the excavators—rashly perhaps—hazard the guess that the whole unwalled and unimpressive city in that period was a sacred area. But it was by no means there alone that evidences of religious interest appeared. The temples thus far discovered have not been so elaborately planned or so clearly marked as at Bethshan. Inscribed lintels and dedicatory stelae have been wanting. But those found do cover a much longer period of time, and the story may be very different when the lower strata are fully excavated.

The sharp difference of opinions as to one supposed temple has been noted. Schumacher, Fisher, and May regarded it as a temple partly because its solid construction suited a temple fortress, partly because of the cult objects found within or near it. Within was a flat stone and another with cup marks which might have served for offering tables, and beside them a layer of charcoal with animal bones. There were two pillars (without tie holes) for *masseboth* and near by were pottery shrines or incense stands. Schumacher's and Fisher's temple

(Rooms 338-340) is in stratum III, May's on the same foundations, but in stratum IV, Room 340 being a holy of holies.

The evidence had largely disappeared when Mr. Guy took the directorship. He with Mr. Shipton and Dr. Engberg believes the majority of the cult objects to be associated with other buildings not far away which belong to stratum V. But there must have been some temple in stratum IV. On Schumacher's evidence May's arguments have more plausibility than his former colleagues allow. The question is too complicated for further discussion here. Much depends upon the interpretation of the "proto-Ionic" capitals. Would they grace a governor's palace or a temple? The latter seems more probable.

On one temple all of the recent excavators agree. South of the disputed building are the stratum V buildings to which the skeptics assign the cult objects found in the neighborhood. One building (10) is called a storehouse. The other (1A) has two rows of four standing monolithic pillars each.[2] The two rows of monoliths may be *masseboth*; they may be the lower sections of roof supports. But the variety and number of cult objects, stands, censers, amulets, and gazelle horns (from sacrifices) found in and near the two buildings indicate indubitably that there must have been a shrine in the immediate neighborhood.

Still another stratum V shrine, with horned altars, offering stands, censers, libation bowls, carved three-footed mortars, and other objects not unlike those already mentioned, was discovered in the 1935-36 excavations near the city gate. Its construction seems not to have been completed. It represents quite a different type of worship from that in the lower strata. A small "proto-Ionic" pilaster capital connects this temple with the stratum IV or V structures where full-sized capitals of this order appeared.

Between 1935 and 1939 excavation in the eastern area of the mound discovered other temples. Perchance a building of strata VIII-VII which lay on the north edge of the mound east of the

---

[2] Another room (1706) still farther to the southwest has a row of four standing pillars.

city gate is such. A low dais of limestone slabs against the west wall, a free-standing square structure of mud bricks, a large circular stone in the center, and two stone vessels for ablutions might suggest such a use.

Under the northeast complex of stables in stratum IX was a temple consisting of a single chamber which was completely rebuilt in strata VIII and VII. Several figurines (one of them gilded) of Resheph, or perhaps rather of the Canaanite storm god, Ba'al, were found within and around these structures. Entirely unique was a pottery model of a sheep's liver, doubtless intended for augury. Numerous fragments of busts of Egyptian rulers were found built into the walls. All lacked inscriptions but probably came from the Twelfth Dynasty. A cache of contemporary jewelry was found in one of the walls. The building's plan suggested Babylonian influence.

Directly below this "eastern temple," the excavations of 1937-39 uncovered a large round structure built of unshaped stones and still standing about 7 feet high. Its diameter was about 30 feet at the base. It tapered toward the top and had in its east side a flight of steps, at the base of which were quantities of animal bones. West of it were two buildings of *megaron* plan and north of it another. The two nearest it, perhaps the other also, had against their south walls, opposite the door which opened from the porch, a dais, or platform. Cult objects were found in none of these rooms, but, particularly in view of the bones by the steps of the round structure, it can hardly be doubted that they were shrines. The round altar may have originated in stratum XVII. It certainly was in use in XV and XIV, that is from 2100 to 1800 B.C. For the Hyksos period (XIII-XI) no shrines are reported.

Another outstanding discovery was a shrine in stratum XIX (*ca.* 3250 B.C.) with a remarkable stone pavement before it in which figures of men and animals had been incised, crudely in some cases, in others with no little skill. Two figures, one a warrior, are dancing. Another plays a harp. The room lay to the east of the site of the later round altar facing the edge of the mound. Against its west wall there was a rectangular altar with a lower shelf or broad step beside it. In front of it lay a stone of peculiar mandolin shape. Within the same period the altar was irregularly enlarged and stones were placed at irregular intervals about the room. This stratum is the first to show real building ability. The shrine is a massive building with strong mud-brick walls on stone foundations of a single course.

Because of their chronological proximity to Old Testament times the cult objects of strata III-V have special interest. They have been fully pictured and discussed in many publications. There were limestone and pottery incense altars, doubtless the sort called *hamman* in the Old Testament and mistranslated as "image," or "sun image."[3] There were pottery shrines which assist greatly in visualizing the appearance of ancient temples. A characteristic object is the *kernos* ring, a hollow pottery ring on which little vessels in the shape of vases, birds, and other animals sit. There were *masseboth*, censers of various shapes, stands of bronze and of pottery, models of chariots, of various animals, legs, phalli, statuettes, rattles, and numerous figurines of gods and goddesses. Many of these objects may have been amulets. This catalogue is inadequate to suggest the wide variety of religious observances and beliefs that prevailed.

Innumerable other small objects of daily use in household, field, and shop were found. Among them interest has centered on the signet rings and scarabs. Schumacher found two with Hebrew inscriptions which, in his day, electrified the scholarly world. An oval seal of jasper read "(Belonging) to Shemaʿ servant of Jeroboam" and bore a vigorous lion with gaping jaws in its center. Shemaʿ is probably an officer of Jeroboam II. Another seal of lapis lazuli had at the bottom the inscription, "(Belonging) to Asaph." It bore a delicately carved winged griffin wearing the crowns of Upper and Lower Egypt. In front of it in a small cartouche were the hieroglyphic signs for "life" and "beloved." Like the other seal it belongs probably to the eighth century, though possibly to the seventh.

[3] Lev 26.30; Is 17.8; 27.9; Ez 6.4, 6; 2 Chr 14.5; 34.4.

A multitude of scarabs, fibulae, cylinder seals, eyelet pins, rings, bracelets, and other pieces of jewelry have contributed to knowledge of the art and fashions of different periods. No more artistic seals have been found in the subsequent excavations, but the ivories and the hoard of gold and electrum found in the palace west of the gate in strata VIII and VII prophesy that the Middle and Late Bronze Age cities, here as elsewhere, will outshine those of Israelite times.

MEGIDDO'S STORY

Unlike Beth-shan and Jericho, Megiddo tells an almost continuous story of Palestinian civilization from 3500 B.C. down to 450 B.C., or a little later. Because of the absence of the unique burnished Khirbet Kerak ware and the characteristic Tomb A pottery of Jericho, it appears not to have been occupied for a time after the middle of the third millennium. There may have been brief gaps at other times. But unlike Tell el-Husn at Beth-shan, it was a most important city all during the Israelite period. The "stables of Solomon" and the walls of cities IV and III testify to its position. It was unfortunate that so many different individuals, German, English, and American, were engaged in the excavation of these areas. Their story is not quite coherent. But if one poor excavator had done all of the work, it would have been far less intelligible.

The history of the period before the United Kingdom is not yet complete. But that it was a significant city with excellent architecture from before 3000 B.C. is clear. At times it had strong fortifications. Its gate moved more than once, apparently always eastward. Its finest buildings were usually at the northwest side of the oval, as Sir Flinders Petrie always insists they must be. Further excavation there and over the remainder of the mound should reveal much more of the ladder of civilization in Palestine.

CHAPTER XIII

LUXURIOUS SAMARIA

❖

SAMARIA-SEBASTE is unique among the cities of Palestine. The wide-spreading dome of its hill is the most beautiful city site in all the land, and it looks out, not only upon the charming "fat valleys" of Samaria, but also over rolling hills to the Plain of Sharon and the sea. Its history is well documented in the Bible and in Josephus. As is true of no other city in the land, the time and circumstances of its founding are definitely given in the Bible. Since it was the capital city of the Northern Kingdom, there are numerous further references to its history. The wealth, luxury, and hard-heartedness of its citizens are bitterly denounced by the prophets. Because of its commanding location it continued to be occupied. It was rebuilt on a magnificent scale by Herod the Great and was a place of importance down into the Arab and the Crusader periods. There is not a shadow of suspicion as to its identification.

THE EXPEDITIONS

Samaria never suffered such destructions as have fallen upon Jerusalem and there is now no city covering its site. Therefore it can be excavated. Difficulties, indeed, are not wanting, for it is a fertile hill covered with magnificent olive orchards. For generations the remains have served as a quarry for the villagers of Sebastieh. It never was a mud-brick village. It always boasted large stone buildings and at each successive reconstruction foundations were dug through the underlying walls and debris—to their serious disarrangement. Strata, therefore, do not lie one above the other neatly separated by layers of ashes. The area is large, and there are masses of stones and earth to

move. The excavator's task is far from easy. But unlike so many
Palestinian sites, Samaria has been fortunate in having only two
expeditions attack its problems, and both of them were remarkably well conducted.

The first was under the auspices of Harvard University and
was conducted by Professor D. G. Lyons, Dr. George A.
Reisner, and Dr. C. S. Fisher during the years 1908-1910. Both
Dr. Reisner and Dr. Fisher had already had valuable experience
as excavators and they prepared a report which was as adequate
as was then possible.

The second expedition, which was due to the initiative of
Professor Kirsopp Lake of Harvard, was placed under the
directorship of Mr. J. W. Crowfoot, director of the British
School of Archaeology in Jerusalem. It was financed by American and British societies and staffed by a notable group of
younger archaeologists, with Professor E. L. Sukenik of the
Hebrew University as assistant director. Dr. Fisher at times
acted as advisor and thus insured a certain continuity. The
expedition worked through three full summer seasons in 1931,
1932, and 1933, and for a short period in 1935.

The earlier expedition made one sad blunder. It dumped its
debris on the highest part of the hill where it made subsequent
efforts to solve the puzzles of the city's history difficult and
expensive. The second expedition disclosed the general accuracy
and conscientiousness of its predecessor, but also the advances
which Palestinian archaeology had made in the intervening
two decades. The two expeditions have unrolled a magnificent
historical panorama stretching from the time of Omri, 875 B.C.,
to the Byzantine period, over 1500 years, or, one may say, even
to the Crusader period, over 2000 years all told.

The chief periods of the city's history appeared amid the
confusion of crisscrossed walls and heaped debris. Israelite was
followed by Assyrian, Persian, Greek, Roman, and Byzantine.
Two, and in places three, strata of Hebrew occupation have been
found over the whole central area of the city. The period which
seems least clearly represented covers the two centuries of

Assyrian rule, following Sargon's capture of the city in 722 B.C. Civilization in Palestine was apparently more nearly uniform and less influenced by the foreign invaders and the imported refugee populations than might be expected. The Persian period also is not too clearly differentiated by reported discoveries. The few expeditions which have worked in materials of that period have failed to discover marks of difference. They should be found at Samaria if anywhere. The final report should clear up many dark places in the city's history and in that of the postexilic period.

CORRECTIONS

The chief corrections made by the second expedition in the conclusions of the first lower the dates of certain structures and strata. It may be that the "palace of Ahab," like the ostraca, will have to be assigned to Jeroboam II. That is not yet clear. But the dates of certain of the most outstanding structures on the mound have been reduced. One of these is the street of columns which every visitor admires. It was formerly said to be Herodian but now to belong to the "third century A.D. at the earliest." Neither expedition made any considerable clearance of the street and further excavation will probably find traces of various reconstructions as was true at Jerash.

Another important reconsideration of dates touches certain great round towers and the "Greek fort wall." In 1933 a semicircular tower of similar construction to one which Reisner had attributed to Jeroboam II was found at the northeast corner of the walls which surround the summit. Mr. Crowfoot was not entirely satisfied with that dating and had already before the new discovery expressed himself privately as believing that reconsideration was demanded. The brief excavation of 1935 was undertaken for the purpose of settling this and other moot questions.

On this point definite evidence was discovered and the uncertainty removed by a beautiful piece of excavation and inference. On the inside of the tower a trench was dug down to its bottom. It was found that, as the courses of the tower were laid, earth was piled against it to serve as a platform for the masons. With each course a thin horizontal streak of chips from the stones showed how the earth had been thrown in. At the top, the debris used was full of Israelite pottery. Toward the bottom there were sherds from Hellenistic wares. They could not be intrusive, for the layers of chips showed that the fill had not been disturbed. It had merely reversed the order of the debris which had been used to make it. Therefore, the earliest possible date for the tower must fall in the Hellenistic period, perhaps about 325 B.C., for that kind of pottery was on top when the fill was begun.

With this tower go also the southwest tower and what the first expedition called the Greek fort wall. These structures all exhibit a different masonry from that of the walls which have been assigned to the Israelite period, and the conclusions based on pottery evidence are thus strongly supported. Miss Kathleen Kenyon, who was especially entrusted with the supervision of the work touching these walls, believes they cannot be earlier than 200 B.C. The towers at the southwest gate were assigned by Reisner and Fisher to the Greek period, but were supposed to hide Israelite defenses. Many now think that there is no Israelite work at the point, and the round towers there are said to be Roman.

The area covered by the city varied greatly through the fifteen centuries of its history. In the beginning there was an almost rectangular enclosure, walled with excellent masonry, surrounding the summit of the hill, and measuring on the inside about 90 by 175 meters, 300 by 580 feet. This wall was soon strengthened by a casemated wall of great strength just outside it. It was a true citadel, or acropolis. Still within the Israelite period the wall was extended eastward to include almost the entire top of the hill as far as the present village and the mosque, which was once the Crusader Church of St. John the Baptist, and the city was probably enlarged also in other directions. These three periods are assigned to Omri, Ahab, and

Jeroboam II. In Persian or Greek times the city was enlarged by building the wall on a still lower terrace of the level limestone strata which form the hill, then again in Herodian times by dropping down to a much lower terrace which allowed the inclusion of a temple and the palestra far down on the north slope of the hill.

SIGNIFICANT RESULTS

The "high lights" of the labors of the two expeditions strike nearly every period, but especially the Israelite, and then the Christian era. A mere list is formidable: ostraca written in Hebrew; the palaces of Israel's kings; a remarkable collection of ivory inlay from furniture and wall panels; imposing examples of Israelite masonry; a series of fortifications repeatedly enlarged to protect the growing city; complicated systems of water supply; a great Augusteum and a magnificent basilica and forum, originally built by Herod the Great; a striking colonnaded street; repeated reconstructions of these buildings, especially in the Severan period; a temple of Kore or the Dioscuri; a palestra; a theater; a half-preserved Christian church; rock-cut tombs; mausolea—this is only a partial catalogue.

The historical results of the excavations emphasize the distinction that ought to be drawn between the legends of the Bible and the historical records which are embedded in its accounts. So far as could possibly be expected, the archaeological findings confirm the statements of the Bible regarding the city. Where, again and again, digging has gone down to the bedrock of the hill, no remains have been found earlier than the Israelite period except sherds and cup marks of the Early Bronze Age. As the Bible indicates (1 Kg 16.24), it was an unoccupied mountain top when Omri purchased it.

THE IVORIES OF SAMARIA

Another interesting correspondence to biblical data was discovered in a mass of fragments of beautifully carved and inlaid ivories found by Mr. Crowfoot near the summit of the hill.

No discovery which the expedition made has attracted so much attention, and that deservedly, for the objects are beautiful in themselves, they tell a fascinating tale of the cultural and artistic achievements of the Israelites and of their international trade relationships, and they illustrate famous biblical passages.

The earlier expedition had discovered three ivory fragments near the western wall of the great rectangular enclosure which formed the heart of the city of Omri and Ahab. The recent expedition found hundreds of fragments scattered over almost the entire city, but especially in the north-central section of the rectangular acropolis. They were, as a rule, smashed into tiny atoms, but many were fairly large. Evidently they had been used as inlay on furniture and on wooden walls. Amos (6.4) denounces the luxury of Samaria's couches of ivory. A Hebrew historian (1 Kg 22.39) refers to the house of ivory which Ahab built, perhaps a pavilion or reception hall having walls inlaid with ivory. Amos (3.15) scornfully predicts its destruction. No such walls were found, but, if the large number of pieces discovered near the center of the north city wall may be taken as evidence, the "house of ivory" stood near the summit of the hill on the north side, where it would receive the best of the cool northwest winds from the Mediterranean. This is not certain, however, for the area was filled with mixed rubbish of various ages and included a piece of unworked ivory.

The ivories are of various types. A small number were carved in low relief while details such as eyes, hair, necklaces, and borders of robes were deeply grooved and filled with colored insets of lapis lazuli, glass, and paste after the fashion of champ-levé or cloisonné. The cloisons were sometimes covered with gold leaf so that almost no ivory was visible. Such pieces made a gorgeous appearance. In others the polychrome insets, molded to give the necessary relief, showed the whole of the figures, while the ivory served only as a background.

A few pieces carved in the round, notably two crouching, roaring lions, were found. The much larger portion consisted of plaques carved in low relief or in open, or pierced, relief without color or gilding. These were usually panels with conventional repeat designs in which palmettes, the lotus, sphinxes, and battling animals predominate. Many of the fragments were marked on the back, often with old Hebrew letters, probably to indicate the order in which they were to be assembled.

A beautiful example of the first class represented the child Horus seated upon a lotus. A striking piece in open relief is a winged sphinx with a human head. In another a lion is strangling a bull whose tongue protrudes most realistically. In a border carved in low relief, the petals of an eight-petaled daisy, or rosette, were polished and stained a pale yellow, while the background was left rough. Description can give no adequate idea of the delicacy and beauty of these pieces.

In technique they are closely related to a group of ivories found by M. Thureau-Dangin at Arslan-Tash in north Syria. An incomplete inscription on one of these carries the name, "our lord Hazael." This dates them to the time of the famous Syrian king who ascended the throne in 842 B.C., according to the Bible with the assistance of Elisha (2 Kg 8). Other similar ivories were found at Nimrud, ancient Nineveh, and are securely dated by an Assyrian tablet of inventory, which lists them as booty from Damascus taken in the time of Hazeal's successor.

The motifs used by the Syrian and Israelite artisans were distinctly Egyptian. But they were not slavishly copying Egyptian models, for their treatment differs significantly at times from the figures and motifs used on Egyptian monuments. The child Horus, for example, was plump in Syria, thin in Egypt. The gods shown are not always those most prominent in Egyptian mythology. The ability and relative independence of these Syrian artists, the connections between Syria and Palestine, and the cultural superiority of the northern capital to Jerusalem are all illustrated by Mr. Crowfoot's fortunate discovery.

OUTSTANDING DISCOVERIES

One of the discoveries most important to the scholar was divided between the two expeditions. The first unearthed a group of potsherds inscribed in Hebrew characters of the time of the monarchy, the Middle Iron period. The second expedition found still more. They were at first thought to date from Ahab's time (850 B.C.), but there is now a strong tendency to drop them down into the reign of Jeroboam II (780 B.C.). Some belong to the Persian period. Intrinsically they are of little historical interest, much less than the Lachish ostraca, for they are only lists and receipts, perhaps connected with the kingdom's fiscal system. But even tax receipts show the kind of handwriting employed and occasionally exhibit grammatical usage. It is something to be able to distinguish the handwriting of Samaria from that of Judea and to know how the first copy of Hosea's prophecies looked. In view of the dearth of Hebrew inscriptional material such documents are most welcome.

A discovery of the first expedition which was enthusiastically received was the palaces of Omri and Ahab. They lay on the western brow of the hill within strong and well-built walls. Omri's less spacious and luxurious buildings served as a core for Ahab's much more magnificent structures. About them was the great rectangular citadel. The characteristic, well-laid and carefully bonded city walls with their margins drafted on three sides only have been the admiration of all and a constant guide to the excavators through the maze of later foundations which interrupted or destroyed them.

The most striking and easily appreciated ruins now visible date from Severan times. They are reconstructions of the great temple erected by Herod the Great to Zeus Olympius in honor of Augustus and of the basilica Herod built. Both structures remind one of Herod's building in Jerusalem, because here as there he built retaining walls and vaults on the slopes of the hill in order to secure level space sufficient for his magnificent structures. Both were built over houses and walls which were destroyed to make room for them.

The Augusteum faced northward toward a huge artificial platform based on large vaults forming double corridors on both sides of the court that spreads out before it and on a great

retaining wall with a similar corridor at the north end, where
the floor of the court was some 40 feet above the rock of the
hill. The court was about 250 feet square. Two spacious flights
of 24 steps led up to the temple itself which stood some 15 feet
higher. It was not a peripteral temple but had an eight-pillared
portico which was flanked by pilasters and, of course, supported
a gabled, tiled roof. Its white limestone columns and walls and
red tiles could have been seen miles away as they crowned the
broad hill top.

The stairway which now appears was built in the Severan
age over the foundations of the Herodian stair. A great altar,
a rectangular core of rubble surrounded by excellent masonry,
was found just below the stairway, a little east of the central
axis of the temple. The torso of a colossal figure bearing a
cuirass and the insignia of an emperor, probably belonging to
a gigantic statue of Augustus, lay near. Its excellent workmanship points to the Herodian period.

Like the temple, the basilica now visible is a reconstruction
in the Severan period of one which had been built by Herod
but which had long lain in ruins. Some of its columns and the
lower part of a beautiful apse still stand, and the excavators were
able to uncover the foundations and the plinth upon which the
columns had stood. Like the temple, the basilica faced toward
the north. East of it was a spacious forum, better called an
agora, for this was a Hellenistic city. The foundations of the
colonnades which had surrounded it could be traced. Underneath were found earlier retaining walls and even Israelite
structures. Herod's stronger walls had enlarged and raised the
area.

One striking feature of the hilltop is the long row of columns
running through the olive orchard on the south side of the summit. Each expedition has made a very limited investigation of
its character. What now is visible is believed to be a Severan reconstruction following the line of a Herodian colonnade. The
well-paved road, 48 feet wide, was bordered by a raised curb-
ing 3 feet wide, on the outside edge of which the columns were

placed. Back of the covered colonnades on each side of the street were shops opening upon the street like modern oriental shops but more regular and elaborate. In places on the north the rock of the hill had been cut away to make room for the road. It ran from the great western gate to a point south of the agora, but does not seem to have turned north to reach the civic center.

The recent expedition cleared a great cistern on the hill near the center of the city and it also discovered the remains of an aqueduct coming in from the east and running west under the south colonnade of the agora and of the basilica. Direct connection could not be traced, but it is reasonably certain that an aqueduct, of which traces were found, ran from en-Naqurah, the present source of Sebastieh's water supply, to a point on the hill to the east opposite the city's mosque. It must have been brought across the valley on arches.

The long oval bay marked by a few standing columns in the hill below the agora was partially excavated. It was found to be a palestra rather than a stadium, or hippodrome. On a plastered wall there were rude graffiti with names such as Roufos, Preimos, and Narkissos and with pictures of athletes, gladiators, and animals. This wall and a colonnade of the Doric order appeared to belong to the Augustan era. A higher pavement and a large altar dedicated to Lady Kore (Persephone) with a Corinthian colonnade were probably erected in the third century, while there were mosaic pavements which seem to belong to Christian memorial chapels of the fifth or sixth century. On the hillside Israelite tombs and a Roman columbarium were found but no traces of tiers of seats such as would have surrounded a hippodrome.

The earlier expedition had supposed the city's theater to lie in a hollow of the hill below the Augusteum. Photographs from the air suggested that it had lain instead at a spot farther east about midway between the Augusteum and the basilica. Excavation proved this to be correct. The remains indicated its size and general character though they were not sufficient to make a reconstruction possible. They were massive, but rough and irregular and are thought to date from the third century. However, it is difficult to suppose that so large and beautiful a city would have remained without this standard form of amusement until so late a date.

MINOR TEMPLES AND SHRINES

Altogether four sanctuaries of Roman times were found, besides the Augusteum, which represents the official cult of Zeus and the Emperor. North of the colonnaded street near the west gate was a building of late Roman construction. Its plan was unique but seemed to indicate a small temple with a paved area before it and sunken trenches, possibly for flower beds (!) on both sides of it. Another shrine just south of the basilica is mentioned but not described. Possibly the basilica itself should be included as a place of public worship for the city.

Below the great northern retaining wall of the Augusteum, or Temple of Zeus Olympius, lies one of the few level areas at Samaria. Excavation proved it to have been so, not naturally, but through quarrying and the building of a large Roman temple and its surrounding temenos. The Roman constructions had destroyed all but meager traces of earlier buildings. A well-cut inscription, dated on paleographic grounds to the third century B.C., carried a dedication to Isis and Osiris. A fragmentary inscription appeared to be a dedication to Kore. But the temple appeared to belong to other deities. Two stones were found with carvings in high relief of star-crested helmets. Mr. M. Narkiss of Jerusalem pointed out that this kind of helmet was an emblem of the Dioscuri. Père Vincent carried the suggestion farther by showing that Helen, sister of the Dioscuri (*Dios kouroi*) was sometimes joined with them as *Dios kourē* and confused with Kore Persephone.

In the palestra a charming statue of Kore, evidently a popular goddess at Samaria, was found. It had been broken into fragments and thrown into a cistern. Somewhat under life size, the goddess wears a veil over a high crown. She carries in her right hand a long torch which rests on the ground and in her left a pomegranate and ears of wheat, symbols of immortality. The work is regarded as dating not much later than 200 A.D. In the same cistern was a headless draped goddess and a nude torso of a youthful god. On a marble fragment painted in red was a Greek inscription which runs, "God is one, the Lord of all; great is Kore the unconquered." The altar set up in the palestra was dedicated to Kyria Kore, "Lady Kore," by a Kalpournianos, son of Gaianos, and the name Pomponios Roufos *hieroktistēs*, "founder of a temple," was found. These documents belong to the third and fourth centuries.

The attribution of the temple remains uncertain. There must have been a Hellenistic temple before the Roman one which was probably built by Herod. It again was reconstructed in the Severan epoch. But to what deity it was dedicated is uncertain. There was no evidence of temple or cella at the palestra, but there can be no doubt that the cult of Kore was carried on there. With its practical monotheism and its promise of immortality it must have been a formidable rival to Christianity. The broken statues in a cistern testify to its eventual defeat and destruction.

The Church of John the Baptist

One of the most engaging discoveries was the Church of the first *inventio* ("discovery") of the head of John the Baptist. Although no trace of buildings appeared above ground, a field on a rather high terrace south of the palace area was called Qata'in ed-Deir, "the lands of the monastery," and in part was used by the small Christian community of Sebastieh as a burial place. Investigation proved it to conceal walls of considerable height. By agreement the cemetery was moved to land purchased elsewhere and a small church with other structures, doubtless belonging to a monastery, was uncovered.

A basilica had been followed by a church with a wooden dome carried on four basalt columns, and that by another with a masonry dome on four masonry piers built around the columns. Beneath was a crypt which was found intact but empty.

In a niche on the east wall there were remains of paintings which show various persons and represent two scenes, the beheading of the Baptist and the discovery of his head.

The church and the crypt with its paintings are quite accurately described by the Cretan pilgrim, Phocas, who visited Sebaste in 1185 A.D. The third structure, therefore, probably belongs to that century. It may have been rebuilt at the time the Crusaders built the much more pretentious church which now serves as the village mosque. Possibly the Emperor Manuel Comnenus (1143-80) co-operated in its rebuilding as he did in the restoration of the Church of the Nativity at Bethlehem. When it began to fall into disrepair, it was crudely mended here and there, and then eventually abandoned by an enfeebled Christianity.

In remarkable contrast to Gerasa, Bostra, and some other cities of Transjordan, Sebaste, magnificent as it was, has left few written records in Hellenistic and Roman times. Very few Greek and Latin inscriptions were found. In contrast to Gerasa, it seems never to have had many churches. The basilica may have been turned into a church; there was the very modest Church of the Invention of the Head of the Baptist; there was a funerary chapel or two where the palestra once had been. No more have been found. But Samaria had its luxuries in certain periods. The ivories tell a tale of wealth and cultural progress. Another tale is told by 2000 unearthed handles from Rhodian wine jars, a story of wide commerce and luxurious indulgence. The second century B.C. must have needed an Amos as greatly as did the eighth. The great structures of the city seem always to have been the work of royal builders. The responsibilities of citizenship sat lightly on the fortunate people of Samaria.

CHAPTER XIV

THE MOUNTAINS ROUND ABOUT JERUSALEM

❖

WHAT is not as yet known about the archaeology of the central mountain range of Palestine will eventually fill many volumes. In the last twenty years, however, a real beginning has been made. Before the first World War Jerusalem was the only site in all the truly Hebrew section of the country in which excavations had been made. Jericho was mainly pre-Israelite. Megiddo and Ta'annak are on the edge of the plain of Esdraelon; Gezer, Tell Sandahanneh, and all the mounds which Bliss and Macalister investigated forty years ago are in the Shephelah or on the edge of the Maritime Plain. None of them was exclusively or even typically Hebrew.

In 1913-4 a German expedition under Sellin had begun work at Balatah, the fortress of ancient Shechem and a place of prime importance in Hebrew history. That work was later continued with American support. As already noted, expeditions at Tell Beit Mirsim and Tell ed-Duweir have thrown unexpected light upon the development of Hebrew civilization on the southwestern edge of the hills. Expeditions at Tell el-Ful (the Gibeah of Saul), at Tell en-Nasbeh (provisionally identified with the Mizpah of Gedaliah), at Seilun (Shiloh), at Beitin (Bethel), at et-Tell (Ai), and at Beit Sur (Beth-zur) attacked from various angles the numerous problems which surround the history of the Hebrews. Each has made its contribution to the history of the Hebrew highlands.

SAUL'S CAPITAL—TELL EL-FUL [1]

A once-famous excavator contemptuously remarked that the labors of the American School of Oriental Research at Tell

[1] Dr. Albright has read this section and that on "Bethel and Ai" and made valuable suggestions.

el-Ful did not appear to have been very productive and that nothing bearing upon the identification of the site had been discovered. The statement revealed a clear misunderstanding of the purpose of archaeology and the value of excavation. To the former director of an expensive expedition, striking museum objects were the only evidence of "production" and inscriptions the only satisfactory proof of a topographical identification.

It is surely something to have shown that the archaeology of Tell el-Ful exactly fits the history of the first capital of Israel, Gibeah of Saul, with which, by common consent, the tell has been identified. It is a real contribution to have determined when the site was first occupied and to have followed the little village and its primitive castle through their numerous stages of habitation and abandonment, which clearly reflect the varying fortunes of Judea and the fluctuations of its northern border. It is both interesting and enlightening to have pictured the crude and primitive life of Israel's first king, even to the pots used in his kitchen. To have done all this with the expenditure of only a couple of thousands of dollars is a real achievement.

East of the modern highway about three miles north of the Damascus Gate in Old Jerusalem there rises a limestone hill with a little mound on its summit. Being on the highest ridge of the central mountain range, it reaches an elevation of 2754 feet. Only Nebi Samwil overtops it. It has, therefore, a fine outlook in every direction and well deserves the epithet "height" (*gib'ah*).

The Arabs call it Tell el-Ful, the "hill of the beans," because beans grow in its soil of marl with unusual luxuriance, whereas wheat and other grains produce only miserable crops. To its identification with Gibeah of Benjamin, the home of Saul, there had been a few dissenting voices, particularly because the village of Jeba' lies only a couple of miles to the east and seems to preserve the ancient name, whereas Tell el-Ful has lost it completely. Only excavation could settle the question. If there should prove to be no remains of the Early Iron Age, 1200-900

B.C., then there could be no question. Tell el-Ful would not be the site of Gibeah of Saul. If the discovered remains should fit the literary references to Gibeah, which run from Samuel down to Jerome, then the arguments for Tell el-Ful would be put on a very plausible basis.

Dr. W. F. Albright as director of the American School of Oriental Research and of the expedition was able to devote only two short campaigns of altogether a little over two months to the task, one in 1922 and 1923 and one in 1933. He was sadly hampered by the contentiousness of the sixty-six owners of the two acres of land involved. At first they asked four hundred pounds rental. Eventually, they went so far as to bring Dr. Albright before the District Magistrate on numerous formidable charges, for which they had no evidence whatever.

In several respects the second expedition corrected the first, for the decade which had elapsed was archaeologically the most fruitful in Palestine's history, and much had been learned. An enlargement of the field of operations in the second campaign inevitably altered the picture also by way of addition.

According to the conclusions reached during the second campaign, the dates assigned to the various strata during the first were slightly lowered, as in nearly all of Dr. Albright's recent chronological studies. In brief, the little village went through seven periods. First, in the twelfth century, there was merely a village of Hebrew peasants which was destroyed by fire, probably in the intertribal warfare described in Judges 19-20. Next came a village with a fortress (I) which according to its pottery should fall after 1050 B.C. Built of massive polygonal masonry, it was probably the "castle" of Saul as Israel's king, and therefore dates a little before 1000 B.C. It was destroyed and rebuilt immediately, of less massive but better-laid masonry, either during Saul's reign or shortly after his death on Gilboa.

This fortress (II) apparently fell into neglect and was abandoned during the period when Jerusalem became the capital, and Ramah, Geba, and Mizpah were the border fortresses of Judah. Sometime in the late ninth or the eighth century a corner tower of Saul's citadel was carefully rebuilt as a *migdal*, a northern watchtower and outpost of the capital. The former citadel walls were otherwise almost entirely removed, either to construct the *migdal* or later to rebuild the village on the top of the hill. The *migdal* was destroyed and rebuilt probably in the seventh century. That the top of the hill was occupied in later pre-exilic times is proved by the presence of the familiar *lemelekh* stamp on jar handles found in the tower and in house ruins outside. Both tower and village were probably destroyed by the Chaldeans.

In the Persian-Hellenistic period (500-100 B.C.) including Maccabean times, the site was occupied by a prosperous village which was larger than any that preceded it, as was proved by Hellenistic potsherds in debris to a depth of ten feet on the eastern edge of the hill. In the century before the fall of Jerusalem a village centered again around the old ruined fortress, to be destroyed probably by Titus as he marched upon Jerusalem in 70 A.D. When Paula made her pilgrimage to Jerusalem about 385 A.D., Jerome described the place as destroyed to its very foundations.

The site thus was occupied before and during the eleventh century by a Benjamite village and the castle of a petty princeling on the border of Jebusite Jerusalem. When Jerusalem became the capital and Judah's frontier moved to the northern boundary of Benjamin, it became a mere outpost and watchtower of the capital city, a role for which its height eminently fitted it. In times of peace and prosperity it could harbor a village, but its small, wind-swept height was not so inviting as the sites of rival villages on all sides and it did not enjoy continued occupation. What is known of its history admirably suits the archaeological findings and the location of the tell. It would be a fallacy of the middle term to insist that the demonstration is logically complete, but there can be little doubt that the earliest fortress which Dr. Albright uncovered represents the royal "palace" and the citadel of Saul.

The first fortress was the most massively constructed of all.

Walls of Tell el-Ful (Gibeah): Lowest wall ninth century fortress of kings of Judah; highest wall, Maccabean fortress; between, possibly Maccabean buttress.

Large house; inner room in foreground, three rooms opening into it. In the background the excavated ruins are being covered up to preserve them. Tell en-Nasbeh.

The Kedron Valley, village of Silwan at right, hill on which the city of David lay at left below city wall, this side of houses (1921). "The Valley" is off the picture to the left.

Piece of typical Herodian masonry in city wall east of the Dome of the Rock. Large stone about 27 feet long.

Its outer walls of large, roughly shaped stones were between 8 and 10 feet in thickness. Its exact size cannot be determined for only the lower walls and foundations of the southwest corner were preserved. Apparently the whole would have covered two or three city lots. A heavy layer of ashes proves that there must have been a second story in the first fortress, as a wide stairway proved for the second. From the ashes Mr. John Dinsmore, botanist of Jerusalem, determined that cypress and pine were the timbers used. Thus it is evident that Judea was not then denuded as it now is, but that coniferous trees of some size grew upon its hills.

The simplicity of the structure and its furnishings must not be overlooked. The best room Saul had for an audience chamber, where David might have played his little harp, barely equaled a modest modern living room, 14 by 23 feet. Some of his pottery was painted with simple horizontal bands, but none of the highly decorated Philistine pottery and no foreign importations were found. Cooking pots of standard size, nine or ten inches across, other ware that had been hand burnished, some of it over a red slip, thin, light saucers, polished black juglets, and well-shaped decanters appear. Some of the ware was of fine clean paste, much of it decidedly coarse. There were the usual finds of spinning whorls, grinding querns, and rubbing stones, a game board and a counter to speak of both work and play. Two bronze arrowheads and numerous round slingstones told of the serious business of war. Wine, oil and grain jars showed that the basement rooms were stored with food. Such are the remains found in a Hebrew "royal palace" of three thousand years ago.

A Border Fortress—Tell en-Nasbeh

Only one expedition since 1920 has attacked a mound, gone systematically through it, and completed the task of excavation—the Pacific School of Religion expedition at Tell en-Nasbeh. Most unfortunately in this case the excavator passed away before beginning the work of publishing his results. The late Dr. W. F. Badè, Professor of Old Testament Literature and Semitic Languages in the Pacific School of Religion, carried through the excavation of the site and founded a "Palestine Institute," to carry it on and to conserve the results for biblical interpretation and instruction.

Tell en-Nasbeh lies on a large, rounded limestone hill about eight miles from Jerusalem on the highway that runs north to Samaria. South of it are Ramah and Gibeah, north and northeast are Beeroth and Bethel. The name 'Attarah is attached to the southern end of the hill. The topographical problem is whether it is to be identified with the Mizpah of Samuel, as various authorities had done, or with Ataroth-Addar, or, as some hold, with Beeroth. The rival for the site of Mizpah is Nebi Samwil, four miles to the southwest, with which Eusebius identified it. When Dr. Badè was seeking a site for excavation, Dr. Albright suggested Tell en-Nasbeh in the hope that excavation might solve the problem. This has been done, so far as is possible until Nebi Samwil is excavated.

The expedition went through five seasons, 1926, 1927, 1929, 1932, and 1935, usually from late March to early July. The last season of work proved too strenuous for Dr. Badè. He suffered a collapse before reaching Marseilles on the return trip and, after a temporary recovery, passed away in March, 1936. Fortunately, Mr. J. C. Wampler, who had been his assistant since 1929 and therefore through three major seasons, has been able to co-ordinate the results as well as was humanly possible without Dr. Badè's own supervision. It is hoped that the first volumes of the final publication, prepared by Mr. Wampler and the writer, may appear in 1943.

The first year's work in a little over two months uncovered the strongest city wall which, up to that time, had been found in pre-Roman Palestine. On the mound itself Early Bronze Age tombs with pottery which at that time was unique came to light. The second expedition continued the clearance of the great wall and discovered what was regarded as a Hebrew sanctuary. The third continued the clearance of the mound and began the search for tombs, which proved most rewarding. The fourth and fifth seasons continued the same tasks.

During the first three seasons, continual search was made for city gates, but they tantalizingly evaded the workmen's mattocks. Since the parcels of ground to be excavated had to be selected and paid for in advance, each season's work represented the best possible prognostication as to where structures of interest, including gates, would be found. The gate was not found until the fourth season, when the last remaining stretches of wall were uncovered, in the least expected place.

When found, it proved to be a perfect illustration of all that could be expected from the biblical references to the "gate" and the activities carried on near it in Hebrew times. But it was unique in construction. It faced, not toward the south and Jerusalem, but toward the northeast, toward Bethel and the Northern Kingdom of Israel. The wall running up from the south overlapped the wall coming down from the north end of the city, leaving a space of 30 feet between them. The gate was placed between these parallel walls at the southern end of the northern one. Thus outside the gate a long expanse of northern wall, and a great tower at the northern end of the southern wall enclosed a sort of court which was almost 30 feet square. The gate had an opening a trifle over 13 feet wide and consisted of two portals separated on each side by a cell-like guard room.

The walls of the external court and the interior guard rooms were lined with stone benches. Quite clearly everything here was prepared for the varied business which, according to numerous Old Testament passages, took place "in the gate." Justice was dispensed, business transacted, markets held, gossip exchanged, and prophetic sermons preached "in the gate."

The walls about the gate were preserved up to a height of from 6 to 9 feet. The sill, the sockets for the pivots on which the leaves swung, and the stop against which they were closed were in place. The stone with a hole in it into which the bar was fastened when the leaves were shut was found in one gate post and, running through the other into the tower, the long slot into which the bar was thrust back when the gates were opened.

The walls of the city were equally interesting. They enclosed an area of some seven acres. Their thickness was astonishing in so small a city, running from 15 to 20 feet. At important salients, towers projecting as much as seven feet beyond the wall and having a length of 30 feet were built, and their bases protected against battering rams by heavy revetments. Where the upper portions of city walls have been found elsewhere, they are of brick. This does not prove that all walls were so constructed. Great heaps of stone were found at the foot of the Tell en-Nasbeh walls and it seems more reasonable to suppose that, in a region where earth is scarce and stone superabundant, as at Tell en-Nasbeh, the whole wall might have been of stone. Be that as it may, the walls, which in places still stand to a height of 25 feet, probably reached a total height of 35 to 40 feet. They were constructed of good-sized, but not cyclopean, blocks roughly shaped and fitted together and laid in clay mortar, with smaller stones to fill in the interstices. The outside was covered to a height of 15 or 18 feet with a lime plaster.

Their crude and massive construction led to their being seriously misdated. In 1926 when the walls were first uncovered, the archaeologists at the International Archaeological Congress held at Jerusalem in that year unanimously agreed in placing them in the Middle Bronze Age, not much later than the megalithic walls of Jericho and Balatah. Subsequent investigation discovered Early Iron Age sherds lying under and through the walls, and therefore proved conclusively that they were not built until near the end of that age, about 900 B.C. The incident shows how difficult it is to date walls from their general appearance unless they have well-marked idiosyncrasies, as Herod's walls, for example, often do.

Another mistake was made in the earlier seasons. Some of the pottery found was dated to the Middle Bronze Age by the most competent experts. However, as further material was collected by successive expeditions, it became apparent that the truly characteristic Middle and Late Bronze types were wanting. It is now seen that practically no Middle or Late Bronze (2100–1230 B.C.) pottery has been found. There is no considerable amount of Early Iron i and Philistine pottery, but this does not prove lack of occupation during these periods, for much less was found at Tell el-Ful only 5 miles away, though this site was occupied from 1200 B.C. or a little earlier.

The site continued to be occupied without any complete or even serious destruction down almost until the Hellenistic period. Over 90 stamped jar handles bearing the familiar *lemelekh* legend prove that it was an important city during the century or so before the Exile and that it belonged to Judah. Their absence at Bethel, only three miles to the north, demonstrates that at least in this later period, the border lay between the two little cities. *Yehud* stamps chiefly on handles with one ridge—the postexilic type—prove that it was likewise inhabited and belonged to Judah in the Persian period.

Twenty-eight handles of the same type bear three letters *m-s-p*, or *m-s-h*. Thereby hangs a tale of archaeological and paleographic uncertainty. Some scholars insist on reading *m-s-p* (Mizpah) and regard this inscription of three letters as proving the identity of Tell en-Nasbeh with the city of Samuel and Gedaliah. Others are equally certain that, paleographically considered, the final letter can only be *he*, even though the meaning of the word is not clear. It seems to be a stamp peculiar to Tell en-Nasbeh for it has been found nowhere else except, in a single specimen, at Jericho.

The discovery of several pieces of Attic pottery and an early Attic coin proves the existence of a settlement here until the fifth century. But the absence of Ptolemaic, Seleucid, and Maccabean coins in any numbers makes it clear that only a few persons have lived on the hill after the Persian period. Possibly there was merely a watchtower, or military patrol outpost, on the hill.

It must be again admitted that, as at Tell Beit Mirsim and Tell el-Ful, archaeology is not able to say the final word on the problem of identification. The remains discovered fit the history of Mizpah, and that very closely. That does not prove the identification but only renders it plausible. Until Nebi Samwil can be excavated, the answer still depends in part upon the dubious topographic references in literature. If Nebi Samwil should be found to parallel the history of Mizpah and Tell en-Nasbeh, the question will remain unanswered. If it does not correspond so well to the history of Mizpah, then it will become perfectly clear that Eusebius and subsequent tradition were mistaken in connecting that site with Samuel and that, as now seems probable, Tell en-Nasbeh was the Mizpah of Samuel.[2]

Entirely apart from the problem of identification, the excavation of Tell en-Nasbeh has abundantly justified itself in the light it has thrown on the cultural history of the Judean kingdom. The great walls, the remarkable gate, the houses, jewelry, pottery, utensils of all kinds, wine and oil presses, dyeing plants, indeed the whole gamut of life in a provincial city passes before one's eyes in the expedition's discoveries. The tombs cover not only the period of the city's history, but, since in the necropolis burials had repeatedly been made from the neighboring Byzantine ruin called Khirbet esh-Shuweikeh, they carry the story on down into Christian times. Even if not Mizpah, Tell en-Nasbeh shows how valuable a contribution archaeology can make to history.

BETHEL AND AI

Three miles in a straight line north of Tell en-Nasbeh and a very little east, on the old road to Shechem, lies Beitin, which is universally identified with Bethel. A mile east of Beitin rises et-Tell, generally identified with Ai. Bethel is more often mentioned in the Bible than any other city except Jerusalem. Ai bulks large in one narrative of Joshua (chs. 7 f.) and is mentioned three times in other books of the Bible. Yet the fortunes of the two cities were inextricably linked together.

[2] The complicated data, inscriptional, archaeological, and literary, touching the identification will be fully set forth by Professor James Muilenburg and the writer in the forthcoming publication.

With regard to et-Tell, archaeology in the twenties made one of its most serious blunders. On the basis of the examination of surface sherds and a little superficial digging here and there by Professor Garstang as director of Antiquities, Albright and Garstang had declared that the ceramic evidence confirmed the biblical account of the fall of Ai at Joshua's hands in the sixteenth or fifteenth century. As Professor Garstang has shown, no incident in the Bible better suits the locale in which it is placed than the story of Joshua's capture of the city.

Imagine the archaeological dismay when in 1934, the late Mme. Krause-Marquet and Mr. S. Yeivin began excavations at et-Tell and made the entirely unexpected discovery that the city was destroyed before the end of the Early Bronze Age and was not occupied for over a thousand years, until the Hebrews had settled in Palestine. The error was due to the fact that little had been known of the period before 1600 B.C. until about 1930, when the lower strata at Beth-shan and Megiddo were reached. Early Bronze Age pottery was frequently dated much too late. New light appeared also on later periods. The sherds which had been taken as proving Ai's occupation in the Late Bronze Age before the Israelites entered were seen to be of a kind which existed also in the Israelite Age, while an overwhelming mass of Early Bronze Age pottery along with Egyptian alabaster vases of the Second and Third Dynasties proved that the main occupation of Ai had fallen before 2200 B.C., or even before 2400 B.C. The palace and latest sanctuary are coeval with Tomb A at Jericho.

As the excavations in both 1934 and 1935 showed, Ai had been a flourishing city in the third millennium. It had strong walls, well-constructed stone houses, and a porticoed palace on the top of the hill. In a small but interesting shrine built against the south wall the remains of a sacrifice lay before an altar. A very seemly collection of pottery came from tombs roughly contemporary with the earliest sanctuary. Ai was a large and flourishing city when, apparently, Jerusalem was still without walls. But how does it happen that the Hebrew historians relate

a circumstantial account of its capture when for 1000 years it
already had been what its name implies, *ha-ʿAi*, "the ruin"?

Various explanations have been offered. Perhaps the Hebrews
received from the Canaanites whom they conquered a more or
less circumstantial tradition explaining "the ruin," and simply
transferred the story to their own hero, Joshua. Perhaps the
story of the conquest of Bethel has been transferred to "the
ruin." As the Judean historian knew the terrain perfectly, it
was easy for him in either case to describe the various movements of the attacking party with complete topographical accuracy.[3]

Another group of considerations enters into the explanation.
While Mme. Krause-Marquet was working at et-Tell, Dr. Albright was directing at Beitin a memorial expedition in honor
of Dr. Kyle, with whom he had labored so happily at Tell
Beit Mirsim. As operations proceeded, it became clear that
Bethel and Ai were archaeological and historical complements,
one of the other. Bethel was founded about the time of Ai's
destruction and flourished throughout the whole of the Middle
Bronze and Late Bronze Ages. This suggests how it was possible for the Hebrew historian to confuse the capture of Bethel
with the age-old tradition regarding Ai.

Dr. Albright had made soundings at Beitin in 1927 sufficient to
prove that it was a valuable site. As the ancient city is largely
covered by the modern village, areas for excavation had to be
rented in a fig orchard. In the second expedition, which ran
from July to September, 1934, plots of ground covering about
970 square yards were investigated.

The results were not startling if "museum pieces" be the
criterion, although a cylinder seal (of about 1300 B.C.) picturing and naming in hieroglyphics the goddess Astarte and a bone
sistrum handle shaped like a Hathor column and capital (15th
century) were found. There was a considerable number of coins

---

[3] The writer accompanied Professor Garstang on the walk which yielded the
picture in his *Joshua-Judges*, pl. XXXI, and was then fully convinced by the
interpretation given, pp. 149-58. See Albright, *BAS* 56 (1934), 11.

running from Alexander the Great to the fall of Jerusalem in 68-9 A.D. The occupation of Bethel, beginning after 2200 B.C., reached its highest prosperity in the Late Bronze Age, when the city presents some of the best-laid masonry of that period as yet found in Palestine. It continued until sometime in the thirteenth century when it was destroyed in a tremendous conflagration, according to Dr. Albright's belief at the hands of the Israelites. There was a complete break in the cultural sequence, followed by three phases of a very different but homogeneous civilization, and then a fourth in which a decided improvement appears. These cover the Early Iron Age. In Middle Iron there are three centuries of more or less uninterrupted development. It is significant that characteristic "Samaria" pottery is wanting and that commercial connections seem closest with Judea. But since not a single *lemelekh* stamp was found, the place clearly belonged to the Northern Kingdom.

Early in the sixth century Bethel was destroyed in a great conflagration, no doubt at Chaldean hands. For a time it lay unoccupied, but during the Persian period it was crudely rebuilt and continued until its destruction by the Romans in 70 A.D. During all of this time Ai lay unoccupied, except for occasional inhabitants in early Israelite times. The story of Ai's archaeological resurrection at least proves archaeology's ability to correct its own mistakes as well as those of Hebrew historians.[4]

ISRAEL'S FIRST SANCTUARY

Largely through the almost fanatical enthusiasm of Dr. Aage Schmidt, a Danish expedition headed by the late Dr. Hans Kjaer of the National Museum of Copenhagen undertook the excavation of Seilun, the site of ancient Shiloh. It is one of the most clearly marked and least disputed sites in all of Palestine. However, the exact location of the ancient sanctuary was quite uncertain. Excavation could possibly settle that question and also reveal something of the character of primitive Hebrew religion.

[4] Père Vincent still holds to the historicity of the biblical account. See *RB*, 1937, pp. 231-66, and Albright, *BAS*, 74, pp. 15 ff.

The task was undertaken with the purpose of applying and adapting the meticulous methods of Danish prehistorians to Palestinian conditions. Excavation was carried on with the collaboration of Dr. Albright and later of Dr. Nelson Glueck as consulting archaeologists during 1926, 1929, and 1932. Unfortunately various circumstances, culminating in Dr. Kjaer's death in September, 1932, as a result of overwork at the task, have prevented the expedition from doing more than prove the site to be much more rewarding than was anticipated.

The remains even before excavation was begun were enough to pique any person's curiosity. At the southern foot of a ruin-covered tell was a *weli*, a Moslem saint's shrine called Jami'a el-Yeteïm, a low, dark building built in part of Hellenistic or Roman materials and shaded by a luxuriant *ballut* tree. A little farther away to the south was a ruin called "Jami'a es-Sittin, consisting merely of some standing walls and fallen architraves. Search soon discovered a little to the west of the last a large circle of stones surrounding a smooth area of rock in which a rectangle had been laid out with a *mihrab*, or prayer niche, to the south. It, then, was also a mosque and the *mihrab* pointed to outdoor worship. There could be no doubt that the Moslems once regarded this as a most sacred spot.

Slightly protruding walls soon directed the excavators to two buildings between the two mosques. The removal of only a foot or two of soil revealed the outlines and well-preserved mosaic floors of two churches with dedicatory inscriptions and Christian symbols. In one of them there lay beside the church two rooms which corresponded in their measurements to the ancient tabernacle. The probability is that in Byzantine times this was shown as the site of the sanctuary of Eli and Samuel. There is both literary and archaeological evidence to suggest that before the Christians the Jews had made it a place of pilgrimage.

Soundings on the mound in 1926 disclosed nothing but Hellenistic and Roman remains. A small excavation on the west side of the mound outside a Hellenistic or Roman city wall uncovered remains of the twelfth and early eleventh centuries but nothing later, thus apparently indicating the destruction of Shiloh by the Philistines about 1050 B.C. or a little earlier (1 Sa 1-4) and fully confirming Jeremiah's reference to it as lying waste in his time (Jer 7.12, etc.).

A month of excavation in 1932 before Dr. Kjaer's death discovered nothing startling. There was an Early Bronze and a Middle Bronze occupation, each followed by a period of abandonment. As the discovered evidence now stands, the Early Iron occupation by the incoming Israelites was the most extensive. A slight investigation of a large level space on the north slope of the tell indicated that, contrary to some learned opinions, the tabernacle could not have stood there. The site of the tabernacle, therefore, remains to be discovered. What has been done merely leaves the desire for a more complete investigation in the hope of discoveries which will place the present somewhat tentative conclusions beyond all doubt.

For the student of the history of religions Seilun is of outstanding interest because of the persistence with which it remained a center of vibration. A highly organized priesthood, countless sacred legends, innumerable great names, endlessly repeated literary allusions, holy and sometimes magnificent buildings combined to make Jerusalem eternally "the Holy City" for Jew, Christian, and Moslem. Shiloh flourished as a sanctuary for all Israel for only two centuries. It came to an inglorious end by a combination of priestly weakness, folly, and dishonesty. Yet, even though for six centuries it lay waste and uninhabited, it was not forgotten. Jew, Christian, and Moslem, one after the other and perhaps all together, came to worship at the shrine where, according to hoary legend, Israel first gathered for united worship in the "Promised Land."

MIGDAL-SHECHEM

The most puzzling and disappointing of all the excavations in Palestine has been that at the site of ancient Shechem. Lying by the village of Balatah a little north of the highway and at the foot of Mount Ebal, the mound was by no means conspicuous, but it has proved to contain remains of the strongest Middle Bronze Age fortress yet uncovered in Palestine. In its day it must have been well able to control the currents of war and commerce which flowed through the pass between Ebal and Gerizim, the easiest and best-watered path through all the central mountain.

The discoveries made can only be described as astonishing. Some of them strike the eye as do very few of the excavated ruins of Palestine. Yet the excavators continued to follow the old technique of trenching which other archaeologists had abandoned. Too little systematic attention was paid to the pottery, apparently none at all during two seasons, 1928 and 1931. As a result almost no chronological results which have been announced can be regarded as final, while much valuable information has been lost forever. Professor Ernst Sellin, already famous for fruitful excavations at Ta'annak and Jericho, began work upon the site in 1913-14. In 1926 and 1927 and again in 1934, supported in part by gifts from Holland and America, he resumed the task. The director who took his place in 1928 and 1931, Dr. G. Welter, a classical archaeologist, only introduced greater confusion. Apparently the last brief excavation by Dr. Sellin and Dr. H. Steckeweh made progress toward greater clarity.

What can be said of the results is that no evidence of occupation before 2000 B.C. has yet come to light. Apparently there was a small Middle Bronze Age town, then a typical Hyksos fortification, and thereafter a much larger, seventeenth-century city with a most remarkable wall and imposing gates of massive cyclopean masonry. Nothing like it has been found in Palestine. Within the city a structure of most unusual strength, interpreted by Sellin as a fortress temple, and above it an Early Iron Age temple were discovered. Two Canaanite cuneiform tablets were found in 1926, and the limestone plaque in 1934.[5] Though the former are only private business documents, they show that writing was in common use and raise the hopes that

[5] See above chap. VIII.

more may come to light. Occupation of the site in Canaanite and early Israelite times was demonstrated and some Israelite incense altars were found. Doubtless after Samaria was founded, it lost its importance. The site was occupied in Hellenistic and Roman times, but again, with the founding of Roman Neapolis a short distance away, it declined.

The walls and gates of cyclopean masonry deserve more than passing notice. The northwest gate is similar in plan to the Iron Age gates of Megiddo and Tell en-Nasbeh, but much more massive. It covers a total area of about 60 by 53 feet. Two parallel walls 60 feet long and 15 feet thick form the sides and project out beyond the city walls as massive towers. Between these walls three portals with openings of about 5¼ feet were placed, separated on each side by two guard rooms or courts which are 13 feet wide by 9 feet deep. The walls and the thresholds were constructed of tremendous oblong blocks of limestone roughly shaped. The foundations, built of similar blocks, go down 15 feet—a sufficient deterrent to mining. The eastern gate had only a double portal, as at Megiddo and Tell en-Nasbeh, but it was much more spacious. Its two guard rooms measured 19 by 16 feet and the portal opening was 11½ feet.

The temple, or *migdal,* within the city—probably it was both—was equally impressive. It was 69 feet wide by 86 feet long. As its walls were seventeen or eighteen feet in thickness, there remained within them a room 33 feet wide by 45 feet long. A narrow passage led into it from a broad open porch. The roof was supported by three pairs of columns, which thus divided it into three equal aisles. Almost at the center were two stone bases which may have supported a cult image and an altar. The building may, therefore, be the temple of Baal-berith (Jdg 8.33; 9.4), the "stronghold of the house of El-berith" (Jdg 9.46).

Abraham's Oak

To the east of the highway a little north of Hebron is a structure bearing the imposing title of Haram Ramet el-Khalil, "the sacred area of the height of the Friend of God" (Abraham). As it formerly appeared, it was only a rectangular enclosure having a well at one corner and consisting of magnificent masonry that vied with the best Herodian walls in the size and fit of its stones. A few short campaigns by Father D. A. Mader for the Catholic Görresgesellschaft revealed a complicated history.

Apparently the structure had been begun by Herod when he was building the Hebron *haram* over the patriarchal tombs. The greater part of the masonry, however, is of distinctly Hadrianic type and literary evidence points to his having built it and made it a great market with a temple of Mercury at its center. Father Mader found evidence of many sacrifices to the god of merchants and travelers. Over the ruins of the temple a church and accompanying monastery were built, and pilgrims came from far to see the place where Abraham pitched his tent under the oak of Mamre (Gen 13.18; 18.1). The oak of Mamre has journeyed to another spot down the valley to suit the convenience of a Russian monastery and pilgrim hostel. But in the pavement near the well is a round opening where a large tree may have grown when this was a famous place of Jewish and Christian pilgrimage.

Outside toward the west Father Mader uncovered insignificant ancient walls which he would assign to a pre-Herodian period and use as a springboard to carry us back to David's time. This ancient shrine, he thinks, might naturally be the place where David was crowned king when he reigned seven years in Hebron. The suggestion is not impossible. Whether it is true or not, Haram Ramet el-Khalil is like Seilun, a revelation of the tenacity with which religious superstition holds to external objects that have some sacred association.

A JUDEAN FORTRESS

A little over four miles north of Hebron lies a site known as Beit Sur, or Burj es-Sur. Not half a mile to the northwest lies a low mound called Khirbet et-Tubeiqah. At Burj es-Sur only Byzantine and Arab pottery appear on the surface. At Khirbet et-Tubeiqah Israelite and Hellenistic pottery was found. Independently in 1924 and 1925 Père Abel, Professor Alt, and Dr. Albright reached the conclusion that Khirbet et-Tubeiqah must be the site of Beth-zur, which, according to the literary references, lay in this region. Professor Gustaf Dalman had reached the same conclusion on topographic grounds as early as 1913. The excavations managed by Professor O. R. Sellers and directed by Professor Albright in the summer of 1931 on behalf of the Presbyterian Theological Seminary of Chicago and the American Schools of Oriental Research proved that the surface reading of ceramic data was correct, and, in addition, made several interesting discoveries.

Beth-zur appears only three times in the Old Testament, all in late passages.[6] It is mentioned in the division of Judah's lot and as a place Rehoboam fortified. Were these references correct? The results of the excavations essentially confirmed the biblical statements. According to the archaeological evidence, Beth-zur was occupied in the times of the Judges. It was destroyed about 1000 B.C. but rebuilt a century later. It suffered a serious decline about 600 B.C., and a little later an entirely different culture dominated by Greek, not Persian, influences appeared. It was an important fortress during the Maccabean wars with Syria but declined when the Judean border was extended southward to include the Idumeans, and its garrison was removed. After John Hyrcanus it appears to have had almost no population. In Byzantine times, its name migrated to the new site at Beit Sur.

The discovery was made of one historical fact which no one had suspected. The place had a considerable population from the late eighteenth to the sixteenth century, that is during the Hyksos period. A few handfuls of Early Bronze Age potsherds were recovered, not enough to prove more than a sporadic occupation. The Middle Bronze Age pottery was sufficient to prove the presence of a real settlement on the hill. But there

6 Josh 15.58; 2 Ch 11.7; Neh 3.16.

was almost nothing of Late Bronze ware. The place had been thoroughly destroyed, whether by Habiru or Egyptians, or rival neighbors, who can tell? A large amount of Early and Middle Iron Age ware proves the city's importance in the period of the monarchy. Still more numerous sherds of the Hellenistic period testify to its still greater population in that period.

A few jar handles with stamps of Hyksos designs appeared. There were 11 handles with *lemelekh* stamps, testifying to occupation during the last century of the Hebrew monarchy, but 23 stamped Rhodian jar handles. A similar tale is told by the coins found. Ten were Greek, 53 Ptolemaic, 173 Seleucid, and 18 Maccabean, 16 of these from John Hyrcanus. The 124 coins of Antiochus IV Epiphanes, out of a total of 173 of Seleucid mint, must indicate vigorous trade before the Maccabean revolt began unless they represent booty from Lysias' army defeated before the city.

A great reservoir with rock-cut steps leading down into it occupied much time but contained few important objects along with much refuse. A room with what appeared to be a bath tub had basins that seemed better to suit a dye plant. Competent archaeological visitors could not agree as to its use. There was much else to point to the activities of the inhabitants, far more than can be chronicled here.

This brief survey indicates how much has been learned and unlearned as a result of excavations in the smaller cities in the mountains round about Jerusalem. It shows also how much more there is to learn as further investigations are systematically prosecuted. No unified picture can be drawn. A little can be restored here, another piece there, and thus the historian's conception of the life of the ancients is slowly growing in clearness and comprehensiveness.

It is noteworthy that so many sites in the mountains reveal clear evidence of the appearance of a new culture at the time when the Hebrews entered Palestine. The present tendency is to date this change in cultural character in the thirteenth or very late in the fourteenth century. New cities or villages, as at Tell en-Nasbeh and Tell el-Ful, emerge in the twelfth century. Professor Garstang still holds to a date early in the fourteenth century for the fall of Jericho and doubtless other cities. It is not possible as yet for archaeology to date such breaks in cultural continuity with absolute certainty. Perhaps future generations of archaeologists may do so.

It is also worth noting that, after a sudden decline at the time of the Hebrew conquest, manual dexterity and the standard of living slowly rise until they eventually reach a new peak in the eighth century. Apparently, the Hebrews never achieved the same heights of material prosperity for the few as the less democratic Canaanites had, though possibly Samaria's ivories suggest it. There never came again such importations of beautiful pottery as in the Late Bronze Age. But there does seem to have come a wider extension of prosperity to the many in the Middle Iron period when industries, such as weaving and dyeing, were added to the pastoral and agricultural economy of the Early Iron Age.

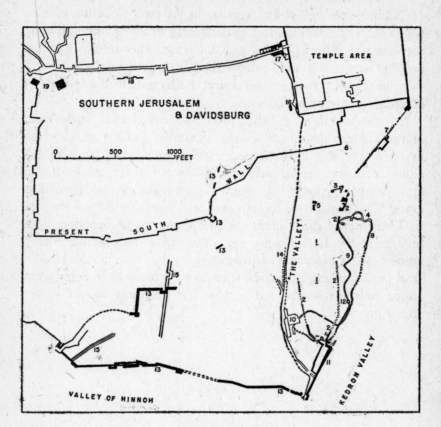

KEY TO PLAN

1. Jebusite Jerusalem, Davidsburg
2. Jebusite Walls
3. Northern Wall
4. "Virgin's Spring"
5. Early Gate
6. Ophel
7. Early Hebrew Wall
8. Early Aqueduct
9. "Hezekiah's Tunnel"
10. "Pool of Siloam," Byzantine Church

11. Early and Later Hebrew Walls
12. Great Round Tower (of Siloam?)
13. Ancient Wall, Date Uncertain
14. Street, Drain, and Stair of New Testament Times
15. Ancient Streets
16. Robinson's Arch
17. Wilson's Arch
18. Line of First North Wall
19. Palace of Herod

FIG. 4

CHAPTER XV

JERUSALEM

THE SEARCH FOR THE CITY OF DAVID

❖

IN ALL of Palestine Jerusalem has been the most alluring place
to excavators, but it has also proved the most difficult. Its long
and tragic history, its intimate associations with Old Testament
story and with the beginnings of Christianity, the inexhaustible
fascination of its holy places for the pilgrim, the glamor of the
Crusades, its sanctity for Christian, Moslem, and Hebrew, all
this makes the problems of its history, topography, and archaeology familiar and attractive to a vast number of people. Small
wonder that the first excavations of French, English, and German archaeologists in Palestine were attempted at the Holy
City!

To render an account of excavation at Jerusalem intelligible,
a preliminary word regarding topography and nomenclature
is necessary. Jerusalem stands on the southern edge of a rugged
plateau which ends in two ridges stretching out like stubby
fingers to the south. Between them lies the valley which
Josephus for some unknown reason names the Tyropean, or
Cheese Monger's, Valley. It is better called simply "the Valley,"
el-Wad, as it is known among Jerusalem Arabs. East of the
Valley lies the Haram esh-Sharif, the "noble sanctuary," or
Temple area. South of this one of the fingers, the "Ophel" hill,
runs now outside the walls. It is in good part turned into veg-
etable gardens belonging to the village of Silwan, which
straggles along the hillside opposite across the Kedron Valley
to the east. West of the Valley is the other finger which has
long been known as Mount Zion, also ending in a hill outside

the southern wall, where are several buildings, new and old. To the west of Mount Zion the Valley of Hinnom begins, then takes a sharp turn to the left, and runs east, covered with a beautiful olive grove, down to the mouths of the Valley and the Kidron, which almost meet just below the so-called Pool of Siloam.

Recent excavators have centered their attention on the southeastern hill, because they were in search of the City of David and the tombs of David and his successors, for it is recorded of David and each of his successors down to Ahaz that he "slept with his fathers and was buried with his fathers in the city of David" (1 Kg 14.31, etc.). The site of the city which David captured from the Jebusites and made his capital has long been one of the moot problems of Jerusalem topography. The discovery of his tomb and the tombs of his successors would excite more interest than that of Jesus himself, for not only Christians but Jews and Moslems also would regard it as a place of the greatest interest. It would at once become an unparalleled cynosure for all tourists. Such tombs, if found undisturbed, would attract as much attention as that of Tutankhamen.

Untutored Beginnings

As it happens, the first recorded modern excavation in Jerusalem was undertaken in search of the tombs of the Hebrew monarchs, but in a very different part of the city. In 1850 de Saulcy persuaded himself that the "Tombs of the Kings," lying back of the Cathedral of St. George, a little north of the American School of Oriental Research, were actually what tradition called them. Eventually returning in 1863, he cleared them and believed that he could point out the very places where the various royal bodies had lain.

With equal lighthearted ignorance of archaeological problems and methods the newly founded Palestine Exploration Fund sent Lieutenant (later General Sir Charles) Warren with a few noncommissioned officers of the Royal Engineers to Jerusalem in 1867 under instructions which prove how little the committee knew. He was to determine the exact location of the Temple of Solomon, the correctness of the site of the Church of the Holy Sepulchre, and the course of history of the city's walls. The fact that only the question regarding the location of the Temple has now been even partially settled illustrates well the difficulty of the tasks so confidently undertaken. The site of the City of David was not specifically mentioned, but it was necessarily involved in the instructions regarding the city walls. In his great volume on *Jerusalem* in the *Survey of Western Palestine* Warren notes the location of the City of David as one of the major problems and remarks with surprise that some would even locate it on Ophel. Since 1867 the search has gone on and a score of scholars and excavators have made contributions toward the solution of the problem until finally in 1927 an excavator of the Palestine Exploration Fund proved beyond cavil that the City of David was where Warren thought it could not be. This chapter is concerned with the long story of this search.

Warren was handicapped by blissful unconsciousness of the intricacy of his problems and complete ignorance of archaeological method, as well as by innumerable obstacles put in his way by Turkish authorities and local inhabitants. He was forbidden to dig within forty feet of the city walls and therefore had to sink shafts and run mines, or tunnels, to any foundations or underground walls he wished to investigate. The work was often interrupted by soldiers. His workmen were attacked, an English sergeant in charge of native workmen was imprisoned, and apparently every effort made to hinder the work and drive the excavators away.

In spite of his many handicaps Warren secured a vast amount of valuable information, some of which will be recounted later. As bearing on the City of David he made two important discoveries. Beginning at the southeast corner of the Haram, he found an ancient wall which he followed for 800 feet toward the southwest, thus proving that the city had once included this area—which nearly all now agree must be "Ophel." In this hill above the Virgin's Fountain, he found the shaft which has since been known by his name, one of those Bronze Age schemes like that at Megiddo for reaching water from within the city walls. It was probably, though not certainly, the *sinnor* by which Joab and his men obtained admission to the city and captured it for David (2 Sa 5.8). Warren also surveyed the tunnel which had been later built, probably by Hezekiah, to bring water down to the Pool of Siloam. Warren's excavations were not confined wholly to the neighborhood of the Temple, and they made some contributions to the problems of other sections. But the prevailing lack of archaeological knowledge caused the destruction of much valuable data and the misinterpretation of others. Jewish pottery and stamped jar handles were ascribed to the Phoenicians, Herodian walls to Solomon, as the guides still do to this day.

Warren did not at any point touch the City of David. The famous French archaeologist, Charles Simon Clermont-Ganneau, was the first modern to set eyes upon the walls of the ancient city. In 1872, workmen in a quarry on the east slope about half way between the spring and the southern point of the hill uncovered a considerable stretch of wall with great foundation stones. Clermont-Ganneau, at that time in Jerusalem as a young French consular employee, observed the wall and discerned its meaning, although he appears not to have published his observations for nearly fifteen years.

Like the Palestine Exploration Fund, the German Palestine Society (Deutscher Palästina-Verein) was led by pious interest in Jerusalem to begin its excavations in this, the most difficult place in the land. In 1881, four years after the founding of the *Verein*, Hermann Guthe, then only a young *Licentiat*, traveled to Palestine full of hopes that by running a few trenches over the Ophel hill he might find the earliest walls of the city and the tombs of the kings of Judah. The discovery of the Siloam inscription the previous June had raised his expectations to the highest pitch and he was unable to await a long-delayed firman from Constantinople, but, with help from Conrad Schick, began digging at once. Fortunately an efficient German consul and an honest and intelligent Turkish governor made it possible for him to carry on without difficulty on telegraphic permission from Constantinople. He devoted himself largely to Ophel. The results of his five months' labors are usually regarded as having been very slight indeed. He just missed several important buildings, walls, and gates. But he corrected previous mistakes, and, if subsequent excavators had known what he did find of walls here and there, they could have worked much more intelligently. If the seemingly meager results discouraged the German society, it was the unfortunate result of having undertaken a too difficult task in the beginning. No other expedition in that region has accomplished more on so small an outlay.

The ordnance survey of Jerusalem made by Captain, later General Sir Charles Wilson, together with the great volume on *Jerusalem* published by the Palestine Exploration Fund in 1884, added tremendously to knowledge of the city, but no further excavating was done until Frederick J. Bliss, fresh from his first major enterprise at Tell el-Hesi, began work for the Palestine Exploration Fund at Jerusalem in 1894. With A. C. Dickie as assistant for two years, he worked until 1897. His excavations were confined almost entirely to the remains outside and south of the present city walls. Here he discovered a series of walls, gates, drains, aqueducts, paved streets, and houses, many of which are not even yet incorporated into any reasonable plan of the ancient city in its numerous vicissitudes. His most interesting single discovery was the church of Eudocia, which once stood over the pool of Siloam. But he also furnished indispensable materials for plans of Jerusalem at various periods in its history.

Bliss's excavations made it perfectly clear that at one time the city wall had included the two southern hills and the Valley between, but he also found a wall running down along the west side of the southeastern hill (the east side of the Valley), and meeting the wall on the east side of the hill so as to include the Pool of Siloam within the city. Plainly the southern limits and outline of the city must have varied greatly at different periods. Unfortunately ceramic chronology was not sufficiently understood to afford any dating criteria, and its value was not sufficiently appreciated to lead even to the recording of the pottery found. Masonry techniques change too little for walls themselves to be datable except in unusual periods, such as those of Herod and Hadrian.

In spite of their many valuable contributions, Bliss's excavations left innumerable points unsettled. Most important of all was the question as to the location of the "city of David," "Davidsburg," as Sir George Adam Smith calls it, the capital which the king occupied after overcoming the Jebusites. Josephus clearly puts this city on the western hill, which, at least since his day, has been called Mount Zion. But there were many who argued that only the eastern hill, south of the Temple Area, had been inhabited by the Jebusites, that Solomon had been the first to occupy the western hill, and that it had mistakenly received the name of Zion, which properly belonged to the eastern hill.

CLAIRVOYANT ARCHAEOLOGY

Until 1909 there were no further excavations in Jerusalem. Then one of the weirdest archaeological expeditions on record was undertaken by an English syndicate under a Captain Parker. The purpose of the undertaking, so it is understood, was not archaeological but commercial. A certain erratic Finnish dilettante asserted that he had discovered in the Book of Ezekiel a cipher which described precisely the location of the Temple treasure which is supposed to have been concealed when the Babylonians captured Jerusalem. With such a prize to be obtained, an abundantly financed expedition was organized which, using its funds freely, easily obtained a permit from the Sublime Porte and began operations on a considerable scale in the Ophel hill.

Fortunately the Dominican fathers of the École Biblique at St. Étienne were soon on the ground, and shortly received ungrudging permission to follow the excavations and record fully whatever of archaeological data might come to light. Père Vincent, who prepared an invaluable report on the operations, gives full credit in private as in print to the generous and courteous treatment he received from Captain Parker and his associates, and equal credit must be given for their publication of the results in both French and English after the failure of their enterprise.

Père Vincent soon found himself greatly puzzled by the erratic course of the excavations. After tunneling had gone in a certain direction for a few days, without any apparent reason a new point of attack would be chosen. Eventually he learned that the operations were actually being directed by a Danish clairvoyant, whose instructions were received from time to time by cable. Needless to say that two years of probing in the hill discovered no treasure.

In 1911 the expedition came to a dramatic, but fortunately not too tragic, end. Whether at the direction of the clairvoyant or not, Captain Parker decided to excavate within the Temple area and, of all places in the world, under the Qubbet es-Sakhrah, the "Dome of the Rock," itself. Bribing the governor of Jerusalem, the chief sheikh, and other officials, he was able to obtain carte blanche for his foolhardy enterprise. After eight o'clock each evening the keys of the Haram were in his hands. But such proceedings allowed too large a scope for blackmail. A disgruntled workman spread the news and soon the Moslems of Jerusalem were in a state of tremendous excitement, threatening a general massacre of Christians. Parker and his aids fled to their private yacht at Jaffa and escaped, while the officials whom he had bribed were arrested and imprisoned.

Having learned to trust the discretion of Père Vincent, Parker had invited him to share their clandestine visits to the holy rock. But the learned father's discretion prevented his accepting the tempting invitation, for he knew the danger only too well. Therefore whether anything of archaeological value was found in this most alluring spot of all we shall never know.

The results of the enterprise on Mount Ophel, however, were valuable, and for that much we can be duly grateful.

One service rendered by the Parker expedition was the cleaning and resurveying of the underground aqueduct of Hezekiah and the Pool of Siloam. Unattractive as the Pool now is to the western tourist, according to all accounts—and the photographic evidence—it was infinitely worse before Parker came and went. Père Vincent surveyed and recorded all the numerous blind canals and caverns connected with the spring, including Warren's shaft, and has presented the clearest picture of the whole which can be found. The expedition rediscovered the beginning of one external aqueduct, found by Schick, Masterman, and Hornstein in 1901, and found a second, new aqueduct. Weill later made the relations of all these water systems clear.

Archaeologically speaking the most important discoveries were certain tombs which contained burials and a few scattered bits of pottery, intensely disappointing, doubtless, to explorers who hoped to find the temple treasures, but, in the hands of one of the foremost ceramic experts in Palestine, Père Vincent, capable of telling a long and interesting story concerning the civilizations which had occupied the hill. Certain burials belonged to the second period discovered at Gezer, the second half of the Early Bronze Age, and therefore, until Damascus can provide earlier materials, indicate Jerusalem as the oldest city in the world which has been continuously occupied. Another interesting and puzzling discovery was a presumably very early gate with monolithic jambs which was found to the east and therefore outside of the eastern line of wall established by the various preceding excavations. Its exact date and its relations to other structures are still undetermined.

THE SEARCH FOR THE KINGS' TOMBS

Two years after Parker's ignominious departure, an expedition of a very different sort attacked the Ophel hill. At the instance of Baron Edmond de Rothschild, Captain Raymond

Weill came in search of the tombs of David and his successors. His avowed purpose has been criticized as unscientific, but his work cannot be. He made adequate use of the labors of his predecessors and reported his own results accurately and fully. Two campaigns were carried on, one in 1913-14, the other in 1923-24.

His procedure was based not upon a secret cipher, but upon the theory, long maintained by Clermont-Ganneau, that the tombs of the kings would be found in the great eastern curve of Hezekiah's tunnel, which had made this bend in order to avoid them. Weill found many tombs, including two containing mass burials of the seventh and sixth centuries in which bodies had been decapitated and the heads placed at gruesome angles to the bodies. He found also four tombs of a peculiar arched construction and unusual size and near them what may have been a funerary chapel. These he believed to be the "tombs of the kings." But his study of Hebrew architecture and engineering led him to abandon Clermont-Ganneau's theory and ascribe his discovery to mere luck. The long bend in the tunnel he thought due merely to bad engineering and laziness. The ancient tunnel diggers had followed the lines of least resistance.

Weill also excavated the series of channels cut in the rock at the side of the hill, channels which had preceded the tunnel. He showed that a complicated system of improvements had followed one another and that the channels had been intended not only to serve the city's population but also to irrigate the king's gardens. He found a series of walls and glacis on the hill slope which proved ancient Jerusalem to have been well defended. He thus made a very considerable contribution to the history of the city and of its inhabitants' struggles with the problems of defense and water supply. He probably has done all that can be done toward discovering the tombs of the kings. But his study of the city's walls is not complete without reference to the last excavations on Ophel, which were undertaken by the Palestine Exploration Fund.

Uncovering the City of David

This venture was due to Professor Garstang, at the time director of Antiquities in Palestine. In 1922 he made a public appeal to archaeologists of all nations to unite in an attack upon the problems of Jerusalem's history. Aside from the resumption of Weill's excavations, the only response came from England. The Palestine Exploration Fund attempted to raise £5000—the minimum sum which Professor Garstang thought at all adequate—and friends interested the proprietor of the London *Daily Telegram*, who offered £1000 on the sole condition that his paper should receive the director's first reports. He was following a worthy tradition, for in 1872 the same paper had sent George Smith to Nineveh in search of "Deluge tablets." The remainder of the sum was secured from various sources, and R. A. S. Macalister, veteran of many Palestinian campaigns, but now professor of Celtic archaeology in Dublin University, was put in charge. The Rev. J. Garrow Duncan was his chief assistant.

In spite of loyal efforts, the expedition was not entirely fortunate. The advance advertising which the undertaking had received led speculators to buy up the fields on the hill and, despite the provisions of the Antiquities law, through someone's incompetence, or worse, the expedition was mulcted of £200 rent for land not worth £20, besides suffering a considerable delay. The time for such an undertaking was also hardly ripe, for the necessary knowledge of ceramic chronology was not available. There is very grave doubt whether the dates assigned to some of the walls uncovered are correct. Some are certainly wrong. However, the expedition, which worked from October, 1923, to November, 1924, and again in the spring and summer of 1925, made its own contribution to enlarging knowledge of the "Holy City."

The show piece of the expedition, the only visible evidence of its work which it has left behind, is a great section of "Jebusite and Solomonic" walls which the visitor can see, standing in lonely grandeur on the hillcrest overlooking the Kidron valley above the Virgin's Fountain. Their date is uncertain, but they are early. The late Dr. H. R. Hall wrote, "They alone would be a sufficient return for the money expended on the excavation . . . , walls that have seen so much of history enacted on and near them." In all 400 feet of the eastern wall were uncovered, bastions, glacis, towers, an inner and an outer wall, ascribed to Jebusite, Davidic, Solomonic, and later periods, all of which makes rich additions to our picture of ancient Jerusalem.

The expedition rendered one very great service. It wrote another most significant chapter in the history of the city by making clear how modest were the original limits of the Jebusite city which David captured. It discovered that there had been a wall and a trench, partly artificial, partly natural, running across the hill from east to west at a point almost halfway between the present city wall south of the Haram area and the southern point of the hill. This trench had been filled with debris containing pottery of the Middle and Late Bronze periods. It must therefore have been dug before 2000 B.C. and must have gone out of use after 1500 B.C. Later a wall was built some sixty feet farther north and this wall seems to mark the northern limit of the Jebusite city which David captured.

In the Tyropean Valley

The expedition conducted by Macalister had determined the northern and eastern limits of the City of David, but the course of the western wall was not known. When in 1927 Mr. J. W. Crowfoot became director of the British School of Archaeology in Jerusalem in succession to Professor Garstang, the task of continuing excavations on Ophel was entrusted to him with the able assistance of Mr. G. M. FitzGerald.

Both men had already had experience with excavation, but neither had reached the point of complacent self-sufficiency which many people, including some archaeologists, attain early in life. They made excellent use of the experience and advice of the several veteran archaeologists of Jerusalem. Neither of them was obsessed with the desire to confirm the Bible or to glorify their work by lugging the Bible in to confirm their conclusions. The result was an excellent piece of excavation scientifically done and intelligently as well as promptly reported.

Mr. Crowfoot undertook what none of his predecessors had dared, an open trench 65 feet wide east and west across the Valley. The unexpected depth of debris made the task much more difficult than had been anticipated. The walls discovered in 1927 led to a southward extension of operations in 1928. Here paucity of debris rather than superabundance tried the excavators' patience. Most trying of all was the discovery that many of the problems which arose could not be solved without going beyond the area leased and that, therefore, they must be adjourned into the indefinite future.

The outstanding discovery of 1927 was a great gate on the western slope of the hill almost directly west of the "North Jebusite ramp" and the "Early Hebrew," or "Solomonic" tower of the east wall. When discovered, it was faced with masonry of Maccabean origin but after the facing was removed the original structure proved to be of Jebusite type, but with evidence of many repairs. The pottery found in the debris which had collected in the lower levels when the gate was in use showed that it must have been built in Jebusite times and continued in use down to the Roman period. A very few sherds of Bronze Age pottery were found. Hellenistic pieces, such as "tear-bottles" and Rhodian jar-handles, were mixed with Early Iron Age sherds. There were "extraordinarily few" fragments of Roman and Byzantine times. A hoard of Maccabean coins came from near the gate. All this is explicable if it be supposed that the gate was kept constantly in use and therefore that little collected. Repairs during the period of the monarchy and again in Maccabean times would account for the turning up and mixture of sherds of various ages. Clearly this region of the city was destroyed and abandoned at the time of the siege of Titus and not again occupied by any considerable populations until the Byzantine period. Then cisterns and the foundations of buildings, dug down to the rock, destroyed a great part of the evidence and mixed in a few later sherds.

The gate was a tremendous affair such as only the Bronze Age produced. The gate towers and the walls on either side ran to twenty-six feet or a little more in width, like those of the east wall, and were still standing to a height of 20 feet above bedrock, on which they stood. The road between the two towers was 11½ feet wide. Gate and wall had been built on a wide platform of rock which allowed space for a road along the wall on the outside approaching the gate and again on the inside. But a sharp, rising rock scarp of the hill inside would have presented an additional obstacle to enemies who forced the gate and would have given the defenders a point of vantage for further resistance. The original construction was not polygonal or megalithic but of roughly hammer-dressed stones laid in fairly regular courses, with mud mortar and a filling of splinters and small stones, masonry typical of the Late Bronze or Early Iron period, but doubtless pre-Hebrew.

The discovery of the great western gate and wall settles quite definitely the general outline of the City of David and of the southeastern section of the city until perhaps Roman times. The city which David captured was shaped somewhat like a gigantic human footprint about 1250 feet long and 400 wide, or like a dolphin headed southward with the end of its tail some distance below the present Haram wall and its nose somewhat short of the Pool of Siloam. At best its area could not have been more than eight acres, which may be compared with the eight acres within the walls at Tell en-Nasbeh, the six acres of Canaanite Jericho and the thirty acres of contemporary Megiddo, but it was defended by stone walls that were impregnable to David's Bedouin and peasant warriors.

Smaller Discoveries

Innumerable small discoveries of more than passing interest have been made by these various expeditions. Among them may be mentioned a Hebrew ostracon, or inscribed potsherd, discovered by Macalister and Duncan. It contains only a list of names, but, coming probably from the seventh century, shows the kind of script used in writing in the capital and so furnishes valuable material for comparison with the more numerous sherds of Samaria and Tell ed-Duweir. A score or more of stamped jar handles, chiefly of the postexilic Jewish province under Persian rule and bearing the letters *y-h*, or *y-h-d*, were found. They stand for the name of the province, *Yehud*, "Judea." Some twenty or thirty stamps bore a pentagram with a letter in each of the five points: *y-r-s-l-m* (Jerusalem), making the official seal of the captured city. These were all in Aramaic, not Hebrew, letters and may be dated possibly in the fourth century, after Ezra according to Jewish tradition introduced the "Assyrian," that is Aramaic, script. They may be as early as the fifth century when Jews in Egypt used Aramaic forms of a much more radical sort.

Two discoveries of interest to New Testament students were made by Weill. In an old cistern he found some architectural fragments carefully piled together and among them a large block with a Greek inscription set up by a certain Theodotus, who came of a Jewish family of Roman freedmen. Many think the inscription belonged to the synagogue of the *libertini*, or "freedmen," mentioned in Acts 6.9. The hypothesis is attractive, even if incapable of absolute proof. Weill also discovered the lower part of a large round tower 24 feet in diameter with walls 4 feet thick, standing well down the eastern slope—over against the village of Silwan. He suggests that it was the tower of Siloam to which Jesus refers as having fallen and suddenly destroyed certain people (Lk 13.4). It is another attractive but undemonstrable hypothesis.

JEWISH TOMBS

Of great interest are the numerous tombs which every one who visits Jerusalem sees. It is perhaps worthwhile to say that excavation has proved what the architecture told the trained

Looking west from American School of Oriental Research. Line of Agrippa's wall, right lower corner west to slender Italian tower.

Gordon's Calvary from wall from which he "discovered" it.

East Tower of Khirbet Minyeh before excavation (1931).

Khirbet Minyeh. Winter palace of Umaiyads under excavation. Qurn Hattin on horizon up Wadi Hamam.

eye, that the Tombs of the Kings by the English cathedral were constructed in the first century A.D., doubtless by Queen Helena of Adiabene. Likewise the tombs in the Kidron Valley belong to the Hellenistic period, long after Absolom, but before the time of James and Zacharias. The familiar guide-book names are totally incorrect.

Professor Sukenik has excavated various Jewish graves and published numerous ossuaries. On Mount Scopus was found an ossuary inscribed in Greek as holding "the bones of Nikanor the Alexandrian who made the gates," doubtless the miraculous gates, whose brass shone like gold, often mentioned in the Mishnah. One ossuary inscription which he published raised a small furor for a time, much to Professor Sukenik's distress. It read (in Aramaic) *Yeshuʿa bar Yehoseph*, "Jesus son of Joseph," and was taken by newspaper reporters to imply that the bones of Jesus, or at least the receptacle for them, had been found. Professor Sukenik used it only to suggest what Jesus would have been called by his contemporaries, how his name would have been written, and also how common the two names were.

Another ossuary caused extended scholarly debate. It was suspected because the Aramaic inscription in archaic square Hebrew characters had peculiar and at first unintelligible phrases and because the ossuary was discovered in an old museum collection which lacked any records. But its authenticity has been sufficiently defended so far as its language is concerned. It reads, "Hither were brought the bones of Uzziah king of Judah—Do not open." When eventually explained, the very linguistic peculiarities which had caused doubts guaranteed the genuineness of the ossuary and its inscription dating from about the time of Christ. Uzziah's tomb must have been cleared out at that time and his bones reverently preserved in the ossuary.

STRATIFICATION IN JERUSALEM

In a chapter on "The Stratification" Crowfoot has rendered all students of the history of Jerusalem a tremendous service in a very few pages, pages which represent a vast amount of keen observation and clear thinking. He points out that because of continuous occupation and continual rebuilding on a somewhat pretentious scale, the stratification discovered in the Holy City differs *toto coelo* from that of the ordinary mound in the Near East. So long as the site was continuously occupied, even after a "destruction" of the city by some enemy, the level of occupation rose practically not at all just as it does not in a modern western city. In England Norman churches are still at the present street level. In Jerusalem building was of stone. Little clay would enter into construction. When a house fell down practically all of the debris could be reused and, therefore, a house was not erected on the ruins of its predecessor. Therefore at Jerusalem there is no tell. Especially on the top of the southeast hill, or Ophel, each succeeding occupation swept the preceding buildings completely away and quarrying has even removed the upper parts of cisterns and tombs which were once underground.

In the Valley, on the contrary, just the opposite has happened. The debris from the hill tops on both sides, from the whole city in fact, has been dumped into it during periods when it was unoccupied by buildings. In places the deposits have grown to a depth of 80 feet. In Crowfoot's 1927 trench across the valley, the depth ran from 35 feet at the east end, just inside the old gate, to 50 feet in the middle of the Valley. Crowfoot's predecessors, who occupied themselves largely with the hillcrest, had very little material to use in determining the stratification. He has been able to make clear what took place.

The great western gate and wall were built on debris of the Middle and Late Bronze Ages before the end of the Late Bronze Age. Then for a period of 1300 or 1400 years the level on the side of the hill, at the gate, and for some distance west of it did not change. No considerable amount of debris collected at the destruction of the city in 586 B.C. or afterward down to 70 A.D. But for 200 years after the destruction of the city by Titus this part of it lay derelict and there was an accumulation of nearly 18 feet. Building was resumed about 300 A.D., but although there was rebuilding, the level did not rise during the next 300 years. During the thirteen centuries since the Arab conquest (638 A.D.), as civilization has gone down, the level of the ground has risen by some 8 or 10 feet, and there have been two building strata. But on the crest of the hill the modern Arabs live at approximately the same level as the ancient Amorites.

In spite of all the money and labor expended, it is still far from possible to write a definite history of the growth of Jerusalem and the extension of its walls. The data are too uncertain and debatable to be detailed here. There can be little doubt, however, that, after Solomon extended occupation northward to include the present site of the Dome of the Rock, where he placed the Temple, the city eventually spread westward, perhaps not, however, until after the Exile. Excavation conducted for the Department of Antiquities under Mr. C. N. Johns has showed that there were Maccabean and perhaps earlier buildings where the Old Turkish barracks were, by the so-called Tower of David. Perhaps all of the western hill had long been occupied. It certainly was before the time of Jesus. Excavation by the Assumptionist fathers on land they own south of the present city wall has revealed a stairway down which Jesus may have walked towards the Pool of Siloam. But where the south wall was in Jesus' day is quite uncertain. Further excavation will eventually solve some problems. The data to settle others are probably lost forever. The questions that have arisen regarding the Jerusalem of Jesus' day are so complicated as to demand a chapter of their own.

CHAPTER XVI

THE SEARCH FOR JESUS' TOMB

❖

THE line of the north wall of Jerusalem is as uncertain as that of the south and this uncertainty touches one of the most thorny of Jerusalem's topographical problems. There can be no doubt that the "Tower of David" by the Jaffa gate marks the location of the Herodian palace and of the three great towers which Josephus describes. But how far north did Herod's city extend? Did the wall run south or north of the Church of the Holy Sepulchre? Jesus died "without the gate." Is the famous church without or within the city wall of that period? Upon this question hangs the authenticity of the site, and innumerable vested interests—sentimental, theological, and economic—are deeply involved.

COMPETING THEORIES

It is unfortunate—not to say ridiculous—that *odium archaeologicum ac theologicum* can be aroused over the location of the site where Jesus was crucified and buried. But, even if the problem is religiously of small moment, it is an interesting historical question because it involves so much of the history of the city. Unfortunately again, it is difficult to settle the problem, for many reasons. It is impossible to excavate in the neighborhood of the Church of the Holy Sepulchre since it is completely surrounded by buildings, chiefly large monasteries and churches. The original identification and selection of the site are suspect because they cannot be dated before the time of Constantine, about 326 A.D., and its genuineness was authenticated by a vision of the Queen Mother, St. Helena. The story of the vision is itself much later than the church. The miracle which authenticated it for fifth-century or sixth-century Christians renders it suspect in the eyes of the modern historian. Actually it would appear that according to some local tradition a temple of Venus had usurped the site of Calvary, and Constantine accepted the tradition. Farther the literary evidence does not go.

It was long held by both defenders and opponents of the present site of the church that its authenticity stood or fell according to the date of the north wall of the Old City as it now runs. According to Josephus, the city had had two north walls before Jesus' day. A third was begun by Herod Agrippa I about 40 A.D., but left incomplete, and it was hastily finished in preparation for the great siege of 68-70 A.D. If the present north wall is that of Herod Agrippa, then there is good reason to believe that the site of the Church was outside the walls before that time. If the present north wall is not that of Agrippa, then it ought to be the second and the Church site must have been within the walls. Strictly speaking neither argument is logical; the conclusions are only possible or plausible, not by any means inevitable, for no one knows what foundations of walls underlie the crowded houses of the northwest section of the Old City. Various walls have been reported from time to time, when new buildings were being erected, but systematic search is impossible.

In the course of the long centuries since Queen Helena's time, there have been millions of Christians who have found the deepest and holiest experience of their lives in a visit to the Church of the Holy Sepulchre. There have been others—not so numerous—for whom "monkish tradition" and all the "mummeries" and quarrels of the sects which squabble over that ugly church have been anathema, as they were for Edward Robinson a century ago.

The famous general and Christian, Chinese Gordon, boarding for a while at the "American Colony" when it was housed on the hill east of the Damascus Gate, came in one day from a walk on the city wall to say, "I have found just the place for Calvary." Like others before him, but quite independently, he

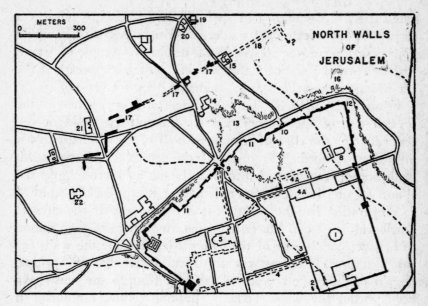

KEY TO PLAN

1. Qubbet es-Sakhrah
2. Robinson's Arch
3. Wilson's Arch
4. First North Wall
4A. Tower of Antonia
5. Church of the Holy Sepulcher
6. Herod's Palace
7. Tower of Psephinus (?)
8. Church of St. Anne
9. Damascus Gate
10. Herod's Gate
11. Suggested lines of Second Wall
12. Burj Laqlaq

13. Gordon's Calvary
14. St. Étienne
15. American School of Oriental Research
16. Palestine Museum
17. Third (Agrippa's) Wall
18. Newly discovered portion (approximate direction)
19. Tomb of Helena of Adiabene
20. St. George's
21. Italian Hospice
22. Russian Church

FIG. 5

had selected the hill lying opposite the great underground quarry known as Solomon's Caverns and over its northern extension called Jeremiah's Grotto. Later a tomb, of which he knew nothing, was discovered behind the hill, called the Garden Tomb, and identified by a small coterie of earnest partisans as the tomb of Jesus.

Another "discovery" was made by an American woman, a second, equally able Queen Helena, to whom it was revealed in a vision that a certain ash heap north of the city was Calvary. In recent years an American tourist guide has been showing this as the true site. Others discovered Calvary just west of the American School of Oriental Research in a hillock which was formed by the earth excavated when the Dominican Monastery and École Biblique of St. Étienne were erected. It is hardly necessary to say that these three recent "discoveries" are all equally without the slightest documentary or archaeological attestation.

THE THIRD WALL

However, the problem of the Third Wall and the Church of the Holy Sepulchre has been put in an entirely new light by recent archaeological discoveries. When Edward Robinson visited Jerusalem in 1838 he discovered, halfway between the "Tombs of the Kings" and the northwest corner of the Old City, very clear traces of a strongly built wall. Other travelers before him and many since, including the American consul, Selah Merrill, Mrs. Flinn, and Professor L. B. Paton, director of the American School in 1903-04, have followed the line, as they believed, of Robinson's wall, and have recorded its gradual destruction and incorporation into modern buildings. Indeed it had so far disappeared that many have believed Robinson to have been deceived by chance piles of debris.

His acumen, however, has been completely vindicated. In 1925 street repairs to the Nablus Road at its junction with Richard Coeur-de-Lion Street, a point almost directly west of the American School of Oriental Research, uncovered a gigantic building block of distinctly Herodian type. It was cleared by the Department of Antiquities, left exposed, and surrounded by a rail. Because of the interest aroused, Drs. E. L. Sukenik and L. A. Mayer undertook excavations on behalf of the Jewish Exploration Society along the line which the stone's position indicated. This led directly to a wall which Dr. Paton had excavated—and misinterpreted—just a little east of the Nablus Road, and to other traces of a wall with similar masonry running almost from the Italian Hospital to the American School of Oriental Research, exactly the line marked "Improbable" in Sir George Adam Smith's *Atlas*.

Just north of the gate in the iron fence in front of the School, the late Professor Romain Butin, when acting director of the School in 1926, discovered that road repairs had uncovered great stones of a tower and gate which proved to fall into the line of the wall which Drs. Sukenik and Mayer were excavating. This portion, which now lies under a hump in Saladin Road, also was excavated and included in their publication. It extended some eight meters inside the fence.

In the autumn of 1940 again road builders, working on the street which runs at the back of the American School, uncovered a portion of the same wall at the northeast corner of the property. Here, that autumn, Drs. Sukenik and Mayer excavated the foundations of a great tower forty-three feet wide, which involved half of the School's tennis court, and they followed the first course of the wall running on to the east. Since no trace of the wall had previously been discovered east of the tower in front of the School, though it had been sought in the grounds of the School, Drs. Sukenik and Mayer had formerly supposed that the wall turned south at this tower and followed approximately the line of Saladin Road to join the present wall a little west of Herod's Gate, the Bab ez-Zahireh. That is now proved wrong. The wall went on to a still larger tower found near the Wadi el-Joz and then turned southward to join approximately the present line of the eastern wall near Burj Laqlaq, the northeast corner of the Old City.

Père Vincent of the École Biblique, with his usual keenness, clarity and thorough scholarship, has marshaled evidence to prove that this could not have been the wall begun by Herod Agrippa and finished by the rebels before Titus began his siege. His arguments were based chiefly on the irregularities and poor masonry in the construction of the wall, whereas Josephus waxes unusually eloquent in his descriptions of the wall as "constructed of stones twenty cubits long and ten broad, so closely jointed that they could scarcely have been undermined with tools of iron or shaken by engines." Père Vincent argued, from Herodian stones found in the present north wall, that this last was the "Third Wall" of Josephus, and that the wall farther north must have been built in the time of the Bar-Kokhba rebellion of 132-35 A.D.

So far as the correspondence of the newly excavated wall with Josephus' description is concerned, conclusions depend upon whether emphasis is laid upon his exaggerated pride over what Agrippa planned or upon his statement that it was left incomplete for nearly thirty years and then hastily finished by unorganized rebels who were fighting among themselves. From personal observation and the study of the excavators' reports, I can only conclude that the new wall fully corresponds, in its mixture of magnificent and absurdly poor masonry, to all that Josephus reports.

Is the Church of the Holy Sepulchre then definitely in the wrong place? Other excavations have set that question in a new light.

THE NORTH WALL OF THE OLD CITY

As long ago as 1925 Dr. Albright and the late Père Alexis Malon of the Pontifical Biblical Institute sought a way out of the impasse regarding the third wall by accepting the newly excavated wall as the third, but identifying the present north wall with that of Aelia Capitolina, Jerusalem as rebuilt by Hadrian in 135 A.D. This allowed the second wall still to be found to the south and east of the Church of the Holy Sepulchre, as Gustaf Dalman does, and saved the faith of those who were concerned for the venerated shrine. Père Vincent and his colleague, Père Abel, who perhaps know Jerusalem better than any other men, insisted that Aelia Capitolina had been undefended and that the new wall was not the third wall.

In recent years the city authorities have been making many attempts to beautify Jerusalem. One of the sore spots, from an aesthetic point of view, was the area along the north wall, especially from the Damascus Gate eastward, where ugly buildings and the debris of centuries had accumulated. In the hope of settling numerous questions regarding the walls, the Department of Antiquities determined to make some soundings before the accumulated rubbish was cleared away.

Various excavations, especially those conducted by Crowfoot and FitzGerald on Ophel and by C. N. Johns south of the Jaffa Gate, have supplied the Department with a vast amount of useful knowledge regarding the pottery of periods just before and after the beginning of the Christian era. Using this knowledge Mr. R. W. Hamilton, as director of the Department, made several soundings by the Damascus Gate and on each side of Herod's Gate (Bab ez-Zahireh). It is unfortunate that they could not have been more extensive, but they have been sufficient to make certain conclusions fairly safe. The findings rest upon a careful and discriminating study of the masonry and of the pottery and coins found in the construction trenches and in the rubbish which accumulated against the walls.

One interesting conclusion was that there had been extensive rebuilding in the third or fourth century and that, therefore, more credit for Byzantine Jerusalem belongs possibly to Constantine and Queen Helena than has been accorded them, perhaps less to Queen Eudocia. This does not affect the question of the Holy Sepulchre, but a second conclusion does. The evidence indicates that the present north city wall represents essentially the line of the north wall of Aelia Capitolina, and in part at least the "second wall" of Josephus.

On the inside of the Damascus Gate, just a little east of the entrance, the top of an arch of moderate size has long been visible. Excavation showed it to be of a size for the side passage of a triple gate. Over it on the outside Mr. Hamilton found a reused stone bearing, in letters of Hadrianic style, the inscription, CO[L](onia) AEL(ia) CAP(itolina) D(ecurionum) D(ecreto), that is "Colonia Aelia Capitolina by decree of the decurions." On the opposite (west) side of the present gate evidence was found of an opening, probably of the corresponding small side passage of a great triple gate. The inscribed stone probably came from this original Hadrianic gateway.

A little in front of this western doorway the lowest course of a wall was found built of large stones of the characteristic Herodian type. A little farther to the west at the foot of the present gateway tower, other Herodian stones were found which may be still *in situ*. In other words, clear evidence of a Herodian structure, probably a gate, preceded equally clear evidence of a Hadrianic triple gateway of the type known from several well-preserved, contemporary examples at Jerash and elsewhere.

The walls, where Mr. Hamilton investigated them near "Herod's Gate," the Bab ez-Zahireh, proved to be built in their lowest courses of Herodian and Hadrianic materials combined. They, therefore, provided no positive evidence as to the time of their building. The pottery in the debris thrown against them gave no evidence of any wall earlier than the building of Aelia Capitolina, but does not positively disprove an earlier construction. This evidence unequivocally points to the building of a wall and gate along this line in Hadrian's time.

If no further inferences are possible, the problem of the tomb of Jesus is still unsolved. If there were no interests vested in the present site, it is unlikely that so much ink would be spilled over it. No remains found within the present Old City clearly prove the existence of the second wall, which was built by Herod the Great, along a line which would leave the church outside the city, although Gustaf Dalman has presented a plausible argument for that hypothesis. The archaeological remains prove the present wall to have been the north wall of the city since early in the second century. The recent excavations of Drs. Sukenik and Mayer and of Mr. Hamilton make it almost impossible to consider it the third wall built by Herod Agrippa.

If the conclusions drawn from the recent discoveries must stop here, then Dr. Albright is justified in saying that the Church of the Holy Sepulchre may still be the genuine site of Golgotha and the tomb of Jesus, although it is not proved to be so. If the Herodian remains found *in situ* at the Damascus Gate and the various evidences of rebuildings and the cutting of scarps along the line of the wall may be taken as sufficient evidence that Herod the Great built this wall (a not unreasonable conclusion), then the Church is not over Golgotha and the tomb of Jesus. In either case, the site is not certainly known, and there are many better places where the Christian may meditate on the city that murdered its country prophet.

PROBLEMS AND POSSIBILITIES

Jerusalem still bristles with unsolved problems. Some of them will be solved if energetic and intelligent archaeologists continue in charge of the Department of Antiquities, for much information comes to light casually, when streets are being made, sewers dug or repaired, or foundations altered or laid anew. Many will depend upon further excavations. Others cannot be solved by archaeological means; many are insoluble. The place of Jesus' trial, Pilate's judgment seat, is an example. It is now generally agreed that Herod's palace lay at the Jaffa Gate. It is quite generally believed that the Ecce Homo Arch belongs to Aelia Capitolina. It was possibly the eastern gate of the city corresponding to the northern gate disclosed by Mr. Hamilton. But, as Père Vincent has demonstrated, the Tower of Antonia was much larger than had been supposed and the pavement east of the Ecce Homo Arch, under the Convent of the Sisters of Zion, is doubtless a part of the courtyard of that Tower, which guarded the Temple in Jesus' day. Did Pilate have his praetorium there or in the palace? Both were at his disposal. No one has recorded his choice. The Herodian palace at the Jaffa Gate is as likely a place as Antonia.

In recent years a great deal of information regarding the life of ancient Jerusalem in all its periods has come through minor excavations of tombs, through the observation of old street levels when any building was in process, and through the clearance of old rubbish heaps. Several Jewish scholars, especially Drs. Sukenik, Mayer, and B. Maisler, who are on the spot and ready to seize every opportunity, deserve great credit for the contributions they have made.

When the path leading down to the road from "St. Stephen's Gate" was widened in the autumn of 1935, a fine hoard of coins of the Second Revolt and some interesting Christian tombs were found. Even more instructive was a vertical section from a block which had carried the Greek inscription set up in the Herodian temple to warn Gentiles not to go within. Although disposed differently on the block, the words were the same as in that discovered by Clermont-Ganneau in 1872 and now in the Museum at Stambul. DeSaulcy found an Aramaic fragment of the same prohibition at the south side of the Temple area. The debris which now partially fills the Kidron and the Tyropean Valleys must be full of such relics of the past which would add immeasurably to our historical knowledge. The Temple area hides many more.

It would require a long catalogue to list the tombs, the mosaic pavements, the foundations of ancient churches and other buildings, the inscriptions, and the small finds of all sorts which have served to make vivid the social conditions and the historical development of this ancient city. One can hardly scratch the surface of the ground without discovering the pulsating life of four millennia of history. For long years to come Jerusalem will constantly bring forth out of her treasury things new and old.

CHAPTER XVII

NEGLECTED GALILEE

❖

ONE of the anomalies of Palestinian archaeology is that, while practically all of the major excavations have been carried on by Christians and have been motivated chiefly by interest in the Bible, no excavation of any importance has been carried on in a Galilean city or at any site which is of predominately Christian interest, unless perhaps Gerasa may be excepted. At Gerasa, as a later chapter will relate, the character of pagan Hellenistic civilization contemporary with the beginnings of Christianity and the process by which Christianity rose and fell in Palestine is excellently documented in speaking ruins. But that little caravan city can tell nothing regarding such a Jewish village as Nazareth or Capharnaum must have been.

As yet almost nothing has been done to make clear the Jewish or Jewish-Hellenistic background of the most fundamental and most appealing of all the books of the Bible, the Gospels. Indeed, the exact character of Galilean Judaism, whether strictly Jewish or decidedly touched with Hellenistic and other outside influences, is entirely unknown. One of the perhaps fortuitous, but decidedly enigmatic, silences of history lets the Galilean followers of Jesus, who must have numbered thousands, drop into complete oblivion, while Jerusalem, the murderer of the prophets and of Jesus, significantly becomes the center of the new faith.

Christians of the nineteenth and twentieth centuries have been as oblivious of Galilee as was the author of Acts, and they have spent thousands of dollars on futile efforts to read the illegible archaeological riddles of Jerusalem, but not one on

Nazareth. The exact site of first-century Nazareth is unknown and even its existence can be disputed. The sites of Capharnaum, Bethsaida, and Cana have long been in dispute. But worse than unsettled questions of topography is complete ignorance of the actual character of the civilization which gave birth to the Christian movement. It may be that the village of Nazareth is buried too deeply for excavation under the multitudinous churches and monasteries that now disfigure the beautiful hillsides above the Virgin's Fountain. But there are various ruined villages now quite uninhabited which could easily reveal the character of Galilean civilization at the beginning of the Christian era.

The Galilean hillsides harbor other secrets which are historically as tantalizing and significant as those which touch Christian history. Problems are involved which are fully as interesting and important to Jews as those already mentioned are to Christians. Galilee gave birth to Christianity. It would be too much to claim that it was the birthplace of Judaism, but it was certainly its *alma mater*. No prophet arose in Galilee. But, if "normative Judaism" was not born in Galilee, it grew to maturity there. The Mishnah was written in Galilee. The "Jerusalem Talmud" was written in Galilee. After the destruction of Jerusalem in 70 A.D., the center of Jewish population gradually moved into the ancient "circle of the nations." Jewish pilgrims journeyed to Galilee to visit and stayed to die on its holy soil. With the people—it would appear reluctantly—went the rabbis. While some still maintained their seats in Lydda, Jamnia, and even in the cities of the Negeb, more and more they gravitated to Sepphoris and even to Tiberias. Today the tombs of Jewish saints are to be found chiefly in the north at Kefr Birim and Tiberias. As the astonishing catacombs of Bethshearim have recently demonstrated, Galilee has much information to divulge regarding the history of the whole Jewish world at the beginning of our era.

CHANCE FINDS

Before the first World War no excavation had been attempted in Galilee except a little surreptitious trenching in the German property at et-Tabigha and the clearance of the synagogue at Tell Hum. In the two decades that followed, chance discoveries and scientific excavations on a small scale at Tiberias, et-Tabigha, Saffurieh, and Sheikh Abreiq have produced interesting and promising, even if necessarily limited, results.

The first excavation after the war was unintentionally carried on by Jewish *halluzim* at ancient Tiberias. While living in tents just below the tomb shrine of Rabbi Meir and building a much needed automobile road south from Tiberias to the railway station at Semakh, they dug into the talus at the foot of the mountains just south of Tiberias to secure ballast needed for the road. When I visited the place in December, 1920, and again in April, 1921, sarcophagi and other evidence which they had uncovered of the presence of a former burial ground were protruding from the half-cleared gravel and earth which had washed down almost to the seashore. Inscriptions in Greek carried names that were clearly Jewish and other indications pointed in the same direction. At one side, building walls had attracted attention, and excavation by Dr. Nahoum Slouschz disclosed the remains of a small synagogue, a building which was hardly to be expected in the neighborhood of a cemetery. Some little distance north of Tiberias the new road cut through the house walls of an ancient, as yet unidentified city, or village.

In December, 1935, Dr. E. L. Sukenik uncovered a round structure, perhaps of Hadrianic date, which had come to light just south of modern Tiberias. It had been used as a lime kiln after the Arab conquest, and its original purpose was uncertain, but apparently it had marked a street crossing in the ancient city. Walls of various dates may be seen between the modern city and the famous hot springs. The discovery of this structure only emphasizes what was already clear to the observant traveler, that ancient Tiberias offers a unique opportunity to the excavator. Since the date of its foundation (21 A.D.) is known, and Josephus refers to various buildings which were standing fifty years later, the excavator may hope to settle vexed problems of ceramic chronology while bringing the ancient city once more to life.

CAPHARNAUM

If excavations in Galilee have been few and modest, nevertheless one long-standing and vexatious topographical problem has been definitely and finally solved by excavation. The result shows what archaeology can do under the proper conditions. Even before the first World War the literature discussing the site of Capharnaum was reaching almost unmanageable proportions but without remotely approaching a satisfactory conclusion as to where lay this little city, which played so large a part in the ministry of Jesus.

Two sites competed for the distinction. One decade the weight of opinion seemed to trend toward Tell Hum, a ruin with a synagogue in beautiful white limestone lying about two miles north of Tell el-'Oreimeh, which occupies the little promontory that walls off the Plain of Gennesaret on the north. Another decade opinion would shift to Khirbet Minyeh, a small ruin consisting of a few heaps of bramble-covered stones scarcely protruding above the little plain just south of Tell el-'Oreimeh. As one now reads the "ancient" literature of twenty-five or fifty years ago, it seems strange that numerous scholars should have been so perverse in their refusal to recognize the superior claims of Tell Hum.

Nearly all of the ancient Christian pilgrims to Galilee recorded visiting Magdala, modern Mejdel, two miles north of Tiberias; then, two miles farther on, the Church of the Multiplying of the Loaves, or Heptapegon (modern et-Tabigha); and still two miles farther north Capharnaum, which, quite clearly then, lay at Tell Hum. Moreover, in 1865 Captain Wilson had done a little digging at Khirbet Minyeh and reported only Arabic pottery. Even more significantly, the surface evidences of a synagogue at Tell Hum and after 1904 the still stronger proof secured by the excavations of the German Orient Society made it perfectly clear that Tell Hum stood on the site of an ancient Jewish city.

However, one or two later pilgrims seemed to reverse the order and put Capharnaum two miles from Magdala. Indeed in the eleventh century the difficulty and danger of travel outside the cities held by the Crusaders led the professional guides to transport practically all of the sacred sites and buildings of the region to Tiberias itself. Such pilgrim itineraries should have been given no weight. But a significant objection to Tell Hum was the absence of springs or other visible water supply there, whereas Josephus had definitely described passing through the place and being impressed with its very large spring. Near Khirbet Minyeh is a beautiful spring of fresh water now called 'Ain et-Tin, and for many that settled the question. Moreover, it was possible to pick up fragments of Roman pottery on the surface by the walls of Khirbet Minyeh. The writer did that in the winter of 1931, had them properly "experted" by Père Vincent, and was temporarily disturbed in his allegiance to Tell Hum.

Both of the disputed sites were acquired by Catholic organizations, Tell Hum about 1894 by the Franciscans, the region of et-Tabigha (Heptapegon) by the German Society of the Holy Land in 1888. Lazarist Fathers as directors at the latter, especially the famous Boniface, Father Johannes Täpper, gradually extended the properties around their delightful hospice until they owned a considerable northern section of the Plain of Gennesaret, including Khirbet Minyeh. They were without funds for real excavations until in 1931 the Catholic organization for scientific research called the Görresgesellschaft sent Father D. A. Mader and Dr. A. M. Schneider to excavate on the property. The society's chief interest had been Tell el-'Oreimeh, the Bronze and Iron Age mound on the promontory called Sheikh 'Ali es-Saiyid, where Canon Bridgeman of Jerusalem had inadvertently found a stela of Thothmes III. Fortunately for New Testament students, the excavators' efforts were turned toward Khibet Minyeh and the "Church of the Multiplication of the Loaves" at et-Tabigha.

KHIRBET MINYEH

The excavators were at first uncertain as to the age of the structures which they gradually unearthed at Khirbet Minyeh. The masonry was so excellent that it was thought to be Roman and the remains of a fort. Once again excellence of masonry proved a poor criterion. As time went on, it was seen that the buildings did not represent a fort, and the character of the pottery began to point to a much later date. Eventually the discovery of gold dinars of the Umaiyads and a mosque which was still perhaps under construction proved beyond the shadow of a doubt that the building was in Moslem hands at the time of its abandonment. A building inscription proves that Calif Walid I ordered the erection of some part of the structure. It belongs therefore to the seventh or eighth century. It was doubt-less the winter palace of some Umaiyad monarch like the some-what similar structure at Khirbet el-Mefjer near Jericho and the hunting lodges on the steppe east of Transjordan.[1] There is a bare possibility that it was originally begun by Ghassanid rulers, but the traces of the Greek architectural and aesthetic tradition which suggested a fifth-century date are probably evidence that, as in the Mosque el-Aqsa at Jerusalem and the Umaiyad Mosque at Damascus, Greek Christian architects and artisans were impressed for the work by their Moslem conquerors. A small room has a mosaic that looks like a carpet. The floor of the mosque has excellent mosaics and the walls and towers, still standing to a height of 27 feet in places, testify to the architectural skill and artistic taste of the workers and to the luxury of the Umaiyad line.

The excavators have uncovered an impressive example of early Moslem architecture where there were only bramble-covered heaps of rocks. More important than that, they have proved

[1] See chapters XIX and XXI.

conclusively that no first-century Jewish village ever existed on the spot, and thus they have definitely proved that Capharnaum could never have stood there.

THE CHURCH OF THE MULTIPLICATION OF THE LOAVES

At the northern edge of the et-Tabigha property, the labors of the same organization and excavators have been rewarded in a very different way. Before the end of the last century the German Catholic director of the et-Tabigha property, Father Z. Biever, had uncovered a mosaic showing a basket of loaves flanked by fishes at a spot not far from the shore west of the great octagonal fountain called Birket 'Ali ed-Daher, one of the "seven springs" of Heptapegon. Karge in 1911 uncovered it again and examined the site carefully, but published nothing because his excavation was done without government permission. The place was marked by walls protruding above the ground and was thus easily found, and its true character was known to the Lazarist fathers. Unfortunately the ruin lay along the disputed boundary between the et-Tabigha property and that of the Franciscans at Tell Hum, and Father Biever and his Lazarist successors kept the matter a dark secret.

Father Mader and Dr. Schneider made the easy clearance of the floor and revealed one of the most beautiful of Palestinian mosaics, along with the outlines of a typical Christian basilica. It was not large, the nave being only about 100 feet in length, but the floor had been paved with mosaics of unusual attractiveness and variety. The nave carried a pattern of crosses in hundreds of repetitions. In the transepts and between the columns which separated nave and aisles there was a very different sort of mosaic, with pictorial representations of great beauty and high artistic quality. In a well-preserved area of twenty by twenty-five feet the north transept has a landscape of oleanders, bullrushes, lotus, and papyrus, through which riot ducks, geese, storks, peacocks, and flamingoes, feeding on flowers and catching snakes. Smaller birds perch on the branches and preen their feathers. Set at random in the landscape are a castle gate, a round, pagoda-like temple, and a square, battlemented tower. Other equally charming *motifs* decorated the intercolumniations and the poorly preserved southern transept. The perspective is not faultless, but the beautifully harmonized colors of the little limestone tessarae and the skill and clarity with which the figures are portrayed are not unworthy of the best artistic traditions of antiquity. The proficiency of the workmanship, the variety of the shades of color, and the felicity of their combination, as well as the genius of the artistic conception, render it perhaps the finest mosaic yet uncovered in Palestine.

The slabs of the marble chancel rail were decorated with three crosses standing upon a hill. The altar covered, but did not conceal, a large unhewn boulder of limestone, supposedly the stone, mentioned by early pilgrims, upon which Jesus placed the five loaves and two fishes while he blessed them. Behind the stone, between the altar and the apse, was the mosaic which the two earlier excavators had uncovered, showing two fish lying one on either side of a basket which holds four little wafer-like loaves of bread, each marked with a cross. The colors of the centimeter cubes of local limestone, black, light gray, brick red, light red, lilac, yellow, ochre, reddish brown, and white, are skillfully blended to give an artistic and lively impression in all of the mosaics.

When, in 1936, the mosaics were lifted in order to relay them in solid concrete and so preserve them indefinitely, one architectural problem was solved and a new chronological element was added. The north wall of the church had run off at a decided angle, making room for a baptistry beside the west end of the north aisle. Under the mosaics were found the foundations of an earlier chapel, which had an orientation approximating that of this oblique north wall. Since Christianity made little progress in Galilee until the time of the *Komes*, or Count, Joseph, about 350 A.D., the chapel may not have been built before his time. The style of the mosaics in the basilica points to a period either a little before or after 400 A.D. for its construction. It seems to have been repaired, perhaps after one of the numerous earthquakes recorded in the fifth century, and to have been destroyed finally perhaps by the Persian invaders of 614 A.D., or the Moslems two decades later.

The uncovering of this building makes possible a remarkable synthesis of documentary and archaeological evidence, such as every excavator longs to achieve. First come accounts of the activities of Count Joseph. Up to Moslem times pilgrims give detailed and accurate descriptions of the road by which they reached the place and of the site itself. After the Moslem conquest the visitors who reach the region no longer describe the church, and eventually the site itself is transported to regions which pilgrims can visit without danger from the Arabs. The later accounts, therefore, cannot affect the identification of the site, but, on the contrary, the site serves as a touchstone of the accuracy of the pilgrim itineraries. As to the Gospel incident itself, in the nature of the case archaeology can say nothing. The situation of the little bay where the "seven springs" lie admirably suits the Gospel narrative, in its original Marcan form. But Jesus and his disciples could have sought solitude and have been followed by multitudes along the lake shore to the north of Capharnaum as well as to the south.

That the early Christians could have preserved for 300 years the memory of the exact spot where Jesus ate a semisacramental meal in a "lonely spot" with a great number of disciples is not impossible, but hardly probable. The discovery of the church is of great value, not for the life of Jesus, but for the history of early Christianity. It throws new light on the vicissitudes through which it passed, while the mosaic is significant of the process by which the church appropriated the art of that ancient civilization to which it fell heir.

In the spring of 1936 the Custodie de Terre Sainte, the Franciscan organization which owns the site of Tell Hum, announced the discovery of a small chapel which is supposed to stand on the spot where the Byzantine world believed the Sermon on the Mount to have been delivered. It lies in the Franciscan property

near the road from Tiberias to Damascus and not far from the
Church of the Multiplication of the Loaves. The apsidal building measured slightly less than 25 by 40 feet. Like so many
Byzantine churches, it was paved with mosaics in geometric
designs. A small monastery lay beside it. Nothing would appear to have been found that would positively identify the
structure, as did the designs and inscription in the floor of the
other church. The identification depends, rather, upon indefinite
statements of Saint Etheria and others, who are thought to
place here a church and a monastery which marked the site of
the Sermon.

SEPPHORIS

The only major expedition undertaken in Galilee by Christians was unfortunately cut short by the course of the depression that began in 1929, and it resulted in but a single short
season of excavation. Professor Leroy Waterman of the University of Michigan visited Palestine on his way to and from
his excavation at Seleucia on the Tigris and, after considering
various sites, chose Sepphoris, the modern Saffuriyeh.

The place lies in beautiful agricultural country four miles
north of Nazareth. It is not mentioned in the Bible, at least
under any name resembling that now in use. But in Josephus
Sepphoris is one of the most important cities in Galilee. He first
mentions it in the history of the second century B.C. It was the
seat of one of the five sanhedrins established by Gabinius in
Palestine (55 B.C.); it was the capital until Herod Antipas built
Tiberias, and again in the middle of the first century. It was a
Jewish city, although Romanophile, and it later became an important rabbinic center. Its significant place in Jewish history
and in the background of New Testament and early Christian
history need not be further emphasized.

The modern village, one of the largest in Galilee, lies on three
sides of a limestone hill which is crowned by a square structure
built as a fortress by the Crusaders and rebuilt in late Arab
times, but now used as a school. It stands where once the ancient

citadel must have stood. The ground around it belongs to the government and, therefore, it was easy to arrange for its use by the expedition—during vacation, from June 20 to August 20. The only part of the hill which is unoccupied adjoins this building on the north, where the sun does not shine and the slope is so steep as to make building difficult. Professor Waterman began work on July 9, 1931, and, by leasing a small strip of private land adjoining the school property, was able to continue until September 9. He did no damage except to some practice gardens started by some of the school boys.

What he could uncover in so short a time affords a glimpse, tantalizing in its meagerness and its promise, of what may be expected if the task can be resumed. Two building complexes were partially uncovered, a Roman theater, with adjoining structures, and a Byzantine church. Some study was given to the neighborhood and especially to the water-supply system, which had been one of the chief points of interest to visitors.

The theater had been cut into the hill on its northern side, looking away from the sun. It was of the usual Roman style, a half circle of seats with a long, narrow stage before it. The latter had gone through at least one period of rebuilding. Near it part of a street was uncovered. Nearly twenty feet of debris had washed down from the hill upon the theater. In the lowest part of this mass, on the floor, were coins of Alexander Janneus. Since it is hardly possible that a theater would have been built here in Hasmonean times and on Roman, not Greek, lines, it would appear that these coins must have been in the earth that was thrown out when the excavation for the theater was made. The theater at the earliest could be the work of Herod the Great or of Herod Antipas when he rebuilt the city after its destruction by Varus in 4 B.C. Other coins, the oldest coming from the time of Seleucus IV (187-175 B.C.), testify to the continuous occupation of the site from shortly after 200 B.C. A few pieces of pottery—unpublished—confirm its occupation from this time, or possibly a little earlier.

The basilica, which was found on the northwestern edge of

the hill top and identified as a church by its eastern apse and one, possibly two, baptisteries, was not large and imposing, and the mosaics found in one room were constructed of crude limestone cubes in black and white laid in a simple pattern. Under the mosaics another floor of lime cement testified to a still simpler preceding stage of construction. The rooms about the church could only be partially excavated. Apparently they were part of a monastery.

One of the prominent archaeological features of Saffuriyeh has been a long, narrow underground reservoir running along the crest of a hill a little over half a mile east of the village. Conder and Kitchener examined it and described it in detail in the *Survey*. They followed in part the aqueduct which filled it. Professor Waterman did likewise and he discovered a watch tower or guard house not far from it a mile and a half away from the village. The *Survey* reports a passage leading from the reservoir toward the village. Waterman found part of the conduit and also three quarters of a mile southeast of the village an open-air masonry reservoir which he thought to have been in some way connected with the aqueduct and underground reservoir. But surely water would not have been led away from the city, but toward it.

Like every Jewish city, Sepphoris is surrounded by tombs dug into the limestone hills. Professor Sukenik excavated one on the northwest slope of the tell which, to judge from graffiti on its walls, was shown to medieval pilgrims as that of Rabbi Jehudah ha-Nasi, who was a famous head of Jewry in the third century.

As is to be expected in a city which is chiefly Hellenistic and Roman, little stratification was found during the excavation. This was, indeed, due in part to the shortness of the period of digging. In one spot three successive mosaic floors appeared, one above another. More such areas are doubtless to be found. Unfortunately also, no pottery appears in the preliminary publication. Therefore it is impossible to check the dates assigned to the buildings. Such a beginning, brought by untoward circumstances to an untimely halt, leaves much to be desired—above all a continuation.

In the New Testament there is no Christian Galilee. It is not to be expected that archaeology will discover it. Evidence of the existence of Christian communities there before the church became well-to-do and fairly influential may not be expected. Though Christian congregations probably existed in Galilee from the beginning, Judaism was dominant until the fourth century. What the historian of Judaism and Christianity needs is knowledge of Galilean Judaism in the period just before and after the time of Jesus. That also is lacking. Excavation will eventually bring to light much to interpret the fairly numerous documents of that period and to reveal the true character of the Judaism of the "second Temple," the matrix out of which both Christianity and "normative Judaism" came. The information already available about the childhood of the latter, to be described in the next chapter, suggests how much more will eventually appear.

CHAPTER XVIII

REMAINS OF "NORMATIVE JUDAISM"

❖

IF ARCHAEOLOGY has little to reveal regarding the beginnings of Christianity and the development of Judaism as it was taking shape before and during its fruitless revolts against imperial Rome, it has at least made some contribution to the history of the early years of Judaism after its development had begun. Some of the features of Jewish society during the comparative peace and prosperity of the five centuries before the Arab invasion are so different from what modern Jews and Christians would have expected that people of both faiths not infrequently refuse to accept the incontrovertible evidence which comes from far-distant sites, such as Dura-Europos, as well as from Galilee in abundant measure.

The one archaeological monument in Galilee which has not been neglected is the synagogue. Unfortunately for the students of Christianity and Judaism, the synagogues as yet uncovered belong to more sophisticated and less combative ages than those which crucified Jesus and defied Vespasian, Trajan, and Hadrian. No synagogue has been found in which Hillel, Jesus, and Paul could have worshiped. Those which have been found, however, are interesting enough in themselves as well as valuable in suggesting the types which must have preceded them.

TELL HUM—CAPHARNAUM

As early as the eighteenth century it was known that there were ruins of a synagogue to be found at Tell Hum. The first excavation was undertaken by Captain Charles Wilson in 1866. He believed that he had discovered the synagogue mentioned in the Gospels as having been built by the Roman centurion

(Lk 7.5), and he thus originated an unfortunate tradition. Lieutenant H. H. Kitchener, later famous for more warlike activities, when assisting in the survey of western Palestine for the Palestine Exploration Fund in 1874-77, adjourned the date of the building to the second or third century. In 1905 Heinrich Kohl and Carl Watzinger, under commission from the Deutsche Orient-Gesellschaft, excavated the synagogue at Capharnaum along with others in Galilee. They gave well-deserved attention to it, twice as much as to any other, and prepared an almost definitive publication. They also dated it after 200 A.D. The excavations which they had begun were continued slowly until the first World War by the owners, the Custodie Franciscaine de Terre Sainte, and finally in 1922, after a further campaign, the late Father Gaudence Orfali, a Galilean-born Syrian and an accomplished scholar, published a thin but sumptuous volume on the synagogue and on a probably Christian structure which they had found near it.

The synagogue and, consequently, the publication have suffered from the depredations of time and man during the long period since the walls were first uncovered. Wilson's excavations convinced the Bedouins, who were the owners and the principal inhabitants of the area about Tell Hum and Kerazeh (Chorazin), that there must be gold in the ruins. Why else should anyone dig into the ground? In search of it they broke up many of the fine Corinthian capitals, the columns, and the building blocks. Neighboring effendis and villagers on the lake used the ruins as a stone quarry. Fortunately no large settlements were near. This spoliation went on until, in 1894, after four years of negotiations, the Franciscans acquired a considerable portion of the ancient site. To protect the ruins they covered them with earth and even planted trees over them.

Thus, in spite of the ravages of a generation, enough of the synagogue was preserved to enable skilled architects to reconstruct its plan and elevations and, it is hoped, eventually the building itself. In anticipation, the northwest corner, where the walls still stood nearly 30 feet high, has been rebuilt. On certain points there is difference of opinion among architects who have studied the remains, differences relating chiefly to the position of some of the ornamental carvings and minor structural elements. On larger matters, such as the now abandoned suggestion that the center of the building was open to the sky, there is practical unanimity.

The building was a gable-roofed basilica eighty feet long, with a single row of interior columns running entirely around the two sides and the north end and carrying galleries for women worshipers. At the south end, in the direction of Jerusalem, the ark of the Law, in the form of a handsome shrine, stood with its back to the great central doorway.[1] A smaller door on each side opened into the aisles. The galleries were reached by a stair which ran around a small square room annexed to the northwest corner. The room was entered only from within and probably served as store room and treasury. On the east side a door opened upon a court which ran the entire length of the building and was surrounded on its three outer sides by a covered gallery. Access to it was gained through three doors on the north, two on the east and two on the south. In the center was a fountain for ablutions.

To those unfamiliar with ancient synagogue architecture, it is an unending astonishment to discover that the synagogue, on its interior frieze and on the lintels of its doors, carried a great variety of ornaments in the shape of animal forms and mythological creatures as well as geometric designs. Evidently the Jews of the three or four centuries before the Moslem invasion understood the second commandment to forbid the worship, not the making, of likenesses of living things, including even human figures, as the remains of Palestinian synagogues almost universally testify. At Tell Hum on one piece of cornice are two eagles, back to back, followed by a horned and bearded sea horse with curving tail. A lintel has two lions facing. Another was ornamented with griffins, or cherubim. These are now

[1] This position of the shrine may be an afterthought. When congregations began worshiping toward Jerusalem is uncertain.

defaced, probably by Moslems. There were the usual Jewish sacred symbols, especially the menorah, or seven-branched candlestick. One of these appears to be surrounded by the body of a serpent which below is tied, head and tail, into a perfect granny-knot. In the frieze is a small pseudo-peripteral temple shrine, which perhaps represents the ancient ark of the Law, but stands on wheels.

The Franciscans purchased the site of the synagogue in the conviction that it was the one built by the Roman centurion. They have, therefore, been more or less at feud with the Lazarists at et-Tabigha, who often preferred to identify Capharnaum with Khirbet Minyeh. They have been proved correct as to the site of Capharnaum, but even Père Orfali's arguments have failed to make a convincing case for the first-century date of the synagogue. Practically all archaeologists, Protestant and Catholic, agree that the remains of Galilean synagogues now known belong to the second or third century, or even later. Their conclusions are based upon the character of the architecture and especially of the ornamentation.

Remains of an earlier synagogue at Tell Hum are reported by some as lying to the east of the excavated synagogue, by others as having been discovered under it, but no definite evidence has been produced. It is most unfortunate that the present owners are bound to a theory which prevents further investigation on this point.

On another score their sentimental interest in the synagogue is obstructive of scientific progress. Their property is ideal for the investigation of the character of a Jewish village in Galilee. But not only have they failed to use this unexampled opportunity; they have thoughtlessly obscured evidence which they had already uncovered. Orfali reports the presence of a basalt-paved street just west of the synagogue and beyond it house walls, mills, and olive presses. This was all visible in 1920 and 1921. But when I returned eight years later, the original remains had been tidied up and the mills, presses, and other household utensils set up, museum-wise, in orderly rows, interesting in themselves, but conveying no knowledge of the appearance of an ancient Jewish village.

The excavations carried on by the Franciscans before and after the war cleared up one problem. A remark of Epiphanius suggested that Count Joseph of Tiberias, presumably about 352 A.D., had built a Christian basilica at Capharnaum over the supposed site of Peter's house. Walls found by the German excavators south of the synagogue had been thought to represent it. But when the spot was more fully cleared, the walls were found not to make a basilica, and below them appeared an octagonal structure floored with mosaics. When excavations were resumed under Père Orfali's direction in 1921, three concentric octagons were disclosed with sparse remains of mosaics in large tessarae worked into simple and conventional, but delicately colored, patterns. This may mark the site of the house of Peter, but it is anything but a basilica. Only more extensive excavation can adequately reveal the history and character of Capharnaum.

The most tantalizing discovery at Tell Hum was an Aramaic inscription which had an unusual history. It was found by the Franciscans when they first acquired the property. It had been hastily scratched on one of the limestone pillars. When they heaped earth over the ruins to preserve them, the inscription was lost and it was not recovered until 1924. In 1925, shortly before his death in an automobile accident, Père Orfali gave an account of it to the Palestine Oriental Society. His reading was disputed by Rabbi Samuel Klein and Dr. Gustaf Dalman, but later Professor Sukenik restudied the lines and reached the conclusion that Père Orfali was right. The inscription reads: "Alphaeus son of Zebedee son of John made this column; on him be blessing." To find three names that appear together in the list of Jesus' disciples and their families (Mark 3.17 f.) on a column in a synagogue at Capharnaum is an astonishing coincidence, but it has no historical significance greater than that of the already mentioned ossuary inscription published by Professor

Sukenik which contained the name, "Jesus son of Joseph." It merely shows how common such names were.

OTHER EARLY SYNAGOGUES

Another, far less beautiful, but equally interesting synagogue was excavated by Kohl and Watzinger at Kerazeh, the site of ancient Chorazin. They covered it up again to save it from the hand of the spoiler. In 1926 the Department of Antiquities once more uncovered it, including a portion which the German excavators could not touch because a Bedouin hut stood upon it. A Bedouin woman and her daughter were set to keep jealous watch over the remains. Unfortunately no adequate publication has as yet appeared.

The general plan was the same as at Capharnaum, but with annexes, the character of which is not entirely clear, at the west instead of the east. The somewhat porous basalt used in the building did not conduce to artistic effects, but the decoration which was attempted is still more surprising than at Capharnaum. Along with rosettes and wreaths and knots and Jewish emblems, there was a series of vintage scenes set in ovals made of intertwined vines. They are similar to scenes which are found again and again on pagan sarcophagi. Great bunches of grapes hang from above. In one oval a man with a staff in one hand holds a large bunch of grapes in the other. In another oval two men are treading out grapes; in another a standing figure hands a drink to a seated person. One figure is interpreted as a centaur holding a wreath. Were these scenes pure *jeux d' esprit*, or do they have some hidden, mystical import? Opinions differ. As to date there is practically no difference of opinion. The building can hardly be earlier than the third century.

One of the significant discoveries at Kerazeh was the "seat of Moses," the stone chair in which doubtless the ruler of the synagogue sat during the service. This one is carved out of a single piece of basalt into the form of a great arm chair. On it is an inscription in Aramaic which names a certain Judan, son of Ishmael, as the builder of the synagogue, so Sukenik believes.

One of the many types of *menorah* (seven-branched lamp) carved on soft limestone
walls of Beth-shearim catacombs.

Remains of white limestone synagogue of third century (A.D.) at Capharnaum, from southeast; partial restoration at northwest corner.

He might be the same as a third-century scribe of that name who is mentioned in rabbinical sources, but there is no means of proving the identification.

Kohl and Watzinger described eleven synagogues, of which two were east of the Jordan and one on Mount Carmel. Professor Sukenik can report twenty-one in western Galilee, six east of the Jordan, and two on Mount Carmel. The greater part of them belong to the same period as those at Capharnaum and Chorazin. While they differ greatly in details, they are basilicas in plan and otherwise show the same general characteristics. The three portals, the rows of columns forming aisles and carrying balconies for the women, the "seat of Moses" for the president and possibly similar seats for other celebrities, these were standard provisions. Benches built one above and behind another in tiers along the walls, as in modern lodge rooms and ancient Mithreums, served the needs of the remainder of the congregation. The floors in the earlier, pre-Byzantine period were paved with stone slabs. The architectural order in the colonnades was almost always Corinthian. In the Byzantine period, to be described later, floors and ornamentation were different.

A synagogue excavated in 1936 by Drs. L. A. Mayer and A. Reifenberg at es-Samu' (Eshtemoa) south of Hebron was originally built in Roman times and then rebuilt in the Byzantine period. The floor was completely destroyed by the local inhabitants in search of treasure. But the western and northern walls were preserved to a considerable height. The entrance was at the east end of the room, but the Torah shrine was on the long side wall to the north, that is toward Jerusalem. Originally it was high in the wall, over 9 feet above the floor, and the excavators, therefore, believe that such synagogues as those at Capharnaum and Chorazin should be reconstructed with a high Torah shrine. The Byzantine reconstruction put the Torah shrine only two steps above the ground level as in the later synagogues elsewhere.

When excavated, this was the only broadhouse synagogue—like that at Dura-Europos—known in Palestine. However, the excavators have since found two others, at Khirbet Susiyyeh near es-Samu' and at Nawa in the Hauran. The building at es-Samu' was well constructed and measured about 65 by 76 feet. When the excavators began, there was very little visible to encourage their venture. At other places in southern Palestine there must be synagogues to excavate, as architectural fragments and literary references testify.

JEWISH CATACOMBS—BETH-SHEARIM

One series of excavations, that at Sheikh Abreiq, partially refutes the charge that Jewish Galilee has been neglected. Since the original *Survey of Western Palestine* Sheikh Abreiq has been known for its "painted caves." In 1921, with the pictures and descriptions of the *Galilee* volume in mind, I visited the site and, in the company of the *mukhtar* and two other Arab citizens, crawled into the great chambers to see the crude traces of red paint on the walls which Conder and Kitchener had recorded. Loculi and seven-branched candlesticks on the walls had shown the surveyors that the caves were Jewish tombs. The earthquake of 1927 rendered these caverns no longer accessible, so I have been told.

When in April, 1936, the Jewish scholar, Dr. B. Maisler, and his father-in-law, Mr. I. Ben-Svi, president of the Jewish National Council and himself a scholar, asked me to accompany them to Sheikh Abreiq to visit some recently discovered tombs, I put everything else aside to seize the opportunity. A large area about the Arab site had been purchased a decade before by one of the Zionist societies, and some of the colonists, investigating a sunken spot developed by the winter rains, discovered a most astonishing catacomb, which, except for its want of paintings, deserves a place beside the Jewish and Christian catacombs at Rome.

The unforgettable impression made during the night and morning we spent clambering about in this great underground, three-storied tenement of the dead has been more than confirmed during the four seasons of excavation which Dr. Maisler has since carried on (1936, 1937, 1938-9, 1940). Eleven caverns or tombs, some of them containing large numbers of rooms, were cleared, and also part of the city. Inscriptions found in tombs clearly proved the city to be the Beth-shearim which is often mentioned in the Talmud and which was for some time the home of Rabbi Judah ha-Nasi and his school. Rabbi and members of his family were perhaps buried here rather than at Sepphoris, where he later lived.[2] The catacombs proved the city to have been famous throughout the Jewish world as a burial place.

They were artificially cut with great care into the soft, chalk-like *nari* limestone common in the neighborhood. The entrances, passages, and rooms had been carved in imitation of Roman buildings. The doorways and arches had their posts or pillars and lintels with accompanying capitals, moldings, and other architectural decorations, some of which were most bizarre. The doors, which turned on great pivots, were carved out of hard limestone—in one case out of basalt—usually in imitation of wooden doors bound with iron and studded with nails or metal bosses. The plans of the various rooms were far from symmetrical or even rectangular. However, a fairly uniform idea dominated. From a long corridor doors opened upon small rooms which had arcosolia or barrel-vaulted chambers on three sides or upon other corridors which gave upon similar rooms. In one case a stairway descended from without through a monumental doorway into a court that had been paved with mosaics and that had passages opening out from it into a great number of corridors and rooms. Usually shallow graves were dug in the floors of the arcosolia and rooms. Sometimes at the end of a pair of graves there was a short grave, probably intended to serve as an ossuary. Evidence in the shape of nails and clamps for holding boards together proved that wooden coffins and ossuaries had been used in some cases.

The walls were decorated with many designs, including the usual sacred Jewish symbols, *shofar, lulab, ethrog,* and especially

2 See above, chap. XVII.

the *menorah*, of which at least twenty-seven varieties were recorded. There were other more astonishing drawings; for example, a man on horseback, lions, human heads, a human figure with a *menorah* on its head, and a ship with large square sail and two rudders. All were crudely scratched in the soft chalk, most of them by quite unpracticed hands.

More enlightenment was afforded by the short but numerous inscriptions in Greek, Aramaic, Palmyrene, and Latin. A marble slab bore the inscription in Greek, "Memorial of Leontius, father of Ribbi Paregorius (the 'Comforter') and of Julianus the Palatine, from the goldsmiths." Another read, "Germanos son of Isaac the Palmyrene." Still another ran, "I belong to Leontius the Polmyrene (*sic*), moneychanger." In a tomb cave a "presbyter" was the head of a family of Himyarites, Jews from Southern Arabia. Nabatean potsherds testified to the burial of Jews from less distant Arab regions. In Aramaic inscriptions the names of well-known Jewish rabbis appeared. It is evident that between the second and fifth centuries Jews from many parts of the Roman world, from Asia Minor to Southern Arabia, from Italy to Palmyra, came to Beth-shearim to die and to be buried in sacred ground. To judge from the inscriptions the dominant language at Beth-shearim in the third and fourth centuries was Greek.

An inscription put together out of 39 fragments of a marble slab from a mausoleum that stood on the hill read, "I, Justus, the Leontide, son of Sappho, am lying dead after having picked (*scil.* the fruits?) of all wisdom. I relinquished the light, my unhappy parents, who will mourn constantly, and my brothers, alas, in my Beth-shearim. After going to Hades, I, Justus . . . am lying here with many of my folk, because such was the wish of powerful Fate. Courage, Justus, no one is immortal." In the debris were fragments of a marble sarcophagus, of an animal frieze, and of other carvings showing Hellenistic motifs, such as Leda and a battle of Greeks and Amazons. Either the Leontides were a thoroughly Hellenized and secularized Jewish family, or Beth-shearim had a population of Greeks as well as

Jews. That Sheikh Abreiq was the ancient Beth-shearim is rendered doubly certain by this piquant inscription. The slab that carried the inscription had been deliberately broken in pieces and scattered over a wide area as had also the sarcophagus, testifying to some tragedy of which we can only imagine the nature. Possibly it was due to a riot of iconoclastic Jews who objected to the presence of a heathenish monument, but it may have been destroyed with the city in the fourth century.

Another significant discovery, made during the third season in the ruins of the city of Beth-shearim, was a synagogue. It consisted of a well-built basilica oriented toward Jerusalem, that is to the southeast. There was a terrace in front of it as at Capharnaum and an open court beside it. The Torah shrine stood near the wall between two doors at the southeast end, the *bema*, from which the law was read, was a stone platform at the other end of the hall. The floor was paved with marble slabs, the walls covered with painted or tinted plaster. Marble slabs which may have been fixed to the wall or used as pavement contained a zodiac among other designs carved in relief. Numerous small objects were found, coins, pots, potsherds, and various metal objects. Two Greek inscriptions show that the synagogue served also as a court house. Apparently a simpler synagogue of the second century had preceded this more elaborate structure which was used in the third and fourth centuries. The synagogue, like the mausoleum of Justus, suffered intentional destruction at men's hands, perhaps at the time of a destruction of the city which Dr. Maisler ascribes to Constantius Gallus in 352 A.D.

LATER SYNAGOGUES

Synagogues of the fourth, fifth, and sixth centuries, found in various parts of Palestine, are in some ways more astonishing—they are certainly more colorful—than those of the third century, for their floors were usually paved with startling and highly colored designs in mosaic. A line which dropped out of the Talmud by homeoteleuton has recently been discovered in a Leningrad manuscript which says: "In the days of Rabbi Abun they began to depict designs on mosaics and he did not hinder them."[3] Since the two rabbis of that name lived in the fourth century, the dates of synagogues with mosaic floors may be assumed to fall some time after 300 A.D. A few fragments of such pavements were found before the first World War at Kefr Kenna and Sepphoris. Since the war such discoveries have been numerous.

The first was uncovered in 1917 by the bursting of a shell as Allenby was driving the Turks across the Jordan and was later excavated by the Dominican École Biblique of Jerusalem. It lies near 'Ain Duq a little north of the Old Testament Jericho at ancient Na'aran. The figures had been so mutilated that little except the outlines was distinguishable. One panel had the twelve signs of the zodiac in a circle surrounding the chariot of the sun. Another showed Daniel approached by two lions, still another linked together polygons, circles, and semicircles within which were pictures of birds, beasts, and plants. A fourth carried a picture of the ark of the law with a seven-branched candlestick on either side.

The inscriptions, of which there were several, were undamaged. They named various figures in the pictures or mentioned donors with the formula "Remembered for good be . . . . ." The Na'aran synagogue is notable also because, while it lies east of Jerusalem, it is oriented north and south and not toward Jerusalem and apparently had its three doors in the north end. Unfortunately it lies on the northern edge of a wadi and the southern end is lost. Possibly the Torah shrine was in the west side, as the synagogue at es-Semu' would suggest.

Another synagogue, discovered in 1928 when an irrigation ditch was being dug, lies on the property of a new Jewish colony at Beth-alpha, a few miles west of Beisan. It has three distinctions. In its mosaic floor is a Greek inscription giving the names of the mosaicists and the date, a year (unfortunately obliterated) in the reign of the Emperor Justin 1 (518-527 A.D.).

[3] Sukenik, *Anc. Synagogues*, 27 f., quoting J. N. Epstein in *Tarbiz*, III, 15 ff.

Thus far this is the only synagogue which can be closely dated. Another distinction is an apse for the ark of the law in the southern end. A third is a stone *bema* built near the apse on the east side. It was built over the mosaic and therefore is later, perhaps dating from the end of the century.

The floor was covered by mosaics which included a picture of the frustrated sacrifice of Isaac at the back, in the center a zodiac surrounding the chariot of the sun much like that of Na'aran, and a third panel with two lions guarding an ark of the law and with various other designs just in front of the apse. The building is irregular in plan and the mosaics colorful but crude in construction.

Still another synagogue of late date was discovered in 1923 by members of the Department of Antiquities at el-Hammeh and excavated by Dr. Sukenik for the Hebrew University. The site lies within a great bend of the Yarmuq River just below Gadara (Umm Qeis). The tell on which the synagogue stood lies near the hot springs which were famous in antiquity as Hammath by Gadara to distinguish them from Hammath by Tiberias. The place is mentioned in Talmudic and Byzantine literature. Soundings made by Dr. Nelson Glueck when director of the American School of Oriental Research showed that the tell was occupied in the Early and Middle Bronze Ages. A partially preserved Roman theater and a small portion of the baths which Buckingham saw and pictured still remain near the springs to tell of their popularity.

In the synagogue an apse for the Torah shrine and mosaic floors testify to a date later than that of the Capharnaum and Chorazin synagogues. One inscription gives the title *komes* ("count") to a donor. Since no Jews were allowed to bear titles after 433 A.D., the building must have been erected before that date. The units of currency recording the donations are not earlier than the fourth century. The building was intentionally demolished and burned, as ashes on the floor and the smashed marble screen testify. It probably stood, therefore, from some time in the fourth century until the sixth, perhaps until the time of Justinian, the severity of whose laws encouraged anti-Jewish riots.

The epigraphic material at el-Hammeh exceeds that of any other synagogue yet found, with the exception of that at 'Ain Duq. It is in Aramaic, set into the mosaics of the floor to commemorate donors. All but two or three of the eighteen names mentioned are Greek. The inscriptions are unique in telling the amounts given. The badly shattered marble screen which stood before the apse bore an inscription in Greek with the name Paregorius, equivalent to Menahem, or Nahum. Unfortunately no date appeared.

The designs in the mosaic were much simpler than those of Beth-alpha and Na'aran. All were geometric except in a panel in front of the apse where two lions, one on either side of a circle containing the record of the chief donation, guard the approach to the Torah shrine. The building and dependencies are curiously irregular in shape. The main hall and the apse look slightly to west of south, directly toward Jerusalem.

Still another synagogue was uncovered at Jerash in 1929 by Mr. J. W. Crowfoot and Mr. R. W. Hamilton. Its mosaic floor came to light about six inches under the floor of a church which was being excavated. In one aisle was an inscription in Aramaic which is perhaps best explained as naming the artisans who laid the mosaics. Inside the door long lines of animals marched across the floor. The names of Shem and Japheth in Greek confirmed the easy guess that the scene came from the story of Noah's ark. An accompanying inscription of benediction was also in Greek. The artistry is better than in any other Palestinian synagogue yet excavated, thus testifying to the wealth of Gerasene Jewry and the proficiency of the Gerasene school of mosaicists.

The building, which was entered from a previously existing court at its eastern end, was oriented slightly north of west, with a rectangular apse for the Torah shrine at that end. The congregation thus faced in the general direction of Jerusalem, although actually toward Samaria. The date of erection must fall in the fourth or fifth century. The Christians took the site

Basalt synagogue at Kerazeh (Chorazin). Carved stones of frieze piled on farthest wall of building. Other ornaments are to be noted. Taken from SE.

Portion of Aramaic inscription on the "seat of Moses."

Photo by D. E. M.

Qasr el-Malfuf. Typical megalithic tower dated in early Iron Age.

Hammam es-Sarakh.

and built a church there in 530-31 A.D. The synagogue had been much better built than the church.

An Earlier Synagogue

A most significant item in the history of Palestinian Judaism has just been published by Professor A. H. Detweiler, who, for several seasons, was architect of the Jerash expedition.[4] When the great Hadrianic triumphal arch was cleared and investigated in 1931-34, several fragments of a Doric order, including architrave and frieze, were discovered, some in the debris at the foot of the arch, others in the topmost layer of the interior fill. Peculiarities of the entablature are held by Mr. Detweiler to prove that the building from which they came was Jewish. They have striking resemblances to the "hybrid architecture" of numerous Hellenistic-Jewish tombs at and near Jerusalem. A relief of what appears to be a seven-branched candlestick adds to the evidence, while a bird which appears on one fragment is paralleled by similar birds flanking a Torah shrine in the decoration of glass vessels of Jewish origin and in synagogue mosaics.[5]

The triumphal arch is dated by its inscription in 130 A.D. The Jewish structure from which the fragments came must have been destroyed, of course, before that time. Mr. Detweiler plausibly suggests that this happened at the time of the attack on Jerash by Lucius Annius in 68 A.D.[6]

This discovery provides a confirmation of Josephus' statement, which has been held in suspicion, and also evidence that as early as the first century Jews were already using symbolic animal figures in the decoration of their synagogues. The confirmation of Josephus fits into other Gerasene inscriptional data in remarkable fashion and adds to our conception of the extent of the Jewish war. The discovery of the use of animal figures settles a moot point in the history of the synagogue and Judaism

---

[4] *BAS*, 87 (1942), 10-17; see below, chap. XX.

[5] See E. L. Sukenik, *The Ancient Synagogue of Beth Alpha*, Jerusalem: University Press, 1932, fig. 35, p. 31; pls. IX and XX.

[6] Josephus, *Jewish War*, IV, 487 f. (ix, 1).

and whets the appetite for more information as to the extent of such use.

This long account shows that much has been learned about Judaism in the period after it recovered from the fall of Jerusalem. What has been found suggests that there is much more to be learned and promises well for the future. If archaeologists can be given a chance in Palestine, many more dark corners in the history of Judaism and Christianity can be illuminated.

CHAPTER XIX

BETWEEN THE DESERT AND THE SOWN

❖

TRANSJORDAN has baffled and beguiled a long series of explorers and archaeologists. To the charm of its limitless stretches of field and moor and steppe and the rippling beauty of the blue streams that murmur in its deep-cut gorges there is added the mystery of hills covered by hundreds of dolmens, lonely menhirs, rude but sturdy block houses, piled up, so it appears, by giant children, and the ruined glory of magnificent cities inhabited only by the ghosts of the past. Because written records of its long history are extremely scanty, the remarkably preserved archaeological documents have roused so much the greater interest. Beginning shortly after 1800 traveler after traveler has brought back reports of its glories.

The discovery in 1868 of the "Moabite stone," the inscription of Mesha, king of Moab, contemporary of Ahab, tantalized biblical scholars by its confirmations and contradictions of biblical statements. The strange "pseudo-Hittite" stela, discovered at Rujm el-'Abd by de Saulcy in 1851, though less known, seemed to promise further revelations. Egyptian stelae appeared in the Hauran region. But most of all, perhaps, the wonders of Petra, Dean Burgon's "rose-red city, half as old as time," focused attention on eastern Palestine. The dramatic fiasco of the forged Deuteronomy, represented as Moses' original manuscript discovered in Moab, could only temporarily dim the attractions of that region.

What most impressed the eye in Transjordan were the Roman and Byzantine remains of the Decapolis, baths, temples, theaters, and Christian basilicas, with an abundance of Greek inscriptions. Selah Merrill for the American Palestine Exploration Society tried to survey eastern Palestine in the seventies. Three American expeditions led by Howard Crosby Butler in the years 1899-1900, 1904-5, and 1909 brought back extensive reports of the monuments and inscriptions that could be found without excavation in northern Transjordan and southern Syria. Rudolf Brünnow and Alfred von Domaszewski performed a similar task with German thoroughness at about the same time. They went much farther south than the American expeditions, following the Roman roads toward the Gulf of 'Aqabah. Gottlieb Schumacher, while surveying the route for the Turkish railroad to Medina and Mecca, secured an entrée to the country which enabled him to make hasty and inaccurate but valuable reports to the Deutsche Palästinaverein.

Charles M. Doughty, Gertrude Bell, Alfred Musil, and T. E. Lawrence traversed the region and the magic of their eyes and pens has transferred to paper something of its mysterious charm. Alfred Musil's adventurous journeys and circumstantial publications recorded extremely valuable data. Fathers of the Dominican Ecole Biblique at Jerusalem have made even more meticulous contributions, for example in Jaussen's "Customs of the Arabs in the Land of Moab." Still more recently Fritz Frank of Jerusalem and Professor Albrecht Alt of Leipzig have gathered invaluable information. The land has been much studied, but piecemeal, never with a comprehensive grasp of the historical problems nor with a technique which offered a means of their solution.

It was not until after the first World War that progress was possible in the history of pre-Roman Palestine. Then, for various reasons, American interest was drawn to that region. After 1928 American scholars made many trips through the region, chiefly in connection with the excavations at Jerash, but also to visit Petra, which had been made accessible to tourists. Especially the development of a Transjordan Department of Antiquities by Professor John Garstang and Mr. George Horsfield and the adequate policing of the region by the Transjordan government prepared the way for a survey of the whole region such as had been impossible before.

Enlightened and intelligent support from English officials has been a most important factor in the success of the excavations and surveys which have been carried on in the last dozen years. The progress which had been made in the determination of ceramic chronology, especially by Dr. Albright and Dr. Fisher of the American School of Oriental Research, was an indispensable item. Previous surveys have had to depend largely upon inscriptions, which are much more numerous in Transjordan than in western Palestine, but still far too few, and almost wanting in pre-Roman times.

The American Palestine Exploration Society, founded in 1870 to supplement the English Palestine Exploration Fund, made a brave, but futile and abortive, attempt to assume responsibility for eastern Palestine. In 1881 Conder attempted to do for eastern Palestine what he and Kitchener had done for the country west of the Jordan. But Turkish suspicions stopped him when he had hardly begun. As to archaeology, the American School of Oriental Research at Jerusalem has eventually made good the promises of that earlier society, and has done it with a success which would have been unattainable seventy years ago. When the findings of the archaeological survey can be fully combined with the Transjordan government's cadastral survey made by airplane photography, the result will be far superior to the great work of Kitchener and Conder in western Palestine. The accomplishment is largely the work of Professor Nelson Glueck of the Hebrew Union College at Cincinnati, who was director of the School in 1932-33, and again from 1936 to 1940.

Selah Merrill and his few colleagues of seventy years ago traveled slowly and painfully on horseback. Dr. Glueck traveled rapidly—and sometimes painfully—by American automobile truck. Conder for the Palestine Exploration Fund made his survey of a small portion of eastern Palestine by moving rapidly enough to keep ahead of Turkish officials who were seeking to arrest and deport him. Glueck made his journeys often with a government official and always with the knowledge and benevolent supervision of the Arab Legion, the Transjordan Frontier Force, and the police, who kept a check on his movements only in order to go to his aid in case of accident or obstruction. It may seem irksome to check in and out of every police station, but when one is on a desert road twenty or thirty miles from food or gasoline, it is comforting to know that your coming has been telephoned ahead, and that, if you do not arrive at the next post within a reasonable time, someone will start out to look for you. Glueck was even flown over the country by a member of the Royal Air Force, Squadron Leader Trail, and has been able to illustrate his reports with scores of aerial photographs taken by the RAF.

Dr. Glueck's preparation for his task had been exceptional. To a thorough theological course in Hebrew Union College, which gave him linguistic preparation, he had added much previous travel in Palestine, and the study of pottery under Dr. Albright's direction, especially at Tell Beit Mirsim and Beit Sur. Dr. Albright had made a beginning of the survey of Transjordan by studying the mounds of the Jordan valley, and among other things, by discovering in 1924 at the southeastern end of the Dead Sea the large camping ground and fortress of Bab edh-Dhra', which dates from the latter part of the Early Bronze Age. In 1929 he had made out a line of Early and Middle Bronze Age mounds along the edge of the steppe east of Gilead.

Glueck has undertaken to apply the technique of the surface observation of ceramic chronological data to the whole region. He was able in his five years as director of the American School of Oriental Research at Jerusalem to cover the whole of the country from the Jabbok (the Nahr ez-Zerqa) south to the Gulf of 'Aqabah. In addition Glueck made two major excavations, at Khirbet et-Tannur and Tell el-Kheleifeh, both extremely enlightening.

The discoveries have ranged from prehistoric rock drawings to medieval Arab castles. Unexpected and highly instructive information has been acquired on pre-Israelite times, on the "wanderings in the wilderness," and on the great pre-Roman Nabatean empire. The history of the Edomites and the story of King Solomon's mines have been illuminated. Obscure passages of the Bible have been fitted into their historical framework and interpreted. Historically speaking, a barren desert has suddenly blossomed as the rose.

THE EASTERN STEPPE

The railway which was intended to carry pilgrims from Damascus to Mecca, and which T. E. Lawrence and his colleagues dynamited with such éclat, marks the eastern edge of sedentary occupation. In the winter of 1932-3 Dr. Glueck began his survey by traveling into the steppe and the desert east of the railroad to determine the nature of the occupation at the various fortresses which, at one time or another, had been built to guard the border of the settled country and to police the caravan routes running east and south. The region preserves an extraordinary record of the fluctuations of civilization.

Keeping of necessity within the safe boundaries of Emir Abdullah's territory, Dr. Glueck visited forts and caravan stations where, in some cases, Greek and Latin inscriptions lying by Moslem mosques and caravansaries testify to the extension of Roman and Byzantine, as well as Arab, protection over the desert routes. Most surprising of all are the winter palaces and hunting lodges in the steppe, as at Hamman es-Sarakh, Qeseir 'Amrah, and Meshetta, where Arab monarchs and their courts, still ostensibly homesick for the free Bedouin life they had recently abandoned, could amuse themselves after a day's hunting, "with poetry, astronomy, philosophy, and wine, women, and song," while they gazed . . . . "on ceilings decorated with fat nudes and with paintings of dancing bears playing musical instruments."[1]

At Kilwa, the Transjordan post farthest to the east, which no one but Gertrude Bell had visited, two surprising discoveries were made. The first was a group of ruins of basalt houses and

[1] Glueck, *The Other Side of the Jordan*, 39 f.

a number of little cells north and east of them. Crosses and Arabic inscriptions appeared to prove that they belonged to a monastic establishment of about 1000 A.D.

Some hundreds of meters northeast of the settlement was a hill of Nubian sandstone. Every smooth surface on the rocks was found to be covered with drawings. Some were very crude. Others showed no little artistic skill. One was of an ibex standing by itself; another was of a wounded ibex with two streams— no doubt of blood—running from its nostrils. The sweep of the horns, the accurate rendering of the head and body, a lifted foot, give a striking vigor and beauty to the carvings. Prehistorians, judging from the style of the drawings and the weathering of the rocks—poor criteria, but the best available—conclude that these and several other drawings probably belong to the Mesolithic period, the time of Natufian I. Others are later, as late perhaps as the Ghassulian or Chalcolithic period. A crudely drawn plow may even be put as late as the Early Bronze Age. Still other drawings with inscriptions are the work of pre-Islamic Bedouins of the Sabean, or Thamudic, period. A German expedition reported by Hans Rhotert later distinguished three Stone Age cultures in the immediate neighborhood: an older Paleolithic marked by extensive deposits of artifacts at the foot of the ridges, a Mesolithic near the drawings, and a crude culture found on top of certain ridges which perhaps was Mesolithic but which was difficult to identify.

The only excavation as yet carried on in the steppe attacked a not very promising site about 25 miles southeast of 'Amman at Wadi Dhobai. It was discovered by Mr. A. S. Kirkbride, then Assistant British Resident, and further investigated by Mr. Lankester Harding, Chief Curator of Antiquities. In 1937-8 Dr. J. d'A. Waechter and Miss V. M. Seton-Williams spent four months searching the neighborhood and making two soundings. Wadi Dhobai is a narrow, shallow valley between ridges of flint and limestone. Its sides and bottom consisted of solidified gravel which stores enough water during the wet season to last six or seven months. A dam built across it in historic times has now been filled to the top with silt. The soil is poor and very little grows except desert shrubs and a few succulents and sparse grasses on the wadi floor. When and how could such a site be inhabited?

Three industries were discovered on the surface and their presence confirmed by the soundings. One, indeed, could not be defined or dated because it was represented only by leaf-shaped blades of flint picked up at the lower end of the wadi. They resembled those from Kilwa but were smaller. Another was Middle Aurignacian, resembling stratum C at Mugharet el-Kebarah. A sounding less than two feet deep was made at one site (K) where this industry was found, but without reaching bedrock. The third industry, called Dhobainian (better Dhobaian) because unknown elsewhere, was similar in some features to an industry found by Mr. Henry Field at Umm Wual in the Nejd, in others to the Tahunian of prepottery Neolithic at Jericho. The Dhobaian sites all had hut circles made by placing slabs of limestone on edge. At the one excavated (B) the rock was reached at a depth of a couple of feet and steps and post holes cut into it were discovered.

Thus further items are added to the story of man's early efforts to meet the challenge of nature. Possibly nature was then more propitious. The Stone Age occupation may belong to a pluvial period. Unfortunately, as Miss Bate points out, too little is as yet known of the fauna of the transition period from Mesolithic to Neolithic for any satisfactory theory to be constructed.

Nothing could seem stranger than the proximity, on the surface, of such a succession of cultures. Yet Paleolithic occupation in the steppe should not be surprising. Mr. Henry Field for the Field Museum has done some valuable prospecting and discovered important stations at numerous places in the desert. It is clear that the desert, perhaps not then a desert by any means, was peopled from the Early Paleolithic period down to the fourth millennium by prehistoric man, who was just emerging into something like agricultural civilization over in the Jordan valley. The artistic urge in the human race is abundantly attested by primitive man's repeated exhibitions of his glyptic skill through ten thousand years. No less surprising is the discovery of a Christian community in the heart of the steppe when Islam was at the height of its glory and power. But it must not be forgotten that there were Bedouin Christians from the earliest Christian times. The wife of Mu'awiyeh and mother of Yezid I was a Bedawiyeh who raised her son in the desert and was perhaps responsible for that nostalgia which took the Umaiyad califs back to it.

SUCCESSIVE CULTURES IN THE SOWN LAND

The discoveries made in the regions between the Jordan rift and the steppe are naturally much more numerous and significant than those in the steppe itself. Dr. Glueck's survey has outlined a succession of seven historical periods: the first covers the end of the Early Bronze and the beginning of the Middle Bronze Age, EB iv and MB i (2300-1900 B.C.). When this flourishing age came to an end, it was succeeded by a second which shows scant occupation, probably by nomads only. Just before the beginning of the Iron Age, in the thirteenth century, the country was occupied by an agricultural population which flourished for four or five hundred years and then declined in the seventh and following centuries. Then came the Greeks and also the Nabateans in the fourth and third centuries, followed by the Romans in the first and second centuries A.D., and the Byzantines in the fifth. Finally in the seventh century the Arabs once more swept away the greater part of the settled population and the land kept continual sabbath. Because there has been no settled population to plunder them for building materials, the standing structures of Transjordan are particularly impressive in their lonely isolation.

To his first period according to Glueck belong the menhirs, massebot, and other standing monoliths discovered at Lejjun, Ader, el-Megheirat, Bab edh-Dhra', and by Khirbet Iskander in Wadi el-Wala; likewise the dolmens of which there are great fields at el-'Adeimeh, in Wadi Heshban, and west of Irbid near Kefr Yuba. Schumacher reports 800 or 1,000 in one section of the 'Ajlun district, 400 in another. Near Kerazeh is an important group. It required no small energy and some organization to place these great stones in position. What race could have possessed the qualities necessary and why did they build such awkward and useless structures? Were there giants in those days as the ancient Hebrews believed? Glueck has found dolmens, menhirs, and cromlechs all near sites that, from their pottery, had to be dated in the first of his periods, EB iv—MB i. De Vaux made a similar discovery at Khirbet Iskander. But the occupied site with its pottery was usually at some small distance. Conclusions from this evidence can, therefore, hardly be accepted as final, even though others have discovered the same pottery.

Two attempts have been made to settle the problem by excavation in the hope of finding under some accidental or intentional tumulus, such as is common in France, preserved skeletons and funerary furniture. In the autumn of 1930 Mr. F. Turville-Petre attacked the Kerazeh dolmen field and excavated 24 dolmens and two other megalithic structures. I can remember the resignation with which he described his finds as Byzantine pottery and Roman coins. It was somewhat better than that in the final outcome, but the flints and crude pottery which came to light allowed no definite conclusions.

In the spring of 1933 Dr. Moshé Stékélis, following up a discovery made by Father Mallon and M. Neuville, excavated 168 small dolmens, or rather stone cists, in the great necropolis at el-'Adeimeh, where for millennia Bedouins have buried their dead. His labors were somewhat better rewarded than those of Turville-Petre. He found a few fragments of bone, and pottery, chiefly handmade, but some apparently shaped on a primitive tournette. Shapes and simple ledge and lug handles were clearly of the Ghassulian type, and Stékélis, in spite of the slight and ambiguous evidence, concluded the burials were contemporaneous with the occupation of the neighboring late Neolithic or Chalcolithic city. They are thus a thousand years earlier than the European dolmens. Albright accepts this view. He regards the menhirs, dolmens, and cromlechs of Transjordan as the work of a nomadic population in a "megalithic phase of the Neolithic period," and calls them "the last great manifestation of the Stone Age in the Old World."[2] They thus came to represent an occupation that is earlier than Glueck's first period by two thousand years.

Neither Glueck's nor Stékélis' evidence can be regarded as conclusive. The tombs which Stékélis excavated are not, strictly speaking, megalithic. They differ markedly from the dolmens of el-'Adeimeh itself and resemble rather the degenerate stone cist of France's late megalithic monuments. There are no bell beakers nor other articles to relate them to any of the multitude of funerary offerings found in European dolmens and other megalithic tombs. Yet some sentences of the descriptions of this latest megalithic culture in France read much like some in the description of Stékélis' el-'Adeimeh necropolis. If the el-'Adeimeh cists are degenerate survivals of the larger and simpler dolmens (according to the usually accepted European typological succession), the true dolmens of Palestine must be extremely early, not one thousand but two thousand years before those of Portugal. If it is "rash to apply to France the Scandinavian typology,"[3] how much more so to apply it to Palestine, and particularly to eastern Palestine.

The whole question as to the date and the builders of these mysterious structures must be regarded as still *sub judice*. Were their makers sea rovers in search of gold, or nomads of the steppe? Do they represent two thousand almost stagnant years or do they belong within a circumscribed period as the work of a particular race or cultural tradition? Perhaps the future will solve the puzzle. It hardly need be said that they were not a race of giants. But it should be noted that not all megalithic

[2] *From the Stone Age to Christianity*, pp. 95 f.
[3] See Gordon Childe, *Dawn of European Civilization*, 2d ed., London-New York, 1927, pp. 280 f. and 277.

structures need to be ascribed to a single race or even successive races.

A third type of megalithic monument found widely in Transjordan has been equally mysterious and puzzling. But it has no necessary connection with dolmens and menhirs. It is what the Arab calls a *rujm*, a "stone heap," or, when it is large, also a *qasr*, a "watch tower," or "castle," or a *khirbeh*, a "ruin." The round ones are sometimes called *qasr el-malfuf*, "cabbage castle." Built of large flat blocks of limestone, only very roughly shaped, they dot the landscape here and there and appear also, though less frequently, on the west side of the rift. While no sufficient excavations beneath them have been made to determine their date, yet, since Dr. Glueck has found them frequently in connection with Iron Age pottery (1200-600 B.C.), it seems safe to assume that they were structures of that age, built by peasants who had no contacts with the more highly developed civilizations of the coast from which Solomon and Ahab imported their masons. In contrast to this architectural lag is their superior skill as potters.

Many of these structures are mere block houses, round or square structures in which a small squad could keep watch and protect themselves while the news of an approaching army or threatening raid could be signaled to the country. Others are huge, irregular walled enclosures covering considerable hilltops and have strong gates and towers. Some, indeed, are of sufficient size to hold flocks and herds as well as people. In the larger enclosures there was usually a strong central structure, essentially an acropolis, around which the houses and tents of the population could be grouped. One fortress, a Moabite site now called el-Medeiyineh, was surrounded by a fosse.

The only excavation which has reached Iron Age strata in the area under consideration is that at Khirbet el-Kheleifeh at the head of the Gulf of 'Aqabah. This most interesting and instructive site is discussed below. Otherwise no architectural monuments of the Iron Age are now known in Transjordan except these great piles of stone. Even if Drs. Stékélis and Albright are correct regarding the menhirs and dolmens, the rough stone towers and fortresses of Transjordan seem to belong to the period when the Israelites were erecting similar structures but also much more durable and artistic temples and palaces and walls on the other side of the Jordan rift. However, only further excavation can settle the question.

The pseudo-Hittite stela of de Saulcy, the Balu'ah stela found by Mr. Head, and the more famous Hebrew inscription of Mesha, king of Moab, as well as superior pottery, seem to be evidence of a much higher civilization in the period between the thirteenth and the ninth centuries than appears on the surface. However, while the EB iv and MB i civilization on the two sides of the Jordan had a relatively homogeneous pottery, in the Iron Age Edom and Moab, on the one hand, and western Palestine, on the other, show pottery types which have individual peculiarities along with basic similarities. It may be, therefore, that intercourse between these neighboring regions was impeded by the growth of nationalistic hatreds, such as come to bitter expression in many a biblical passage, while the chief lines of trade, running north and south, allowed Syria and southern Arabia to exercise decisive influence on Edom and Moab.

On the basis of these differences, Dr. Glueck believes it possible to assert that the Edomites did not settle west of the rift in the Negeb, or southern steppe of Palestine, until the Persian or Hellenistic period. They did not even occupy the great gorge except where they worked its copper mines, but held certain strong fortresses along the edge of their plateau to the west and to the south along Wadi Hismeh. Both Edom and Moab developed a fairly continuous line of fortresses along their eastern borders for defense against maurauding Bedouin bands from the steppe, and along their other borders for defense against one another and the Israelites.

KING SOLOMON'S MINES

A constant source of dispute must have been the scant supplies of metal in the Wadi 'Arabah, which were valuable in

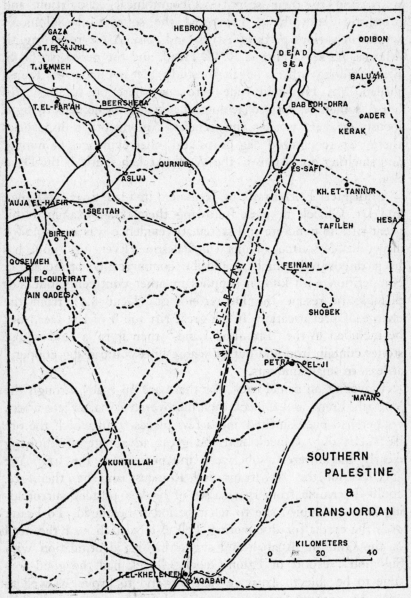

GAZA
T. EL AJJUL
T. JEMMEH
T. EL-FAR'AH
BEERSHEBA
HEBRON
DEAD SEA
DIBON
BALU'AH
BAB EDH-DHRA
ADER
KERAK
QURNUB
ASLUJ
ES-SAFI
KH. ET-TANNUR
'AUJA EL-HAEIR
SBEITAH
TAFILEH
HESA
BIREIN
QOSEIMEH
'AIN EL-QUDEIRAT
'AIN QADEIS
FEINAN
SHOBEK
PETRA EL-JI
MA'AN
KUNTILLAH

SOUTHERN
PALESTINE
&
TRANSJORDAN

KILOMETERS
0   20   40

WADI EL-ARABAH

T. EL-KHELEIFEH
'AQABAH

FIG. 6

proportion to their scarcity. Geographical speculation and novelistic fancy have discovered the sources of Solomon's wealth in various parts of Africa and Asia. After 1920 English officials, A. S. Kirkbride, R. G. Head, and the geologist, G. S. Blake, among others, began to study the resources of Transjordan. Mr. Horsfield rode here and there on his beautiful horse, sometimes on archaeological missions, sometimes to fight locusts or meet various emergencies. Among other discoveries these men recognized slag heaps and other evidences of mining and smelting operations in the Wadi 'Arabah south of the Dead Sea.

Until Herr Fritz Frank of Jerusalem in 1932, 1933, and 1934 and Dr. Glueck in 1934 following their trails, examined this great rift, no concrete and systematic evidence was available for any valuable sources of metal in Palestine. Even now none has been discovered which would be commercially profitable in competition with known supplies in other continents, but it is possible to rescue the Deuteronomist (Deut 8.9) from the charge of prevarication. If the great rift south of the Dead Sea be included in the "Promised Land," then it is "a land whose stones contain iron and out of whose hills you can dig copper," at least in small amounts.

Traveling on camel back, for there are no roads through the 'Arabah, Frank and Glueck each discovered site after site where copper had been smelted and a few places from which the ore had been dug. Glueck had the great advantage of knowing clearly the differences between the pottery of the Iron Age and that of the Nabateans and Romans, and he, therefore, could determine from the masses of broken pottery surrounding every occupied site to what period it belonged. To Frank goes the credit for discovering Tell el-Kheleifeh near the head of the Gulf of 'Aqabah and suggesting its identification with Solomon's seaport of Ezion-Geber. Glueck had the good fortune to be able to excavate that site and to prove, as well as one can without inscriptions, the identification correct. The discovery of mines and smelters up and down the great wadi

Specimens of dolmens from the great fields west of Irbid (ca. 3000 B.C.?).

Roman milestones of the road from Damascus to 'Aqabah, each showing repairs to the road probably built after 105 A.D.

Pluto and Persephone in frescoed tomb at Marwa; Cerberus at left, wool basket at right.

Room at 'Auja el-Hafir in which papyri were found.

goes far to explain the long and bitter warfare between the Edomites, whose border fortresses overlooked it, and the Israelites, whose immediate borders touched no such source of wealth.

Actual mines were not numerous. One, now called Umm el-'Amad, "mother of pillars," may be taken as an example. The modern name is derived from the pillars which support the roof in the great cave. In the sandstone of the walls and pillars veins and nodules of copper were visible. A specimen contained 6 per cent iron and 8 per cent copper with a stain of malachite and black particles giving a good test for manganese. In this case no pottery was to be found on the surface, but the near-by site of Feinan, where plentiful water was available, offered every advantage for smelting. Feinan supplied Dr. Glueck with a few handfuls of EB iv—MB i pottery, with an abundance of Iron Age sherds, and with large quantities from the Nabateans and the Romans. Its mines may have been exploited during all of these periods as well as on down into medieval Arab times.

SOLOMON'S PITTSBURGH—SAN FRANCISCO

At numerous places in the wadi crude furnaces built of unhewn or rudely shaped blocks of stone were found in such relations to slag heaps that there could be no doubt as to their use. The most interesting spot was the insignificant mound of Tell el-Kheleifeh, which Glueck excavated in 1938, 1939, and 1940.

The mound lies half way between the cliffs that rise on both sides of the great gorge and about five hundred meters (one third of a mile) back from the waters of the Gulf of 'Aqabah, completely surrounded by a waste of sand. The spot seems to have been chosen for three reasons. Approached from the west it is the first spot at which a well can be dug to sweet water. None is to be found for some miles in that direction. Why, then, was the little city not built farther to the east, where good water is obtainable? Apparently because the builders sought to benefit by the full sweep of the winds that blow up and especially down the narrow gorge, regularly and often with tremendous force. The construction of the furnaces was such as to secure the best possible draft from these winds. The third reason for the choice of location was that the spot was near the sea. The strong winds which obviated the need of mechanical bellows have doubtless blown much sand into the sea in the course of 3,000 years. As to the strength of the winds I can testify for I slept on those sands one "quiet" night and wakened with small drifts about me and in my mouth, nose, and eyes. The connection of the ancient city with the sea was proved by the discovery in the tell of fishhooks, pitch, six-inch spikes, and thick, heavy rope made of fiber from the bark of palm trees.

The city and its smelters were of unusual interest for no such structures had been known. The walls were entirely of sun-dried brick. The gates and outer walls were of very considerable strength, for doubtless the city, rich in its copper, was exposed to raids both by sea and land. The walls of the smelters were pierced by an elaborate system of flues which allowed the fierce winds coming down the great gorge to find ready entrance to the burning wood, or probably charcoal, which heated the ore. Possibly a preliminary refining process was carried on at the crude stone furnaces near the mines, which then was completed in these more elaborate and effective smelters.

The excavation of such a site presented unusual problems. The heat becomes intense in May. Sand storms which make work impossible are frequent. However, workmen were obtainable at the neighboring town of 'Aqabah, where a police post gave protection and communication. A government guest house was most generously put at the expedition's disposal, even to the discomfort of traveling government officials. The results of the dig were most gratifying.

Numerous finds determined the date of the little city. The earliest pottery belonged to the tenth century, the time of Solomon. The city gate was like that of the Solomonic Megiddo and the contemporary Lachish, and the fortifications were remarkably strong. It was the seaport that brought the Hebrews into touch with the gold and spices of Arabia Felix, and its copper smelters that furnished the exchange for those costly importations. The place was in miniature both the Pittsburgh and the San Francisco of Israel for a few prosperous years. Not for long, however, for it was soon destroyed, possibly by Shishak (Sheshonk I, 954-924 B.C.). It was rebuilt on the same plan and may not have lain waste for any considerable time.

When this second city was destroyed by fire, a third arose which was on a different plan and may not have been Israelite. This may be the Elath of 2 Kings (14.22; 16.6), and a seal "of Jotham" found at Tell el-Kheleifeh may be that of the king of Judah. A couple of jars bearing South Arabian letters may mean that connections were stronger with the Mineans than with the Israelites. There are many examples of importations, articles of carnelian, agate, amethyst, faience, alabaster, testifying to trade with Sinai and Egypt. Its Edomite occupation (2 Kgs 16.6) is attested by pottery and seal impressions with an Edomite name, "Qos'anal, the slave of the king." Slight remains of a fourth city could be discovered on the top of the low mound. Whether Tell el-Kheleifeh was occupied or not, the mines of Wadi 'Arabah probably contributed to the richest civilization ever developed in this region, that of the Nabateans.

THE NABATEANS

In the sixth or fifth century, driven perhaps by nomadic inroads, the Edomites crossed the 'Arabah into the Negeb of western Palestine and, known by their Greek name as the Idumeans, they occupied all of southern Judah up to Hebron. Moabite civilization declined at the same time, probably under the pressure of the same nomads from the steppe, doubtless those who eventually appear as the Nabateans.

The glories of Petra with its tombs, temples, and palaces cut out of rose-red and marvelously variegated sandstone cliffs have been known for over a century. Since Burckhardt discovered it, adventurers and travelers in long succession have come back to describe its unique charm. It remained for the Honorable Agnes Conway (later Mrs. Horsfield) to initiate an expedition which was to have gone beyond maps, pictures, and adjectives. An elaborate preliminary survey was made in the spring of 1929, but the financial crash in the United States in the autumn immobilized the funds which were to have been used, and only a very little excavation has been carried on. However, the identification of Nabatean pottery by this expedition was an event of major importance. It made it possible within the next decade to draw for the first time the boundaries of the truly extraordinary realm of which the "rose-red city" was the capital. The thin, brittle, reddish-buff, eggshell ware, often highly decorated with characteristic palmettes, floral designs, and vine trails, or rouletted in various patterns, is easily recognized once it is seen. Where it was made and how it originated is still unknown. In Transjordan it is almost always found with "sigillata," or "Samian," ware, which indicates that it belongs to the Hellenistic-Roman and Roman periods.

The fascinating subject of Nabatean, Hellenistic, Roman, and Byzantine civilization in Transjordan must be passed by with only the briefest mention. It will in part be discussed later. Two matters call for treatment here because they are intimately connected with the problems of the economic exploitation of the marginal lands between the desert and the sown, and because recent archaeological research has made great advances possible in the solution of their problems. The history of the Nabatean kingdom and the Byzantine occupation of the Negeb of western Palestine are subjects upon which much new light has recently been thrown.

Mr. and Mrs. Horsfield with Dr. Albright and members of the American School of Oriental Research cleared the "Conway High Place" in November, 1934. This cult site, discovered and provisionally identified as such in 1929, was found to consist of a sacred stone and a processional way around it, somewhat in the style of the Kaabah at Mecca. The pavement was of a very hard crystalline limestone brought from a distance, probably for ritual reasons, though the sacred structures were of local sandstone. In the Christian era, offerings in pots were buried under the pavement. The place was built after Edomite times, perhaps in the fourth century when the Nabateans entered, and it survived, with some reconstructions, down to about the fourth Christian century, when, after a period of decline, it was destroyed by fire.

Dr. M. A. Murray for Sir Flinders and Lady Petrie excavated two small caves and a tomb in March, 1937. Miss Murray's volume, *Petra, the Rock City of Edom* (1939), gives an interesting and dependable description of Petra and history of the Nabateans and closes with a racy and amusing, if somewhat "popular," account of the peculiar problems of the excavator at this unusual spot. The isolation, naïveté, and poverty of the people rendered them much more difficult to manage than the more industrious and intelligent peasants of Palestine. The "short and intensive excavation" of a tomb and two small caves with chambers seemed to prove that the chambered caves belonged to a street of small houses. By the entrance to the tomb an altar in the shape of a mass of rock 18 feet long, 5 feet wide, and from 1 to 3 feet high was uncovered.

These two brief excavations have added some items to modern knowledge of the Nabateans. Numerous monuments, some with Nabatean inscriptions, lie open to view in Petra. Assyrian records mention a Nabatean king in the seventh century. Coins and inscriptions bearing the names of their monarchs, along with ancient literary references, gives an almost complete list from 169 B.C. to 106 A.D. Otherwise knowledge of their history and civilization rests upon surface exploration and the partial excavation of three or four sites, chiefly temples. Appearing in the fifth or fourth century the Nabateans played no small part in the politics of the Near East in the centuries just before and after the birth of Jesus. They reached the zenith of their prosperity under Aretas (Harithath) IV (9 B.C.-40 A.D.), whose territory extended from Meda'in Salih to Damascus, and from the Dead Sea and the 'Arabah to the Euphrates. It was his deputy who attempted to arrest Paul (2 Co 11.32). The Arabia into which Paul went briefly after his conversion and in which he probably began his career as a Christian missionary (Gal 1.17) was doubtless the land of the Nabateans. In 105 A.D. Trajan made their land into the Roman province of Arabia and, although the region continued to be fully occupied all during the Roman and Byzantine periods, its political influence came to an end and its prosperity gradually but surely decreased.

The prosperity of the Nabateans is usually ascribed to their control of the caravan routes which came to Egypt and the Mediterranean across the steppe from the east and up from the south. No doubt their role as the bearers of commerce was an important factor in their wealth. But Dr. Glueck's explorations have shown that they exploited more fully than any people before them the resources of the land, and very probably they used also the mines of the Wadi 'Arabah. Their characteristic pottery, which practically stops at a line running from the north end of the Dead Sea through Madeba eastward to the steppe, appears in the 'Arabah south of the Dead Sea, reaches to some extent over upon the western side of that great cleft, and spreads much farther into the eastern steppe than that of any of its predecessors or immediate successors.

Dr. Glueck has examined it in more than five hundred sites. The significant thing is that these sites are nearly always in the midst of cultivated fields. They are nearly always marked by terraces now fallen into disrepair and by ingenious and sometimes laboriously erected aqueducts, dams, and reservoirs for the conservation and use of the scant rainfall of that region. Their forts for the protection of their cities and villages and their caravan routes were more numerous and more widely spread than those of their predecessors. Whatever they may have been in the beginning, they became far more than mere Bedouin caravan traders. Their ability to assimilate culture is proved by Petra. They spoke their own Arabic language and spoke and wrote Aramaic also. Their script, derived from Aramaic, became the ancestor of the round Arabic script.

A NABATEAN TEMPLE

The progress which the Nabateans were making is strikingly—and amusingly—illustrated by their temples. One of Professor Glueck's most satisfactory achievements was his clearance of the temple of Atargatis and Hadad at Khirbet et-Tannur. Jebel Tannur, a high and lonely peak, rises above Wadi el-Hesa some sixteen miles south of Kerak and the same distance southeast of the Dead Sea. The peak where the temple stood is accessible only on one side where a road—in part a stairway—was built, doubtless a sacred way up which long processions of worshipers used to toil for the great festivals of their deities. When some earthquake shattered the temple and it was abandoned, its inaccessibility and distance from settled civilization preserved its stones almost intact. Only an occasional lone shepherd, frightened at a peering idol face, has obeyed the law of Islam and smashed such as he could see.

The temple went through several phases of rebuilding without any complete alteration. Broad steps led up to a gateway in the center of the east wall of a large paved court. On the north and south sides were platforms two steps higher than the court and carrying colonnaded porches. At the right as the worshiper entered was a large altar. In front of him, at the west end of the court, four steps led to the central gateway of the temple proper. The shrine, standing in the center of the higher platform, was oriented almost due east. A stairway led to its flat roof, for what purpose one can only guess.

Amid the mass of architectural fragments which covered the temple area and the top of the hill was a whole pantheon of deities. The decorative carving of geometrical designs and of conventionalized leaves, flowers, and arrows was excellent. The attempts to reproduce animal and human forms, while not positively crude like the Tell Beit Mirsim lion, were far from expert, especially if compared with Hellenistic sculpture which they clearly imitated. A striking example is a magnificent life-size head of Zeus-Hadad with a beautiful thunderbolt on his left arm but with a three-quarter-length body. The bulls at both sides of his throne were even less successful. Sculpture in the round was hardly attempted, but the figures, usually busts, were shown in high relief. Many of the faces were partly conventionalized. In part this may have been intentional, for the religious value of the various deities was symbolized by accompanying attributes. When two dolphins appear above the rippling hair of an "Atargatis," it is natural to think of the rippling hair also as suggesting her connection with the sea or with life-giving waters.

That the chief interest of the worshipers was a fertility cult is proved by the heads of wheat which border another "Atargatis" head and especially by one in which the face and breast of the goddess are covered with a mass of finely carved foliage, while the abundant hair is done in thick, short tresses that imitate heads of grain. The head of another goddess is surmounted by a mural crown and the whole bust surrounded by a circular panel bearing the signs of the zodiac, while in the free space over one shoulder is a crescent moon, over the other possibly a quiver with arrows, thus pointing possibly to identification with Artemis.

The variety of connections and influences which were at work is evident. Greek and oriental meet here on the edge of the steppe. One of the male heads wears a Parthian turban. There are resemblances to the Atargatis and Hadad of a Dura shrine. Palmyra, Baalbek, Bambyke, and Askalon are suggested. An altar bearing on its sides full-length figures in relief of winged Tyches, a Zeus-Hadad with staff and thunderbolt, and in Greek a dedicatory inscription from "Alexander, son of 'Amr" is a sufficient indication of the cultural combinations which took place here. The piety of the Nabateans is demonstrated by the number of such temples which have already come to light.

When Trajan set up his Provincia Arabia in 105 A.D., Rome came in, not to destroy or replace the Nabateans, but to rule and exploit them. In practically every Nabatean site Roman

Photo by D. E. M.

Corner of the large theatre at Jerash, with end of the pillars of the *scaena frons* back of the stage.

Portion of the Maiumas theatre at Jerash under excavation. The oleanders in the right foreground grow out of the orchestra.

Inscription recording gifts of 10,000 drachmae and the dedication of two sons and a daughter to Zeus by a certain Theon. More than 360 inscriptions have been found at Gerasa.

potsherds appear. When the eastern empire with its own civilization succeeded the western rulers, Byzantine pottery styles and Christian shrines begin to appear. The importance of Petra declined, for trade began to flow in other channels under the Roman and the Byzantine emperors, since they made other and easier trade routes safe.

Roman Painted Tombs

In recent years, due to the better organization of government and the vigilance of the authorities, many interesting tombs have come to light. The number in which frescoes have been found is as astonishing as the animal friezes in Palestinian synagogues. The painted tombs of Marisa and the slight remaining traces in the old caverns at Sheikh Abreiq should have been sufficient portents to lead to great expectations.[4] A very finely decorated tomb recently came to light near Askalon. Many tombs which showed no decoration have been valuable because of the groups of pottery and other vessels which they contained, since such groups often give the archaeologist a fairly certain date within definite limits. The frescoed tombs are merely more spectacular.

The only frescoed tomb of Transjordan was discovered in 1935 by some peasants of Marwa, a village northeast of Irbid. Unfortunately the Moslem villagers, true to their religious tradition, mutilated the faces before the Department of Antiquities was notified and protected the tomb. It was a roughly rectangular chamber cut in the rock and furnished with sarcophagi and loculi and thus, in its architecture represents more nearly indigenous tradition than the Askalon tomb. But it was decidedly Roman in its decoration.

At the right of the entrance a niche had been made in the wall so as to form in an arcosolium a grave with a sarcophagus-like top, above which on the curving surface of the niche were two figures seated on a double camp stool. At the left was a male figure, at the right a female figure. Her right arm lay over his shoulders, her left held up a torch. His right carried a short

[4] See above pp. 148, 274-277.

staff, or scepter, which rested upon his knee. At his right was a three-headed Cerberus, at her left a basket full of either flowers or wool. That the figures represent Pluto and Persephone is obvious. Probably the father and mother of the family which built the tomb, represented as the gods of the underworld, are thought of as happily ruling over their children and children's children in the next life as in this.

Aside from three masks on the wall below the grave, the tomb had no other decoration. Evidently this tomb, as also that at Askalon, had been cleared of all tomb furniture and perhaps used as a dwelling. Traces of frescoing on walls in partially collapsed tombs or caves not far away showed that there had been more than one such tomb. The clothing and coiffures of the frescoed figures point to approximately the period of Alexander Severus (*ca.* 200 A.D.) as the probable date of the painting. As abundant evidence from other cities to the south, east, and northeast shows, at this time there was a very lively Roman civilization on this far-distant border of the Roman Empire.

THE NEGEB

The Negeb of the Hebrews, the steppe to the south of Judea, has almost the same character as ancient Edom, and, indeed, as already noted, when the Edomites were driven out by the Nabateans, they settled in this territory, which, for Hellenistic and Roman times, was Idumea. The assumption, doubtless justified, that this was part of the "wilderness of the wanderings" of the Hebrews has led many ancient and modern travelers into it. The region some 45 miles south of Beersheba, where three springs, 'Ain el-Qoseimeh, 'Ain el-Qadeis, and 'Ain el-Qudeirat, lie within five or ten miles of one another may well be the Kadesh Barnea of the Bible.

The only extensive survey of the region was made by Woolley and Lawrence just before the last war. Developed knowledge of ceramic chronology was not then available. Therefore they could do little more than record the surface evidence of extensive Byzantine occupation. Frank, Glueck, and others have examined parts of the region, enough to establish the fact that the pre-exilic Edomites did not occupy it, but that the Nabateans had settled along the trade routes which their caravans must have used on the way to Egypt and to their chief seaport, Gaza. Like Transjordan, it was extensively occupied in Roman and Byzantine times.

Excavations have been carried on at two places by an expedition under the direction of Mr. Dunscombe Colt of New York, colleague of Mr. Starkey and formally a part of his expedition. Mr. Colt began work at Sbeitah, about half way between Beersheba and Qoseimeh in 1935. Heavy rains early in the autumn filled the ancient cisterns and the expedition regarded their position secure for the winter. But, exercising their immemorial rights, the Bedouins of the neighborhood came in, used all of the water up in a few weeks, and then wandered off again. Since no more rains came, the expedition had to wander also. The work had opened most auspiciously. Three churches and some other structures had been cleared, numerous Greek inscriptions and graffiti found, and various constructions for the conservation of water discovered. With heavy hearts the staff moved to 'Auja el-Hafir, where Turkish and German construction during the war appeared to have destroyed nearly all the ancient structures, but where water was available.

After a few weeks of routine labors, mourning turned into joy at the discovery of a mass of papyri, the only finds of the sort ever as yet made in Palestine. They were uncovered in a room filled with earth and debris at one side of the chief church along with various small objects, including a dead mouse which had found the papyri indigestible. The documents were of the sixth and seventh centuries in Greek and in Arabic.

The crudely written Arabic, among the earliest documents in that language known, were in striking contrast to the beautiful caligraphy of the Greek translations which accompanied them. The Greek business documents were, moreover, written with such abbreviations that they were almost impossible to understand, whereas an American business man in Jerusalem to whom I showed an Arabic letter read it with little difficulty. The documents were of all sorts, letters, deeds, receipts, contracts, Christian legends, a Greek glossary of Latin words from Vergil, and some New Testament fragments. As a product of Byzantine civilization on the edge of the desert they are most illuminating. They also raise the hope that further excavations in similar sites on both sides of the Jordan rift may discover other and older documents such as Dura-Europos has preserved.

For eight hundred or nine hundred years these lands, lying between the desert and the sown and partaking of the qualities of both, were populated more thickly than ever before or since. Forts far out in the steppe protected the little cities with their wide-stretching terraces and fields and the reservoirs and the aqueducts which made life possible in these marginal lands. Only when a new wave of nomads, fired with a zeal for religion and for plunder, swept in upon the decrepit Byzantines, did the land lapse once more back into the pastoral quiet it had known before Israelites, Moabites, and Edomites entered it 2,000 years before.

CHAPTER XX

GERASA—A ROMAN CARAVAN CITY

❖

IN THE early thirties, when a score of expeditions were excavating in Palestine, the most stately and imposing of all the ruins that were once more coming to life were those at Jerash in Transjordan. The paleanthropic stalwarts of Wad' el-Mugharah, the widespreading stables of Solomon's horses at Megiddo, the successive temples where Egyptians and Canaanites had worshiped at Beth-shan, the massive walls that had defended Judah's border at Tell en-Nasbeh are a few outstanding examples of many instructive discoveries. But of all the expeditions in Palestine, the one which has dealt with the most spectacular and artistically satisfying remains is the joint undertaking of Yale University, the British School of Archaeology, and the American School of Oriental Research at ancient Gerasa of the Decapolis, the "Pompeii of the Near East."

The striking ruins that mark the margin of the Arabian steppe have long enchanted the traveler. Palmyra, Baalbek, Petra, Bostra, and a score of others, standing gaunt and deserted, like giant skeletons guarding mysterious treasure, testify to the artistic imagination, constructive skill, and unestimated wealth of the ancient world. Baalbek is more gigantesque, Palmyra more spacious, Petra more exotic, but none of them has greater charm and none preserves more that is of historical interest than Gerasa.

In Italy the archaeologist thanks Vesuvius for the devastating flood of lava and ashes which preserved Herculaneum and Pompeii. In Transjordan the desert itself has protected the dead guardians of the civilization which for centuries sowed and reaped where once the steppe had been. Nature in her wilder

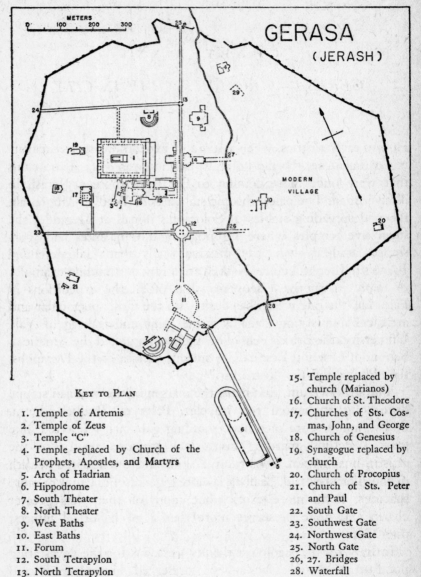

KEY TO PLAN

1. Temple of Artemis
2. Temple of Zeus
3. Temple "C"
4. Temple replaced by Church of the Prophets, Apostles, and Martyrs
5. Arch of Hadrian
6. Hippodrome
7. South Theater
8. North Theater
9. West Baths
10. East Baths
11. Forum
12. South Tetrapylon
13. North Tetrapylon
14. Propylea Plaza replaced by church

15. Temple replaced by church (Marianos)
16. Church of St. Theodore
17. Churches of Sts. Cosmas, John, and George
18. Church of Genesius
19. Synagogue replaced by church
20. Church of Procopius
21. Church of Sts. Peter and Paul
22. South Gate
23. Southwest Gate
24. Northwest Gate
25. North Gate
26, 27. Bridges
28. Waterfall
29. 'Ain Kerawan

FIG. 7

moods destroyed that ancient civilization. The demons of destruction that lurk under the earth shattered its imposing cities. The fiery outburst of Moslem hordes from the steppe swept away the commerce that nourished their strength. Then the Bedouins pitched their "houses of hair" about them and by keeping the civilization that builds with stone at bay, they excluded the hand that destroys while it renews. Nature in her milder moods has preserved their ruins to the present day, when the West is again invading the East.

Because Gerasa, lying on the edge of the steppe, was abandoned for nearly a thousand years, it largely escaped the frequent rebuildings and consequent destruction of antiquities which have visited every ancient site in Palestine. Roman engineers erected it with such solidity that large portions of its principal buildings have withstood the frequent earthquakes that shake the mountains on which it stands. The rains of winter have washed the soil of the hills down upon its ruins; the winds of summer have covered them with dust; the red anemones and poppies, the pink hollyhocks, and the wan and stately asphodel of spring have spread a gay mantle above them and preserved them almost as if they had been covered by the ashes of another Vesuvius.

Abundant waters and fertile fields made Gerasa an important station on the great caravan route from Nabatea (Petra), Southern Arabia, and India to the cities of Palestine, Syria, and the western world. The city, though much smaller, was more artistically planned and as magnificently built as Pompeii. Some of its public buildings are better preserved and more imposing. Although its houses, for the most part, do not stand so high above their foundations as those of Pompeii, some are deeply buried and, when cleared, will serve admirably to illustrate the private life of this border city of Hellenistic, Roman, and Byzantine times.

Gerasa is a remarkable monument to the colonizing ability of ancient Graeco-Roman civilization. Its ruins speak of Alexander's conquests and the woes of the Jews. They picture the rise and fall of Rome more graphically than Gibbon. They tell a moving tale of the phenomenal rise and fall of Christianity in the land of its birth. They chant the strange epic of the Arab hordes which all but blotted the faith of Jesus of Nazareth from the face of the earth.

THE PROCESS OF EXCAVATION

Beginning in 1925 Professor John Garstang and Mr. George Horsfield for the Transjordan Department of Antiquities and later, owing to the efforts of Benjamin Wisner Bacon, Professor of New Testament Interpretation at Yale Divinity School, Mr. J. W. Crowfoot for the British School of Archaeology and Yale University undertook various tasks of clearance and restoration. In 1930, when Mr. Crowfoot went to excavate Samaria, through Mr. Horsfield's good offices a liberal permit was given by the Transjordan Government to an all-American expedition, a joint enterprise of Yale University and the American School of Oriental Research in Jerusalem, the Directors being Dr. C. S. Fisher, Professor of Archaeology, and the writer, then Director of the American School. Succeeding Directors and Fellows of the School and representatives of Yale University continued the work until 1935. The results were published in part in the volume *Gerasa* in 1938 under the editorship of Professor C. H. Kraeling, who spent a year in Palestine before completing the task.

The aim of the expedition was to discover every possible scrap of evidence as to the life of the people who for generation after generation thronged the colonnaded streets of this ancient metropolis, and, so far as possible, to restore the ruined buildings. The problems of the excavator are largely set by the very wealth of the remains. The expedition illustrates a totally different technique of excavation from that employed in a Hebrew city. The great wall of Gerasa, which is nearly two and a quarter miles long, encloses 210 acres, of which much less than half is covered by a modern Circassian village. Over a good part of the area are great buildings, stones and column drums, weighing from a few hundredweight to many tons. Not a few of the buildings are protected by a mantle of earth and stones over twenty feet thick. It is estimated that to clear the great courtyard of the Temple of Artemis, one of the chief buildings, it would be necessary to move 727,000 cubic feet of earth, besides many tons of huge column drums and building stones. Not only must they be moved but a place must be found for them, and, amid acres of ruins all calling for excavation, it is almost impossible to plan a dump which will not cover valuable material. As experiment with native labor proved, restoration is impossible without the aid of modern machinery and trained engineers.

Laborers are many; Circassians, surly, slow, demanding high wages, but steady and usually careful; Arabs, lighthearted and careless, but loyal and lovable. From 5:30 to 8:00, from 8:30 to 12:00, and from 1:00 to 5:00 they work, and the boys who carry the baskets of earth sing as they go to and fro throughout the day, while the Circassians grunt and tug grimly at the big stones which they must move.

An incident of the autumn expedition of 1930 illustrates the character of the natives. Since few of the tasks involved demanded skill, the expedition had refused to pay the twenty piastres (one dollar) a day demanded by Circassian labor, but some had remained at fifteen piastres. The Arabs were paid from eight to twelve piastres. Four Arabs were excavating a cave over which the dump was soon to spread and the Circassians were building a wall above it to prevent the dump from covering the mouth of the cave and a small temple beyond it. Suddenly one day the wall buckled and covered the cave. One Arab was caught in the mouth of the cave by the rolling stones and painfully though not permanently injured. Three others were imprisoned inside. They were dug out unharmed but badly frightened, and they spent the next four or five days feasting all of their friends in celebration of their escape. One of the Circassians remarked when taxed with poor wall-building, "What can you expect for fifteen piastres a day?"

The work of clearance and restoration is only in its infancy. Yet a marked transformation has taken place, so those say who saw the place before the war, and enough has been discovered to give some inkling of the buried treasures still awaiting the workman's pick. But little of the pre-Roman city has come to light; only the piers of a great gate below the north entrance to the Roman forum, some caves and some scattered remnants of pottery. The Roman city of the first three centuries of the Christian era constitutes for many the chief center of interest. From its many features it is possible to single out here only its remarkable plan, its wall and gates, its colonnaded streets, its temples, its baths, its stadium, and its theaters. Of even greater interest to the student of historical development and church history is the Byzantine city with its dozen churches and its eloquent evidences of physical deterioration and social degeneration. One outstanding feature of the little city's 700 years of life is its hundreds of inscriptions in half a dozen languages which document its history more completely than is possible as yet for any other city in all Palestine or Syria. The following summary will emphasize the new items of knowledge which the recent excavations have added to what formerly could be seen on the surface.

THE CITY PLAN

The city as it now stands was laid out in the first century, A.D., and built mainly in the first and second centuries, with many subsequent rebuildings and alterations, as inscriptions and coins abundantly testify. Its plan was a remarkable one, more remarkable on close examination than at first appeared. The city lies high in the mountains in an open valley with a fine spring at its northern side and a stream—the Chrysorrhoas—which is fed by other abundant springs still farther north, and which flows in a narrow gully southward through its center. Two small lateral valleys came down to this stream from the west. The Hellenistic business center seems to have lain in the southernmost of these two valleys a little above the main stream and at the foot of a sanctuary which stands on a prominent knoll at the south side of the city.

The architect who planned the Roman city filled up the southern lateral valley, on the lower side to a height of over thirty feet, and thus buried the Hellenistic market place. Here, just at the foot of a great temple and its colonnaded courts, he placed an open plaza or forum, ready, doubtless, to receive the camel trains of Nabatea and Arabia Felix which came swinging up from the crossing of the Jabbok five miles to the south. To make connection between the forecourt of the temple and the main north-south street, the forum was shaped like the smaller half of an egg, open southward toward the temple. From the northern, smaller end of the forum, the central street, the *cardo*, excavated into the hillside and carried over a small fill in the northern lateral valley, ran over half a mile, level and straight, to the north city gate.

The city's focal point was a temple to its tutelary deity, Artemis, which stood on the slopes of the highest hill within the walls to the west of the center of the *cardo*. The *decumanus*, the other chief street of the Roman plan, crossed the *cardo* near its center to give access to the temple. Beginning on the eastern brink of the stream, this sacred processional way climbed up a great stairway and crossed the solid Roman arches of a stone bridge to reach the higher western bank. Here it passed through the successive triple gates and between the colonnades of another forum and civic center.[1] Then, through magnificent propylea and up a stairway sixty feet wide, it climbed to the Artemis precinct, which was cut into the hill behind and carried on enormous vaults in front so that the imposing temple stood in a great open courtyard covering over four acres and surrounded by colonnaded halls. Just south of it was another sanctuary also entered by a beautiful propyleum and spacious stairway, and between the two there was erected a gorgeously decorated, semicircular, two-staged fountain of the type called a *nympheum* because in Roman times it was usually decorated

[1] Later converted into a church, now called the "Propylea Church."

with figures of water nymphs. About half way between the city's center and its walls ran other important east-west and probably north-south streets paralleling the two central co-ordinates.

No occidental city can give any conception of the appearance of ancient Gerasa. Not the finest modern oriental city, such as Cairo or Damascus, can approach it. Only the modern arcaded streets of Hong Kong or Colombo or Milan can suggest something of its appearance. Long lines of standing columns, many still carrying their great stone architraves, testify to the luxury and comfort provided for the shoppers of ancient Gerasa. The spacious streets, the wide forums, and the temple precincts were paved with limestone slabs and were bordered on both sides by covered colonnades from which the shops and public buildings at either side were entered. The ancient Gerasene could walk and window-shop for some five miles, sheltered from the rains of winter or the sun of summer by spacious galleries.

Roman Building

The number of imposing public buildings in this provincial city on the edge of the desert is almost unbelievable. Many still lie under their protecting mantle of earth, with only a row of column ends or the corner of a wall projecting to tell of their existence. The ancient city planner took care that beautiful and imposing vistas should grace his city. The west end of the central east-west street and the south end of the north-south street were marked by the two great temples which still stand with walls and columns partly upright and partly fallen in impressive confusion around them, and two, probably three, other temples are known. Two half-ruined baths lift lofty domes and arches to the sky. There are three theaters with seating capacity for eight or ten thousand people. Two, if not three, bridges threw great arches across the stream. Each of the forums, like the streets, was bordered by covered colonnades and opened out upon the shops, *exedrae*, and buildings for the commercial activities or the civic administration of the city. Where the two east-west streets crossed, there were domed tetrapyla marking the intersection and breaking the vista, while the possible monotony of the long colonnades along the streets was avoided by an occasional change in height or by setting back the line of columns where the entrance to some great building needed emphasis.

The care and thought which the builders expended upon details were enormous. For the most part the paving blocks were laid diagonally so as the better to avoid wearing into ruts. In the oval forum the stones were cut so as to be laid in curves concentric with the curves of the stylobate of the colonnade. But at certain points, where higher columns and architraves indicate the entrance to some important building, the blocks were rectangular, so that a broad straight path led through the elsewhere curving lines. The street crossings likewise were paved with blocks running straight across, not diagonally.

To one who knows only the indifferent community planning of many an American town or the utter lack of public services in large oriental cities, it comes as a distinct surprise to discover the attention given to sanitation and water supply in Hellenistic-Roman cities such as Gerasa. Excavation disclosed that the hill west of the *cardo* was honeycombed with water and sewer pipes. One tunnel built of stone was about five feet high. Three-inch terra cotta tiles looking much like the drain tile used on an American farm were everywhere in evidence. Under the *cardo* from the north gate to the southern border of the city ran a sewer, Gerasa's *cloaca maxima*. Its course is marked by a row of manholes, some of the round cover stones still showing the iron staple and ring by which they were lifted.

Gerasa's water supply, especially for pools and fountains and the villas of the rich, which graced the west side of the city, came by a long aqueduct which followed the hill contours from great springs and a stone-built pool a mile north of the city. What sort of public fountain first adorned the civic center by the Artemis propylea is not indicated by the inscription which mentions it. In 190 A.D. a new and gorgeous nympheum was erected—a two-story semicircular structure roofed by a half dome—each story bearing niches, the one above doubtless for statues, the lower for figures, lions' heads and what not, from which the water spouted into a huge rectangular masonry basin and from this again through lions' mouths into large circular basins of pinkish limestone.

Outside the city, on the south, at a point where the caravan road came within full sight of the city, an imposing triple-gated triumphal arch was erected in 130 A.D. in honor of Hadrian's visit to the city where his personal bodyguard and perhaps the emperor himself had spent at least part of the winter. The mighty stadium lay beside and between it and the city. The careful city planning of those days is illustrated by the fact that a traveler approaching from the south looked straight through the central gateway of the arch along the wall of the stadium, over a triple city gate which was a replica of the arch, and eventually to the temple of Artemis crowning the slope of the city's loftiest hill.

The stadium, or hippodrome, had all the usual appurtenances of a circus and an amphitheater. It was 860 feet long and 250 feet wide, being noticeably smaller than that at Caesarea Stratonis (1056 x 264 ft.) or that at Antioch (1625 x 205 ft. inside measurements). But it would hold 15,000 people—not small for a city which occupied only a third of a square mile. The stadium lay in a shallow valley which opened out southward from its head near the city wall not far from the southern temple. Its straight eastern wall and the semicircular wall at the northern end were based on the native rock. The most of the western side wall and the southern end were based on the earth which had filled the widening valley. The wall at the south end against which were built ten starting stalls for chariots, and a central box for officials was slightly curved and placed at such an angle that each quadriga was headed directly toward the starting post and would have had the same distance to go as it raced toward it. No *spina*, or starting post, however, was found. As now seen, the southern portion of the interior shows a great depression. A careful study of the ruined walls led to the conclusion that it was never filled in and that, therefore, the structure partially collapsed or some other obstacle arose to prevent its completion. Projecting rock left unleveled in the racecourse confirms this conclusion. Later the northern third was made over into an amphitheater.

TEMPLES

The Temple of Artemis is an especially magnificent example of Roman industrial organization and technical precision. The foundations were laid upon the solid rock and built with such care and solidity that the structure might have been standing today but for an overlarge doorway which proved a source of weakness. The blocks were all cut at the quarry exactly to size and laid without mortar, a "header" and a "stretcher" so alternating throughout each course and from course to course that no joint in the masonry of one course ever appears above one in the course below. The blocks were all marked with the letters ΔIH (*delta, iota, eta*), evidently the label for this particular job. In strange contrast to the faultless masonry of foundations and walls is the fact that the column drums and the Corinthian capitals which went to make the graceful portico of the temple were either not accurately measured, or else not properly set together, for the twelve columns vary several inches in height. However, they were so perfectly fitted and the foundations so well laid that only one has fallen although some of them sway with the boisterous breezes that blow over the Transjordan highlands.

Whether the temple was ever completed is as yet uncertain. It certainly was originally planned as a peristyle edifice, since part of the base for one of the great columns at the side of the building is in place. But none are standing except in the portico and the remains of capitals and great drums which should appear around the structure have not yet been discovered.

The other great temple, which was probably sacred to Zeus,

stood on a prominent knoll at the south end of the city's *cardo*. It represents a simpler and even nobler tradition of architecture than the Artemis temple. But the foundations for its great peristyle were not so well laid. The knoll which may have been adequate for the building of a more modest Hellenistic temple was too small. The magnificent columns lie in wild confusion all about it, only one of them still being in place.

Another temple of generous proportions stood just east of the stream on the north side of the town near the city's chief spring, which was also decorated with a nympheum. Just south of the central nympheum was another sacred enclosure. Both of these temples were early occupied by Christian churches. The excavations of the autumn of 1930 discovered a small temple, or *heroön*, about 100 yards south of the Artemis temple. Nothing has been found to indicate certainly to whom any one of these three temples was dedicated. Inscriptions in various places in the ruins mention Serapis, Isis, the Arabian god (Dusares), a new Semitic deity, Pakeidas, who had Hera as his consort, and other deities, beside Zeus and Artemis.

In front of the Artemis temple and just to the right of its central axis, excavation discovered the base of the corner of a structure with well-cut moldings. Unfortunately litigation with rapacious owners of the land over compensation for its use prevented sufficient excavation to discover the character of this structure. But when the little temple farther south was uncovered, the complete base of a small altar was discovered in front of the temple steps and likewise just north of the central axis of the building. Doubtless the base before the Artemis temple once carried an altar.

The wall of the little city was admirably built of moderately large stones with wide marginal drafting about rough bosses. They were laid in alternating pairs of headers and stretchers with well-broken joints. The wall was quite uniform in construction, about three meters (10 ft.) thick, with towers six meters square built into it at varying intervals of from 17 to 22 meters. It followed the best line of defense which could be chosen without enclosing too great an area. Two of its original gates still stand on the west side at the ends of the two main east-west thoroughfares.

The northwest gate has preserved part of its inscription with the date 138, or 75-76 A.D. This probably marks the time when the wall was completed. Another inscription, unfortunately incomplete, may refer to its erection in 66-67 A.D. Probably all the gates were like the northwest gate, single arched portals. In 115 A.D. the north gate was rebuilt, still as a simple single gate. Doubtless in connection with Hadrian's visit and the building of the triumphal arch in 130 A.D., the south gate was torn out and a triple gate which was a smaller replica of the great arch standing only a short distance away was introduced into the wall. Only these four gates are known. If there were any lying east of the stream they have been completely destroyed or are covered by debris.

THEATERS

Besides the stadium and the baths, the latter not yet excavated, three theaters provided for the amusement of the Gerasenes, all three of them probably, two of them certainly, connected with temples. The largest lies by the south wall just west of the Zeus temple. It was a typical semicircular Roman theater seating some three or four thousand people. Its highly ornate two-storied *scaena frons* was backed by a large stage house. The niches back of the stage for statuary, the doorways opening from the stage house upon the stage, and many of the columns of the *scaena frons*, even of the second story, are preserved. Underneath the flooring of the stage—now gone— are remains of an earlier structure. Two inscriptions indicate that the present theater was under construction in the early eighties.

A much smaller theater, which lay on the northern edge of the Artemis temenos by the northern *decumanus*, is not so well preserved as to its proscenium. It evidently was provided with either a permanent or a temporary roof. It may have served as an *odeum,* and, since it seems to have been near the administrative center of the city, it may have held meetings of the *bulē,* the city council, or of the citizens, the *dēmos.*

Still another and even smaller theater serves to connect the Graeco-Roman with the Christian age. It lies a mile north of the city on a hillside facing a rectangular reservoir intended to conserve the waters of rich springs which gush out at the foot of the hill just north of the theater. It was a very small theater, especially if, as appears probable, it contained no second tier of seats rising above the one preserved. It was once supposed that the structure represented a *naumachia.* Then the discovery of an inscription which was interpreted as recording the building of a Maiumas theater led to the supposition that it provided the setting for the festival Chrysostum describes as including the watching of naked harlots swimming in a pool. Neither supposition can be correct, for a considerable space including a road and a portico or colonnade separates theater and pool. There would probably have been a wall and possibly a stage building back of the stage also to obstruct vision.

BYZANTINE GERASA

What the inscription actually records is the celebration of "the most joyful Maiumas" festival in November, 535 A.D., "after the lapse of years." Evidently the reference is to the permission of the festival in the code of Justinian published in 533 A.D. after its long prohibition since the days of Arcadius and Honorius (399 A.D.). An inscription discovered in the neighborhood indicates that a temple of Zeus Epikarpios, "Zeus the bearer of fruits," once stood near by. It seems probable that the Maiumas (the word is not explained) was a Hellenized form of some Semitic fertility cult which Byzantine Christendom inherited from its ancestral paganism. It is an interesting commentary on sixth-century Christianity that it hastened to revive a pagan, ribald, drunken, and probably lascivious festival as soon as "prohibition was repealed."

In this account, the pagan festival revived by Christians may serve to bridge the gap between Roman and Byzantine times. The expedition has discovered nothing to throw direct light on the process of change or to indicate definitely when Christianity came to power. After about 250 A.D. inscriptions become very few and remain so for two hundred and fifty years. A colonnade and altars were set up about 256 A.D. About 300 A.D. the south tetrapylon was rebuilt. Other records fail. Dated inscriptions are almost entirely wanting and others which belong in this period are few. The great church of St. Theodore was dedicated in 496 A.D. The great majority of the churches which Mr. Crowfoot successfully excavated are dated in the late fifth or early sixth century. Especially under a Bishop Paul, between 526 and 533 A.D., the erection of four or more churches testifies to the piety of various Gerasenes.

The impractical but self-centered nature of their piety is well illustrated by the three churches placed side by side and dedicated to Saints Cosmas and Damianos, St. John the Forerunner, and St. George. The long dedicatory inscriptions in the mosaic floor and the mosaic portraits of the donor and his wife, also with inscriptions, fully document the fact which the placing of the three churches so close together clearly implies, that they were erected, not to serve crowding congregations, but to glorify the bishop and the wealthy donors who sought by this use of the mammon of unrighteousness to assure themselves friends in the eternal habitations.

Even if these churches are no evidence of the progress of ethical monotheism, their mosaic floors are most welcome to the archaeologist and historian, for they picture—with some unfamiliar conventions to be sure—various cities in Egypt and especially their churches. These brilliantly colored representations, therefore, in spite of their architectural crudity, and their lack of perspective, are of no small value in depicting the appearance of ancient cities and the nature of early Christian architecture.

These were small churches and hardly intended to serve congregations. But the two great Gerasene churches were erected with hardly more regard for the needs of worshipers. Sometime, perhaps in the fourth century, the temple of Pakeidas and Hera was destroyed and its site, with its fine propyleum and stairway almost duplicating those of Artemis, fell into Christian hands. In place of the temple and using its building stones, a Christian church, probably dedicated to the martyr Marianos, was built in basilica, or cathedral, style. The Artemis precinct was also denuded of paving and building stone to provide for the new structure. As its altar had to be placed at its eastern end toward the street, its chief door turned away from the street toward the west. Here a considerable court, paved with fine limestone blocks, was located around a little fountain in a square basin. Back of the court to the west, on a higher terrace of the hill, another cathedral, dedicated to the militant St. Theodore, was built at the end of the fifth century, as the long metrical dedicatory inscription on the inner face of the lintel over the western door still relates. There were side chapels and baptisteries for both churches, and, to the north and west, a monastery and other ecclesiastical buildings arose where once Roman villas had stood. Bishop Plankos built a fine bath here in 454 or 455 A.D.

Water for the fountain in the "Fountain Court" between the two churches was piped to it from the aqueduct that ran to the Maiumas pool. It poured into a stone funnel at a height of seven or eight feet behind a wall on the north side of the court and then was conducted through a small lead pipe to the fountain itself. The lead pipe allowed the pressure from the water which collected in the stone funnel to force up a small, wavering jet of water into the air. One cannot repress the suspicion that a miracle which Epiphanius relates of turning water into wine at Gerasa on the anniversary of the miracle at Cana is connected with the open stone funnel behind the wall of the Fountain Court.

Crude Christian plaques made from molds, of which two have been found, depicting the baptism of Jesus, and Daniel in the lion's den, represent Christian art. They replaced the beautiful

Hellenistic-Roman statuary which had graced the colonnaded streets and forums, but which Christian and Arab almost totally destroyed, and the charming figurines of which a great number were discovered in a cave. Byzantine art has an interest all of its own, but it is not aesthetically satisfying to modern eyes.

Only the mosaics of Gerasa compel the respect of the artist. One, of which fragments are in Berlin, belongs to the third century perhaps. More should eventually be found. The early sixth-century mosaics of the churches are from a school of mosaicists who knew how to achieve lively and striking effects by a vigorous treatment and bright colors. The "Gerasene school" was one of the best in Palestine.

No documents record in words the immediate effect of the Arab conquest which occurred about 635 A.D. The Persians had conquered the city in 614 and held it for fourteen years. The only traceable effect of their occupation was the reconstruction of the northern part of the hippodrome into a polo field. The Moslem conquest was a different matter. It has left few traces in writing: a seal of the Calif 'Ali, a few lamps with Arabic inscriptions, some Arabic graffiti. But the destruction of all representations of living creatures in all the exposed mosaics of the churches probably represents the iconoclastic fervor of the reign of Yezid II (720-24 A.D.). The injured mosaics were repaired in plain tessarae or in concrete, and no church was ever turned into a mosque. Islam did not attempt to blot out Christianity, but it did destroy Byzantine civilization by isolating it from the west and destroying its natural commercial connections. Sometime, in the ninth, or possibly the tenth century, the wretched hovels that had been built in the aisles of the great churches and the tall colonnades of Gerasa's streets were abandoned, and the land reverted to the Bedouin.

CHAPTER XXI

BYZANTINES, ARABS, AND CRUSADERS

ARCHAEOLOGICAL OPPORTUNITIES

✣

THE interest which the average Christian feels in Palestine stops at the death of Jesus, or, at best, at the fall of Jerusalem, when he has shuddered over Josephus' lurid story of the siege or, perhaps, gone so far as the horrible suicide of the last remnant at Masada. Interest revives again at the mention of the Crusades and Saladin, but carries no farther. For the average Jew, Palestine is the land of the Old Testament. He will give money for the excavation of Samaria, but Sephoris would be as unknown to him as to the Christian. Galilean Judaism in Roman times means little to him. Yet some of the most attractive opportunities for an archaeologist fall in the later periods.

The whole surface of Palestine is sown with ruins that belong to the periods after the beginnings of Christianity. The remains are easily reached, for they are near the surface, if not in part above it. They are better preserved and often much superior, artistically speaking, to those of pre-Christian times. They often have in their keeping valuable data on the development of civilization. They are unusually important to the student of Judaism, as a previous chapter (XVIII) has shown. They are equally valuable to the student of Byzantine Christianity and Islam.

The churches at Gerasa, the octagon at Capharnaum, the remarkable mosaic of the Church of the Multiplying of the Loaves at el-Tabigha, the great cathedrals of Scythopolis (Beth-shan), the Church of St. John at Sebaste-Samaria, and the cities and churches in the inhospitable Negeb, these, as well as the

326

synagogues and their mosaics already described, are outstanding examples of the achievements of later Roman and of Byzantine civilization. Untouched sites, like Yajuz in Transjordan, display their invitation to every eye. A few further illustrations of Byzantine art and architecture, of Arab adaptation of that culture, and then of the Crusader and Saracenic contributions to Palestine's culture are collected here.

The extent of the opportunities which Palestine still offers is suggested by a hasty survey with some soundings made at the site of ancient Pella in 1933 by Mr. John Richmond, son of the director of the Department. Gottlieb Schumacher had made a brief survey of the site which he published in 1889. Mr. Richmond's slight soundings discovered various items in which Schumacher's report was incorrect. He added much new information. His topographic survey made clear the situation of the ancient city. It lay in a beautiful little valley and on the hills bounding it. The hills all around are full of caves of which some certainly would repay excavation. The cemeteries have the majority of their tombs plundered, of course, but some await an excavator. A basilica and a church, with adjacent buildings, probably monasteries, are easily recognizable, as well as a theater and a temple, and there are many other buildings which must be excavated to be identified. The pottery was chiefly Roman and Byzantine. However, Tell el-Husn on the south side of the valley appears a likely site for an Iron Age and probably a Bronze Age settlement. A thermal spring about a mile north of the ruins has some ancient stones built into its present bath house and doubtless would also reward investigation. Thus the city to which the Christians of Judea fled when Jerusalem was surrounded by armies shows a tantalizing variety of inducements to the archaeologist.

The Palestinian Department of Antiquities has often filled the breach left by those whose interests were centered on the earlier periods of the country's history. Whenever any Byzantine mosaic is uncovered by some farmer's planting or building, a member of the Department is sent to investigate and record the find, in case no qualified institution is ready to undertake the task. Tombs of all dates are continually being discovered. The Department excavates and records them in order to avoid clandestine operations which put their contents on the market without any account of the circumstances under which they were preserved. Many tombs of all periods have thus been made to contribute toward the history of Palestine.

The interests of Mr. E. T. Richmond, former director, led him to send members of the staff to investigate also various castles and other buildings of later periods. The result has been a long series of reports, usually concise and interesting, in the *Quarterly* of the Department of Antiquities. Mr. M. Avi-Yonah of the Department has made contributions in two fields, among others: in a study of mosaics and in his "Map of Roman Palestine." The map attempts to record all roads and places as of 300 A.D., whether known from archaeological remains or from literary mention. It includes materials that belongs to the two or three centuries when Roman influence was predominant in Palestine, but before Christian churches and monasteries appeared. An enormous amount of detail is crowded upon the map and into the accompanying text even more in bibliographical references. Such a work is of inestimable value to the student of the archaeology and history of Palestine during the period chosen.

Another service rendered by Mr. Avi-Yonah has been the listing of all mosaic pavements which have ever been found in Palestine. Chance finds excavated by the Department have been adding continually to the list, which now reaches well over four hundred. Not all by any means, but a very large proportion are church pavements. The beauty, their number, and their wide distribution in fifth-century churches testify to the wealth and taste of Byzantine civilization as it was ripening for destruction by the Persians and the Arabs. One recent discovery in particular must be mentioned, the mosaic pavement beneath the modern floor of the Church of the Nativity at Bethlehem.

Père Vincent believes that a simple stone pavement of the Constantinian basilica was replaced in the time of Theodosius and Eudocia by the sumptuous mosaics of which fragmentary remains were found. Destroyed in the Judeo-Samaritan riots at the end of the fifth century, the church was reconstructed by Justinian, who raised the floor level and paved the building again with stone. The brief references I have made to mosaics are quite inadequate to suggest the wealth of material available for those interested in Byzantine art.

An ambitious Roman, Byzantine, and Crusader church site has been carefully excavated and sumptuously published by the Dominican fathers, Vincent and Abel. Excavations were actually begun in 1875, apparently by Clermont-Ganneau, but, fortunately, they were pursued very slowly, leaving the completion to times of greater archaeological experience. The ground had been occupied in the second and first centuries B.C. Then a Roman villa of the first and second centuries had spread its mosaics with their animal figures over the place. In the third century a basilica with three apses had been built over the ruins of the villa and had used some of its mosaics. In the sixth century it was rebuilt on a smaller scale. When the Arabs arrived they turned the site into a cemetery. Finally in the twelfth century Crusaders had used the central apse and some of the walls for a similarly small but very respectable structure. A cruciform baptistery with mosaic floors occupied a small neighboring structure.

The site is that called Emmaus or Nicopolis in Roman and Byzantine times. Whether it was the Emmaus named in Luke's narrative of the appearance of Jesus to two disciples cannot be discussed here. Certainly the church was an important one for some centuries, partly because the name appeared in the Gospel, partly because of various other traditions which attached themselves to it, partly because Nicopolis was a city of some size. Both its various mosaics and its repeated rebuildings give the church archaeological interest.

BOSRA—THE CATHEDRAL

The development of church architecture is an attractive subject. The Church of the Nativity is only one of many which deserve study. The great cathedral at Bosra is the center of interest in a story of archaeological investigation which covers much over a century. The first modern travelers, Seetzen, Burckhardt, and Buckingham, mention it. The earliest visitors, Burckhardt for example, had seen that it was a large church with a circular plan inside a square building. It was long an almost unique example of such a plan and therefore piqued the curiosity of architects and historians. It was historically important because the dedicatory inscription gave its exact date, 512-13 A.D.

In 1857 the French explorer E. Guillaume Rey essayed the first draft of the plan with fair success, for much more was visible then than now. Since then visitor after visitor has attempted his reconstruction based upon what could be seen without excavation. But the enigma proved insoluble. Buildings and rubbish within and without completely hid the plan. The problem was darkened by a supposed discovery of H. C. Butler whose expeditions to Syria rendered the greatest possible service in other areas. He saw the base of a composite pier in a hole which some of the inhabitants were digging in the rubbish covering the floor. Apparently some error in working up his notes led him to misplace it and thus to confuse the problem still more.

Mr. J. W. Crowfoot became interested in the problem when excavating churches at Jerash and Sebastieh, the more so as at both places he came upon small churches with a "circular nave." Eventually in 1934 and 1935 he undertook two short trips to Bosra with trained assistants and, by making soundings in several places, he succeeded in finding evidence which settled the long debated problem on quite unexpected lines.

The church was a great square structure with an extension to the east containing a long apse and four rooms, two on each side, which probably served as sacristies. The "nave," as it may be called, was a circle within the square and the corners thus left were filled, each with a large semicircular exedra and niches. The shed roof and a central tower were carried on four heavy L-shaped piers supplemented each by four columns which curved out beyond each pair of piers to make a quatrefoil. A clerestory in the tower contained more windows than wall space. This, fortunately, is proved by a small remnant, now fallen, which is to be seen in a drawing made by de Vogüé in 1862 and in a photograph taken by Selah Merrill in 1875.

Mr. Crowfoot thinks that this large church, like the small church of St. John at Jerash, never had a masonry dome but was completed by a round, pointed tower in timber. In spite of its intricate and interesting floor plan, it was not a beautiful building, but with its large, brilliantly lighted floor space it would have served a large congregation. It was built of basalt, much of it reused from older buildings. But ornaments and moldings were properly placed, so that the result was excellent.

Numerous inscriptions in several languages and various buildings of which extensive ruins still stand give Bosra a special interest. Only Gerasa surpasses it. It has a great theater standing out on the open plain and remarkably well preserved. The now-abandoned "Umaiyad Mosque" was once a Christian church and its columns carry crosses and Christian inscriptions while a side aisle still exhibits stone roofing slabs such as must have been used when the church was built.

Byzantine and Umaiyad Jericho

A series of discoveries at Jericho may serve to illustrate discoveries which are being made over the country. Mr. D. C. Baramki of the Department has been intrusted with the excavation of several later ruins. Three of them were found near Jericho. At Tell Hassan an early Byzantine basilica was discovered when the land owner was digging an irrigation ditch. Even the foundations of the walls and the bases of the rows of columns had disappeared but enough of the mosaic floor remained to allow the plan of the building, which was quite conventional, to be determined. The mosaics were all in conventional geometric patterns, those in the nave having smaller tessarae and more colors (eight) than those of the aisles and rooms which adjoined on the north side. A half dozen coins found covered the period from the later fourth until the sixth century. If the building was, as he intimates, the church of the Virgin Mary which Justinian restored at Jericho, it is no great credit either to the Virgin or to the emperor.

Another building recorded by Mr. Baramki was a Jewish synagogue discovered near Tell es-Sultan, the ancient Jericho, by a farmer when digging trenches to plant bananas. Fortunately both the mosaic floor and the walls to or above floor level were preserved. The building, a basilica in plan, is only roughly rectangular; no corner is quite a right angle, and the apse, which points southwest—roughly in the direction of Jerusalem—shows a very irregular curve. The mosaic is in conventional geometric patterns of a somewhat involved character. The half of the nave nearest the apse had a design of its own with a conventional representation of the ark of the Law in the center and back of it, within a circle, a *menorah*, *lulab*, and *shofar* with an Aramaic inscription which said, "Peace upon Israel." In front of the door was a long Aramaic inscription in early square characters which began, "May . . . . the congregation be remembered for good . . . ." and named no individual donor. The tessarae varied greatly in size in different sections of the floor, and the variety of colors was not great but, on the whole, the effect was pleasing. Since, aside from a single, badly worn late Roman coin, all those found were Cufic coins of the eighth century, Mr. Baramki would date the building at that time.

One of the chief undertakings of the Department in the field of early Moslem archaeology is a large palace at Khirbet el-Mefjer three miles north of Jericho. The building lies just beyond Wadi Nuwe'meh, and still beyond it for over 600 yards stretch other ruins not yet investigated. The identity of the structure at first was entirely in doubt, like its fellow at Khirbet

Minyeh. Dr. A. M. Schneider, basing his conclusions on a surface survey and literary allusions, had identified it with Byzantine Gilgal, and, in 1935 and 1936, at the beginning of the excavations, the discovery of columns bearing finely carved Maltese crosses in relief seemed to confirm his hypothesis. At the same time, the presence of numerous names in Arabic in ink on pieces of masonry pointed to its construction after the Arab invasion. Eventually a slab of marble was found bearing an inscription praising the "prince of the faithful," Hisham, whose caliphate ran from 724 to 743 A.D. Apparently the building was under construction at the time of an earthquake in 746 A.D. Since with Hisham the Umaiyad line came to an end, the unfinished and damaged building was not completed and was only partially reoccupied in later times.

One portion of the structure was particularly puzzling when I visited it in 1935 and 1936. At one side of the large central court was a stairway leading down to a small sunken court which gave upon a long vaulted room with what looked like a brick bathing pool built across the farthest end. It evidently was an afterthought, judged from the awkward way in which it fitted into the room. In a Christian monastery it seemed entirely out of place. When the building became instead an Umaiyad winter resort, its purpose was clear.

Umaiyad Mosaics

After the first World War the establishment of settled conditions under enlightened governments made possible many archaeological studies both with and without excavation in Near Eastern countries other than Palestine, and Palestinian archaeology has profited immensely therefrom. Among such enterprises was a study made by Major Creswell, under the patronage of King Fuad I of Egypt, into the history of Moslem architecture in a considerable portion of the ancient Arab world. Among the results, published in two magnificent volumes, were descriptions of the Dome of the Rock in Jerusalem and of the hunting lodges in the steppe which contribute greatly to the understanding of Arabic architecture in Palestine.

Since Major Creswell worked under the patronage of King Fuad, he was given special facilities by Moslems everywhere. He was able to take hour-long photographs of dark corners in the Dome of the Rock and reveal features which were hitherto entirely unknown. The French authorities in Damascus removed large patches of plaster from the ceiling of the great Umaiyad mosque and the study of these mosaics by Mlle. Marguerite Van Berchem, published in Major Creswell's first volume, added decidedly to knowledge of the development of art and artisanship in the early years of the Caliphate. Mlle. Van Berchem showed that not Byzantine Greeks but native Syrians were employed in making these beautiful mosaics.

A Ninth-Century Nestorian Hermitage

In February, 1933, a workman engaged in road repairs uncovered a mosaic floor 60 meters beyond kilometer 42 on the way from Jericho to the Allenby Bridge. When cleared by Mr. Baramki the structure was discovered to consist of a large rectangular living room opening on its south side into a small, almost square room, doubtless a chapel. The walls were of sun-dried brick coated inside and out with several layers of plaster. The floor of the large room had a pavement of pebbles with a cross of flagstones in the center. The smaller room, which had a square apse at the east, was paved with a crude mosaic in the center of which within a circle was an inscription in Estrangelo Syriac naming four otherwise-unknown persons each of whom came from a place well known in Nestorian history. One had the characteristic Nestorian name of Iso'dad. The site is sprinkled with Byzantine potsherds. The building is tentatively dated in the ninth century.

So small and mean a building should not be taken as characteristic or representative of Nestorian Christianity, but, since little is known of Nestorians in Palestine before the Crusades, the buildings and the inscription have a special value. Three or four other Syriac inscriptions in western Palestine are extant; several names crudely cut on tombstones were found at Khirbet es-Samra on the edge of the steppe in Transjordan, and fragments on potsherds appear at Jerash. It is strange that, in a country where Syriac is said to have been spoken until the seventeenth century, so few traces of its use should have been discovered.

'ATHLIT AND ITS PILGRIMS' CASTLE

Among the places which have always attracted attention, but which have recently become centers of especial interest, one of the most impressive is 'Athlit. The great Crusader stronghold, Castellum Peregrinorum, or "Pilgrims' Castle," was made the chief seat of the Templar order in 1218 and it was the last Crusader fortress to fall to the Arabs, in 1291 A.D. It lies on a small, low, rocky peninsula which projects into the Mediterranean between two little bays. A little east of the peninsula, a rocky ridge which follows the coast for many miles had for some years previously provided a perch for a Crusader fort, now Khirbet Dustrey, from le Destroit, Latin Districtum, so called because it overlooked and defended a narrow passage which ran through the ridge just north of it.

Before excavation began, indeed when the *Survey* was made, a great pile of ruins with tremendous vaults below and walls standing in one place 110 feet high was visible. An outer enceinte having four gates, with corner towers and a fosse, and, across the neck of the peninsula, an inner defense wall, also protected by a fosse, were traceable. In the castle itself the towering wall on the northwest side still showed three ribbed, pointed arches supported on corbels, one of which represented a bearded head, one a shaven face with curling hair, and the third, at the center, three lilies in low relief. On the southwest side a beautiful Templar church, decagonal in plan, was easily recognized. Even its roof was intact until the earthquake of 1837. The next year Ibrahim Pasha took the fallen stones to rebuild 'Akka, Jaffa, and Beirut. The castle itself was occupied by an Arab village. The area between it and the outer wall was almost entirely covered with hillocks of blown sand overgrown with bushes.

The Department of Antiquities has declared the place an "Antiquities site" and is gradually moving the Arab villagers out. The excavations, which were in charge of Mr. C. N. Johns, have cleared vaults and rooms in the castle, studied its architecture and its defences, and revealed a small city under the sand hummocks in the *faubourg*.

One building, of which three vaults appeared above the sand before excavation began, proved to be a bath, probably of Mamluk times, the fourteenth and fifteenth centuries. But it was a reconstruction of a thirteenth-century building. In restoring a fallen corner of the building a local mason was discovered to be using Arabic corruptions of French architectural terms, and probably medieval French techniques, just as the women of the neighboring villages still wear costumes which are replicas of medieval European attire.

In the southern part of the castle suburbs Crusader stables covering an acre and offering accommodations for some 200 horses came to light. The building has a unique plan, which resembles that of an oriental khan, and it contained a larger number and variety of objects of daily use than have been found anywhere else. It was built, according to coins found, early in the Templar occupation, and burned shortly before their evacuation. Since it therefore gives a secure dating for the objects discovered including the pottery, it has special values for the archaeologist.

Against the eastern *enceinte* wall 120 yards north of the corner fortress lay a church within a church yard of standard size, thirty feet around the building. It was, unfortunately, left unfinished and had been robbed of all easily available squared building stones. However, the plan was plain and its resemblance to French and Cypriote churches built in the thirteenth century allow fair inferences as to its character—a matter of some value since very few Crusader churches are preserved. Its eastern apse

The apse of the circular cathedral at Bosra.

Portion of the Umaiyad Mosque at Bosra, formerly a church.

Unexcavated ruins of a round building with a semicircular eastern apse, doubtless a Byzantine church, at Yajuz in Transjordan—an archaeological opportunity.

Broken arches of the Castellum Peregrinorum at 'Athlit, looking out to sea.

was unusual, like those in the castle chapel, having five, instead of the conventional three or six sides. A shallow bay came next and then the one main bay, which was practically square (32 x 34 feet). The temporary wall which closed the west end of this bay evidently awaited the addition of one, or perhaps two more, similar bays which the plan would demand. Toward the end of the Templar occupation the idea of completing the structure had evidently been adandoned, for burials of Crusader date had been made across the line along which the north wall would have been continued. Many features of the interior also indicated that the building had not been completed according to the original design and exhibited a haste or carelessness that revealed the decay of the Crusaders' energy and their growing insecurity.

Excavations at 'Athlit were begun because of interest in the Crusader castle. Even the discoveries bearing on the Crusader period, the thirteenth century, went quite beyond anticipations. But eventually it became clear that the site was occupied at a much earlier period. The Crusader castle was built on a low hill which actually was a tell. It had occupied a spine of rock which paralleled the shore throughout the area where the castle suburbs were built and ran out into the sea. By no means has all of the town lying on this tell and within the *enceinte* wall as yet been excavated, but pottery indicating fairly continuous occupation from the late Middle Bronze down to the Hellenistic Age has been found.

The periods so far best represented fall at the end of the Middle Iron Age and in the Persian-Hellenistic period. Excavation of the southeastern fortress and the stables discovered burials covering three or four hundred years, from the ninth to the fourth centuries. Phoenician and Cypriote pottery and Phoenician coins tell the story of a Phoenician settlement here running at least from 700 down to 300 B.C. Most unusual of all, a little farther north on the tell there was found a series of cremation burials which also belong to the Phoenician settlement of perhaps the seventh century or a little earlier. Few such burials have

appeared in Palestine, chiefly at Tell el-Far'ah and Tell el-'Ajjul.
The smooth shelving sandy beach south of the castle must have
received the visits of scores of little Phoenician vessels during
the long centuries when that race produced the most enterpris-
ing mariners in the East. Scarabs, pottery, and other objects
testify to extensive commerce with Egypt and Greece.

Qal'at er-Rabad—'Ajlun

Still less attention has been paid to Saracenic and Mamluk
remains in Palestine than to Crusader. For the average visitor
they are eclipsed by the places of Christian and biblical interest,
just as these, now, for the majority of excavators must give way
to Bronze Age sites. The great Crusader castles at Kerak east of
the Dead Sea, at Banias (Caesarea Philippi), and a few other
places have always been tourist shrines. It seems strange that the
well-preserved castle built near 'Ajlun about 1185 A.D. by
Saladin's able emir, 'Izz ed-din Usama, does not appear in some
of the most famous of guide books to Palestine.

In 1929 Mr. C. N. Johns examined it carefully for the Transjordan Department of Antiquities which had already cleared
and consolidated it to prevent further deterioration and make it
accessible. Since its history is documented by contemporary
references and by building inscriptions, it is possible to trace its
construction, enlargement, and repairs with some degree of
certainty.

The Qal'at er-Rabad, "castle with the suburbs," was so called
because in its prime the now-deserted slopes below its hilltop
carried a considerable village. Built on one of the most outstanding mountain tops in all eastern Palestine, it easily vies with the
traditional Mount Nebo (Jebel es-Siaghah) and with Jebel Osha'
by es-Salt in its commanding view of the Jordan Valley, from
the Dead Sea to the Sea of Galilee, and of the mountain range
from Jerusalem to Tabor and Safed. In Mamluk times it was one
of a series of stations by which messages could be sent by fire
beacon and pigeon within twelve hours by day or by night
between Baghdad and Cairo.

The slopes around the building are comparatively gentle, but the great square towers of the original keep surrounded by a fosse made it a fortress of no small strength. A large tower, added on the south in 1214-5, as an inscription relates, by Aibak ibn 'Abdullah, Mamluk and Major-domo of al-Malik al-Mu'azzam, increased its defensibility. But, when the Latin kingdom of Kerak had fallen following the battle of Hattin in 1187 A.D., the castle had ceased to have any great strategic value and it became chiefly a center for the collection of taxes and the storing of supplies. It may be that one of its chief values lay in its nearness to the iron mines on the north side of the Zerqa, which were worked up until modern times.

A few architectural and sculptured fragments built into the walls and one piece of very fine masonry laid bare at the southern angle indicate that a much earlier building occupied the site. A lintel with a crudely carved cross may have come from a Byzantine town on the site of modern 'Ajlun. But in the present building aside from one or two stones with diagonal chisel dressing, there are no signs of direct western or Crusader influence. It is a typical piece of Arabic construction.

In some now-distant future the buildings of Turkish overlords may pique the curiosity of archaeologists, perhaps largely because of a desire to distinguish them from those of earlier and later periods. The more recent invasion of the west, both before and still more since the first World War, will add new problems which can be appreciated from what is apparent in antiquity. As it is, Palestine offers a long and instructive past to the student of history such as can be found within the same compass in no other land.

CHAPTER XXII

WHAT TO BELIEVE

❖

ARCHAEOLOGICAL CANARDS

WHAT not to believe might be a better subject for a final chapter. The account of Palestinian archaeology which has been given is intended to assist the nontechnical reader in understanding and judging archaeological publications concerning Palestine. It is often difficult for one long familiar with the field to know what to expect and to believe. If one had first read a newspaper blurb regarding the papyri found at 'Auja el-Hafir,[1] relying on past experience one would have doubted the possibility of such a discovery even though small fragments had been found there previously by German scholars. The presence of "ossuaries" under strata of sandstone at Khudeirah[2] seemed quite impossible until all the circumstances of the discovery were known. Undue skepticism is possible. Yet it is not true, even in such a land of archaeological magic as Palestine, that, as Apuleius said, "Anything can happen."

Some amusing newspaper canards may illustrate the need of caution. The best recent example had a perfectly natural basis. Early in 1929 the Sunday edition of a San Francisco daily carried a full-page, illustrated story telling of the discovery in a tomb at Jerusalem of a roll written by Solomon himself. In it he related how, when enemies had attempted to poison him, his Egyptian queen had seized the poison cup and drunk it herself to save her master. In loving affection he had written the story and buried it with her. To anyone who knew the dampness of

[1] See above, pp. 307 ff.
[2] See above, pp. 65 ff.

340

Jerusalem's climate the story was plainly fictitious, in spite of the drawings with which the page was embellished. As it was related, however, it seemed a strange story and difficult to explain. The explanation, when it came, was more interesting than the story itself.

Some months later in Jerusalem, when talking with the very reliable representative of a leading New York newspaper, I mentioned the story and expressed my surprise. He said, "I know who wrote it and, indeed, was present when it was being written." (Since he has a gifted wife, the anonymous author may easily be guessed.) He went on to explain how it came about. The story first appeared in December, 1928, in the *Palestine Weekly*, a Jerusalem literary periodical. That it was intended as an amusing piece of fiction was quite apparent.

However, an Arab vernacular paper in Cairo, attracted perhaps by the reference to an Egyptian queen, published a brief news item on the "discovery." Some foreign journalist picked it up and used it. Soon reporters in the Near East began to receive telegrams from their editors demanding to know why they had failed to report such a sensational find. Thus the item traveled across the world.

Fortunately the reporters in Palestine and Egypt were as a whole reliable, though far from being archaeologically expert, and did not seriously distort the news. One "release" of my own was badly garbled, but the reporter showed me his telegram, and it proved that not he, but the copy writer at home, was responsible. The traveling free-lance correspondent who came to Jerusalem for sensations proved far less reliable, although there were honorable exceptions.

At best, however, newspaper accounts are not satisfactory sources of information. In an Australian newspaper an "Orientalist" published the "translation" of tablets found at Bethlehem recording a very ancient treaty of universal peace. The story was manufactured out of whole cloth, for no one had even been excavating at Bethlehem. An American paper carried a full-page Sunday account of an expedition which was proceeding to

Palestine to find the burial place of Aaron, a site which is much in dispute but regarding which this unknown archaeologist had complete information. However, for some reason, he abandoned the attempt and never appeared in Palestine. Such stories might be multiplied.

FAMOUS FORGERIES

Of real hoaxes there have been few. Spurious antiquities are numerous. At Tyre in 1921 a man who was known to his fellow townsmen as a manufacturer of "*antikes*" made no objection to having his picture taken or to showing his wares, which consisted of well-cut seals and gems. In the eighties of the last century the business was, for a time, active and profitable. Spurious inscriptions, especially attempts to reproduce the famous "balustrade" inscription prohibiting Gentiles entering the Temple courts, were many.

The most famous forgery was again a roll, said to be the original copy of Deuteronomy. After the discovery of the Moabite Stone in 1868, Moab became the cynosure of archaeology. It was a mysterious, little-traveled land and was expected to provide solutions for all sorts of biblical problems. Clandestine excavations were said to have produced real Moabite pottery and other antiquities and eventually this roll. It was the period when, not only the Moabite Stone, but the Temple "balustrade inscription" and the Siloam inscription were found, and everyone was in a receptive mood.

The pottery forgeries were at first successful. A Jerusalem antiquities dealer, a Jewish convert to Christianity named M. W. Shapira, put them on the market, and the "Shapira collections" became world famous. Perhaps because the French had secured the Moabite Stone, Germans welcomed the "Moabite antiquities." When the genuineness of the "discoveries" was challenged, Pastor Weser of the German church and the German consul general, appropriately named Freiherr von Münchhausen, were completely deceived by expeditions to Moab in which more of the same pottery was excavated in the presence of

Pastor Weser and other Europeans. Eventually, moved especially by the arguments of a prominent scholar, Professor Constantin Schlottmann, the German Oriental Society accepted the discoveries as genuine. Lieutenant Conder and Mr. C. F. Tyrwhitt Drake, then engaged in the Palestine Exploration Fund survey, were also for a time deceived. Emil Kautzsch and Albert Socin, then young professors, published a discussion in which they declared the "discoveries" unauthentic, yet, with scholarly caution, left the door open for further evidence. But for the time being Pastor Weser and Professor Schlottmann held the field.

A former American consul, Rev. Frank S. DeHass, D.D., still in 1883 could enthusiastically acclaim the discoveries. He reported that the collection had reached the astonishing sum of "about fifteen thousand kiln-burnt urns, idols, vases, tablets, and other articles, many of them small images and coins."[3] A thousand carried inscriptions which showed strange combinations of letters. They found their way into the best museums on both sides of the Atlantic after the first collection was bought by the Prussian government for a thousand pounds. Some pieces are even still in the hands of dealers.

Scholars in England, however, never accepted them as authentic, and over a period of nearly ten years controversy broke out repeatedly in communications to the *Times* and the *Athenaeum*. Charles Clermont-Ganneau, who, as an attaché of the French consulate, had rescued the remnants of the Moabite Stone for the Louvre and in 1873 returned to Palestine as agent of the Palestine Exploration Fund, traced them to their originator, a painter named Selim el-Gari. The latter used all the means known to the Orient in an effort to discredit Clermont-Ganneau, and Mr. Shapira arranged the expeditions which convinced Pastor Weser and his friends.

Eventually Clermont-Ganneau was vindicated by Shapira's crowning achievement. About 1883 he offered to the museums

---

[3] *Buried Cities Recovered*, p. 420; see pictures also on p. 345. In 1874 there were 1600.

at Berlin and London his chef-d'oeuvre, fragments of a roll of Deuteronomy written in archaic Hebrew characters and suggested to be from the hand of Moses himself. The price was a million pounds.

Enough skill and ingenuity were expended on the pieces to have won fame in a legitimate task. In a day when Hebrew paleography was in its infancy they might well have deceived the very elect. But even Professor Schlottmann pronounced them forgeries on the basis of a copy of a fragment sent to him and both Jewish and Christian scholars in England unhesitatingly agreed to that judgment when Shapira took them to London. He had cut off the wide lower margins of a synagogue roll and copied on these narrow strips his own version of parts of Deuteronomy in a script imitating the now well-known characters of the Moabite Stone. A charming but tragic fictional version of the story has been included in an autobiographical novel by a daughter of the forger, who, under the pen name of Myriam Harry, became an accomplished authoress.

That few such controversies have recently arisen in Palestine speaks for the dependability of the results which archaeology has achieved. The speed with which mistakes and attempted forgeries have been detected proves the acumen of the excavators. It is easy still to buy forged antiquities and copper coins that have been silvered, if the tourist tries to be cunning and buy of peasants or clandestine dealers. But dishonest workmen are now easily caught by the skilled excavator and the whole enterprise is so well guarded by law that serious frauds are almost impossible.

Pitfalls

One of the chief difficulties, even for the instructed student of archaeology, is to keep up with new information which cancels old. This account, written over a period of a decade, has had to be repeatedly revised, even so perhaps not sufficiently. There are but three or four scholars in Europe, England, Palestine, and America who can be trusted to know all that is going on and even the best of them makes mistakes. Sound and critical judgment, wide linguistic and philological learning, indefatigable industry, and a prodigious memory are necessary in the real "authority" in a field which now is so enormous. It cannot be held surprising, therefore, that a newspaper feature writer has recently published Professor Garstang's "Jerash head" as the earliest known head of Christ. The identification was, indeed, made when the head was discovered in the atrium of the Propylea church[4] and the arguments for it seemed sound, but the objections urged by numerous scholars have been so weighty that the idea has now been long abandoned. The "Antioch chalice" is another case in point.

To know what to believe, anyone, whether an "interested reader" or merely an archaeologist, must use dependable publications, including periodicals published under the aegis of established and well-proved societies.[5] The reader must be prepared for differences of opinion and debate. Uncritical longings for certainty, for final conclusions, must be dismissed. The serpent in the archaeologist's Garden of Eden is also the desire for forbidden knowledge, knowledge which the past left unrecorded because it was regarded as unimportant. The vicious strife of sects over the place of the Nativity and the Church of the Holy Sepulchre, the superstitions that defile scores of saints' tombs in Palestine are sufficient warnings. The endless controversies and the bitter feelings that have arisen over such matters should prove that no valuable truths are lost by leaving some problems unsettled.

The traveling free-lance writer, the theological professor who has spent a few months in Palestine, and especially the pious tourist, even with the best of intentions, are a prolific source of error. Perhaps least of all to be credited are the accounts which from time to time are published heralding great discoveries which prove the Bible true. Some widely known men whose claim to recognition is their generosity have repeatedly rushed

[4] See above, p. 315 and note 1.
[5] Some of these are listed in the accompanying general bibliography.

into print in an effort to "steady the ark." Naturally the truth about the Bible is best learned from the qualified excavator and orientalist, not from rich merchants and manufacturers.

Archaeology does not discredit the Bible as a record of religious faith, neither does it prove that all its historical statements are literally true. Archaeological research and historical study go hand in hand to make the Bible intelligible, to correct false notions about it, to rectify wrong ideas derived from misinterpretations of it, and to give added force and beauty to its teachings. Archaeology is the handmaid of history and interpretation. Like any science its one purpose is a search for the truth. The Bible needs no other support.

What to Expect

What, then, can be expected of this search for the truth? First of all that there is still much to be learned and that many ideas now accepted will be changed by further excavation and by fresh consideration of the discoveries that have been made. Neither the lay reader nor the professional archaeologist should accept the conclusions of the present hour as final truth from heaven. The discoveries of the past twenty years, the greater part published only recently, have been too numerous for their bearing upon many phases of Palestinian history to be properly estimated and appreciated. There are many new discoveries to be made. The very successes of recent years and the progress made should be a warning against any tendency to strike a final balance now.

However, it would be a mistake to overemphasize the tentative character of present conclusions. Changes will be made chiefly where conclusions have been based, as they too often have had to be, on scanty or negative evidence. New excavations will constantly enrich the student's opportunities; they will fill in the picture of ancient civilization; but they will not overturn the structure which the study of recent years has erected. Modifications will be introduced, not complete destruction and rebuilding.

It is true that the prewar reconstruction of Old Testament Jericho was wrong in essential points. When a conspicuous fortification is misdated by a thousand years, the resulting picture is false. But the contemporary excavations at Samaria made no such egregious blunder. There certain towers and walls have had to be given a date that is lower by a few hundred years and the resulting conceptions of Israel's civilization have accordingly been modified. The street of columns ascribed to Herod has also been tentatively assigned to a later period. Much more precise dating of much of the pottery is now possible. But such errors were inevitable in the beginnings of such a science. The changes are by no means so serious as those which a generation has brought about in physics and chemistry.

If it is admissible to prognosticate on the basis of past experience, it is probable that certain tendencies now operating will be reversed by a return of the pendulum. The present inclination to lower dates is possibly as mistaken as was the former proclivity, of Sir Flinders Petrie and his period, for example, to make everything ancient as ancient as possible.

There is not the slightest probability that the chronology as a whole will again be radically changed as that of Sir Flinders has been. It is more than probable that some problems now easily solved on the basis of meager evidence will become insoluble as more data are discovered. Yet this difficulty cannot be so great where the data are material and not dependent on the fallibilities of human vision and memory, as in the case of written documents. With the accumulation of archaeological materials and the development of scholars able to appreciate and interpret them many historical problems will vanish. In practically every case this will be possible only by the application of the strictest scientific method.

In the past archaeologists have depended too much on "general impressions," a hazy group of memories accumulated through years of experience, but actually dependent upon varying degrees of attention which the mind happened to devote to the material excavated and upon uncritical associations of these

fugitive and random memories. One famous archaeologist whom
I knew well could never explain why he dated pottery as he
did. He seemed to depend upon a kind of clairvoyance. He
could not have been far wrong in his conclusions, for he usually
agreed with others, but as a teacher he was unsatisfactory and
he left one with a decided impression of uncertainty. Unfortunately others, of lesser gifts and experience, emulated his
example with more *ex cathedra* assertiveness. Another used to
taste his ancient fragments to determine their date. Archaeologists will have to condescend to even greater drudgery than
in the past, they must make much more numerous and meticulous records than in the past if many of the problems of date
and relationship are to be settled. Statistics must take the place
of general impressions if fact is to replace fancy.

THE SERVICE OF ARCHAEOLOGY

With the development of archaeological method and the
accumulation of information the total life of the ancient Near
East will be better and better understood. Many individual
statements in ancient authors that have meant nothing to the
reader or have meant the wrong thing will suddenly be illuminated. Statements that have seemed impossible will appear
perfectly natural. Places will fit into Palestinian topography,
events will fit into their chronological sequence, names will
become persons. But this is the smallest, though the most
emphasized service of archaeology.

The real contribution of archaeology is in the vivid picture it
enables the student to draw of the social life of the past. The
remark which Dr. Albright's Tell Beit Mirsim workmen made
when they found that what they had supposed to be a treasure
cave was a mere grain bin will be more and more emphasized
as archaeology continues to interpret the past: "They were
poor people like us." If some of the glamor of the past is dis-
pelled, the true character of common life and the nature of the
problems which then had to be solved will appear in their true

perspective. Consequently the lessons of history will be more and more truly understood.

To history the student of society must turn to discover the laws of social evolution. But history based on written records alone is faulty in many regards. It necessarily ignores the thousands of years of human social evolution before writing was discovered and it equally misses all those vast areas of life which written records overlook. The present writings of antiquity are naturally in the main the work of the great literary artists writing for the rich who could support them and the educated few who could read and understand them. Even the documents from the hands of the common man, of which Egypt has preserved vast quantities, ignore many of the fundamental factors in society just because they were the common everyday matters known to everyone and taken as a matter of course. Archaeology discovers and reveals to the student this often-neglected background which is essential to a proper interpretation of the written documents.

Innumerable illustrations might be given to show the service of archaeology to the development of social wisdom. One can be drawn from ancient Gerasa. In this beautiful Graeco-Roman city, the dozen churches built between the fourth and the seventh century, five of them within a period of six or eight years, were nearly all of them erected, as their inscriptions testify, to the glory of the donors. Evidence was found of priestly deception in miracle mongering. Does not this explain the weakness of Christianity which led to its fall before the conquests of Islam? Does it not, indeed, explain the very rise of Islam?

A second illustration may be drawn from pottery itself. Like other arts it everywhere reveals crude beginnings, a period of development, then of high originality and artistic excellence, and finally decay until some new idea or method revives it. So history passes through its various cycles. Can modern civilization and current Christianity discover new principles which would prevent their decadence?

A third illustration may be drawn from the fact that written history is but a fragment of social evolution. The prehistorian and the geologist agree that what may be called human beings began to live on the earth 500,000 or 1,000,000 years ago. Yet modern man is only perhaps 10,000 years old, while written history goes back only 5,000 years or less. It is not after all surprising that so little progress has been made in social organization when biological evolution has required countless millennia before human beings appeared.

One important fact emerges from archaeological and historical studies and further excavation will surely only illustrate and confirm it: man has made progress, even in this brief space of time. A far larger proportion of mankind have a relatively satisfactory standard of living than ever before. Even the worst that the wars of the twentieth century have brought has not been worse than the evils of the past, while, what is even more significant, the standards of the present are incomparably higher and the area of moral obligation incomparably broader than ever before. Archaeology, which records the ruins of past civilization, is equally replete with evidence of the rebirth of the better out of the good of the past.

GENERAL BIBLIOGRAPHY—Selected

❖

Albright, William Foxwell. *Archaeology of Palestine and the Bible.* 3d ed. New York: Fleming H. Revell Company, 1935.
——. *From the Stone Age to Christianity.* Baltimore: The Johns Hopkins Press, 1940.
——. *Archaeology and the Religion of Israel.* Baltimore: The Johns Hopkins Press, 1942.
Barrois, A. G. *Manuel d'archéologie biblique.* Paris: Picard, 1939.
Barton, George A. *Archaeology and the Bible.* 7th ed. Philadelphia: American Sunday School Union, 1937 (excellent collection of ancient literary materials).
Burrows, Millar. *What Mean These Stones? The Significance of Archeology for Biblical Studies.* New Haven: American Schools of Oriental Research, 1941.
Garstang, John. *Joshua-Judges. The Foundations of Biblical History.* London: Constable & Company, Ltd., 1931.
Graham, W. C. and H. G. May. *Culture and Conscience. An Archaeological Study of the New Religious Past in Palestine.* Chicago: University of Chicago Press, 1936.
Watzinger, Carl. *Denkmäler Palästinas,* 2 vols. Leipzig: Hinrichs, 1933, 1935.

AAS   Annual, American Schools of Oriental Research
AJA   American Journal of Archaeology, American Institute of Archaeology
AJSL American Journal of Semitic Languages and Literatures; see now *JNES*
BA   Biblical Archaeologist, American Schools of Oriental Research
BAS   Bulletin, American Schools of Oriental Research
JAOS Journal American Oriental Society
JNES Journal of Near Eastern Studies
JPOS Journal Palestine Oriental Society
PEQ   Palestine Exploration Quarterly (formerly Quarterly Statement), Palestine Exploration Fund (PEF)
PJB   Palästina Jahrbuch
QDAP Quarterly of the Department of Antiquities in Palestine
RB   Revue Biblique, École Pratique d'Études Bibliques, Jerusalem
ZAW Zeitschrift für die alttestamentliche Wissenschaft
ZDPV Zeitschrift des deutschen Palästina-Vereins

Brief official reports on all excavations in progress have appeared in each volume of *QDAP*. *BAS* and *AJA* carry news items and discussions of Palestinian discoveries, in the former usually by W. F. Albright. In *AJA,* beginning in Vol. XXXII (1928), the first number each year carries a report by the director of the American School of Oriental Research in Jerusalem on archaeological activities in Palestine and Syria during the previous year. Each number of *AJSL* from 1933 to 1941 carried brief reports on archaeological activities and publications in the Near East. *The Journal of Near Eastern Studies,* which replaced *AJSL* in 1942, will for the present publish an annual summary. *QDAP* has published a series of succinct but complete bibliographies on excavations at various sites in Palestine, Vol. I (1932), pp. 86-94, 139-149, 163-199; thereafter at the conclusion of each volume (except Vol. II) for the previous year.

SELECTED BIBLIOGRAPHY

CHAPTERS II-IV: PREHISTORY

❖

"Ancient Fauna and Early Man at Bethlehem," editorial, *Nature*, 140 (3540), p. 381 (Sept. 4, 1937).

GARDNER, ELINOR W. and DOROTHEA M. A. BATE. "The Bone-Bearing Beds of Bethlehem: Their Fauna and Industry," *ibid.*, p. 431 ff.

GARROD, DOROTHY A. E. "Excavation of a Palaeolithic Cave," *PEQ*, 1928, pp. 182-185.

———. "The Stone Age of Palestine," *Antiquity*, VIII (1934), pp. 133-150.

———. "A New Mesolithic Industry: the Natufian," *JRAI*, 62 (1932), pp. 257-269; *L'Anthropologie*, 44 (1932), pp. 143-146.

GARROD, DOROTHY A. E. and DOROTHEA M. A. BATE. *The Stone Age of Mount Carmel; Excavations at Wady el-Mughara.* Vol. I. Oxford: Clarendon Press, 1937.

KEITH, SIR ARTHUR. *New Discoveries Relating to the Antiquity of Man.* New York: W. W. Norton & Company, Inc., 1931, pp. 173-224.

KÖPPEL, R., "Das Alter der neuentdeckten Schädel von Nazareth," *Biblica*, 16 (1935), pp. 58-73.

McCOWN, THEODORE D. and SIR ARTHUR KEITH. *The Stone Age of Mount Carmel: The Fossil Human Remains from the Levalloiso-Mousterian.* Vol. II. Oxford: Clarendon Press, 1939.

MACDONALD, EANN, "Prehistoric Fara," in *Beth-pelet* II (London, 1932), pp. 1-15.

MOIR, J. REID, "Flint Instruments of Lower Paleolithic Types from Palestine," *JRAI*, 60 (1930), pp. 485-499.

TURVILLE-PETRE, F., "Excavations in the Mugharet el-Kebarah," *Journal Royal Asiatic Society*, 62 (1932), pp. 271-276.

———. *Researches in Prehistoric Galilee.* London: British School of Archaeology at Jerusalem, 1927.

WRIGHT, G. ERNEST. *The Pottery of Palestine from the Earliest Times to the End of the Early Bronze Age.* New Haven, 1937.

French discoveries have been published in many articles, a few of which are listed:

BUZY, DENIS, "Une industrie mésolithique en Palestine (Ouâdy Tahouneh)," *RB*, XXXVII (1928), pp. 558-578.

NEUVILLE, RENÉ, "Notes de préhistoire palestinienne," *JPOS*, X (1930), pp. 64-75, 193-216.

———. "L'Acheuléen supérieur de la grotte d'Oum Qatafa (Palestine)," *L'Anthropologie*, 41 (1931), pp. 13-51, 249-263.
———. "Le préhistorique de Palestine," *RB*, XLIII (1934), pp. 237-259.

CHAPTER V: MAN BUILDS CITIES

MALLON, A., R. KOEPPEL, and R. NEUVILLE. *Teleilat Ghassul* I (1929-1932). Rome: Institute Biblique Pontifical, 1934.
KOEPPEL, R., *et al. Teleilat Ghassul* II. Rome, 1940 (not seen).
———. *Biblica*, XVI (1935), pp. 241-256; XVII (1936), pp. 393-406; XIX (1938), pp. 260-266.
V(INCENT), L. H. "Les fouilles de Teleilat Ghassul," *RB*, XLIV (1935), pp. 69-104, 220-244 (Rev. of *Ghassul* I).
ALBRIGHT, W. F., *JPOS*, XV (1935), pp. 199-208.
WATZINGER, CARL, *ZDPV*, LIX (1936), pp. 155-159 (Rev. of *Ghassul* I).
WRIGHT, G. ERNEST. *The Pottery of Palestine from the Earliest Times to the End of the Early Bronze Age.* New Haven: American Schools of Oriental Research, 1937, esp. pp. 14-41.
———. "Palestine in the Chalcolithic Age," *BAS*, 66 (1937), pp. 21-25.
SUKENIK, E. L., "A Chalcolithic Necropolis at Hederah," *JPOS*, XVII (1937), pp. 15-30.

CHAPTER VI: JERICHO

ALBRIGHT, W. F., *AAS*, IV (1924), pp. 146 f.; VI (1926), p. 53.
———. *BAS*, 58 (1935), pp. 10-13; 74 (1939), p. 18 ff.
GARSTANG, JOHN. Reports in *Annals of Archaeology and Anthropology*, XIX-XXIII (1932-1936).
GARSTANG, JOHN and J. B. E. GARSTANG. *The Story of Jericho.* London: Hodder & Stoughton, Ltd., 1940.
SELLIN, ERNST and CARL WATZINGER. *Jericho.* . . . Leipzig, 1913.
VINCENT, L. H., "La chronologie des ruines de Jéricho," *RB*, XXXIX (1930), pp. 403-433; XLI (1932), pp. 266-276; XLIV (1935), pp. 583-605.
———. "L'aube de l'histoire à Jéricho," *ibid.*, XLVII (1938), pp. 561-589; XLVIII (1939), pp. 91-107.
WATZINGER, CARL. "Ieriko . . . ," *Svenska Orient Arsbok*, 1923, pp. 100-105; cf. *Zeitschrift des deutschen morgenländischen Gesellschaft*, 1926, pp. 131-136.
WRIGHT, G. E., "Epic of Conquest," *BA*, III (1940), pp. 25-40.

CHAPTER VII: TELL BEIT MIRSIM

ALBRIGHT, W. F., in *AAS*, XII (1932), pp. 1-165; XIII (1933), pp. 55-127; XVII (1938), pp. 1-96, pls. 1-56; XXI-XXII, (1943).
———. *BAS*, 23 (1926), pp. 2-14; 31 (1928), pp. 1-11; 39 (1930), pp. 1-10; 47 (1932), pp. 3-17.
———. in *Journal of Biblical Literature*, LI (1932), pp. 77-85.

ALBRIGHT, W. F., in *JPOS*, XV (1935), pp. 193-234.
———. The Archaeology of Palestine and the Bible. 3d ed. New York, 1935, pp. 63-126, 190-204, 235-239.
———. *AJA*, XXXVI (1932), pp. 556-564.

CHAPTER VIII: THE ALPHABET

PETRIE, SIR W. M. FLINDERS. *Researches in Sinai.* London, 1906.
LAKE, KIRSOPP, et al. *Harvard Theological Review*, XXI (1928), pp. 1-68; XXV (1932), pp. 95-203.
GARDINER, ALAN H. *PEQ*, 1929, pp. 48-55.
SPRENGLING, MARTIN. *The Alphabet: Its Rise and Development from the Sinai Inscriptions* (OIC 12). Chicago: University of Chicago Press, 1931.
ALBRIGHT, W. F. *JPOS*, XV (1935), pp. 334-340.
———. *BAS*, 53 (1934), pp. 18 f.; 55 (1934), pp. 27 f.; 58 (1935), pp. 28 f.; 63 (1936), pp. 8-12.
BAUER, HANS. *Entzifferung der Keilschrifttafeln von Ras-Schamra.* Halle, 1930.
———. *Der Ursprung des Alphabets* (Der Alte Orient 36:1, 2). 1937.
VIROLLEAUD, CHARLES. *Syria*, X (1929), pp. 304-310; XII (1931), pp. 15-23; etc.
BÖHL, F. M. TH. "Die Sichem Plakette," *ZDPV*, LXI (1938), pp. 1-25.
BARTON, GEORGE A. *BAS*, 52 (1933), pp. 5 f. ('Ain Shems cuneiform tablet).
MAISLER, B. *JPOS*, XVIII (1938), pp. 173-181.
OBERMANN, JULIAN. *The Archaic Inscriptions from Lachish.* Supplement to *JAOS*, 58 (1938).
———. *JBL* LVII (1938), pp. 239-253.
ULLMAN, B. L. "The Origin and Development of the Alphabet," *AJA*, XXXI (1927), pp. 311-328.
YEIVIN, S. *PEQ*, 1937, pp. 180-193.
FLIGHT, JOHN W. Haverford Symposium (New Haven: American Schools of Oriental Research, 1938), pp. 111-135, with valuable bibliography.

CHAPTER IX: ON THE EGYPTIAN FRONTIER

PETRIE, SIR W. M. FLINDERS. *Ancient Gaza.* 4 vols. London: British School of Archaeology in Egypt, 1931-1934.
———. *Anthedon* (with J. C. Ellis). London, 1937.
———. *Beth-pelet* (Tell Fara). Vol. 1. London, 1930.
———. *Gerar.* London, 1928.
———. *Seventy Years in Archaeology.* London: Low, Marston and Co., 1931.
———. *Tell el Hesy* (Lachish). London: A. P. Watt, 1891.
PHYTHIAN-ADAMS, W. J. *PEQ*, 1923, pp. 12, 140-146.
GALLING, KURT. *ZDPV*, LIV (1931), pp. 93-100.

MACDONALD, EANN, J. L. STARKEY, and LANKESTER HARDING. *Beth-pelet* II. London: British School of Archaeology in Egypt, 1932.
ILIFFE, J. H. *QDAP*, IV (1935), pp. 182-186.
ALBRIGHT, W. F. *AJSL*, LV (1938), pp. 337-359 (Revision of chronology).

CHAPTER X: BORDER CITIES OF THE SHEPHELAH

TELL ED-DUWEIR—LACHISH

TORCZYNER, HARRY, et al. *The Lachish Letters* (*Lachish* I).
TUFNELL, OLGA, CHARLES H. INGE, and LANKESTER HARDING. *The Fosse Temple* (*Lachish* II). London: Oxford University Press, 1938, 1940.
STARKEY, J. L. and CHARLES H. INGE. Reports in *PEQ*, 1933-1938.
VINCENT, L. H. *RB*, XLVIII (1939), pp. 250-277, 406-433, 565-583.
ALBRIGHT, W. F. *BAS*, 73 (1939), pp. 16-21; 82 (1941), pp. 18-24.
KEITH, SIR ARTHUR. *PEQ*, 1940, pp. 7-12.
WRIGHT, G. E. *AJA*, XLV (1941), pp. 634 f.
DIRINGER, DAVID. *PEQ*, 1941, pp. 38-56, 81-109.

'AIN SHEMS—BETH-SHEMESH

MACKENZIE, DUNCAN. *Annual* Palestine Exploration Fund, I (1911), pp. 41-94; II (1913).
GRANT, ELIHU. *Beth-Shemesh*. Haverford, Pa., 1929.
———. *'Ain Shems Excavations*, Vols. 1-5. (Vols. 4 and 5 with G. Ernest Wright). Haverford, 1931-1939.

EARLIER EXCAVATIONS

BLISS, F. J. and R. A. S. MACALISTER. *Excavations in Palestine during the years 1898-1900*. London, 1902.
MACALISTER, R. A. S. *The Excavation of Gezer, 1902-1905 and 1907-1909*. 3 vols. London, 1912.
ROWE, ALAN. *PEQ*, 1935, pp. 19-33.

CHAPTER XI: BETH-SHAN, THE MOUND OF THE FORTRESS

FISHER, C. S., ALAN ROWE, and GERALD M. FITZGERALD. Reports in *Museum Journal*, 1922-1935.
ROWE, ALAN and G. M. FITZGERALD. Reports in *PEQ*, 1927-1929, 1931, 1932, 1934.
———. Publications of the Palestine Section of the Museum of the University of Pennsylvania. Philadelphia, 1930-1939. Four volumes in five (final reports).
VINCENT, L. H., A. G. BARROIS, ALAN ROWE, G. M. FITZGERALD. *RB*, 1922-1933.
ALBRIGHT, W. F. and ALAN ROWE. "A Royal Stele of the New Empire from Galilee," *Journal of Egyptian Archaeology*, XIV (1928), 281-287 (Thothmes III).

GALLING, KURT, "Archäologische Bemerkungen zum Löwenrelief von Beth Sean," *ZDPV*, LVII (1934), pp. 153-156.

THIERSCH, HERMANN, "Ein hellenistischer Kolossalkopf aus Beisan," *Nachrichten d. Gesellschaft d. Wissenschaften, Göttingen*, Phil.-hist. Klasse, 1932, vol. I, pp. 52-76.

WRIGHT, G. ERNEST, *AJA*, XLV (1941), pp. 483 ff. (Wright lowers the dates of stratum V to the Eleventh-Tenth centuries).

CHAPTER XII: ARMAGEDDON-MEGIDDO (TELL EL-MUTESELLIM)

FISHER, C. S. *The Excavation of Armageddon* (OIC, 4). Chicago, 1929.

GUY, P. L. O. *New Light from Armageddon* (OIC, 9). Chicago, 1931.

MAY, H. G. *Material Remains of the Megiddo Cult* (OIP, 26). Chicago, 1935.

LAMON, ROBERT S. *The Megiddo Water System* (OIP, 32). Chicago, 1935.

ENGBERG, ROBERT M. and GEOFFREY M. SHIPTON. *Notes on the Chalcolithic and Early Bronze Age Pottery of Megiddo* (SAOC, 10). Chicago, 1934.

GUY, P. L. O. and R. M. ENGBERG. *Megiddo Tombs* (OIP, 33). Chicago, 1938.

LAMON, ROBERT S. and GEOFFREY M. SHIPTON. *Megiddo* I (OIP, 42). Chicago, 1939.

SHIPTON, GEOFFREY M. *Notes on the Megiddo Pottery of Strata VI-XX* (SAOC, 17). Chicago, 1939.

LOUD, GORDON. *The Megiddo Ivories* (OIP, 52). Chicago, 1939.

VINCENT, L. H., *RB*, XLIII (1934), pp. 403-431; XLIV (1935), 416-437.

ENGBERG, R. M., "Historical Analysis of Archaeological Evidence: Megiddo and the Song of Deborah," *BAS*, 78 (April, 1940), pp. 4-7, with notes by W. F. Albright, pp. 7 ff.

CROWFOOT, J. W. *PEQ*, 1940, pp. 132-147; rev. of *Megiddo* I.

ALBRIGHT, W. F. *AJA*, XLIV (1940), pp. 546-550; rev. of *Megiddo* I.

For excavations at a neighboring site see:

HAMILTON, R. W. "Tall Abu Hawam," *QDAP*, III (1934), pp. 74-80; IV (1935), pp. 1-69.

CHAPTER XIII: SAMARIA-SEBASTE

REISNER, G. A., C. S. FISHER and D. G. LYON. *Harvard Excavations at Samaria 1908-1910*. 2 vols. Cambridge, 1924.

CROWFOOT, J. W., KATHLEEN KENYON, and E. L. SUKENIK. Articles in *PEQ*, 1931-1935.

SUKENIK, E. L., *Archäologischer Anzeiger des deutschen archäologischen Instituts*, 1933, columns 85-115.

CROWFOOT, J. W. *Churches at Bosra and Samaria-Sebaste*. London: British School of Archaeology in Jerusalem, Supplementary Papers No. 4, 1937.

CROWFOOT, J. W. and GRACE M. CROWFOOT. *Early Ivories from Samaria*. London, 1938.

HAMILTON, R. W. *Guide to the Historical Site of Sebastieh.* Jerusalem: Dept. of Antiquities, 1936.

JACK, J. W. *Samaria in Ahab's Time.* Edinburgh, 1929.

GALLING, K. *ZDPV*, LIX (1936), pp. 242-246.

VINCENT, L. H. *RB*, XXXIV (1925), pp. 436-441; XLV (1936), pp. 221-232.

NARKIS, M. *PEQ*, 1932, pp. 210 ff.

CHAPTER XIV: THE MOUNTAINS ROUND ABOUT JERUSALEM

TELL EL-FUL-GIBEAH

ALBRIGHT, W. F., *AAS*, IV (1924), pp. 1-89.

———. *BAS*, 52 (1933), pp. 6-12.

TELL EN-NASBEH-MIZPAH(?)

BADÈ, W. F. *Excavations at Tell en-Nasbeh, 1926 and 1927.* Berkeley, 1928.

———. *Some Tombs of Tell en-Nasbeh Discovered in 1929.* Berkeley, 1931.

———. *Werden und Wesen des Alten Testaments* (Beiheft 66 to *ZAW*), Berlin, 1936, pp. 30-36.

———. "The Seal of Jaazaniah," *ZAW*, 51 (1933), pp. 1-7.

McCOWN, C. C., JAMES MUILENBURG, AND J. C. WAMPLER. *Tell en-Nasbeh* (in press).

AI (ET-TELL) AND BETHEL

ALBRIGHT, W. F. *AAS*, IV (1924), pp. 140-149.

———. *BAS*, 29 (1929), pp. 9 ff.; 35 (1929), pp. 4 ff.; 55 (1934), pp. 23 ff.; 56 (1934), pp. 2-15; 57 (1935), pp. 27-30; 74 (1939), pp. 15-18.

GARSTANG, JOHN. *Joshua-Judges. The Foundations of Bible History.* London: Constable & Company, Ltd., 1931, esp. pp. 153-159, 355 f.

KRAUSE-MARQUET, JUDITH. "La deuxième campagne de fouilles à Ay (1934). Rap. sommaire," *Syria*, XVI (1935), pp. 325-345.

NOTH, M. "Bethel and Ai," *PJB*, XXXI (1935), pp. 7-29.

VINCENT, L. H. "Les fouilles d' et-Tell," *RB*, XLVI (1937), pp. 231-266.

SEILUN-SHILOH

KJAER, HANS. *I Det Helige Land: de Danske Udgravninger i Shilo. . . .* København, 1931.

———. "The Excavation of Shiloh, 1929, a Preliminary Report," *JPOS*, X (1930), pp. 87-174.

BALATAH-MIGDAL SHECHEM(?)

SELLIN, E. *Anzeiger der Akademie der Wissenschaften, Wien,* Phil.-Hist. Classe, 1914, pp. 35-40, 204-207.

———. *ZDPV*, XLIX (1926), pp. 229-236; pp. 304-320; L (1927), pp. 205-211, 265-274; LI (1928), pp. 119-123; LII (1929), pp. 141-148.

BÖHL, F. M. TH. *ibid.*, XLIX (1926), pp. 321-327; LXI (1938), pp. 1-25.

WELTER, G. *Archäol. Anzeiger, Beiblatt zum Jahrbuch des Arch. Insts.*, XLVII (1932), cols. pp. 289-316.

THIERSCH, H. *ZAW*, IX (1932), pp. 76 ff.; cf. pp. 303-308.
HEMPEL, JOH. *ZAW*, X (1933), pp. 156-169.
SELLIN, E. and H. STECKEWEH. *ZDPV*, LXIV (1941), pp. 1-20.

BETH-ZUR

SELLERS, OVID R. *The Citadel of Beth-zur.* Philadelphia: Westminster Press, 1933.

HARAM RAMET EL-KHALIL—ABRAHAM'S OAK

MADER, A. E. *Oriens Christianus,* Ser. 3, I (1927), pp. 333-351; II (1928), pp. 360-379.
———. *Archäol. Anzeiger, Beiblatt zum Jahrbuch des Arch. Insts.,* XLII (1927), pp. 452-458.
———. *RB,* XXXIX (1930), pp. 84-117, 199-225 (Tr. by A. Barrois).

CHAPTER XV: JERUSALEM

"Concise Bibliography of Excavations in Palestine: Jerusalem," *QDAP,* I (1932), pp. 163-188 and pl. LX (map).
GUTHE, HERMANN. "Ausgrabungen bei Jerusalem," *ZDPV,* V (1882), pp. 7-204, 271-378.
BLISS, F. J. *Excavations at Jerusalem 1894-97.* London, 1898.
VINCENT, L. H. *Jérusalem sous Terre.* (Eng. trans.) *Underground Jerusalem.* London, 1911.
WEILL, RAYMOND. *La Cité de David.* Paris, 1920.
———. "La pointe sud de la cité de David et les fouilles de 1923-1924," *Revue des Études Juives,* 82 (1926), pp. 8-22.
MACALISTER, R. A. S. and J. G. DUNCAN. *Excavation on the Hill of Ophel.* (Ann. PEF IV). London, 1926.
CROWFOOT, J. W. and G. M. FITZGERALD. *Excavations in the Tyropean Valley Jerusalem,* 1927 (Ann. PEF, V). London, 1929.
SUKENIK, E. L. *Jüdische Gräber Jerusalems.* Jerusalem, 1931.
DALMAN, GUSTAF. *Jerusalem und seine Gelände.* Gütersloh, 1930.
VINCENT, L. H. "Acra," *RB,* XLIII (1934), pp. 205-236.

CHAPTER XVI: THE SEARCH FOR JESUS' TOMB

MACALISTER, R. A. S. *A Century of Excavation in Palestine.* London, 1925, pp. 89-94 (on the "Garden Tomb").
DALMAN, GUSTAF. *Sacred Sites and Ways.* New York: The Macmillan Company, 1935, pp. 270, 346-381.
———. *Jerusalem und seine Gelände.* Gütersloh, 1930, pp. 88-111.
SUKENIK, E. L. and L. A. MAYER. *The Third Wall of Jerusalem. . . .* Jerusalem: University Press, 1930.
HAMILTON, R. W. *QDAP,* VI (1938), pp. 78-83, 153-156; X (1940), pp. 1-54.
SOLOMIAC, M. "The Towers and Cisterns of the Third Wall of Jerusalem," *BAS,* 84 (1941), 5 ff.

Vincent, L. H. "Garden Tomb: Histoire d'un mythe," *RB*, XXXIV (1925), pp. 401-443.

———. "Autour du rampart d'Agrippa," *RB*, XXXIV (1925), pp. 588-591.

———. "Le troisieme enceinte de Jérusalem," *ibid.*, XXXVI (1927), pp. 516-548; XXXVII (1928), pp. 80-100, 321-339.

———. "L'Antonia et le Prétoire," *ibid.*, XLII (1933), pp. 83-113.

———. "Autour du Prétoire," *ibid.*, XLVI (1937), pp. 563-570.

Albright, W. F. *BAS*, 19 ff.; 20 (1925), pp. 12 f.; 25 (1927), pp. 1-3, 22; 26 (1927), pp. 8 f.; 81 (1941), 6-10.

Palestine Post, Oct. 14, 1940, p. 4 (Kindness of Miss Katherine Wambold).

Fisher, C. S. and E. L. Sukenik, *BAS*, 83 (1941), pp. 4-7.

Duncan, J. Garrow, *PEQ*, 1925, pp. 172-182.

Chapter XVII: Neglected Galilee

Mader, A. E. "Die Ausgrabung der Brotvermehrungskirche auf dem deutschen Besitz et-Tabgha am See Genesareth," *Das Heilige Land*, 78 (1934), pp. 1-15, 41-66, 89-103, 129-149.

Schneider, Alfons M. *Die Brotvermehrungskriche von et-tabga am Gennesarethsee*. Paderborn: Schöningh, 1934. (Eng. trans.) *The Church of the Multiplying of the Loaves at Tabgha on the Lake of Gennesaret*. Ed. by A. A. Gordon. London: Alexander Ouseley, 1937.

Sukenik, E. L. *Ancient Synagogues in Palestine and Greece*. (Schweich Lectures, 1930.) London: Oxford University Press, 1934.

Waterman, Leroy. *Preliminary Report of the University of Michigan Excavations at Sepphoris, Palestine, in 1931*. Ann Arbor: University of Michigan Press, 1937.

Vincent, L. H. *RB*, XXXI (1922), pp. 115-125.

Albright, W. F. *AAS*, II-III (1923), pp. 17-46.

McCown, C. C. *AAS*, II-III (1923), pp. 109-115.

———. *JPOS*, X (1930), pp. 32-58.

Schneider, A. M. *ZDPV*, LX (1937), pp. 133-135 (a Crusader *mensa Domini* of Scandinavian origin).

Chapter XVIII: Remains of Normative Judaism

Kohl, Heinrich and Carl Watzinger. *Antike Synagogen in Galilaea*. Leipzig: Hinrichs, 1916.

Orfali, Gaudence. *Capharnaum et ses ruins*. . . . Paris: Picard, 1922.

Sukenik, E. L. *Ancient Synagogues in Palestine and Greece*. (Schweich Lectures, 1930.) London: Oxford University Press, 1934.

———. "The Ancient Synagogue of el-Hammeh," *JPOS*, XV (1935), pp. 101-180 (also separate).

Maisler, B. "The Excavations at Sheikh, Ibreiq (Beth She'arim), 1936-7," *JPOS*, XVIII (1938), pp. 41-49.

Avi-Yonah, M. "A Sixth-Century Synagogue at 'Isfiya," *QDAP*, III (1934), pp. 118-131.

DETWEILER, A. H. "Some Early Jewish Architectural Vestiges from Jerash," *BAS*, 87 (1942), pp. 10-17 (from destruction in 68 A.D.).

CHAPTER XIX: BETWEEN THE DESERT AND THE SOWN

TRANSJORDAN

GLUECK, NELSON, "Explorations in Eastern Palestine (I) II, III," *AAS*, XIV (1934), pp. 1-114; XV (1935), pp. 1-202; XVIII-XIX (1939), pp. 1-269.

————. "Christian Kilwa," *JPOS*, XVI (1936), pp. 9-16.

————. *On the Other Side of the Jordan*. New Haven: American Schools of Oriental Research, 1940.

————. "Recently Discovered Ore Deposits in Eastern Palestine," *BAS*, 63 (1936), pp. 4-8.

————. "The Nabatean Temple of Khirbet et-Tannur," *BAS*, 67 (1937), pp. 6-16.

————. "The Early History of a Nabatean Temple: Khirbet et-Tannur," *BAS*, 69 (1938), pp. 7-18.

————. Campaigns at Tell el-Kheleifeh, *BAS*, 71 (1938), pp. 3-17; 72 (1938), pp. 2-13; 75 (1939), pp. 8-22; 79 (1940), pp. 2-18; 80 (1940), pp. 2-10.

FRANK, FRITZ. *Aus der 'Araba I*. Offprint from *ZDPV*, LVII (1934). Leipzig; Hinrichs, 1934.

ALT, ALBRECHT. *Aus der 'Araba II-IV*. Offprint from *ZDPV*, LVIII (1935). Leipzig: Hinrichs, 1935.

JENSEN, AD. E. and HANS RHOTERT, *Verlauf und Ergebnisse der XII. deutschen Inner-Afrikanischen Forschungs-Expedition 1934-1935. . . . Vorgeschichliche Forschungen in Kleinasien und Nordafrika. Bd. I. Transjordanien. Vorgeschichtliche Forschungen, mit Beiträgen von Franz M. Th. Böhl und K. Willmann*. Stuttgart: Strecker u. Schröder, 1938.

WADI DHOBAI

WAECHTER, J. D'A. and V. M. SETON-WILLIAMS, "The Excavations at Wadi Dhobai, 1937-1938, and the Dhobaian Industry," *JPOS*, XVIII (1938), pp. 172-186, 297 f.

BATE, DOROTHEA M. A. "Vertebrate Remains from Wadi Dhobai, 1938," *Ibid.*, pp. 292-296.

PETRA

HORSFIELD, GEORGE and AGNES CONWAY, *Geographical Journal*, LXVI (1930), pp. 369-390.

————. "Sela-Petra, of Edom and Nabatene," *QDAP*, VII (1938), pp. 1-42, 74 pls.; VIII (1938), pp. 87-115, 56 pls.; IX (1941), pp. 105-204, 49 pls.

FRESCOED TOMBS

PETERS, JOHN P. and HERMANN THIERSCH. *Painted Tombs in the Necropolis of Marissa*. London, 1905.

MOULTON, WARREN J. *AAS*, II-III (1923), pp. 95-101.
ORY, J. B. *QDAP*, VIII (1938), pp. 38-44.
McCOWN, C. C. *QDAP*, IX (1939), pp. 1-30.

NEGEB

WOOLEY, C. L. and T. E. LAWRENCE. *The Wilderness of Zin* (Ann. PEF, 1914-1915). London, 1915.
ALT, ALBRECHT. *Beiträge zur historischen Geographie u. Topographie des Negeb*, *JPOS*, XI, XII, XV, XVII, XVIII (1931-1938).
KIRK, G. E. Articles in *JPOS*, XV, XVII, XVIII (1936-1938); in *PEQ*, 1938, 1939, 1941.
DE VAUX, R. and R. SAVIGNAC. "Nouvell recherches dans le région de Cadès," *RB*, XLVII (1938), pp. 89-100.

CHAPTER XX: GERASA

KRAELING, CARL H., ed. *Gerasa, City of the Decapolis*. New Haven: American Schools of Oriental Research, 1938.
————. "The Nabatean Sanctuary at Gerasa," *BAS*, 83 (1941), pp. 7-14.
FISHER, C. S. and C. C. McCOWN, *AAS*, XI (1930), pp. 1-59, 131-169.
McCOWN, C. C. *JAOS*, 54 (1934), pp. 178-185.
————. *AAS*, XIII (1933), pp. 129-166.
CROWFOOT, J. W. *The Churches at Jerash* (British School of Archaeology in Jerusalem, Supplementary Papers, no. 3). London, 1931.
VINCENT, L. H. "Le dieu saint Paqeidas a Gérasa," *RB*, XLIX (1940), pp. 98-129.
Père Vincent's conclusion that the little temple (C) was that of Paqeidas seems unjustified.

CHAPTER XXI: BYZANTINES, ARABS, AND CRUSADERS

ʿAJLUN

JOHNS, C. N. in *QDAP*, I (1932), pp. 21-33, with plates.

ʿATHLIT

JOHNS, C. N. in *QDAP*, I (1932), pp. 111-129; II (1933), pp. 41-104; III (1934), pp. 145-164; IV (1935), pp. 81-86; VI (1938), pp. 121-152, with plates.

BETHLEHEM

VINCENT, L. H. "Bethlehem, le sanctuaire de la Nativité," *RB*, XLV (1936), pp. 544-574; XLVI (1937), pp. 93-121.

BOSRA

CROWFOOT, J. W. *Churches at Bosra and Samaria-Sebaste*. British School of Archaeology, Supplementary Papers, No. 4. London, 1937.

EMMAUS

VINCENT, L. H. and F. M. ABEL. *Emmaüs, sa basilique et son histoire,* Paris: Leroux, 1932.
VINCENT, L. H. *RB,* XLV (1936), pp. 403-415.

JERICHO

Khirbet el-Mefjer:

SCHNEIDER, A. M. *ZDPV,* LIV (1931), pp. 50-59.
BARAMKI, D. C. *QDAP,* V (1936), pp. 132-136; VI (1938), pp. 157-168; VIII (1938), pp. 51 ff.; X (1942), pp. 65-103.

Nestorian Hermitage:

BARAMKI, D. C. and ST. H. STEPHEN, *QDAP,* IV (1935), pp. 81-86.

Synagogue:

BARAMKI, D. C. *QDAP,* VI (1938), pp. 73-77.

Tell Hassan:

BARAMKI, D. C. *QDAP,* V (1936), pp. 82-88.

MOSLEM ARCHITECTURE

CRESWELL, K. A. C. *Early Muslim Architecture, Umayyads, Early Abbasids, and Tulunids.* 2 vols. Oxford, 1932, 1940, with section (Vol. I, pp. 149-228) by Mlle Marguerite Van Berchem.

MT. NEBO—SIAGHAH

SALLER, S. "L'église du Mont Nébo," *RB,* XLIII (1934), pp. 120-127.

CHAPTER XXII: WHAT TO BELIEVE

Shapiro and His Forgeries, *PEQ* 1873, pp. 13 f., 79 f.; 1874, pp. 114-124, 201-207; 1878, pp. 41-45, 88-105; 1883, pp. 195-209.
CLERMONT-GANNEAU, CHARLES, "Genuine and False Inscriptions in Palestine," (Repr. from the *Times*), *PEQ,* 1884, pp. 89-100.
———. *Les fraudes archéologiques en Palestine.* Paris, 1885.
DIRINGER, DAVID. *Le inscrizioni antico-ebraiche Palestinesi.* Florence, 1934, pp. 319 f.
DEHASS, FRANK S. *Buried Cities Recovered.* 5th ed. Philadelphia and San Francisco, 1883.
KAUTZSCH, E. and A. SOCIN. *Die Aechtheit der moabitischen Altertümer geprüft.* Strassburg and London, 1876.
HARRY, MYRIAM (Mme Perrault-Harry). *La petite fille de Jérusalem.* Paris, 1914. (Eng. trans.) *Little Daughter of Jerusalem.* New York, 1910.
BURROWS, MILLAR. *What Mean These Stones?* esp. pp. 250-292.
ALBRIGHT, W. F. *BAS,* 74 (1939), pp. 11-15.
———. *From the Stone Age to Christianity,* pp. 1-47.
———. *Archaeology and the Religion of Israel,* pp. 59-67, *et passim.*

INDEX OF BIBLICAL CITATIONS

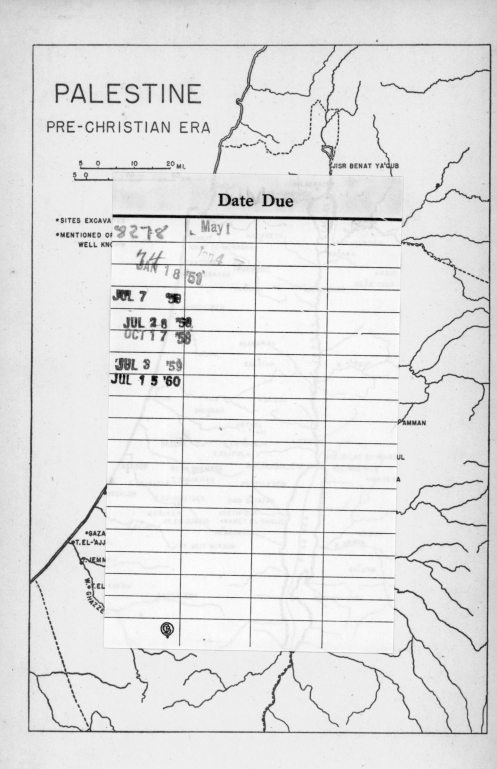

PALESTINE
PRE-CHRISTIAN ERA

5 0   10   20 MI.
5 0

JISR BENAT YA'QUB

• SITES EXCAVA

•MENTIONED OF
  WELL KNO

•GAZA
T. EL-'AJJ

T. JEMN

W. EL
GHAZZE

PAMMAN

UL

A

Date Due

8278   May 1

74   '74
JAN 1 8 '51

JUL 7   '58

JUL 2 8 '58
OCT 1 7 '58

JUL 3   '59
JUL 1 5 '60